D0945184

THE RISE
AND FALL
OF THE
BRANCHHEAD
BOYS

To Patsy Robertson

Thank you for your interest in Tar Heel politics.

Bob Clinton

The Rise and Fall of the Branchhead Boys

NORTH CAROLINA'S SCOTT FAMILY AND THE ERA OF PROGRESSIVE POLITICS

ROB CHRISTENSEN

THE UNIVERSITY OF
NORTH CAROLINA PRESS
Chapel Hill

*This book was published with the assistance of the
Luther H. Hodges Sr. and Luther H. Hodges Jr. Fund
of the University of North Carolina Press.*

Designed by Richard Hendel
Set in Utopia and TheSerif
by Tseng Information Systems, Inc.
Manufactured in the United States of America

The University of North Carolina Press has been a member
of the Green Press Initiative since 2003.

Jacket illustration: the Bull Calf Walk from Kerr Scott's 1954 Senate campaign;
courtesy of the State Archives of North Carolina.

Library of Congress Cataloging-in-Publication Data
Names: Christensen, Rob, author.
Title: The rise and fall of the Branchhead boys : North Carolina's Scott family
and the era of progressive politics / Rob Christensen.
Description: Chapel Hill : The University of North Carolina Press, [2019] |
Includes bibliographical references and index.
Identifiers: LCCN 2018049279 | ISBN 9781469651040 (cloth : alk. paper) |
ISBN 9781469651057 (ebook)
Subjects: LCSH: Scott family. | North Carolina—Politics and government—1951- |
Progressivism (United States politics) | Politicians—North Carolina—Biography.
Classification: LCC F260 .C577 2019 | DDC 975.6/043—dc23
LC record available at https://lccn.loc.gov/2018049279

To my parents, Chris and Arlene Christensen

CONTENTS

FIGURES

THE RISE
AND FALL
OF THE
BRANCHHEAD
BOYS

INTRODUCTION

Governor Kerr Scott was riding high when he arrived in the coastal town of New Bern to speak to the Young Democrats Club convention in September 1949. During his first nine months in office, Scott had launched a transformative road-building program, begun a major school construction effort, improved teacher salaries, pushed for extending electricity and telephone service to the countryside, and supported ongoing efforts to improve health care in the state. He had also shown himself an ally of blacks, women, and organized labor. He voiced support for an Equal Rights Amendment to the Constitution for women and stood up to powerful corporations that ran the state.

In the process, Scott had outraged conservatives by naming liberals to high posts, whether it was an African American to the State Board of Education, the former press secretary of Franklin Roosevelt and Harry Truman as the state's Democratic National Commiteeman, or Frank Porter Graham, the president of the University of North Carolina and the South's leading liberal, to the U.S. Senate.

Kerr Scott's accomplishments were also in service to the grooming of future generations of Democratic progressives like those in the Young Democrats Club at New Bern who gathered to hear him speak. The YDCs elected as their chairman Terry Sanford, a thirty-two-year-old Fayetteville attorney who would become Scott's heir apparent. Soon, a fifteen-year-old Jim Hunt, another future governor, would be ushered into Scott's office to have his photograph taken with the governor. Scott's own family would be part of the rural progressivism, too—his son Bob would follow him as governor; his brother, Ralph, would become one of North Carolina's most influential state lawmakers; his daughter-in-law would run for labor commissioner and lobby for the ERA; and his granddaughter would be elected agriculture commissioner. Speaking to about three hundred Young Democrats after a barbecue supper at the Trent Pines Club, Scott said that North Carolina's future rested in the hands of a "liberal Democratic Party." He warned the Young Democrats to avoid "getting yourself lined up with conservatism. . . . Let us be an aggressive, progressive people." The Democratic Party should avoid putting any hindrance in the way of developing every resource. To return to conservatism would mean reestablishing "new breeding grounds for Republicanism."[1] No statewide opinion polls were conducted in those days, but there can be little doubt that Scott had a large and loyal following. "There never was a time in the history of our state when there was a general 'shaking up' of the machine rule rottenness as at this time," wrote C. C. Burns from the small Pender County town of Atkinson. "The late governor and senator Huey Long did the same for Louisiana, bucking the Standard Oil Co., along with the rest to build a new state, along with the confidence of the people of that state. . . . We are with you, one hundred percent, governor, and are expecting, like the people of Louisiana referred, to send you on up to the U.S. Senate."[2] Burns's enthusiasm was echoed by Harry Golden, editor of the Charlotte-based *Carolina Israelite*, who wrote in a letter to Scott: "I think that you are the first major political figure in the South, since the days of Reconstruction, who could conceivably receive the vote of the Lower East Side in New York, the Black Belt in Chicago, and the trade unionists of Pennsylvania and Ohio."[3]

Among Scott's other admirers was Raleigh radio reporter Jesse Helms. In an "off the record" letter to the governor, Helms wrote, "I think the present governor of North Carolina ought to set his cap for an even greater achievement. Our present governor, as far as I am concerned, is the first North Carolinian in my life time who has had the vision and the ability to become president of the United States. And he may represent North Carolina's only chance for that honor in my life time. Won't you have a heart-to-heart talk with the Governor in the hopes that he may set his cap for that accomplishment? This is the political era of the 'Little Man.' You have a way of getting along with the little man. Make the most of it." It was signed, "Admiringly, Jesse."[4]

The North Carolina of 1949 was a far different place than the one today. It was among the most agrarian states in America, with two-thirds of the population living in areas officially designated as rural. The population was overwhelmingly composed of Tar Heel natives, and Charlotte, the largest city, was home to 134,930 people. The Sun Belt migration was decades in the future. But Kerr Scott, a rough-hewn dairy farmer from Haw River, helped foster a brand of rural progressivism that burnished North Carolina's reputation as among the most moderate and forward-looking in the South. As a result, for much of the second half of the twentieth century, North Carolina was led by Kerr, his son Bob, and their political allies, such as Terry Sanford, a lawyer from the small farming community of Laurin-burg, and Jim Hunt, who grew up on a dairy farm outside Rock Ridge.

This was redeye-gravy progressivism—not big-city liberalism. Scott called his supporters Branchhead Boys, or those rural residents born at the head of a creek or branch. The movement was born among some of the nation's poorest, most isolated farmers, nurtured in country churches, and powered by agriculture movements such as the Farmers' Alliance and the North Carolina Grange, which welded the highly individualistic farmers into a single voice. When unleashed, the rural progressivism could erect great universities, build vast road networks, create new ports, force the utility companies to extend electricity and telephones into the country-side, and build housing for the poor. During Kerr Scott's term as governor, many rural North Carolinians saw government as a vehicle for improving their lives.

But at every step of the way, this rural progressivism was confronted by a deeply ingrained conservatism—much of it emanating from those same fields and church pews. On the inflammatory question of racial equality, in particular, there was often a reactionary pushback. Well before Kerr Scott's time, during the Farmers' Alliance and Populist push of the 1890s, the first wave of rural progressivism faced opposition in the form of the white su-premacy campaigns of 1898 and 1900. Likewise, Kerr Scott's Populist Go Forward program led to the racially charged Smith-Graham Senate cam-paign in 1950. And when his son Bob became governor, many came to dis-trust governmental power, especially when it came to forced racial inte-gration of the public schools. Bob Scott's term as governor, from 1969 to 1973—with its rise of black activism—led to the election of sharply conser-vative Jesse Helms to the U.S. Senate.

What happened in North Carolina is not unique to the state or even to the South. The progressive ruralism of the Midwest and the West—the phe-nomenon that gave rise to such movements as the Populist Party and orga-nizations such as the Grange and the National Farmers' Alliance—faded with time. Indeed, the small, embattled farmer—the Branchhead Boy sup-porter of Kerr Scott—began to disappear as far fewer people earned their living from the land and farming became more mechanized and corporate.

The religious undertone of the rural self-improvement movement morphed in many cases into a religious fundamentalism that saw govern-ment—especially the federal courts—as a foe of those with socially con-servative sensibilities who saw the legalization of abortion, the outlawing of prescribed group prayer in the public schools, equal rights for women, and, later, gay marriages and transgender rights as antibiblical. Preceding this, too, the war in Vietnam ripped the country's sense of unity, creating divisions that were difficult to heal; and the rise of the counterculture helped sow the seeds of suspicion between—as Ralph Scott put it—the fellow pumping gas and the perceived campus elites. Moreover, large swaths of rural America became more homogenized, particularly those locales surrounding growing metro areas, with farm fields being turned into strip malls and residential subdivisions. Today, many rural residents no longer see themselves as underdogs in need of a friendly government.

Some noted historians, such as Julian Pleasants, have labeled Kerr Scott a populist, and there is certainly an argument to be made for that. Kerr Scott, and his father, known as Farmer Bob, led pitchfork rebellions of rural voters seeking a better life, much of it through the power of government to extend services into the countryside. Throughout his career, Kerr Scott often fought the power companies over rural service, the oil companies over gas prices, and the banks over state deposits. Although his politics had a Populist flavor, in many ways he was equally influenced by Franklin Roosevelt's New Deal and Harry Truman's Fair Deal progressive philosophy for the forgotten American. Unlike many Populists, Kerr Scott did not propose to soak the rich, rail against Wall Street, or campaign against African Americans or other minorities. Similarly, the Democrats who followed in his footsteps—most notably his son Bob Scott, Terry Sanford, and Jim Hunt—were progressive but not Populist. But Bob Scott would confront a conservative backlash among many of those same voters, dealing with a landscape populated by players keen on pushing the country in a new, more conservative direction—Jesse Helms, Jim Gardner, George Wallace, Richard Nixon, and Roger Ailes.

The Scott family provides a unique lens through which to view both North Carolina politics and rural progressivism. From Reconstruction into the early twenty-first century, the Scotts of Haw River, a rural community located in the middle of the state, were center stage in North Carolina's political narrative. But perhaps more important, the Scott story provides a very human story of the rural South as it struggles with how to overcome the legacies of poverty and isolation, racism and segregation. The Scotts demonstrate that the rural South was a far more complicated and nuanced place than often resides in the public imagination.

1 ★ HAW RIVER

The farmers seem like unto fruit—you can gather them
by a gentle shake of the bush. —Col. Buck Barry, a former
Texas Ranger on organizing in North Carolina

As long as he lived, W. Kerr Scott remembered the farm bells tolling long into the night among the farms scattered along the Haw River, which flowed through the gently rolling hills of central North Carolina. By prearrangement, the farm bells—big iron dinner bells with dangling ropes to set their clappers in motion—were rung as a signal that the local referendum passed in 1903, raising a tax to pay for the area's first public school. It was a small step for progress, but its passage had been in doubt. The campaign was so close and hard-fought that Governor Charles Brantley Aycock had traveled the forty-six miles by train from Raleigh to campaign for it in the small rural community.

What Scott particularly remembered was not just that the referendum passed but how it passed. In the segregated Jim Crow South, where the vast majority of black voters were newly disenfranchised by a literacy test, the school mandate had come down to the vote of one aging black farmhand. Lawson Chavis, a bachelor and ex-slave, was one of relatively few African Americans who were literate and therefore eligible to vote. But the choice was not easy for Chavis. The owner of the farm where he worked opposed the levy and had threatened to evict Chavis if he exercised his franchise. Shortly before the polls closed, James Covington, who owned the farm next to the Scott place, visited Chavis and arranged for him to move to a log cabin on land owned by his mother-in law. Covington took Chavis to the polls and, after supper, moved him to his new home. The measure passed 26–24, and the tolling of the bells began.[1]

"When I think back I can't recollect anything that has ever happened in my life that made a deeper impression on my mind or influenced my public acts more than the ringing of farm bells," Scott told a radio audience in 1953, a year after he stepped down as one of the most progressive southern governors of the mid-twentieth century.[2] The lesson, Scott wrote decades later, was "that our people wanted to go forward. Our community, like thousands of others, has done so."[3]

Kerr Scott and his brothers and sisters would attend that school, and so, albeit briefly, would his son, Robert W. Scott, a future governor, before it closed in 1936. Although just a simple country school, for Kerr Scott it represented something larger—the push of a poor rural people to build a better life. It was a task the Scott family devoted much of their lives to, using the power of government to build schools and roads, and to push power and telephone companies to extend lines deep into farm country. In a state that had no big cities and little in-migration, this rural progressivism helped shape North Carolina's politics and gave the state the reputation as among the most moderate and forward-looking in the South in the twentieth century.

BEGINNINGS

Kerr Scott was born April 17, 1896, in the handsome, sizable country home built by his grandfather Henderson Scott before the Civil War. Visitors remarked about the grove of impressive old oaks and the stately row of boxwoods in the semicircular driveway.

The Scotts were part of the great Scots-Irish immigration, or Ulster Irish, that had arrived in Philadelphia and then made their way down the Great Wagon Road to North Carolina in the mid-1700s, drawn to the sassafras- and hickory-covered red hills around the Haw River. But it was Henderson Scott (1814–1870), the modern patriarch of the Scott clan and a figure out of the Old South, who firmly established the family in the middle class. A self-made man, Kerr Scott's grandfather started out as an eighteen-year-old mechanic in a textile mill before becoming one of the richest men in the county, opening a general store, operating a blacksmith shop, a tannery, and a chewing tobacco factory, and doing a little farming. He also served as justice of the peace and was one of the builders of Hawfields Presbyterian Church, where much of the Scott family still worships and where most of them are buried.

By 1860, Henderson Scott was one of the largest slaveholders in the county, with thirty-seven enslaved people, ranging in age from one to eighty. Although it was common for Haw River farmers to own slaves, most white households in Alamance County (65.1 percent) owned no slaves.[4] Crippled in 1857 when he was thrown by a mule, Henderson Scott did not

The old Scott family home, built before the Civil War by Henderson Scott and where Farmer Bob raised his family. Farmer Bob stands on the steps. Kerr is one of the two children seated in the middle next to their grandmother. Photo taken around 1900. (Courtesy of State Archives of North Carolina)

see combat during the Civil War, although his tannery provided shoes and leather for the Confederacy.[5]

After the war, Henderson Scott joined one of the most active Ku Klux Klan organizations in the state. The group included much of the old white power structure, and membership in Alamance County numbered an estimated five hundred to seven hundred individuals. Particularly fervent and brutal, the Alamance KKK terrorized blacks who sought advancement and any whites who helped them, including lynching and murdering a black town councilman and white state senator. Henderson Scott's Klan activity landed him in jail when Republican governor William Holden sent in former Union troops to help restore order in what became known as the Kirk-Holden War, but Scott was soon released. Several months later, his leg deteriorated. A Hillsborough doctor ran out of anesthesia during an operation to amputate his foot, and Henderson Scott died from shock three days later, on October 11, 1870, at age fifty-six.[6]

To understand Henderson Scott's grandson, Kerr Scott, one must first understand Kerr Scott's father, Robert W. Scott (1861–1929). Everyone who knew the two men said so: the father's life was devoted to farming, politics, and the church—and so was the son's. The father was involved in a pitchfork rebellion; so was the son. The father ran for state agriculture commissioner, and so did the son.

Educated largely at private academies in an age with few public schools, by age seventeen Robert W. Scott was already managing his mother's farm. Two years later in 1880, Scott bought out the interests of his brothers and sisters in the home place of 668 acres for $4,250, excepting his mother's dower interest of 213 acres.[7] Apart from the acquisition of land, a young farmer had few options to improve himself in the years before North Carolina had an agricultural school or county farm extension agents. So Scott did something unusual for the time. In late 1881, he apprenticed himself for six months to an experimental farm in the Hudson Valley region of New York that was owned by a wealthy northern industrialist.

Returning to North Carolina, he married his girlfriend, Lizzie Hughes, in 1883, and set about building a model farm. Under the management of tenants, Scott's family acreage had deteriorated, with badly washed gullies, half the fields in timber, and its irregular fields full of stones. But with his new knowledge, Scott practiced diversity, self-sufficiency, and crop rotation, vastly improving the farm's output of wheat, corn, oats, cattle, and sheep.

After transforming his own farm, Scott began traveling across North Carolina as a missionary for good farming methods. He wasn't alone: a wave of late nineteenth-century agricultural reforms gave rise to the practice known as scientific farming as well as to agricultural fairs and publications. In time, Scott became one of the founders of the Farmers' Institute program, forerunner of the extension service, which at its height in 1912 held 502 institutes around the state. He was also the first president of the North Carolina Farmers' Convention; selected a "Master Farmer," he gained such a reputation that he became known across the state as "Farmer Bob." It was a short step from being a farm proponent to becoming a lieutenant in a powerful agrarian political movement that upended Tar Heel politics and helped set the course for rural progressivism for the next century.

The pitchfork rebellion began in Lampasas County, Texas, in 1875, led by a group of small frontier farmers who combined to protect themselves against foreign-owned land syndicates, cattle kings, and rustlers.

The Farmers' Alliance and Industrial Union advocated taxing and controlling the railroads, establishing interstate commerce regulation, and expanding the currency. By 1886, the Texans decided to spread their gospel across the South and Midwest. Although allied with unions, the alliance was primarily driven by farmers. The South in particular faced a farming crisis, and no state was more fertile territory for the Texans' message than North Carolina, where farmers were still feeling the effects of economic destruction caused by the Civil War, the emancipation of 350,000 slaves, an overdependence on cotton, and the lack of credit that led to the exploitive sharecropping system.

The Texans moved into North Carolina in May 1887 under the leadership of sixty-six-year-old former Texas Ranger J. B. "Buck" Barry. A North Carolina native, Barry had fought in the Mexican and Civil Wars, led vigilante groups against Indians and horse thieves, served in the Texas legislature, and operated a farm in Bosque County, Texas. By August, Barry had organized thirty Farmers' Alliance chapters, or suballiances, in Wake County alone. In Harnett County, he organized eleven chapters in twenty-one days, and in fourteen days he organized ten more in Moore County. By 1890, the Farmer's Alliance had 2,147 local organizations in North Carolina and ninety thousand members.[8]

Among the farmers going into politics was Farmer Bob, the head of the Alamance County Alliance, who was elected to the state House in 1888 at the age of twenty-seven with the alliance's backing. In North Carolina that same year, the alliance elected eight congressmen and seized control of the state legislature. In 1892, the head of the alliance, Elias Carr, a farmer from Edgecombe County, won the governorship. Similar developments occurred across the South: the alliance won other state and legislative offices, including Benjamin "Pitchfork Ben" Tillman as governor of South Carolina and James "Big Jim" Hogg of Texas as governor. In total, Farmers' Alliance strength took over eight southern legislatures, elected six alliance-pledged governors, and seated more than fifty congressmen.[9]

The revolutionary "farmers' legislature" of 1891, in which Farmer Bob served, passed an extraordinary slate of progressive measures. Many were related to education: the legislature increased the tax rate to finance public schools; created a normal school for white girls that would later become Woman's College and is now the coeducational University of North Carolina at Greensboro; and initiated an agricultural college and normal college in Greensboro for blacks, now known as North Carolina A&T State University. The Farmers' Alliance also played a role in establishing what would become N.C. State University in Raleigh. The legislature's other focus was the railroad, which for many years had enjoyed nearly unfettered power. The legislature put into place regulations forbidding railroad rebates and rate discrimination, and it created a three-member railroad commission empowered to reduce rates and to eliminate the special tax exemptions and lower assessments enjoyed by the railroads.[10]

The alliance's influence would not last, however, as the group splintered into factions. The more radical Farmers' Alliance members broke from the Democratic Party and formed a coalition with Republicans, then strongly influenced by African Americans, to form a Populist party called Fusionists. The more conservative alliance members, including Farmer Bob, stayed with the Democrats. He lost reelection to his House seat in 1894 to a Fusionist-backed candidate.

THE POPULIST

The Fusion election upended twenty years of Democrat rule in Raleigh, and the new legislature passed a series of progressive reforms, including a 6 percent interest ceiling on loans, a tax hike on railroads and other businesses, and increased spending for public school and colleges. Legislators also made North Carolina's elections laws the fairest in the South, which led to a surge in black elected local officials.

The Fusion government sparked a brutal conservative reaction. In a campaign financed by business interests opposed to the farmers' revolt, the Democratic Party in 1898 ran a virulently racist and sometimes violent campaign that drew a wedge between the white Populist farmers and their new allies, the black Republicans. After winning control of the legislature, the Democrats in 1900 elected a Democratic governor and passed a constitutional amendment requiring a literacy test designed to disenfranchise most black voters, ensuring that Democratic power would not again be threatened by a biracial coalition. The white supremacy campaigns of 1898 and 1900 established a pattern in North Carolina politics of progressive reform followed by a race-tainted white backlash.

Nowhere in the country did the farmers' rebellion have such far-reaching political effects as in North Carolina, a state dotted with small subsistence farmers. Even when the Democrats regained control, it was a changed Democratic Party—no longer quite as reactionary and much more willing to consider spending for education and to consider other reforms. The Farmers' Alliance for its part refused to give up and hung on in North Carolina longer than anywhere else in the country—a one-time prairie fire reduced to embers. Farmer Bob, a Democrat in good standing but still an old alliance man, returned to the Raleigh in 1901, this time in the Senate. He was elected to the House in 1902 and remained active in politics, pushing for increased funding for education and serving under six governors on the state Board of Agriculture, an important body in a farm-centric state.

In 1908, Farmer Bob unsuccessfully sought the Democratic nomination for agriculture commissioner at a marathon Democratic convention in Charlotte in which sixty-one ballots were cast for governor over four days and four nights. The agriculture commissioner's race didn't take that long, with William A. Graham winning the nomination on the sixth ballot in a five-man field. Farmer Bob finished fourth and dropped out after the fourth ballot. He remained active in the Farmers' Alliance until his death in 1929 and was often joined at its annual meetings in the coastal town of New Bern or at N.C. State University in Raleigh by his son, Kerr, and his daughter-in-law, Mary.[11]

Farmer Bob and his wife, Lizzie, had fourteen children, three of whom died as infants, one of whom fatally rolled into the burning coals of the fireplace as a baby. Of the children who survived, it was a remarkably high-achieving family. All graduated from college, and many had distinguished careers. Kerr became governor and U.S. senator, while Ralph became a businessman and one of the most powerful North Carolina state legislators of the mid-twentieth century. Elizabeth Scott Carrington helped create the nursing school at the University of North Carolina at Chapel Hill, and Carrington Hall still houses the program and bears her name. Ivy League–educated Floyd Scott worked as a country doctor and delivered an estimated seven thousand babies; Henry Scott, a farmer and businessman, served as chairman of the Alamance County board of education and president of the state school boards association.

Both parents emphasized education. Farmer Bob, who attended the University of North Carolina for one year, served as chairman of the local school board, as a trustee of Flora MacDonald College for women, and as a member of the board of what would become N.C. State University. Lizzie was the daughter of a college-educated schoolmaster, Samuel Wellwood Hughes, who founded Hughes Academy for boys. Similar to a prep school, Hughes Academy drew students from as far away as Texas; it is also where Lizzie met her future husband.[12]

Because of Farmer Bob's wide connections, the Scott farm received well-known visitors such as Aycock, Josephus Daniels, the Raleigh publisher and Woodrow Wilson's secretary of the navy, and Clarence Poe, the editor of the *Progressive Farmer* and a leading agriculturalist.[13] And yet, the Scotts wore their education and connections lightly. If anything, they tended to camouflage their intelligence behind a bale of hay and a wisecrack. The children called their father "Captain," or sometimes "Colonel," and he was often described as a stern taskmaster. From an early age, the youngsters shared in the farm work with little time left for leisure. The boys were up at 5:00 A.M. to milk the cows before school, and there was plowing and other chores.

The grandchildren of a slave owner and a Klansman, the children grew up on stories of Yankee soldiers stealing horses, of hard times during and after the Civil War, of children playing with useless Confederate money. As was the custom of the time, the black help was called "Aunt" and "Uncle," while the Scott children were always addressed by the black help as "Mister" or "Miss."[14] At the same time, farm life was far more integrated than many might imagine today, and the Scott boys often ate in the homes of their black playmates, sharing meals of cornbread and molasses. They also worked in the fields alongside both white and black farmhands. One day when he was young, Ralph Scott was out in the field when the sheriff arrested a black field hand, taking him away at gunpoint. Ralph never forgot the fear of the moment, and when he later asked a black neighbor what had happened, the man replied: "Boy, don't never argue with the man who has the gun." Ralph refused to accept the answer and, when he grew up, never hesitated to stand with those who were powerless against those in authority.[15]

If the family didn't produce anyone who would challenge the racial status quo—and there were few white civil rights crusaders anywhere in the white South of that era—it did turn out people who seemed fairminded for that day and time. Kerr and Ralph would become leaders in pushing for more equitable treatment of African Americans in the political arena and in education. On the domestic front, at least a third of the babies delivered by Dr. Floyd Scott in northern Alamance County were African American. Henry Scott, a farmer, served on the board of historically black N.C. A&T State University for nearly twenty years. Anderson Hughes Scott, when managing a dairy in Raleigh (1947–53) after World War II, hired the company's first black deliveryman. Kerr's brother-in-law Rex Hudson, who directed the county extension agent program at N.C. State, was forced to flee Raleigh and live in High Point for three months after the Klan threatened his life for hiring a black extension agent.

Two of the sisters lived most of their adult lives in integrated environments: Elizabeth, both nursing and teaching nursing at the University of Pennsylvania in Philadelphia, and Agnes as a public health nurse in Newark, New Jersey. If they had any reservations about such arrangements, they didn't mention it in their memoirs. Before retiring to North Carolina, Agnes took in a black South African mother with two small children who had been abandoned by her husband and had showed up unannounced on her doorstep one day. One of her Catholic friends dubbed her "St. Agnes," and she that said her New Jersey neighbors "had ten thousand fits." But Agnes said that she was simply responding to the Haw River upbringing that she and her siblings had received from Farmer Bob and Lizzie. "We were raised with the understanding that we were expected to do something worthwhile for others," Agnes later recalled.[16]

On March 27, 1914, after having been in poor health for years, Lizzie Scott died at age forty-eight following a gall bladder operation at Rex Hospital in Raleigh. Farmer Bob's unmarried sister, Mary, known as Mamie, moved from Asheville to take over the large household. Living with the family were two maiden aunts and as many as four public school teachers who boarded at the house. The teachers were housed in a wing separated from the residency by what we would call today a breezeway. The Scotts boarded the teachers not only for the extra income but because they thought they would be a good influence on their children.[17] The following year after Lizzie's death, Farmer Bob married Ella Anderson of Cedar Grove, a tall, slim, quiet, soft-spoken teacher who had taught many of the Scott children and whom Farmer Bob, as local school board chairman, had had a role in hiring.[18]

KERR SCOTT

When he arrived at N.C. State University in 1913, although academically behind students who attended prep or city schools, Kerr Scott graduated in four years with honors and a degree in agriculture science. His courses included algebra, plane geometry, physics, quantitative analysis in chemistry, organic chemistry, and four years of allied scientific studies.[19] But he was not a grind. At five feet, ten and a half inches tall and 170 pounds, he ran on the state track team for four years and won several cross-country medals. He started the school debating team, served as president of the YMCA, and was elected junior class president. One way he managed to accomplish so much is that he went home only at Christmas. His sophomore year, he walked the fifty miles home from Raleigh to Haw River for the holidays so that he would have money to buy presents for his family. He spent the first two days back home soaking his blistered feet in hot water. "I found the giving of those Christmas presents very painful," Scott recalled.[20]

After graduation, Scott took a job as an agriculture extension agent, helping to organize and promote wheat and oat clubs across the state. He resigned his position with the extension service and enlisted on September 7, 1918, reporting to Field Artillery Camp Zachary Taylor near Louisville, Kentucky. World War I ended while he was still in camp, and he was honorably discharged.[21] Scott immediately visited an elementary school in Taylorsville, N.C., where Mary Elizabeth White was teaching. The couple married on July 2, 1919, in the Hawfields Presbyterian Church, where both families had been members for five generations; afterward, Kerr and Mary honeymooned in Wrightsville Beach.[22] It was hardly a whirlwind romance since the two had known each other practically all their lives. Mary White's parents, Alamance farmers, lived a mile down Highway 119 from the Scotts and had deep roots in the community. Kerr Scott remembered that their first date was when they attended a school function—he age twelve and she eleven. But Mary said it was hard to tell because they had been walking together to school and church for years. When they hit their midteens, they graduated to buggy rides.

Scott and Miss Mary—as he always called her and as the public later came to know her—were opposites. A graduate of Woman's College (now the University of North Carolina at Greensboro), she was quiet, loved peace, books, and gardening, and appreciated old friends and neighbors. Kerr towered over Miss Mary, who stood five feet tall and weighed ninety-five pounds.[23] Reading interested him, too, but he preferred current events and history books. He also relished crowds (the more the better), enjoyed a good fight, and liked to rib people. Sometimes Mary picked up the pieces.

In October 1921, Farmer Bob conveyed the legal title of his 692 acres to his eleven surviving children, dividing it equally. He hoped that doing so while his children were alive might encourage them to settle near him. And to some extent, it did: Kerr and his brother Henry farmed their land, while three sisters sold their portion. Elizabeth Scott Carrington, on the other hand, rented her portion to Kerr and later donated it to Alamance Community College as the site of their new campus.[24] After the title changed hands, Farmer Bob largely gave up farming himself but retained a life interest in his farm, charging his children rent and continuing to live there.[25]

While still in college in 1917, Kerr Scott had borrowed $4,000 ($66,000 in 2018 dollars) from his father to buy a 224-acre tract of undeveloped land

as well as a few head of sheep and cattle. The parcel featured gently rolling hills with deep woods and was located near the Haw River and its con-
fluence with Back Creek. To farm the land required backbreaking work—
clearing stumps and felling trees—which Kerr accomplished with a farm
laborer's help.[26] He also bought from his father and moved to the property a two-room, log-built house that had been constructed by a relative
during the Civil War. Kerr's carpenter neighbor added four rooms and a
front porch. With the help of a farmhand, Kerr Scott sawed trees to provide
wood for construction. However, despite the improvements, when Kerr
and Miss Mary set up house, there was no electricity, no running water,
and no heat—and they had no car. The oil stove in the kitchen—a wedding
gift from Farmer Bob—produced so little warmth that Mary could hardly
bear to stay in the kitchen. After living in the house for several years, Scott
built an upstairs addition that provided the house with a total of 2,900
square feet.

By adding on to the small antebellum farmhouse, Scott created a modern, circa 1919 bungalow, with a common bond brick foundation, weather-
board walls, and a standing seam metal roof. While substantial, it would
hardly draw a second look from a motorist, let alone strike someone as the
home of two North Carolina governors. Today, the farmstead rests just off
the current Interstate 85 at the Haw River exit, about ten miles southeast
of Burlington—about a thirty-minute drive from Greensboro, Chapel Hill,
and Durham. Kerr Scott lived there the rest of his life, and when he died,
his widow, Miss Mary, lived there until her passing, too.

During nearly his entire life, Scott held a full-time government job while
continuing to live and work on the farm, leaving much of the daily tending
of his cows and crops to managers, hired hands, and tenant farmers. Starting with 224 acres, twenty-five cows, and twenty-five sheep, by the time he
was governor in 1949, he owned 1,300 acres, one hundred Holsteins, and
eighty Jersey cows. Three hundred of those acres served as pasture, and 47
acres grew alfalfa. At the time of his death in 1958, the farm operation—
actually several farms—had grown to 2,200 acres.

In early 1920, Scott took a job as Alamance County farm extension agent,
a post he held for the next ten years, making $3,000 per year (or $37,433 in
2018 dollars). He started by touring Alamance County farms by horseback,
which took him four days. During the decade, Kerr Scott estimated that
he traveled 150,000 miles in the county, attending meetings, lecturing and
assisting organizations, and promoting projects.[27]

After getting up at 5:00 A.M. to milk the cows and taking the milk to town, he drove his pickup to his office in the basement of the old court-house in Graham—pleasantly cool in the summer in those days before air conditioning—where his first desk was a nail keg. He packed his lunch to save money. Often there were night meetings.[28]

He developed a countywide pasture campaign, ordering a carload of grass and clover seed. He also took a special interest in 4-H work and organized the largest 4-H Jersey calf club in the world, helping more than 244 boys and girls obtain Jersey calves.[29]

Miss Mary taught school during the couple's first year of marriage. But after one cold winter in which she rode horseback six miles roundtrip to her school, she quit her teaching job and became a full-time mother and farm manager.

The young couple also started their family. Osborne was born in 1920, Mary Kerr Scott in 1921, and Robert W. Scott, the future governor, in 1929. Robert Scott was born less than a month after his grandfather and name-sake, Farmer Bob, serving one last term in the Senate, died on May 16.

Among the honorary pallbearers at his funeral were Josephus Daniels, Clarence Poe, and state agriculture commissioner William A. Graham. Although he had been a model farmer, by the time Farmer Bob died, he had little money. He had educated his large family, had devoted increasing energies to politics and less to farming, and had dispersed much of his land to his children.[30]

When Kerr Scott outlined his plan for rural improvements, his neighbor Jim Covington said that he was just following the path of his father. "Course, it's Kerr's program, but it's also the program his daddy worked for all his life—this thing of better schools and roads."[31]

2 ★ HARD TIMES

I enter the campaign as a Progressive New Deal candidate for farm people,
as against an ultra-conservative candidate, one whose main qualification
has been the greatest hand shaker and vote getter of this generation; one
who has spent his life-time building political fences. —W. Kerr Scott in 1936,
announcing his campaign for agriculture commissioner

During the 1920s boom times, North Carolina's cities and towns saw lights coming on, telephone lines strung, trolley tracks laid, and the first skyscrapers erected. Across the piedmont, thousands of textile spindles and looms hummed as North Carolina became the South's leading industrial state. But the countryside remained mired in poverty and backwardness. In fact, rural North Carolina was one of the last places in the country to acquire electricity, telephones, running water, or paved roads. Meanwhile, most North Carolina farmers were producing just one crop, either tobacco or cotton, which provided only a subsistence-level existence. "Living from hand-to-mouth as most of our farmers live—both tenants and operating owners—the problems of farming as a business are well-nigh insolvable," wrote Samuel H. Hobbs Jr., a noted rural social economist at the University of North Carolina.[1] The chief problem, Hobbs argued, was the sharecropping system, which "is perhaps the next step up after serfdom or peonage, neither of which exists in this country."[2]

With the 1929 stock market crash and the Great Depression, farming soon got unimaginably worse. Flue-cured tobacco prices fell from 17.3 cents a pound in 1928 to 8.4 cents a pound in 1931. Cotton, which was selling for 22.5 cents per pound in 1925, fell to 6 cents a pound in 1931.[3] The crisis would produce North Carolina's second great agricultural movement, which, like its predecessor, would become a powerful influence on state politics.

The organizer was Clarence Poe, who had taken over the *Progressive Farmer*, the publication started by Leonidas Polk, the former Farmers' Alliance and Populist leader. The son of a Chatham County cotton farmer, Poe built the *Progressive Farmer* into the leading agricultural publication

Tobacco sharecropper family outside their home in Person County in July 1939.
Photo by Dorothea Lange. (Courtesy of the Library of Congress)

in the South, with a circulation reaching 1.4 million in the 1930s. Before reaching that success, however, in 1927 Poe brought together farm leaders to discuss how to best organize themselves. While the old Farmers' Alliance and Farmers' Union still existed on paper, they were now remnants of their former selves. So the farm leaders chose to affiliate with the National Grange, an organization that had disappeared from the state decades earlier. But as the nation's oldest farm organization, with chapters in thirty-three states, the Grange seemed a natural choice with its family-oriented focus and strong support among former Farmers' Alliance members. Lewis Taber of Columbus, Ohio, the national Grange master, agreed that North Carolina was "fertile soil" and sent in organizers.

Just weeks before the stock market crash, the Grange held its first organizational meeting in the House chambers of the State Capitol on September 26 and 27, 1929, with 225 people from seventeen counties attending.[4] Poe agreed to serve one year to help the Grange get under way. At the group's next convention, in Salisbury on October 2, 1930, the group chose the youthful and dynamic Kerr Scott, who had recently resigned his job as Alamance County extension agent, to become state master. It is probable that Poe—a longtime friend and admirer of Farmer Bob—played a role in the choice.

It was a meeting of the man and the times. The farmers were ready to get out their pitchforks, and Kerr Scott—raised on the stories of his father and the Farmers' Alliance and the Populists of a generation earlier—had the personality to lead the march. As master of the North Carolina Grange for three years, Scott emerged as the chief spokesman in the state for struggling Depression era farmers. He served as their lobbyist in Raleigh and spoke regularly across the state, building the connections he would later use to launch his political career.

In time, the Grange became a proving ground for three North Carolina governors who came out of the rural progressive movement—Kerr, his son Bob Scott, and Jim Hunt. The three ultimately occupied the executive mansion for twenty-four years of the last half of the twentieth century. Although the Grange was a fraternal organization rather than a political one—it didn't endorse candidates, and it included both Democrats and Republicans—it had a world view. It believed in helping rural people better their plight through electrification, telephones, better schools, and better health care; it saw government as an instrument to help accomplish those goals. It also had prolabor sympathies. Hunt in 2016 remarked,

> They [Depression-era farmers] saw in the Grange and in the leaders of the Grange a big powerful effort to help rural people, rural families to improve their lives in terms of having a good income from their farms, public policies that would get them good schools, good roads and better health care and nationally supporting good farm programs helping farmers get a good price for their products. . . . It fit right in with FDR's agricultural programs and those that the Democrats supported all these years. . . . And out of the Grange work, helping farm families, came a family that went into politics, championing all of those things. That's why we were for him [Kerr].[5]

Lots of people, it turned out, were for Kerr Scott. He presided over the fastest-growing Grange state chapter since the 1870s; organizing thirty-two new chapters with five thousand members in just the first year.[6] In his address to the Grange convention in 1931, Scott demonstrated his commitment to the organization's principles, calling for greater rural electrification and rural telephones. His agenda would change remarkably little over years—largely borrowing his Grange program for his political agenda.[7]

While in the 1930s a huge gap existed between urban and rural America everywhere, farmers in North Carolina experienced a particular disadvantage. In 1935, only 10.9 percent of American farms had electricity. But that was triple the rate of North Carolina, where only 3.2 percent of farms had power.[8] And life on a farm without electricity involved backbreaking work. For farmers, it meant milking cows and lifting feed and cotton by hand. Families split wood by ax and fed dirty, hard-to-regulate woodstoves; they hand-pumped water from wells. For farmwives, no refrigeration meant that vegetables had to be canned shortly after picking. No washing machines meant bending over cast-iron tubs and boiling the family's clothes, not to mention using lye soap to scrub the dirt out of clothes on washboards until knuckles were raw. The garments then had to be rinsed several times—the water pumped from wells—and then the clothes hung on lines. When everything was dry, then began the ironing: several heavy irons heated on the woodstove. Women aged before their time.

The daily, personal struggles of North Carolina farming families took a backseat to the power companies' bottom lines. Slow to extend service to the thinly settled countryside, companies said that it was impractical to string a line unless it would pay for itself in three years. The companies often demanded that prospective customers agree to buy refrigerators and washing machines before they would extend the lines.

Impatient with the progress of private power, in a speech in Statesville in 1931, Scott as Grange master called for the creation of a state agency to help finance construction of rural electric lines. He also composed a letter encouraging several hundred local Grange leaders to write to Governor J. C. B. Ehringhaus to begin a rural electrification push.[9] Finally, at the Grange's behest in May 1934, Ehringhaus named a four-member committee headed by Poe and including Scott to study the problem of rural electrification. Based on the committee's recommendations, the legislature created the N.C. Rural Electrification Authority in 1935. Scott was one of five people Ehringhaus appointed as initial members.[10]

At the same time that North Carolina created a state agency, Congress passed the Rural Electrification Act, and FDR created the Rural Electrification Administration to provide loans to local cooperatives to build more electric lines. Slowly, with the help of federal money and local co-ops, the lights began to come on in the North Carolina countryside. By July 1937, 11.3 percent of North Carolina farms had electricity, compared to 16.8 percent nationally. By 1940, 24.3 percent of North Carolina farms were connected compared to 30.4 percent nationally. By 1948, 66.4 percent of the North Carolina farms had power, compared to 68.6 percent nationally.[11] Much of the electrification was due to public power. Of the 72,096 miles of electrical lines built in the state's rural areas by 1950, 44 percent was built by privately owned utilities, 50 percent by Rural Electric Membership corporations, and the rest by municipalities and public institutions.[12]

Electric power transformed rural life. People could now turn on the spigot to get hot water. They had electric stoves, refrigerators to preserve food and milk, and radios—playing the news or the Grand Ol' Opry—to break the rural isolation. Simple lightbulbs brightened previously dingy homes in astonishing ways, and one no longer had to trim greasy, oily wicks or wash the sooty globes of kerosene lamps. Children could do homework by lamplight.

While electricity began to bring relief to some North Carolina farmers, the Depression brought other challenges. With the collapse of farm prices, many farmers found it difficult to pay their property taxes, and some faced foreclosure. They turned to Grange Master Kerr Scott—not once but twice—to lead pitchfork rebellions in Raleigh as they pressured lawmakers to provide tax relief.

In the first rebellion, in March 1931, an estimated five thousand farmers marched on the State Capitol—forcing lawmakers to move a hearing to Broughton High School, then Raleigh's largest venue. The subject was how to finance a reorganization of state government. "The speeches and even more, the attitude of the gathering, convinced every observer that the money should be raised 'from sources other than ad valorem taxes on property' or there will be a powerful revolution such as the State witnessed in 1894," said an editorial in the *News and Observer*, referring to the Populist takeover of the state. It is "Relief or Revolt," the headline announced.[13]

Two years later, in March 1933, Kerr Scott helped lead about 1,500 farmers before the legislature, again demanding tax relief. He said one third of the state's farms had been sold within the past eighteen months. "I am asking the government to cut expenses, not reasonably, but drastically," Scott urged. "I am hoping to keep the schools open and other government functions running, but at lower cost, especially the schools."[14]

Scott was also guiding the farmers' fight on another front—although not in his capacity as Grange master—in a showdown with big dairy that fore-shadowed his future as the most prolabor governor in twentieth-century North Carolina. The Pet Milk Company of St. Louis in 1930 purchased the Alamance Cooperative Creamery and its dairy plant in Greensboro, which had been buying their milk from the Guilford County Milk Producers Association. Pet Milk officials said they would deal with the farmers individually but would no longer do business with them collectively as of January 1, 1931. The dairymen balked. They insisted that unless they could bargain collectively, they would be at the mercy of the creamery company. Friction increased when Pet Milk cut the price it paid farmers for milk.

Scott led a group of farmers in a meeting with the Pet Milk manager, which went badly: the manager came to the four-and-a-half-hour meeting armed and full of "abusive reprimand," according to Scott. "Alamance County is not going to prosper as a dairy county when the price for milk forces the farmer to take his wife and daughter to the field with him to produce feed for family and livestock because his income will not justify hiring labor," Scott wrote in a letter to a Burlington newspaper. "This producer-be-damned policy is not going to work much longer in North Carolina."[15] But the Pet Milk Company did not budge, and the farmers declared a "milk holiday," pouring milk into the streets of Greensboro. "The farmers literally struck," recalled Bob Scott, Kerr's son. "They said, 'no, we just can't take it anymore.' So they poured their milk out on the streets of Greensboro. I'm told the fire department had to come and hose it down because it was freezing. For a number of days after that, the farmers just kept their milk at home and fed it to the pigs and the chickens and threw the rest of it out."[16]

Bypassing Pet, about fifty farmers formed the Guilford Dairy, a cooperative of dairy farmers in Greensboro, to sell their milk directly to consumers in early 1931. Scott was one of the co-op's charter members, and through acquisitions and mergers, the cooperative eventually became part of Flav-O-Rich Dairies, a Kentucky-based chain.

"Organized labor leaders will observe the foregoing with interest," said an editorial in the *Statesville Record and Landmark* during the dairy fight. "The principle of collective bargaining is the principle on which organized labor rests its case. The Guilford County dairymen may not have thought of it before, but hereafter when employees of labor refuse to deal with labor organizations and insists on dealing with individuals directly, the Guilford milk producers will have a fellow feeling."[17] One dairyman in particular, Kerr Scott, had been placed on the side of the workers in what primarily had been a labor-management dispute.

As Grange president, even as his interests were focused on state farmers, Scott made valuable connections at the national level. He brought the national Grange convention to North Carolina for the first time, holding a ten-day meeting in Winston-Salem in 1932. At the close of the conference, Scott was the only southerner among the Grange leadership to travel to Warm Springs, Georgia, to meet with President-elect Franklin Roosevelt, a longtime Grange leader, on November 26, 1932, to discuss farm problems.[18] Out of such meetings came a series of New Deal programs that slowed the rush of farm foreclosures, extended electricity to the countryside, and created production controls aimed at stabilizing prices for tobacco and other crops.

Scott then went to work for the New Deal, starting as an investigator for the Farm Credit Administration and moving up in October 1935 to become five-state director of the Farm Debt Adjustment Administration, Resettlement Administration, where he drew a salary of $4,800 per year (or $87,000 in 2018 dollars).[19] He dealt with the thousands of farmers facing foreclosure because they could no longer make their mortgage payments. Nash County, a tobacco-growing area east of Raleigh, alone reported 3,500 foreclosures of its 5,280 farms in 1930. Working out of Raleigh, Kerr Scott oversaw a debt specialist in each state as well as hundreds of volunteers who worked to keep farmers on their land, by negotiating to give them time to pay off their debt.[20]

AGRICULTURAL COMMISSIONER

Scott had long been thinking about running for state agriculture commissioner. His father had sought the post in 1908, and according to family lore, the elder Scott on his deathbed in 1929 had urged Kerr to avenge his defeat—a story that sounds more like a political fable than fact. In any case, as early as June 1935, newspapers speculated about him challenging Commissioner William A. Graham Jr. in 1936. The speculation heightened when Kerr turned down a promotion to become national director of the Farm Debt Adjustment Administration in November 1935. But Scott hesitated. Graham was regarded as one of the ablest politicians in the state: he had been appointed commissioner in 1923, upon the death of his father, William A. Graham Sr., the man who had defeated Kerr Scott's father. But political circumstances changed in Scott's favor.

A major battle for control of the state was taking shape in 1936. The Democratic organization, headed by former governor O. Max Gardner, now a high-powered Washington super lobbyist, was attempting to nominate Shelby attorney Clyde Hoey as governor. Hoey, Gardner's brother-in-law, was the Democratic primary's conservative. Hoey was challenged by Ralph McDonald, a college professor and New Dealer, and by Lieutenant Governor A. H. "Sandy" Graham. The Gardner organization worried that Commissioner Graham would work against Hoey and for Sandy Graham, his cousin, in the governor's race, and the Gardner organization was recruiting a candidate to run against Graham in the Democratic primary to keep him occupied. The Hoey campaign approached several potential candidates before settling on Scott. It was risk, to be sure: later, during the campaign, Scott would have to fend off charges that he was a "spite candidate" run by Hoey.[21]

It wasn't until April, seven weeks before the primary, that Scott requested a leave of absence from his federal job and entered the race on the last day of candidate filing.[22] In announcing his run for office at the Alamance County courthouse, where he once worked as a county farm agent, Scott argued that he would be a stronger voice for the farmer. "I enter the campaign as a Progressive New Deal candidate for farm people, as against an ultra-conservative candidate, one whose main qualification has been the greatest hand shaker and vote-getter of this generation; one who has spent his life time building political fences," Scott said.[23] He also argued that he would overhaul an agency that he said had become known as "the Funeral Parlor of Agriculture ideas." His "progressive" department, by contrast, would be open to fresh ideas, encourage rural churches by working to boost endowments for houses of worship and cemeteries, and advocate for better rural schools and roads, more electricity to the countryside, and more rural telephone service. To further his position as a farming advocate, Kerr tied his opponent to the poor farm conditions of the Depression.[24] His campaign also emphasized that he was still a practicing farmer, and Scott sometimes demonstrated his skills by peeling off his coat, rolling up his sleeves, and helping a farmer with the milking; he was known to pay a campaign debt with a goat.[25]

Scott's farming roots didn't keep him from the backing of the Gardner machine, a powerful organization with the financial support of most of the state's industrial, banking, and utility interests, as well as the courthouse organizations of the piedmont and the mountains. In 1936, the courthouse organization had a well-deserved reputation for stuffing ballot boxes and mobilizing state employees and federal Works Progress Administration workers for campaign work.[26]

Scott also put together a broader coalition. He created an extensive farm network through his Grange connections and through the county extension agents, many of whom he had worked with. In addition, he carried the good name of his father, the pseudo-endorsement of the *Progressive Farmer*, and the backing of some New Deal Democrats who liked Kerr Scott's message for change. And he had the support of some business leaders, including S. Clay Williams, chairman of R. J. Reynolds, George Holderness, president of Carolina Telephone and Telegraph, and Wachovia Bank's Robert M. Hanes.

Kerr was at home on election night. In a highly improbable victory against a popular and entrenched incumbent, he won the primary 52–48 percent, carrying sixty-two counties to Graham's thirty-eight.

When well-wishers telephoned the next morning, they were told he was "down at the barn" working with one of his farm staff.[27] Even after the primary, visitors would sometimes find him sweating behind two mules planting corn.[28] With this approach, and throughout his campaign, Scott demonstrated the political skills and common touch that would cause him never to lose an election. In the fall, he won by the widest margin of any candidate, taking 70 percent of the vote against Republican John L. Phelps.[29] In sum, the North Carolina elections in 1936 ended with two notable events: the Gardner organization was in complete control and would remain so for another dozen years, and the man who would eventually supplant the Shelby Dynasty—the nickname for the powerful Democratic machine headed by Max Gardner—had arrived in Raleigh. But no one knew that at the time, for Scott had entered political office not as a rebel but as a card-carrying member of the state's political establishment.

The job of agriculture commissioner was far more important in 1936 than it is today. North Carolina was still a mostly rural state in 1936, with only Texas having more farms.[30] As agriculture commissioner, Scott set a persona and agenda that he later followed as governor: he was an activist, unafraid of using the power of government to better the lives of rural people. He was a practitioner of patronage politics. And he often courted controversy, rubbing people the wrong way. He started with wholesale firings—something virtually unknown in state capital circles, where Democrats had been in control for a generation. Promising to "clean house," Scott said that city slickers must go, meaning that he preferred people with rural backgrounds. He also expressed doubts about married women, and brother-sister, brother-brother, and sister-sister teams. He wanted to cut nepotism and give jobs to the main earners in families during the Depression.[31] Yet he replaced veteran state employees with loyalists, some of whom he would take with him to his governor's administration.

By most accounts, Kerr Scott breathed new life into the agriculture department. In almost every area, the department became more active—whether building a modern cotton-grading warehouse, stepping up seed testing, making more plant inspections, or conducting more butterfat tests. Scott urged farmers to support the New Deal tobacco program, allowing the federal government to purchase tobacco for later resale.[32] He also returned the state fair to state control—after several years of the fair having been privately run—in part to make it more of an agricultural exposition and less of a carnival. Under Scott's leadership, North Carolina became the first state to rid itself of brucellosis, also known as contagious abortion, among cattle. Scott also forced unscrupulous feed manufactures to stop using sawdust and rice hulls in their livestock feed and fertilizer manufacturers to discontinue putting sand in their product—and in doing so, he incurred the wrath of the feed and fertilizer interests. On the other hand, Scott won praise from bankers such as George Watts Hill of Durham and Robert M. Hanes of Winston-Salem, from farm leaders such as Clarence Poe, and from prominent black leaders such as James Shepherd, president of the North Carolina College for Negroes in Durham, who thought he was fair in his dealings with black farm extension agents.

But critics attacked him for his firings, for his expansion of the agriculture department, and for raising his salary (from $4,500 per year in 1937 to $6,000 per year in 1941, or, in 2018 dollars, from $77,985 to $101,858). He feuded with the N.C. State agriculture extension department about who should be assisting farmers, and he raised eyebrows when he allowed state employees to pass the hat to buy him a new car, noting that his old flivver had ninety-eight thousand miles on it.[33]

Scott's most serious contest came in 1940, when he was opposed by state senator C. Wayland Spruill, a big farmer from Bertie County, widely known as "Cousin Wayland," an old-fashioned orator who was famous for saying that he represented the area "from the rippling waters of silvery Chowan to the windswept shores of Dare." Spruill promised, "After the election, my opponent will be singing: 'When the moon comes over the cowshed, I'll be milking my cows once again.'" Yet Scott easily defeated Spruill, winning 61 percent of the vote in the Democratic primary. Scott never had a serious primary challenge after that, and he won the fall campaigns by more than 70 percent of the vote.[34]

Scott never stopped milking his cows. In the days before interstate highways, he commuted the fifty miles each way daily—an hour-long trip—between his office in Raleigh and his farm in Haw River on the two-lane N.C. 54. Before leaving at 7:00 A.M., Scott met with his foreman to discuss farm business, usually returning home by 6:00 P.M. unless he had a night meeting.[35] Although Scott did not rent a hotel room or an apartment in Raleigh like most state officials, he rented a room in the YMCA, a block from his office in the Agriculture Building. Y employees remembered him coming in at 2:00 A.M. after long trips. Even after he was elected governor and senator, he kept the room for out-of-town guests who did not feel comfortable staying at the executive mansion or, if unused, for anyone who might need a room.[36]

Not only did Scott continue farming, he expanded Melville Farm from 224 acres to 1,300 acres, buying more tracts of land so that by the time he became agriculture commissioner, he owned five farms. He often borrowed money to buy the land, accumulating debt. Kerr Scott didn't understand stocks and bonds, but he did understand land, and he used his savings to buy more farmland whenever he could.[37] Kerr Scott expanded in other ways, too. In 1929, with the help of neighbors, he erected a large dairy barn with sixty-four stalls. In 1949, he added a wing, hoping the completed barn would hold one hundred cows, but he was disappointed: it held only ninety-eight when he switched from Jerseys to larger Holsteins imported from Wisconsin after his herds were twice wiped out by brucellosis.[38] By 1948, he had two hundred cows and several barns, making it one of the largest dairy farms in the state. The farm also boasted 350 acres of pasture, 700 acres of corn, wheat, oats, and alfalfa, and large areas devoted to timber.

The enterprise required fifteen tenants and farmhands directed by a foreman with the help of Kerr Scott's wife, Mary, and later his son, Bob.[39] From 1933 until 1968, Melville Farms was run by Cecil Johnson, a Chatham County native six years younger than Scott who lived with his family on the farm in a house not far from Kerr's. He supervised a racially mixed group of farmhands, including thirty people during the warm months—although that number expanded during the harvest and shrank to fourteen or fifteen during the slack winter season. Some lived as tenant farmers on the Scott property, others on nearby farms.

During World War II, Scott like many farmers faced a severe labor shortage as many men served in the armed forces or left the area in favor of higher-paying defense industry jobs. Governor Melville Broughton rejected Scott's pleas that he use the state's prison population for farmwork, saying they were needed for road gangs. Instead, Kerr Scott received help from German prisoners of war trucked by Kerr's son Bob to the farm daily from a POW camp at Butner. The largest of eighteen German POW camps in North Carolina, Butner held five thousand prisoners—half of the ten thousand POWs in the state.[40] Bob Scott recalled the POWs as quite gifted and able to fix anything; they entertained themselves at lunch by playing a violin and singing German songs. Kerr Scott also obtained guest workers from the Bahamas to help work his farm.[41]

State officials were shocked during World War II when North Carolina had the nation's highest Selective Service rejection rate (57 percent) because of physical deficiencies. The health problems ranged from poor teeth and bad eyesight to chronic infections, malnutrition, tuberculosis, hookworm, and malaria. Broughton appointed a study commission, headed by Clarence Poe, the editor of the *Progressive Farmer* and a rural progressive, to study the problem. The Poe Commission recommendations in 1945, which became the Good Health Plan, identified three pressing needs: more doctors, more hospitals, and more health insurance. The commission proposed a four-year state medical school, a $4 million appropriation to build and expand hospitals, and state encouragement for group medical insurance plans. In 1947, the decision was made to create a four-year teaching hospital at the University of North Carolina at Chapel Hill.

In selling the Good Health Plan, a high-powered PR campaign began on November 9, 1946, with a live radio broadcast that featured popular bandleader Kay Kyser, a North Carolina native, on the state's forty-seven radio stations. He used his Hollywood connections to get celebrities, such as actor Randolph Scott of Charlotte and actress Ava Gardner of Smithfield, to endorse the program.[42] But Agriculture Commissioner Scott wasn't on board. Rather, he told 2,500 farmers meeting in Raleigh that the major purpose of the good health program was "to build a medical school at Chapel Hill to keep up with the Joneses" and that "all of the rest of us were sucked in to serve this end." He even singled out such political allies as the North Carolina Grange and its master, Harry Caldwell, as among those who had allowed themselves to be misled. The speech earned Scott some of the worst press of his career. "Scott's speech may go down simply as the most unpolitic public address made in modern North Carolina history," wrote the *Salisbury Post*. The *Durham Herald* said that the speech "is so shocking that one wonders that it could be uttered by a responsible state official."[43] However, after his election to the governorship in 1948, Scott reversed field and supported the Good Health Plan, taking political credit for many of the rural hospitals the program helped to build. Scott was known for being bull-headed, but he also knew when to retreat.

The politically ambitious Scott first considered running for the U.S. Senate in 1944 against Senator Robert Reynolds but ruled it out when former governor Clyde Hoey entered the race. "At the present moment I have the feeling that since Governor Hoey and his organization sponsored me for Commissioner of Agriculture and since I served under him while he was Governor, I would not be showing him the proper appreciation if I entered the race for the Senate," Scott wrote to a supporter. By early as the fall of 1947, supporters were urging him to consider jumping into the governor's race the following year.[44]

During the 1930s and 1940s, North Carolina's political leaders often gave lip service in supporting President Roosevelt, who was highly popular in the state. But while taking federal funds, they mainly steered the Tar Heel State on a more conservative course. Meanwhile, North Carolina survived the hard times of the Depression, and electric lights were slowly being extended into the countryside. Yet rural North Carolina remained a landscape barren of telephone lines and blacktopped roads and with poor country schools. Now North Carolina was about to get its first true New Dealer in the governor's mansion, and he was determined to use the power of government to improve rural life.

3 ⋆ 1948

I was not invited by the self-anointed king-makers of politics to run
for governor. —Kerr Scott, News and Observer, *February 25, 1948*

For the first half of the twentieth century, the Democrats controlled North Carolina—with Republicans mainly a regional
party in the western part of the state and with blacks largely
disenfranchised. The state's political machine had been run
first by U.S. senator Furnifold Simmons and then by Governor O. Max Gardner—with strong support from business aristocracy of the textile, tobacco, furniture, banking, insurance, and utility
executives of the rapidly industrializing piedmont. "Industrialization has
created a financial and business elite whose influence prevails in the state's
political and economic life," wrote political scientist V. O. Key in his classic 1949 study *Southern Politics*. He continued, "An aggressive aristocracy
of manufacturing and banking, centered around Greensboro, Winston-
Salem, Charlotte and Durham, has had a tremendous stake in state policy
and has not been remiss in protecting and advancing what it visualizes as
its interests."[1]

The machines had spurred business growth by financing a huge road-
building program in the 1920s, earning North Carolina the nickname "The
Good Roads State," and by making the state university system one of the
best in the South. For its day, North Carolina had a reputation for clean
government—although the political machine was not above stealing elections when necessary. From 1928 to 1948, the key figure had been Gardner,
a moderate lawyer and textile owner from Shelby, who after a term as governor had moved to Washington, where he was one of the first superlobby-
ists and an intimate of President Roosevelt. In a South filled with mounte-
banks and demagogues, North Carolina stood out for its sober-minded,
business-oriented leadership.

But the political machine had been losing its grip. Gardner died in February 1946, a day before he was to set sail for England, where he was to

assume his post as U.S. ambassador to Great Britain. In December 1946, Senator Josiah Bailey died, and William B. Umstead of Durham, who was to have been the machine's candidate for governor in 1948, was appointed to his seat. In short order, the Shelby Dynasty had lost both its leader and its gubernatorial candidate. "The machine this year finds itself in much the same plight as a ship without a rudder," wrote newspaper editor George Haskett.[2]

Moving to fill the void was state treasurer Charles Johnson, who soon got the stamp of approval from the Democratic machine. A white-haired, handsome fifty-seven-year-old who looked like a governor out of central casting, Johnson was born on a Pender County farm near Burgaw in eastern North Carolina. He had started out as a clerk in the state auditor's office and, although lacking a college education, had worked his way up to increasing positions of responsibility in state government. Gardner appointed him state treasurer in 1932, which gave Johnson the backing of the majority of the legislature, the courthouse machines, and most of the state's corporate titans. But Johnson was the perfect foil for the charismatic Scott—a colorless bureaucrat and a wooden public speaker who appeared humorless. "He was the most pompous son-of-a-bitch I have ever met in my life," recalled Lauch Faircloth, a twenty-year-old farmer at the time, who later become a U.S. senator.[3]

In many ways, Johnson spoke for the North Carolina where things were going well, the North Carolina that was receiving bouquets as the most progressive state in the midcentury South. As journalist John Gunther wrote in 1947, North Carolina is "beyond doubt one of the most important, alive and progressive states in the union."[4] In the past, that would have been enough. Scott never articulated why he thought he could pull off one of the biggest upsets in North Carolina history, but there were several plausible reasons why he might have thought it was possible. Having served with him for twelve years in Raleigh, Scott knew that Johnson lacked the common touch. As someone constantly traveling North Carolina's byways and backwaters, Scott understood that the growing prosperity from the industrialization of the towns and cities was not filtering into the countryside, where most people still lacked either paved roads or telephones or electricity—or in some cases all three.

Despite his later reputation as a maverick, Scott's first instinct was to see if he could get the support of the Democratic organization—a group that, after all, had backed him for agriculture commissioner. By several accounts, Scott approached Robert M. Hanes, the president of Wachovia

Bank and the de facto head of the Shelby machine after the death of Gardner, about running for governor in 1948. Scott was told that it was not his turn and he would have to wait eight years; furthermore, under the state's informal geographic rotation system, it was the turn of an easterner because Greg Cherry, the current governor, was from the western town of Gastonia.[5]

Scott showed signs of uncertainty about undertaking such a large political gamble of bucking a political machine that had run the state for the first half of the century—and one that had helped make him agriculture commissioner. He approached several high-profile Democrats, including Raleigh corporate attorney Willis Smith and Secretary of the Army Kenneth Royall, and urged them to get into the race. Both turned him down.[6]

Then, amid the aroma of cooked rabbit, squirrel, and venison at the Department of Agriculture's annual game dinner on January 9, 1948, Scott told 250 guests that he was returning to his farm rather than seeking re-election. "I just thought it was time for a change," he said. "I have 200 cows there and I don't have to hunt for a job." Scott's announcement immediately prompted speculation that he was running for governor, something Scott did little to discourage as he formed an exploratory committee and gave several speeches around the state while his wife's cousin textile manufacturer B. Everett Jordan and his brother Ralph Scott took soundings on whether he could raise enough money for a race.[7]

"The Democratic Party in North Carolina needs some stirring up," Scott announced on February 6 in Burlington. As a candidate for governor, he said, he was resigning as agriculture commissioner immediately because a high-ranking official should not run for another office—a step Johnson declined to take. Asked whether Johnson had the nomination sewed up, Scott replied: "If someone has something sewed up, I guess your wife can rip it out and sew it up the way you want it."[8] But how do you win a primary when your opponent has lined up the local politicians in nearly every courthouse in the state, the big-name state political figures, and the business community? You get the other folks.

Twenty-year-old Lauch Faircloth was working on his father's Sampson County farm when the local agriculture extension agent asked if he would attend a county organizational meeting with Scott in 1948. Only five or six people showed up. "There were a couple of blacks who looked like they were lost, a cripple, a drunk, and me," Faircloth recalled. When Scott asked Faircloth to manage his county campaign, Faircloth said he didn't know anything about politics. "Son, you can do it," Scott replied. "All you have to do is nail up a couple of placards." Faircloth left that night as county manager. Only later did it dawn on him "that I was a fool because everybody in the county was for Charlie Johnson. It was already predetermined that he was going to be governor. The county Democratic organization was for him."[9]

But Scott was better positioned than many people realized. Although he may not have had the courthouse organizations, Scott had built an extensive network of contacts in communities and crossroads across North Carolina during his twelve years as agriculture commissioner, his four years as Grange master, and his decade as a county extension agent. Although polling didn't exist then, his headline-grabbing ability and outspokenness made him among the best-known political figures in the state. The agriculture commissioner's job also had a far higher profile in the 1940s than the state treasurer. Seeing him as a threat, the Johnson camp tried, unsuccessfully, to convince Scott to run for lieutenant governor.

Scott called his rural supporters "Branchhead Boys," or the people who lived at the head of a branch. A reporter once asked where the term came from. "Well, the way I campaign, I go into a county, and I don't go to the courthouse the first thing like most of them do to pay my respects to the powers that be," recalled Bob Scott, quoting his father. "I go up to the head of the branch. And I start working back down. By the time I get to the courthouse I've got my votes. He said it's the branch head, the boys at the head of the branch that got me elected. I don't have to pay any attention to the folks in the courthouse. They weren't working for me. You know, there are some exceptions to that, but very few."[10]

Kerr Scott, although a relatively prosperous farmer, lived on a dirt road on Back Creek, one of a series of tributaries such as Meadow Creek, Moles Creek, and Otter Creek that fed into the Haw River, and he always identified with the land and his neighbors. About two-thirds of North Carolina was rural, and in 1948, it had 302,000 farms—nearly agriculture's high-water mark in the state. But North Carolina farmers remained among the poorest in the country—which meant that the Branchhead Boy was likely to be a subsistence farmer. The total capita income per farmworker in North Carolina in 1945 was $3,091, compared with a national average for a farmer of $7,167. Only one in ten Tar Heel farms had a tractor, one in twenty had a telephone, 15 percent had running water, 38 percent had electricity, and 60 percent had radios, mainly battery operated, according to a report prepared at Governor Cherry's request. There were simply too many people trying to scratch out a living on too little land, the report concluded.

Only one in four heads of the farm families had gone to school beyond the seventh grade.[11]

From the beginning, Johnson worked the courthouses and ran a cautious incumbent's campaign while the plainspoken Scott, whose talent for making headlines attracted reporters, went on the attack. His brother Ralph recalled that one Sunday morning he expressed regret to Kerr that most of the editorial pages were supporting Johnson. "That's alright," said Kerr. "As long as they keep me on the front page, the other side can have the editorial pages." It would be a formula long followed by candidates with populist appeal, including the 2016 presidential campaign of Donald Trump.[12] Taking another populist strategy, Scott campaigned against what he called the "crown princes in state politics" who had picked Johnson as their candidate. "I am happy to greet you as an aggressive candidate for governor," Scott said on statewide radio. "I was not invited by the self-anointed king-makers of politics to run for governor. They demanded that I wait eight years. In effect, they said they had already picked your governor for you. They want you to confirm their choice in the Democratic primary on May 29. I say to you, a true Democrat, you ought to be allowed to pick your own governor. We fought two wars within memory of a good many of us to preserve that democratic right."[13] In addition, like most Bible Belt politicians, Scott emphasized his religious ties, campaigning as a "God-fearing, God-loving farmer" who had been a deacon, church treasurer, and Sunday School teacher and was an active Presbyterian.

Johnson tried to echo some of Scott's talking points, noting that he owned a 220-acre farm in Pender County. He also posed for a photograph behind a plow during the campaign—unfortunately dressed in a coat and tie—to show voters that he still knew how to use the farm implement. But it was hard to out-country Scott, who filled his talks with farm expressions like "plowing to the end of the row" or "toting fair" or "hoeing out."

Taking another tack, just five days after Scott entered the race, Johnson sought to undercut Scott's rural appeal by proposing a $100 million rural road construction bond issue and calling for a special legislative session to consider it. Governor Cherry rebuffed the call, saying the state was already doing "an enormous amount of work" on rural roads and had $12.5 million budgeted for maintenance and another $11 million for construction.[14] In a stance that came back to haunt him, Scott rejected the bond proposal. "It is ridiculous to advocate plunging the state into debt with a hundred-million-dollar bond issue," he said. He added, "The proposal of the ring candidate to float a hundred-million-dollar issue, despite the huge surplus piled up in the banks, is indicative of the kind of government to be expected if State Treasurer Charles M. Johnson should be elected." Scott proclaimed, "In all my travel over the state, the only persons I have heard who are in favor of state bond issue are the state treasurer and his big bank backers."[15]

The 1948 Democratic primary was more a factional battle than an ideological contest. With the electorate harboring a pent-up demand for public services, the Scott and Johnson campaigns shared similar views about increasing teacher salaries, reducing the size of classrooms, stepping up school and road construction, and backing a statewide referendum on the liquor sales—a move pushed by the churches and the prohibitionist forces.

Where Scott drew blood, however, was through his portrayal of Johnson as both a machine politician and a tool of the big banks, which were mismanaging the taxpayers' money. When the Scott campaign learned that the treasurer's office had deposited up to $171 million in state money in 239 banks without earning interest, Scott criticized Johnson for not investing the money more wisely and suggested that he was rewarding the bankers, a key political ally. "I tell you that the state treasurer has been piling up funds for two years to ensure his nomination," Scott charged. "He has been using up to $170 million of your money, placed with banks at no interest, to help him fill that war chest." Scott also attacked Johnson for allowing Wachovia, the state's largest bank, to hold state money without paying interest, calling it "lazy money" that, because of Johnson's practices, was costing the state $1 million per year.[16]

Johnson first ignored the charges, but he began to respond as Scott gained ground. Johnson explained that the treasurer had little discretion in how to handle the funds because of a 1943 state law that said surplus funds could only be invested in state or federal bonds or notes. Johnson also said that for the state to earn $1 million annually it would have to have $40 million on hand (at 2.5 percent interest), and at no time did state coffers have that much. He insisted, "I have not violated either the spirit or the letter of the law. Kerr Scott has violated the ninth commandment. He has borne false witness against a neighbor."[17]

Johnson was indeed within the law, but it looked like favoritism. The Federal Deposit Insurance Corporation had in 1937 freed banks from paying interest on deposits of public funds, and state law did not authorize the state treasurer to require banks to pay interest on state interest.[18] After being elected governor in 1948, Scott pushed through a law requiring the state treasurer to charge the market rate for state money deposited. By 1965, that had earned the state $88.3 million in interest.[19]

Although Johnson had a financial advantage in the campaign, Scott was competitive, using mailing lists from Roosevelt's 1936 campaign to raise money. Alamance County textile manufacturer B. Everett Jordan used his broad contacts in the business community and became Scott's key fundraiser. Scott rewarded Jordan by naming him chairman of the state Democratic Party and retaining his brother, Henry Jordan, as chairman of the state Highway Commission.[20]

R. Mayne Albright, a minor candidate in the race, attacked "the big money candidates" and said Scott and Johnson had vastly outspent the state's 1931 law, which limited gubernatorial and Senate candidates to $12,000 each. However, the law did not limit what other persons could spend on behalf of a candidate. In his final report, Scott listed donations of $11,407.70 and expenditures of $11,796.16, both sums just under the limit. But this was fiction. After the 1954 Senate race, Scott admitted that the cost of running his headquarters alone in 1948 was $62,000. Plenty of contributions showed up in personal papers that were not listed in the campaign finance reports. Historian Julian Pleasants estimates that Scott spent more than $150,000 and Johnson at least $100,000.[21] Scott told the legislature in 1951 that the campaign spending limit needed to be raised. "It is a matter of general knowledge that the present law is very largely ignored," Scott said.[22]

Whereas some rural populists used racial appeals to win the support of country people, Scott quietly sought to build a biracial coalition. Only 14 percent of eligible blacks were registered to vote at the time, and their representation at the polls differed dramatically across the state: blacks organized in the cities, while most African Americans still found themselves disenfranchised in rural areas. As the Populists learned in the 1890s, putting together a coalition of white farmers and black citizens required a skillful balancing act. Scott walked a fine line in segregated North Carolina when civil rights issues were heating up nationally; he quietly sought the support of urban blacks while attempting not to alienate white segregationists.

Scott liked to tell a story of campaigning in a rural northeastern county where in a country store he came across a local political "big shot" who controlled a lot of local votes. "How do you feel about this here race situation?" the man asked. (Sometimes the story is told more crudely: "Commissioner, how do you feel about the nigger issue?") Scott remembered, "I was in a pickle. It was damned if you did and damned if you didn't. I needed votes from the colored folks and I needed them from the whites. I just prayed for a minute, 'Lord, if you've ever helped me, help me now.'"

"Let me put it this way mister," Scott replied. "I'm a North Carolina Democrat. I was born south of the Mason Dixon line, and I was raised here. My daddy before me was a southerner, and a North Carolina Democrat. Does that answer your question?" The fellow jumped off the nail keg in the country store and said, "By golly, that's good enough for me. You're my man."[23]

On primary day, Scott's appeal to rural residents and his aggressive campaign, combined with Johnson's lackluster effort, paid off. Johnson led the first primary with 170,141 votes, Scott received 161,293 votes, and R. Mayne Albright had 76,281 votes. Johnson carried fifty-one counties compared to Scott's forty-one. Johnson had run well in the machine-controlled counties of the west, while Scott took most of rural eastern counties and fared well in some urban ones, such as Wake, Guilford, and Forsyth, where there was support both in the rural precincts among farmers and in the black precincts of Raleigh, Greensboro, and Winston-Salem.

But Johnson was in trouble. He had won 40 percent but failed to win a majority despite his establishment backing. Scott, with his 38 percent support, was the candidate with momentum. Under North Carolina law, if no candidate received 50 percent, then the second-place finisher could call for a runoff.

THE RUNOFF

Scott quietly picked up the endorsement of organized labor that had backed Albright in the first primary, and he doubled down on his criticism of Johnson as the handpicked candidate of "a few powerful men" and "kingmakers." North Carolina did not want to adopt "the Russian system under which you can vote for or against only one man for each office," Scott said in a June radio address.[24] "It amounts to oligarchy when a ring-controlled candidate can be pushed into the highest office in the state against the desires of the people," Scott said.[25]

Johnson hit back, saying that Scott didn't seem to have any problem with the machine when it backed him for agriculture commissioner in 1936 and in subsequent elections. Johnson further cried hypocrisy and remarked that Scott "seized upon this opportunity to ride into office on the coat-tail of Hoey. Mr. Scott had nothing to say about a machine at that time.

But now that he is the candidate for governor, he can talk of nothing else but machines."[26] Johnson further accused Scott of practicing wedge politics, attempting to "align the rural population against the city population, one class of citizens against another."[27]

No runner-up had won a runoff in North Carolina since the primary system's creation in 1916. But 1948 was different. Scott defeated Johnson 54–46 percent, winning sixty-five counties to Johnson's thirty-five. Not only did Scott win in the eastern rural part of the state, where populist sentiment went back to the days of the Farmers' Alliance, but he won in such cities as Raleigh, Durham, and Greensboro with the help of the black vote and organized labor. Scott even won all seven counties that voted for Albright and picked up sixteen counties that had previously voted for Johnson, who in the runoff ran strongest in the machine-controlled western counties. On election night, a Raleigh elevator operator, a black man, summed things up: "I done figured this out. Mr. Scott got in there to run for governor. Mr. Johnson, he just walked, but Mr. Scott he ran."[28]

Political shenanigans undoubtedly occurred in the vote counting. Watauga County political bosses told Scott that he would lose the second primary but get a good vote because "we can't afford to have a governor mad at us." Sure enough, the mountain county on election day reported that Johnson had narrowly carried the county. Two days later after it became clear that Scott had won statewide, county officials announced that a mistake had been made and that, in fact, Scott had carried the county by 120 votes. "They just jockey the figures to make the result right," Scott said. He later estimated that 180 of the state's 1,900 precincts "can be tampered with."[29]

Scott's insurgency was not isolated. Moderates who promised to shake up the old courthouse crowds began winning across the South. World War II had made people less satisfied with the status quo; the boys had gone off to war, women been exposed to new freedoms in the workplace, and blacks had been given new responsibilities in the armed services. The fourteen new military bases constructed in North Carolina created an influx of people from outside the state; Hitler's ideology of racial superiority had raised questions about the South's own white superiority; and people of color across the world were stirring against white control, whether in India, Indonesia, or South Africa. Moderates elected in the postwar South included "Big Jim" Folsom as governor of Alabama in 1946 and Earl K. Long in 1948 as governor of Louisiana. Fuller Warren became governor of Florida. Postwar voters were also sending New Dealers to the Senate, including John Sparkman of Alabama, Estes Kefauver of Tennessee, and Lyndon Johnson of Texas.

The day after the election, Scott returned to Haw River, where he set up a chair under a Spanish oak in his front yard and greeted hundreds of well-wishers. The same tree had served as a campaign war room. Scott often greeted constituents during his term as governor under the same tree on Sundays. Scott was the first farmer elected North Carolina governor since the Farmers' Alliance had elevated one of their own, Elias Carr, in 1892. This time the alliance's successor, the Grange, had helped elect one of their own. In some ways, Scott had reconstituted the old Populist coalition of small white farmers and blacks. But this window of postwar liberalism proved to be a narrow one, because even as the soldiers returned from overseas, events in motion began to undercut rural progressivism.

THE BLINDING OF SERGEANT WOODARD

One of those events involved Technical Sergeant Isaac Woodard Jr., who grew up in Goldsboro. Woodard, a twenty-seven-year-old black man, served fifteen months in the U.S. Army working as a military longshoreman during World War II. He had received a battle star for unloading ships under enemy fire during the campaign against the Japanese in New Guinea.

On February 12, 1946, Woodard received his discharge from Camp Gordon, Georgia, and boarded a Greyhound bus to return to his wife. What exactly happened next is unclear, but Woodard and black soldiers intermingled with white civilian passengers, and the bus driver testified that a bottle of whiskey passed hands. Woodard denied drinking, and his fellow soldiers backed him up. At some point, Woodard asked the driver if there was time to "take a piss" at the next stop. "Boy, go on back and sit down and keep quiet and don't be talking out so loud," the driver warned. Woodard, who only hours before had been an army sergeant, replied: "God damn it, talk to me like I'm talking to you. I'm a man just like you," he testified.

When the bus pulled into Batesburg, South Carolina, Police Chief Linwood Shull and an officer were waiting to take Woodard off the bus. Woodard testified that one of the policemen struck him with a blackjack when he tried to tell his side of the story—a version backed up by a soldier. An arrest was made, and what happened next occurred around the corner out of sight of the bus passengers and witnesses.

But the facts of what happened are not in doubt. Woodard was struck multiple times, which ruptured both his eyeballs. He was taken to jail, and the next morning he could barely see. He was charged with drunk and disorderly conduct and fined fifty dollars, then driven to a veterans hospital in Columbia, where after two months of treatment, he emerged blind for the rest of his life.

There the issue might have rested—another in long line of racial injustices. But instead the blinding of Sergeant Woodard had a powerful effect on southern politics in general, and on North Carolina in particular, causing wrenching divisions that would take generations to heal, if they ever have. It began when the National Association for the Advancement of Colored People (NAACP) spread the word about Woodard's case. Orson Wells, the famous movie actor, helped bring the story to national attention by discussing it on at least five of his ABC radio shows. For a benefit performance for Woodard, folk singer Woody Guthrie wrote a song, "The Blinding of Isaac Woodard." Twenty thousand people attended the New York performance, including heavyweight boxing champion Joe Louis and actor Paul Robeson. Unlike victims of lynching, Woodard had survived his ordeal, and supporters took him to eighteen mass meetings across the country to raise money for his expenses.[30]

President Harry Truman became aware of Woodard after an NAACP delegation met with him in September 1946 to complain about the mistreatment of returning black veterans. Truman ordered the U.S. Justice Department to investigate the case, which resulted in charges being brought against Linwood Shull, the South Carolina police chief. In the closing argument, the defense lawyer argued: "If you rule against Shull, then let this South Carolina secede again." The all-white jury found Shull not guilty.

Truman was an unlikely champion of southern blacks. Both sets of grandparents had been slave owners and his mother bore a lifelong grudge against President Abraham Lincoln. Privately, Truman still used the word "nigger." But Truman was deeply offended by the mistreatment of returning black servicemen, and in personal correspondence he would cite the blinding of Sergeant Woodard and the subsequent acquittal of the police chief as evidence that there "is something radically wrong with the system."[31] In December 1946, Truman signed an executive order creating a fifteen-member President's Committee on Civil Rights. The committee included two southerners, University of North Carolina president Frank Porter Graham and M. E. Tilley of the Women's Society of Christian Services of Atlanta. The Graham appointment would come back to haunt North Carolina politics.

The Truman commission issued its bombshell report in October 1947, calling for an end to discrimination. It was the first time a top-level government report outlined widespread racism in the United States. The report, called *To Secure These Rights*, contained thirty-five recommendations, including federal antilynching, anti–poll tax, and antidiscrimination measures; desegregation of the armed forces and the end of segregated seating on interstate buses and trains; a guarantee of voting; and the creation of a variety of antidiscrimination mechanisms, including a revived Fair Employment Practices Commission, a commission on civil rights, a civil rights division of the Justice Department, and a joint congressional committee on civil rights. For the first time, a report said that the federal government—not the states—had a major responsibility to protect the civil rights of its citizens. Graham issued a minority report calling for goodwill and education—not a federal law—to solve discrimination.

In February 1948, Harry Truman became the first president to submit a special message on civil rights to Congress. Based on the recommendations of his civil rights committee, Truman proposed a federal law against lynching, a ban on poll taxes then being used in seven southern states (not North Carolina), an end to discrimination in interstate travel by bus, rail, and airplanes, and the creation of the Fair Employment Practices Commission (FEPC) with power to end job discrimination. It essentially laid out the agenda for the civil rights movement over the next generation—even coining the term "civil rights." The legislation had no possibility of passing a Congress dominated by powerful southern committee chairmen. But it was politically explosive nonetheless.

By March, southern Democrats threatened a revolt against the party if Truman was to be nominated for a full term. "Southern senators are solid all right in their fight against anti–poll tax, anti-lynching, anti-segregation and fair employment practices commission proposals," said North Carolina senator Clyde Hoey.[32] The state's other senator, William Umstead, suggested that Truman quit the race. Yet North Carolina's political leaders were not among the segregationist hard-liners. Neither Scott nor Charles Johnson made Truman's civil rights report an issue in their primary campaigns, although many southern candidates did that year. And when a group of southern governors met in Washington and vowed to "fight to the last ditch" the civil rights proposals and work to block Truman from getting the nomination, North Carolina's Cherry skipped the meeting, citing pressing business back in North Carolina.

The atmosphere crackled when three thousand delegates to the state Democratic convention gathered in Raleigh's Memorial Auditorium on May 20, 1948, in the middle of the Democratic primary. To help keep the convention in line for Truman, the party leaders trotted out their oldest warhorse: seventy-nine-year-old Cameron Morrison, the former Red Shirt leader, governor, and U.S. senator. "I swear that I'll never vote for the nomination of Truman," Morrison said. "[But] I don't want any more of this revolting business. . . . If we can't beat Truman [at the national convention] let's step under the Democratic flag and elect him. Then we'll let our congressmen and senators beat him down when he needs beating down. We should stand together. Let's not throw away our power. Let's not permit any accidental president of the United States to run us out of the party."[33] The state convention followed Morrison's advice and largely avoided the civil rights issue, voting to send an uninstructed delegation to the national convention in Philadelphia.

In Philadelphia, a fierce platform fight over civil rights ensued. Party leaders feared a southern walkout when Minneapolis mayor Hubert Humphrey advocated a strong civil rights plan that called for the end to the poll tax, an end to lynching, an end to segregation in the armed forces, and fair employment legislation.[34] The Alabama and half of the Mississippi delegation did indeed walk out, but Cherry grabbed the North Carolina banner to prevent a walk out of the Tar Heel delegation.[35] All thirteen southern votes for Truman were cast by North Carolina delegates, with the Tar Heel delegation splitting 19–13 for favorite southern son Senator Richard Russell of Georgia. Among those voting for Russell were Senators Hoey and Umstead. Cherry and Jonathan Daniels, editor of the *News and Observer*, the state capital paper, voted for Truman. Although a Truman ally, Scott was a nonvoting member of the delegation.

DIXIECRATS AND WALLACITES

On July 17, two days after the Democrats met in Philadelphia, the hardline segregationists formed a rump convention in Birmingham and nominated South Carolina governor Strom Thurmond as the States' Rights Democratic Party presidential candidate and Mississippi governor Fielding Wright as his vice presidential running mate. Thus emerged the Dixiecrat Party. Thirteen southern states were officially represented, but hardly anyone from outside Mississippi and Alabama attended.[36]

Thurmond opened his campaign for president at North Carolina's Cherryville Watermelon Festival, on July 31. "If the segregation program of the president is enforced," he told a crowd of fifteen hundred people, "the results of civil strife may be horrible beyond imagination. Lawlessness will be rampant. Chaos will prevail. Our streets will be unsafe. And there will be greatest breakdown of law enforcement in the history of the nation. Let us all tell them, that in the South, the intermingling of the races in our homes, in our schools, and in our theaters is impractical and impossible."[37] Later, in October, Thurmond made a two-day, eleven-stop tour across North Carolina and argued that the proposed FEPC was "communistic in principle and would be an effective tool for Russia to use in placing agents in our industries."[38] He also used radio ads to generate support. The script for one that aired in North Carolina said: "Mill workers and office workers of NC. Do you want to work side by side with Negroes, share your restrooms with Negroes and give up your job to a Negro? Of course, you don't, you are a southerner. But remember. President Truman has boasted he is training a federal police force to make you do just those things. He is trying to stir up trouble in North Carolina. Let's don't let him do it." This time, the ads didn't work. But a year and half later, the state would be blanketed with similar advertisements to far greater effect.[39]

Thurmond wasn't the only third-party presidential candidate barnstorming through North Carolina in 1948 and stirring up racial passions. Henry Wallace was a lifelong progressive Republican from Iowa. His father had founded the magazine *Wallace's Farmer* and served in the cabinet of Presidents Warren Harding and Calvin Coolidge. Young Henry took over the editorship of the magazine and made millions in the science of corn breeding. Blaming President Herbert Hoover for the death of his father, Henry Wallace backed Democrat Al Smith in the 1928 presidential race and Franklin Roosevelt in 1932, which landed him the post of agriculture secretary, where he helped design the New Deal's farm programs. In 1940, FDR named him his vice presidential running mate. But Wallace proved an embarrassment, which included making naive comments about the Soviet secret police during a trip in Siberia. Roosevelt dumped him in 1944 for Truman and then made Wallace his commerce secretary, a move Kerr Scott wholeheartedly endorsed, saying that Wallace "through his crop-control ideas did more for the tobacco farmer than any other one man in the nation." Then, Truman fired Wallace.

In announcing his candidacy for the presidency in 1948, Wallace attacked Truman's Democratic Party as a party of "war and depression," denouncing its support for the cold war, segregation, the Marshall Plan, and the universal military draft. As Wallace drifted leftward, his campaign was increasingly influenced by Communist Party members who took prominent positions in his organization.[40]

It made little sense for presidential candidates to campaign in the one-party South. But Wallace launched a twenty-eight-city, seven-state tour of the South on August 29 as a way to reinvigorate his support among northern blacks. Accompanied by folk singer Pete Seeger, Wallace insisted on speaking only to racially integrated audiences, staying in mixed hotels, and eating in integrated restaurants. Reactions to his campaign swing offered a sneak preview of the power of reds and race in Tar Heel politics.

The North Carolina portion of the trip started at the City Armory in Durham, where about fifteen hundred people were attending a Progressive Party convention supporting Wallace. There were so many protestors that National Guard Sergeant Calvin Hackney—his .45 caliber revolver drawn—escorted Wallace to the podium. Demonstrators held placards with such messages as "Send Wallace Back to Russia" and "Wallace Alligator Bait." Shouts of "Hey, Communist! Nigger lover!" filled the air. When James D. Harris, a twenty-four-year-old war veteran, University of North Carolina student, and Wallace bodyguard, tried to prevent a crowd of twenty protesters from entering the building, someone pulled a knife, and he was cut eight times. Police threatened to arrest Harris after he had been attacked.[41]

Everywhere Wallace stopped—in Burlington, Greensboro, Winston-Salem, High Point, Hickory, and Charlotte—mobs pelted the former vice president with eggs, tomatoes, peach pits, and green peppers. In many places, such as Burlington, Wallace was not permitted to speak. Stepping from his car on Main Street, Wallace began: "I'd like to take this opportunity . . . ." Then he was met with a hail of fruit and tomatoes from a crowd of 2,500 people who had been waiting one and a half hours for the opportunity to run him out of town. When Wallace tried to speak a second time, a roar of boos drowned out his voice. Livid, Wallace turned to a man in the crowd, put his hands on his shoulder, and asked: "Are you an American? Am I in America?"

"Get your hands off me," the man replied, giving him a slight shove.

"Get your communists and your Negroes out of this town," someone else shouted. The crowd broke past police, shouting and pounding on the car windows and blocking the path of the motorcade. A motorcycle patrolman brandished his pistol before the crowd gave way.[42]

The violence in North Carolina made national headlines, and in Asheville, Wallace was allowed to speak only after Governor Cherry ordered police reinforcements. Cherry said, "A man ought to have the right to talk." Truman called the treatment of his former vice president "a highly un-American business."

To support Wallace's candidacy, the state Progressive Party was founded in January 1948 in Greensboro. An integrated group of about three hundred people held their first convention in a Winston-Salem tobacco warehouse in April, and they sang a version of the spiritual: "Black and white together, we shall not be moved." Besides supporting Wallace, the Progressive Party fielded North Carolina's first racially integrated ticket of the twentieth century, nominating blacks for the U.S. Senate and attorney general. The Progressive Party's gubernatorial nominee was Mary Price, a thirty-nine-year-old white woman from Greensboro, who lobbied for progressive causes in the state legislature. After earning a journalism degree from the University of North Carolina, she moved to New York City, where she became involved in left-wing circles after joining the labor movement. As it turned out, the first women candidate for governor in North Carolina was a Soviet agent.

In July 1948, during a Senate investigation, a former Soviet agent turned FBI informant testified that Price had spied for the Soviet Union while working as a secretary for influential nationally syndicated columnist Walter Lippmann. Price denied it at the time, but in 1995 the U.S. government declassified the files of what was known as the Venona Project—the decoded secret cables between Moscow and its agents in the United States. The files disclosed that Price's code names were "Dir" or "Kid" or "Arena," and she supplied the KGB with information about Lippmann's contacts with high government officials, assisted in Soviet recruitment of agents, and was a Soviet courier.[43]

Truman, facing an uphill reelection battle, worried about losing white southerners because of his civil rights proposals and losing the northern black vote to the left-wing Wallace. Since World War II, scores of blacks had migrated from the South, and now there were now 2.5 million northern black voters—many in such key states as New York, Illinois, Pennsylvania, Michigan, New Jersey, California, and Ohio.[44] That may have been one reason why Truman on July 26, 1948, signed an executive order desegregating federal employment, particularly the military, which once again raised the South's hackles.[45]

After the Democratic convention in Philadelphia, Capus Waynick, Scott's handpicked state party chairman, called for a strategy session at the O. Henry Hotel in Greensboro. Waynick heard strong anti-Truman feeling. "Waynick, you can't possibly hope to carry North Carolina for Harry Truman," said Senator Umstead. When Waynick asked why, Umstead replied: "Well, people around me in Durham say that they'll never vote again for that civil rights S.O.B."

Congressman Robert "Farmer Bob" Doughton, the chairman of the

House Ways and Means Committee, added, "Mr. Chairman, you can't help Harry Truman. If you try, you're going to get us all whipped. He's through and if you try to do anything about him, you'll get the whole ticket defeated." A wary Kerr Scott told Waynick that he was too busy with his own gubernatorial run to help much, and Senator Hoey offered only token support. Some at the meeting didn't even want Truman signs at state Democratic headquarters and argued against the ticket campaigning in the state.[46]

Scott continued to keep his distance from Truman and tended to his own campaign. When Scott brought four to five thousand Democrats to his Haw River farm in September for a rally, it was army secretary Kenneth Royall, a native North Carolinian, who plugged the national ticket. "I finally wrote a speech for Scott and pushed him on the radio with which he endorsed the ticket, but he was reluctant to do it," Waynick recalled.[47]

With the South up in arms over his civil rights proposals, Truman avoided the region except for Texas and North Carolina. Truman made a campaign appearance on October 16 in Raleigh, the first presidential visit to the state since Teddy Roosevelt in 1905. An estimated twenty-five to thirty thousand people greeted his motorcade. He unveiled the monument to the three presidents on the Capitol grounds and opened the state fair in front of seventy-five thousand people.[48]

By this time, Scott had warmed to Truman and appeared with him on a platform at the state fair, where they shook hands and began a close political friendship. After the event, Scott had to leave early for a speaking engagement in Pender County, but when he tried to leave by a back gate, the president's security detail blocked his exit. "Orders to keep it closed," said an officer. "Take my name boys, I'm going over," Scott said as he climbed over the wire fence.[49]

Scott won 73 percent of the vote that November, defeating Republican George Pritchard, an Asheville attorney, and Progressive Party candidate Mary Price.[50] In the presidential race, Truman carried North Carolina with 58 percent of the vote compared to 33 percent for Republican Thomas Dewey, with Thurmond receiving only 9 percent and Wallace less than 0.5 percent. It was Truman's second-highest margin of victory in the country, surpassed only by Texas. Nationally, Truman's civil rights policy, which many thought politically risky, helped win him a close election. Black voters provided Truman with the crucial margin of victory in Ohio, Illinois, and California.[51] Overall, Truman garnered 49.5 percent to Republican Thomas Dewey's 45.1 percent; Thurmond received 2.4 percent and

Wallace 2.38 percent. The third-party efforts had collapsed, with the Dixie-crats winning just four states and Wallace's campaign fizzling.

The election marked the beginning of the post–World War II era in politics, one where the tectonic plates of southern politics began shifting—with Jim Crow coming under attack for the first time from the White House and the old courthouse machines beginning to lose their grip. "Thus 1948, the year of the National Democratic Convention that marked the end of the Solid South, also marked the decline and the fall of the fifty-year regimes of the Simmons Machine–Shelby Dynasty organization," R. Mayne Albright reflected thirty-five years later. "It ushered in a new era of more open, if less predictable, politics with better opportunities for bipartisan debate and decisions."[52]

4 ★ MUD TAX

The people are demanding that something be done to lift them out of the mud. — *Governor W. Kerr Scott, January 17, 1949*

Raleigh was a small, pleasant, white-collar city of about sixty-five thousand people when Kerr Scott became governor in January 1949. The governor's office rested on the ground floor of the 1840 Greek Revival Capitol, spared by Union general William Tecumseh Sherman when his troops marched through. Although admired for its classic design, the cramped Capitol also housed the state legislature, which met on the second floor. There was no room for legislative offices or committee rooms, and the lawmakers had neither secretaries nor filing cabinets. The Appropriations and Finance Committees convened in the Revenue Building across the street, and some committees met at the Ambassador Theatre, a nearby movie house on Fayetteville Street. Lawmakers held session only three months every other year—and if they met for any longer, they weren't paid.[1]

Most lawmakers stayed at one of the two main downtown hotels, the Sir Walter and the Carolina, and they often ate at the S&W Cafeteria, which catered to the lawmakers' taste for inexpensive country cooking. In deference to Baptist sensibilities, there were no saloons where politicians hung out. But every Monday morning the liquor lobby dropped off nine cases of booze in Room 215 of the Sir Walter Hotel, to be distributed in brown paper bags to slake lawmakers' thirst. For his part, Scott headed out every Friday to his Haw River farm and returned Monday mornings.

As in the rest of the South, Raleigh was a segregated city. If you wanted to hear Marian Anderson, the great African American contralto, perform at Memorial Auditorium that January, you bought tickets at Stephenson Music on Fayetteville Street if you were white and at Hamlin Drug on East Hargett Street, Raleigh's black main street, if you were not. The seating, of course, was separate. So was everything else in the caste system—the bathrooms, the water fountains, and even the Bibles used at county court-houses.[2]

Raleigh's small size wasn't surprising despite North Carolina's standing as the tenth most populous state: in 1950, North Carolina was one of the most rural places in the United States, outranked only by Mississippi, Arkansas, Alaska, and the Dakotas.[3] Of North Carolina's four million people, 39 percent farmed and another 22 percent lived in the country or in towns or villages of less than 2,500, according to an N.C. State study. This meant that 61 percent were classified as rural—and country people, for the most part, lived poor and without the basic services that many Americans took for granted.[4]

So when a champion of rural North Carolina took office, a record fifty thousand people turned out to celebrate the inauguration. The affair had a Jacksonian flavor to it—a man of the people was being installed after so many corporate lawyers. Scott shook the hands of an estimated fifteen hundred well-wishers at the executive mansion. The only thing amiss was the state flag at the Capitol, which was inadvertently flown upside down in the international sign of distress. "Don't worry," Scott told the head grounds-keeper. "Half the people are in distress because I was inaugurated."[5] Yet there was nothing amiss about Scott, resplendent in traditional striped trousers, a fork-tailed coat, and a high silk hat—or what he called "a two-cow suit": "It took two cows to pay for it," Scott explained.

Leading up to his inauguration, Scott had sent signals that he would be a different breed of governor. For the previous half century, North Carolina governors had been products of the same Democratic organizations. Often top-level officials in the state bureaucracy kept their jobs for decades, regardless of who was sitting in the governor's mansion. North Carolina's business community had also been used to preferential treatment. Historian George Tindall called North Carolina's reigning philosophy "business progressivism," with a close working relationship between the politicians in Raleigh and the corporate wheels in Charlotte, Winston-Salem, Greensboro, and elsewhere. But Scott sent shock waves through those boardrooms when before the inauguration he spoke to the state's chamber of commerce—then called the N.C. Citizens for Business and Industry—at a December luncheon. Instead of extending an olive branch to a group whose members had largely supported Johnson in the primary, Scott lectured them. He said the business group's magazine, called *We the People*, should be renamed *We the People against the People*.

"I see we have telephone representatives here today," Scott said. "If you can't get telephones to the people I'll join with others, using any powers I have as governor to see that something is done about it. If it takes reorganization of the Utilities Commission, I'll try that too. Rural areas need telephones, and I'm going to go to work to see that they get them. I see we have representatives of the power companies here today too. If they had the vision of the founder of Duke Power Co., we would not have any real need for the REA today. Remember that."[6]

People were therefore primed for more than a cliché-ridden inaugural address, and Scott did not disappoint. In a forty-four-minute speech at Memorial Auditorium, Scott laid out a vision for his Go Forward program in which he asked the state to cast aside two decades of cautious spending. He called for a giant rural road-building program to get the farmers out of the mud, for big pay hikes for teachers, for a new dental school, for revisions or repeal of the state's 1947 right-to-work law, for the creation of a junior college system, and for an increase in unemployment benefits. "During the war and postwar years, when neither labor nor materials were available, I think our state leadership wisely husbanded tax resources," Scott said. "Our state is in sound fiscal position. But we cannot overlook the vital factor: In amassing a hoard of tax dollars we accumulated a vast backlog of urgent public service needs. We must conclude that we do not have a real surplus, but actually a deficit in public services. To go forward, we must wipe out this deficit." He promised to push to get electricity and telephone service into rural areas, and he said he would reorganize the state utilities commission and pressure the companies to live up to their responsibilities as public franchises. It was "a blunt challenge to a hostile General Assembly dominated by pro Johnson men," wrote C. A. McKnight, editor of the *Charlotte News*. And if the liberal coup succeeded, McKnight wrote, "it will give this state a small-scale 'Fair Deal' without parallel in Dixieland." The Fair Deal was what Truman called his program.[7]

Scott moved his office just half a block, from the Agricultural Building to the Capitol. But it was, as he put it, "the dangdest, roughest detour I've ever taken."[8] This was the era of the one-party South, and the legislature was overwhelmingly Democratic, with a 48–2 margin in the Senate and a 109–11 margin in the House. But conservative-leaning Democrats, who didn't see the need for a large jump in both spending and borrowing, controlled the legislature. Nor were most of the lawmakers, having backed Johnson, invested in seeing the upstart Scott succeed. Some legislative leaders, such as Lieutenant Governor Pat Taylor and House Speaker Craig

Ramsey, despised Scott. The governor also faced a business community that had largely backed Johnson, always hired the best lobbyists in Raleigh, and regularly oiled the legislative machinery with free booze, movie tickets, and campaign donations. "Everything was stacked against him," recalled his brother Ralph Scott. "The old crowd still dominated the legislature. The lobbyists hung around that railing in the Capitol like Grant did around Richmond. They were against everything he was for, good or bad."[9]

Scott held office in one of the constitutionally weaker governor's offices in the country. He had no veto power and was limited to one term; furthermore, independently elected officials held a large number of state offices. But Scott did have seven hundred appointments. He also had the bully pulpit, holding at least a weekly news conference that almost always left reporters with good stories. Scott benefited from good timing, too. The Great Depression and World War II had resulted in a pent-up demand for public services and a healthy state surplus. Despite Scott's criticism of the machine, the 1947 legislature had passed a record state budget that included a 30 percent pay increase for teachers and a 20 percent pay hike for state employees. More secondary roads had been paved under Cherry than all the years before 1945. Moreover, Scott came into office during a healthy economy.[10]

Scott used every tool at his disposal to get his program through. He repeatedly went over the heads of the legislature and appealed directly to the voters. He asked his Branchhead Boys to descend on Raleigh in a show of support. He cut deals. He attacked the legislature, he called out lobbyists by name, he needled civic clubs and newspapers that opposed him, he resurrected images of carpetbaggers, and he railed against big corporations—including oil, electric power, and telephone companies. Johnson had called Scott "the wild bull of Alamance" during the campaign. Now, in the view of political scientist and historian Tom Eamon, Scott faced the worst relations with a legislature of any North Carolina governor since Daniel Russell, the last Republican governor (1897–1901), who kept a loaded pistol in his desk in fear of attacks from the white supremacist Democrats who controlled the legislature.[11]

The legislature convened on January 5 and stayed in Raleigh until April 23, 1949, making it the fourth longest session on record. Before it was over, 60 percent of Scott's agenda would be approved.[12] No issue was more important to Scott than roads—the issue on which he made his reputation.

ROADS

Before the 1920s, the best way to get around North Carolina was by train. The railroad served fifteen hundred communities across the state, and even rural Anson County, with a population of just twenty-eight thousand, had thirteen railroad stations. Traveling by car on unpaved country roads with no highway signs was an adventure.[13]

North Carolina became a national leader in road building in the 1920s after the General Assembly passed the first Highway Act in 1919, which created a highway commission and adopted motor vehicle registration fees. Under the leadership of Governor Cameron Morrison, the state borrowed $115 million—a staggering amount at the time—for road construction in an effort to stimulate industrialization. North Carolina thus forged a reputation as a "Good Roads State," attracting visiting officials from fifty-five nations and governors of five states. Italian dictator Benito Mussolini sent his highway expert to North Carolina, and Louisiana governor Huey Long raided North Carolina's highway department for top engineers. But by the end of the 1920s, North Carolina's roads left the state with the highest debt in the country except for New York. After 1927, the state reverted to pay-as-you go on highways, and with the Great Depression in the 1930s and then World War II in the 1940s, there was not enough money or material for road building. And even during the 1920s, only primary roads had received attention, not the secondary road system that served much of the countryside. By the harsh winter of 1945, most roads except for major highways were impassable for days, and 150,000 schoolchildren lost eleven or more school days. The year 1947 was worse. A large part of the problem was that only a third of the miles traveled by school buses were blacktopped. And more school buses traveled the roads as small country schools consolidated.

Under Cherry, the state had stepped up road building as money and materials became available after World War II. But a lack of aggressiveness characterized road building. As historian Walter Turner noted, when in 1947 North Carolina drew up its request for the new interstate highway system, it asked for less mileage than most of its neighboring states. Raleigh was one of only six state capitals not included in the initial interstate system, and North Carolina's two ports weren't included, either.[14]

As an Alamance County farm agent, Scott wore out twenty-two sets of car chains traveling the roads. Commuting daily from his Haw River farm to his office as agriculture commissioner in Raleigh gave him first-hand knowledge. "I know of no one who could more fully appreciate your need of a better road," Scott wrote to a constituent in 1946. "From daily experience in trying to get to my office from my farm, I understand readily the situation in which you find yourself. Part of the time I am having to have my own car pulled by a tractor for two miles in order to get to the highway from my home. Since I have no authority in the matter of roads there seems little that I can do other than to stress the urgent need for them."[15]

Now he had authority. When Scott took office in 1949, the state was responsible for 62,000 miles of roads, of which only 16,000 had been hard-surfaced. The picture was even worse for secondary roads—with only 5,100 of 52,000 miles paved.[16] "Hell, there weren't any paved rural roads," remembers Lauch Faircloth of rural Sampson County. "I mean there were none. There were some arterial roads paved. But as far as farm-to-market or rural roads there were none that were paved."[17]

In a special message to the legislature on January 17, Scott called for a $200 million road bond issue for secondary roads and a one-cent-per-gallon tax increase to retire the bonds (raising it from six to seven cents per gallon). They were the first state tax levy increases since 1933, when J. C. B. Ehringhaus convinced the legislature to adopt the sales tax during the Great Depression. "A great percentage of North Carolina's population is rural," Scott told the legislature. "Masses of the people are living on dirt roads—many of which are impassable in bad weather. This condition affects the lives of so many of our people and affects them so importantly that the need for secondary road improvement is foremost in their thinking." Scott said the removal of what he called "the mud tax" would promote industrial development across the state, make farming more profitable by improving farm-to-market roads, improve access to schools and churches, and generally help end some of the hardships and isolation of rural life.[18]

Scott's bond proposal reversed his campaign stance of the previous spring. Having ridiculed Johnson for proposing a $100 million road bond, Scott doubled down on Johnson's plan by recommending a bond issue twice the size. He asked state highway officials what it would take to "blacktop" twelve thousand miles of highways and to treat another thirty-eight thousand miles so that they would become passable. In December, Scott received a four-page memo from the highway department saying that it would take $193 million to accomplish the goal. The memo said the state had $31.8 million available for road construction and would likely get another $10 million per year for county road construction—and therefore was $153 million short.[19]

The governor's proposed gas tax hike also flew in the face of his campaign rhetoric when he had declared: "There is no need to increase taxes at this time." In fact, Scott had promised to cut taxes, emphasizing that the sales tax from meals served in restaurants should be abolished. That promise also went by the wayside once he took office. He blamed the legislature for failing to cut taxes, but Scott himself failed to push it.[20]

Having spent years traveling the back roads of North Carolina, Scott knew the terrible isolation and hardship that dirt roads meant for people. And what he had not seen with his own eyes, people wrote to tell him. Dirt roads were sometimes not just a matter of inconvenience. They could be a matter of life and death. D. Reeves Noland, a state agriculture agent from Haywood County, wrote Scott about the loss of his son: "A number of years ago when we had only one boy which was our first son, he had an attack of illness and the country doctor (no country doctor now) advised us to rush him to a hospital in Asheville. We started out in a car in the morning, the roads were so bad we could not get through across the mountains. So a team pulled us back and we started up a very rough road in another direction and arrived in Asheville late that night but it was too late." Noland later almost lost his daughter to pneumonia while he was away on business and the roads became impassable. His wife had some leftover sulfa tablets, which saved their daughter's life. "You see from experience that I am a believer in the secondary road program," Noland wrote.[21]

Sometimes people became stranded on dirt roads and died. Charles D. Thorne, principal of Rodanthe schools on the Outer Banks, wrote to Scott to tell him about Millard Douglas, a resident of Salvo, who became stuck on the main road to Manteo: "He was unable to secure aid during the night, although he suffered a hemorrhage from the strain of trying to push his car out of the sand. Within a few days, he died. Of course, this is a somewhat unusual occurrence, and yet it should not be allowed to happen in our state. It is not rare for people to have to spend the night in an automobile on these banks. To be precise, there was a Coast Guardsman who froze to death last year because he was stuck trying to get to his home on this road."[22]

Dirt roads often made getting to school an adventure. That was the case for Finley L. German, owner of F. L. German Motor Company in Granite Falls, who wrote Scott encouraging his candidacy. "I am one of those who got up at 4 A.M., trudged three miles through mud and all that goes with it to catch an uncertain scheduled cattle truck which was open, with the exception of flapping side curtains of black oilcloth, and in turn rode a mud road, sixteen miles of mud road each way to and from high school," wrote German, continuing:

> Often we missed classes due to lateness on arrival. Often we unloaded, girls as well as boys, into a mud hole and pushed a stalled and steaming truck. Hours after arrival at a school room, poorly heated itself, I could not hold a pencil due to frozen hands. Sixteen miles by cattle truck and three miles wading, returned me home by lantern light where I studied by oil lamp. In spite of the handicap and suffering I was able to make an honor grade. Today, at the age of only 38 years I suffer partial deafness, mastoiditis, chronic sinus trouble and other health impairments as a result of my high school exposure and experience. May the nightmare such as I struggled through never come to my son, and others for that matter. . . . More power to you, Brother Scott. You will be one of our all-time great Governors. May God Bless you.[23]

But it was not just in the remote mountains or coastal areas where bad roads were isolating. It was a problem all over the state. Consider Mrs. William H. Wood of Route 1 in Morrisville, a Wake County town that is now in the middle of the Research Triangle, one of the state's major metropolitan areas, about the isolating effects of bad roads during lousy winter weather. "My little girl has had an infected throat, and the doctor said it was important that he examine her again yesterday," she wrote to Scott. "However it was impossible for me to take her to him or for him to come out to her. My mother has a very serious heart condition. You can imagine the dread I feel knowing that we would be helpless in case of an emergency." The Woods spent $25 ($259 in 2018 dollars) to bring in some fuel oil for their farm where they raised chickens and livestock and to tow their car to the highway so that her husband could drive to work.[24]

But Scott faced considerable skepticism: from conservatives opposed to borrowing to build roads or borrowing that much; from urban lawmakers who didn't want to see all the money going to rural areas; from the energy industry, which opposed a gas tax hike; and from political foes who wanted to see the upstart governor fail. To build support, Scott went on the radio and urged road bond supporters to appear at a public hearing in Raleigh. Some fifteen hundred people, many of them farmers in bib overalls and hobnail boots, descended on Raleigh's Memorial Auditorium in February to support the road bonds.

The Senate Roads Committee in February cut Scott's $200 million bond proposal to $100 million and made it contingent on voters approving a one-cent-per-gallon tax increase—in what many viewed as a poison-pill provision to scuttle the entire plan. The committee was chaired by Senator Oscar Richardson of Union County, who had been comanager of Johnson's gubernatorial campaign. Scott went on the attack against what he called "the obstruction clique" and "the-can't-do club" in a way that had rarely been seen by a governor in North Carolina. "The whole idea is to muddy the water, get the people confused and kill everything," he declared.[25]

Scott went over the heads of the legislature with a statewide radio broadcast, saying that it was time for "a showdown between a few of the hesitants in and outside of the General Assembly and the forces who believe North Carolina should take the steps necessary to build a better future. While there are those who talk about dangerous spending, I think the time has come to give some thought to dangerous withholding," Scott said. "Your Bible tells you that, 'there is that scattereth, and yet increaseth; and there is that withholdeth more than is meet, but it tendeth to poverty.'" Then he targeted the petroleum industry, which had been opposing the bill because it increased the gas tax. "So long as I am governor, this oil monopoly, headed out of New York, will not be allowed to push our people in the mud," Scott said. "Let us run the affairs of North Carolina ourselves."[26] Nor was he done lobbyist bashing, criticizing what he called "the Third House" of the legislature, which he said was trying to sabotage his program. Scott singled out by name four lobbyists, Gilmer Sparger, lobbyist for the gasoline industry; H. E. Buchanan, lobbyist for the movie theater industry; Fred Bowman, lobbyist for the bottling industry, and Sam Blount, lobbyist for the beer industry. "I don't doubt that Gilmer Sparger and Harry Buchanan, Fred Bowman and Sam Blount are behind it all," Scott said at a news conference. The *News and Observer* obliged with a front-page photograph of the four lobbyists posing together with their arms on each other's shoulders. Accompanying the article was a photograph of a movie pass given to legislators.[27]

The public pressure resulted in legislative passage of a $200 million bond issue referendum—contingent on approval by the voters of both the bonds and raising the gas tax from six cents per gallon to seven cents per gallon. Scott's opponents thought that they had sabotaged the effort, believing that voters would not voluntarily raise their taxes. But Scott also was wheeling and dealing. The governor gained the support of truckers for his plan, at the same time backing an increase in the maximum weights for trucks traveling on state roads from 50,000 pounds to 56,000 pounds. Critics charged Scott with making a quid pro quo deal.[28] He also convinced the legislature to pass a $50 million school bond issue. At the time, North Carolina had one of the highest teacher-pupil ratios in the country—if not the highest—and was facing a baby boom that would swell enrollment. Many children also went to small, inadequate country schools. It was estimated that 400 schools for white children and 1,000 schools for black children "should be abandoned and a total of 17,500 new classrooms be provided for them," according a report prepared for the governor. Of the 700 high schools for white children, 550 had fewer than two hundred students enrolled, and 275 had fewer than one hundred. Of the 230 black high schools, 175 had fewer than two hundred students enrolled.[29] The school bonds, when combined with $66 million in local construction funds, would provide 8,000 new classrooms, 174 gymnasiums, 350 lunchrooms, and 1,500 other facilities.[30] On March 3, nearly five thousand people answered Scott's call and jammed Memorial Auditorium once again to support the school bonds. J. Y. Joyner, a frail, aging man who was Governor Charles Brantley Aycock's superintendent of public instruction, told the audience to "deny not the cry of a million children crying for a better chance," and had everyone rise and sing the opening stanza of "The Old North State," the state's official song since 1927.[31]

The legislature adjourned on April 23, 1949, and despite the harsh words, Scott got much of what he wanted. In addition to bond issue referendum, the legislature approved a pay raise for teachers, a 20 percent pay hike for state employees, the creation of a new state personnel department, and further funding of the ongoing four-year medical care improvement program of new hospitals. It also increased social spending for old-age assistance, unemployment benefits, and aid to dependent children.

On April 26, Scott launched his fourth statewide campaign in less than a year to push not only a road bond issue but a school bond as well. The school and road bonds were tied together because Scott believed that the education bonds would have broad appeal and would make it more likely that voters would approve the road bonds. To promote the bonds in the June referendum, Scott formed a nonprofit organization called Better Schools and Roads Inc. The group's two hundred members included prominent North Carolinians from across the state. It established headquarters in Raleigh, had cochairs in each county, and purchased newspaper and radio advertisements.[32]

The chief strategist for the bond campaign was Ben Roney, a tough, shrewd, hard-drinking Rocky Mount oil jobber, who became the leading political operative for the Scott family and, to a lesser extent, would be an important aide to Governor Terry Sanford. "Ben Roney is the smartest man politically that I've ever dealt with," Kerr Scott once remarked to his brother Ralph. "He can sense what the people are thinking and doing and saying."[33] "He had a feel that was amazing," said Roy Wilder, Roney's long-time political sidekick. "He was always having ideas, some were good and some were bad. He had a bad habit of calling you up at 2 or 3 o'clock in the morning. He had not even gone to bed. He was always thinking."[34]

The petroleum industry set up headquarters in Raleigh to distribute literature and advertise across the state opposing the bond issue. The oil companies argued that North Carolina had enough money to pave rural roads without borrowing more, that the state would be burdened with debt, and that hurried construction would lead to shoddy roads. Scott sprang into action and wrote a letter to the nine major oil companies that marketed gas in North Carolina, asking them why they had increased gas prices "in the face of the largest net earnings in the history of their company." They denied Scott's suggestion that there had been "a secret agreement" to raise prices.[35] When the oil industry sent Ed Leary, a New Jersey oil research expert, to Raleigh to help with the opposition, the move provided Scott with more fodder. Campaigning for the road bonds, Scott likened his opponents in the gasoline industry to "carpet baggers." "New Jersey never has helped North Carolina," he told a farm group in Sanford. "It's not going to help us now. I want you to rise up and let these oil people know we want to be allowed to handle things ourselves in North Carolina."[36]

In Charlotte, North Carolina's largest city, Scott admonished his urban critics. "This has been the coldest section in North Carolina towards better schools and roads," he told a joint meeting of the Charlotte Chamber of Commerce and the Charlotte Lions Club. "The intelligentsia of this town, particularly the editors, need to get up early and find out what the working man thinks."[37] But opponents reminded Scott of his previous obstruction of road improvement. They ran an ad with the headline, "Candidate Scott Was Right," in a Charlotte newspaper, reminding voters that Scott had challenged Johnson's $100 million bond.[38] Opponents also accused Scott of planning to pile up a $217 debt for each family of four in the state, charged that North Carolina would have the largest debt of any state except New York and Illinois, and accused Scott of trying to build a personal political machine.

The governor drove himself as if his legacy depended on it—giving at least fifty scheduled speeches, traveling five thousand miles, smoking six cigars a day, and making seventeen radio broadcasts.[39] The pro-bond campaign was financed largely by companies that would benefit from road construction. Of the 176 contributors to the Better Schools and Roads Committee, 33 percent were highway contractors, equipment distributors, and suppliers of other materials. This group contributed nearly 80 percent of the $68,000 of the total money raised. (That is $713,000 in 2018 dollars.) The oil industry financed the campaign against the bonds.[40]

With no organized opposition, the school bonds passed with 69 percent, and the road bonds with 57 percent, on the strength of the rural vote. The counties with the four largest cities—Charlotte, Winston-Salem, Greensboro, and Durham—voted against it by a 4–1 margin. Afterward, Scott blasted North Carolina's civic clubs, dominated by city businesspeople, saying, "They're not worth a damn when it comes to doing something really worthwhile for country people." He later added, "Chambers of Commerce are not so hot either. It's nothing new. I saw the same thing when I was a county farm agent. Civic clubs are great on eating barbecue with the farmers, but of course there'd be a 'trade day,' too and they'd let the farmer know to bring his pocketbook along."[41]

Scott's comments and tactics created a backlash among some, including Democratic congressman Thurmond Chatham of Elkin, the wealthy, Yale-educated chairman of the world's largest blanket manufacturer. "I am sick and tired of people trying to array class against class," Chatham said in a speech in Reidsville. "We in North Carolina are all in the same class—Tar Heels."[42] To which the governor rejoined: "The conveniences I'm trying to get for rural people, Thurmond Chatham has never done without. He doesn't know what it means."[43]

The $200 million road bond issue (or about $2.1 billion in 2018 inflation-adjusted dollars) was the largest in American history up to that point, according to *Better Roads Magazine*.[44] In July, the Scott administration began preparing for a massive public works project that would change the face of North Carolina, or at least the map, from the mountain peaks along the Tennessee border to the coastal swamps. It put out bids for 162 tractors, 166 motor graders, more than 1,000 dump trucks, and 177 other road machinery, such as loaders, mixers, and scrapers. That was even though private contractors would handle 60 to 70 percent of the construction.[45] "Overnight North Carolina became the world's greatest market for road building machinery, equipment and supplies," declared the Ford Motor Company.[46] The Highway Commission also built on the east side of Capitol Square a striking, new, five-story, 61,000-square-foot, Italianate marble highway department building, which is still in use today. It was twice the size of the 1921-era highway building remodeled to accommodate the new North

Carolina Museum of Art.[47] Just as the highway department's headquarters grew, so did the number of employees: the highway staff increased from 9,395 employees in 1948 to 12,369 by 1953. Two hundred road engineers and their assistants oversaw the roadwork, and they pushed the highway workers hard. North Carolina was one of only four states that put highway workers on a fifty-five-hour workweek, spanning five and a half days, which drew complaints from the state employees' association.[48]

In 1950, thirteen-year-old Jim Hunt watched as the graders paved N.C. 42, the two-lane country road that ran by the Hunt family farm in Wilson County. "When you lived on a dirt road as I did, probably the biggest thing that could happen in your life is to get a paved road," recalled Hunt. "I remember people used to get stuck in the middle of the dirt road, the mud was so bad. The dust in the summer when everything was dry, you couldn't keep the washing out on the lines. We didn't have any dryers in those days. Country people would just give their right arm to have their road paved. I stood at the end of the driveway and watched the road paving machines come along and pave my country road. It just hit me—if you work in politics you can do some wonderful things to help people—tangible things that people really need and want."[49]

Of course, some people had mixed feelings about the improved roads, including those farmers who had a lucrative sideline using their tractors to pull stranded motorists out of the mud. Others, such as future judge James H. Pou Bailey, worried that Scott was creating a political machine by hiring so many highway workers. "It doesn't require much imagination to realize that a tremendous number of workers had to be hired by the state to carry out this gargantuan project which has touched every hamlet in North Carolina," Bailey wrote. "Potentially this vast army of highway laborers is politically powerful."[50]

Always keenly attuned to public perception, Scott set benchmarks by which constituents could measure his success or failure. In a statewide radio broadcast on January 6, 1950, Scott said he had asked the Highway Commission to finish ten miles of paved road and thirty miles of stabilized road on the secondary system each working day during the year. At the height of the program, in September 1950, five hundred rural road building projects were underway across the state.[51] In the end, Scott built 14,810 miles of new hard-surfaced roads—or more than all previous North Carolina administrations combined—although he had promised to build 12,000 miles. At the end of his term, only five states had more paved mileage than North Carolina: Texas, California, New York, Ohio, and Pennsylvania.[52]

A Johnston County farm family watches the black-topping of a road bordering their farm as a result of Kerr Scott's road-building program. (Courtesy of North Carolina Museum of History)

Measuring the impact of Scott's road-building program is difficult, but the Highway Commission tried. A 1956 report found that daily vehicle-miles of travel on hard-surfaced secondary roads grew from 1.8 million miles in 1949 to 5.8 million miles in 1953. The additional 4 million miles, the report said, had made a tangible improvement in rural life. Farmers could now get their products more easily to market, so egg production was up 16 percent and milk production was up 68 percent. The living index for North Carolina farm families increased 20.4 percent between 1950 and 1954 while increasing only 10.2 percent nationally. The percentage of rural births occurring in hospitals increased 20 percent. School enrollment went up 10 percent. Voting, too, was up, and the birth rate dropped—all signs of more affluence, and affluence meant that it was easier to go the movies, to church, to 4-H clubs, to Future Farmers of America meetings, to sports events and scout meetings.[53]

A few people complained about roads that were only twelve feet wide, but those stretches of pavement were the exception and mainly built in areas with light traffic. Most roads stood between sixteen and twenty-two feet wide.[54] Even so, the Scott administration roads turned out to be dangerous because people used them as speedways. Most of the 20,500 miles of unnumbered surface roads were meant to link the Branchhead Boys with their markets, country churches, and country stores—that is, the road builders assumed that the people who knew the roads' every twist and turn would be the ones driving them. But this wasn't the case. In some instances, roads were widened and curves straightened and bridges enlarged, but the state generally saved money by keeping roads in the same roadbeds with their "death" curves and suicide bridges. By 1954, 229 people were killed on unnumbered surface roads, 37 more than on the numbered state highways.[55] "They paved a lot of little old cart paths and a lot of those roads, the vertical and horizontal alignment is terrible," Faircloth said. "But it was a helluva lot better than what was there."[56] Even though Kerr Scott met his goal in road paving, two-thirds of the state's secondary roads remained unpaved at the end of his administration.[57]

PORTS

Scott wanted not only to improve farm-to-market roads but also to find an easier way to get North Carolina products to larger markets. That prompted him to launch the state's long-cherished dream of building a deepwater port. Unlike neighboring Virginia and South Carolina, North Carolina had never had a natural port because of its jagged coastline, marked by treacherous inlets and shifting barrier islands.

In 1924, Governor Morrison made a major effort to develop the ports by putting an $8.5 million bond issue on the ballot, but it was defeated by the voters. The North Carolina State Ports Authority was created by the 1945 legislature, but no funds were appropriated to carry out the task. Nothing moved forward until 1949, when the legislature, at Scott's urging, unanimously approved $7.5 million in revenue bonds ($78.6 million in 2018 dollars) for developing the port facilities at Wilmington and Morehead City.[58] Then, after three years of negotiations, the U.S. Maritime Commission signed a fifty-year, one-dollar-per-annum lease transferring to the state fifty acres of the Wilmington shipyard established during World War II. In 1950, President Truman interceded to ensure that the state received an eighteen-thousand-ton surplus dry dock for light ship repairs, transferred from the Pacific Coast to the Wilmington port. It was economic development on the cheap.[59]

Two decades later, $738 million had been invested in the two ports, and eight hundred merchant vessels a year, flying the flags of twenty nations, visited annually.[60] But because it lacked deep water, among other factors, the ports would not become the major economic players that Scott had hoped. In 2016, Wilmington, the larger of the two ports, was the nation's seventy-third largest port, and Morehead City was the ninety-fourth largest.[61]

All told, North Carolina in 1949 had an eye-popping $626.4 million in construction projects under way (or $6.5 billion in 2018 dollars). That included $200 million in rural road bonds, $50 million in state school construction bonds, $7.5 million for the state ports, $72.8 million of permanent improvement appropriations from the 1949 budget, $51 million from the 1947 budget, $150 million in locally financed school construction, and $33.6 million in local and federal hospital money.[62] All the projects were arguably North Carolina's largest public works project ever—much of it designed to help what Scott called the forgotten part of the state. But there was more than just earth to be turned. There were lines to be strung.

5 ★ LOW-VOLTAGE SUTTON

Electricity, the telephone and the system of farm to market all-weather roads we are building, free the farmer from the shackles of economic slavery. —Kerr Scott

Scott's ability to articulate important issues—not generated artificially by focus groups or polls but growing out of his own experience—drove much of his political success. After getting his road program under way, Kerr Scott turned his attention to extending more electric power and telephones to the countryside. He had championed rural electrification since his Alamance County farm agent days; he had also lobbied as North Carolina Grange president, as a charter member of the state Rural Electrification Authority, as agricultural commissioner, and as a gubernatorial candidate. By the time Scott became governor, North Carolina's rural residents had nearly caught up with the farm communities of the rest of the nation in electrification, thanks largely to the New Deal's REA program of providing loans.[1] Despite the progress, there were still one hundred thousand farms that had been waiting for years—in some cases decades—for electricity. In some instances, areas had electric power, but of the reliability that one associates with developing nations.

"It is extremely doubtful that I would ever have run for governor if I had been able to persuade the power and telephone people to give me and my neighbors electricity and telephone service on our farms," Scott told a rural audience in 1952. "The Haw River country, where I was born, raised and still live, was one of the unmarked deserts on the maps of the public utility companies. It made no difference to them. They had their reserved territories, fenced in by franchises, which they could serve, or not serve, as they pleased. They did not have to pay any attention to the voices crying in the utility wilderness. But it is different now."[2]

Although Scott signaled his intense interest in utility expansion in his inaugural address, it was not until the legislature adjourned and he got his road program under way that he focused on the issue in July 1949. In a fifteen-minute statewide radio announcement, Scott said the time had come to get on with the "unfinished business" of putting telephones and electricity into rural areas. He appealed to families who needed phones and power "to write in here and tell me about it. North Carolina is greater than any organization of utility companies." The governor also promised that he would ask the state Utilities Commission and the Rural Electrification Authority to call on each company and cooperative for a study of unserved areas. "If the private companies won't supply them," Scott warned, "the government will have to. I definitely feel that the people in the utilities field have too long had a negative approach. Instead of fighting everything, they need to get a positive approach and do something about filling those needs. If we had to depend on these people to win a war we'd never win one. If we had to depend on them, North Carolina would have never developed."[3]

Scott's belief in public power put him in opposition to the nation's influential utility executives, who saw government-subsidized electric power as verging on socialism. Among them was L. V. Sutton, the chief executive of Raleigh-based Carolina Power and Light Company, who was also president of the Edison Institute, the national association of privately managed electric power companies. Yet Scott had no reservation about needling the powerful. At one news conference, he made fun of Sutton's initials L. V. by referring to him as "our friend, Low Voltage Sutton."[4] On a personal level, their relations were somewhat warmer, with the men exchanging cigars at Christmas. (Much to the amusement of their families, Kerr Scott's granddaughter Susan Scott married L. V. Sutton's grandson Louis Sutton, and the couple became Christian medical missionaries in Africa. Bob Scott offered a toast at their 1980 wedding that said in part: "Let's raise a toast to Louis Sr. and W. Kerr, looking upon us from wherever they are: Disbelief and astonishment, thinking on days of old; But beaming their approval at that what they behold").[5]

Scott convinced the legislature to reorganize the state Utilities Commission, increasing it from three to five members, which allowed him to name new commissioners and take control of the board. In July, he called the five utility commissioners into his office and told them to "put a little more speed behind your work." He then asked the commission to have the utilities draw up plans for connecting power to the unserved areas.[6]

In the fall of 1949, Scott gave a much-anticipated speech at the opening of CP&L's new Lumberton steam generating plant, located on the Lumber River, where he shared a stage with Sutton. Scott praised the opening of the plant and the expansion of power companies such as CP&L, but he noted they had not done enough to help the rural areas of eastern North Carolina; after all, a million North Carolinians had no electric service. "The power companies were not interested in extending their lines beyond thickly populated areas, where they could skim the cream from their product," Scott said. "This power shortage is particularly acute from Goldsboro to the coast. An example of the insufficiency of power in this eastern area is Little Washington, where electric service is at times about on par with a European city after a bombing raid—you veterans know what I am talking about." He added that the lack of power was a major reason why only 5 percent of the state's industry was located east of Raleigh.[7]

Scott asked the public to write him, and hundreds complied. The Reverend Herman Minnema, pastor of Terra Ceia Christian Reformed Church in the eastern town of Pantego, lived in one of those eastern towns Scott had discussed in Lumberton. "Without warning our electric may be turned off for as long as 48 hours; at present we can expect to be without electric about 2 or 3 hours every day," Minnema wrote the governor. "That the electric is turned off on occasion is understandable, but when we do have electric we never know whether it will be so strong that the bulbs will burn out in a week or so weak that the motors will not turn over. With such poor service this brazen Commission has the nerve to charge the highest rates I have ever paid."[8] Other people wrote about waiting decades for electricity to come to their homes, schools, or family members' houses. Scott's favorite letter came from a farmer's wife after electricity arrived in her home: "Been married 40 years and for the first time I can see what my husband looks like."[9]

Scott kept the pressure on the power companies throughout his administration. In a January 1951 speech to the General Assembly, he proposed legislation requiring utilities to apply to the state Utilities Commission for franchise certification, which would give the state more leverage.[10] Scott's efforts appeared to pay off. In 1948, 190,826 farms, or 66.4 percent, were connected to power compared to 68.6 percent of farms nationally. In 1952, Scott's last year as governor, 260,811 farms, or 90.4 percent, had electricity compared to 88.1 percent nationally.[11]

While Scott's populist tactics—and support for public power through the REA—caused heartburn in the corporate boardrooms of the utility companies and their allies, it was hardly bad for business. "There was a great hue and cry about Mr. Scott's 'playing' around with 'creeping' socialism," wrote Charlotte commentator Harry Golden. "So what happened?

That creeping socialism brought about a tremendous capitalistic boom in North Carolina. Suddenly, we discovered 100,000 new customers for things to put into those electrical outlets. The first thing they bought was a radio. Then came the washing machine on the porch; then came the refrigerator and finally the television set. So here we had millions of dollars' worth of appliances sold only because Mr. Scott used public financing to provide electric outlets to 100,000 people who had still been living in the last decade of the nineteenth century."[12]

TELEPHONES

Although the lights were finally coming on, rural North Carolina was still one of the last places in the United States to get telephones. In 1945, only 5.1 percent of North Carolina farms had telephones, the lowest percentage in the nation except for South Carolina. By comparison, the average for U.S. farms was 31.8 percent, and in prosperous farm states such as Iowa, 79.3 percent of farmers had phones. Those figures don't begin to tell the story of how the absence of telephones hurt almost every aspect of rural life—garages, filling stations, implement dealers, repair shops, blacksmiths, stores, doctors, ministers, schools, and churches.[13]

In today's connected age of smartphones, tablets, and Skyping, it is hard to imagine the isolation of mid-twentieth-century rural North Carolina. Vast areas lacked all phone service. R. H. Holden, a dentist in Shallotte in the southeastern part of the state, wrote to Governor Scott "that we have a forty-square mile area here without a telephone."[14] This also meant that whole towns were without service. "We are a family of six living at Addie, a mountain community of about 300 just five miles east of Sylva," wrote Mrs. Frank Terrell. "Our community has no telephone. There is no phone within two miles of us. We have tried for years to get the telephone company in Sylva to install one in our house, but to no avail. A telephone in our community would be of great service to all. It would save everyone from having to drive five miles for a doctor when someone is sick. It would save everyone from a lot of trouble."[15] In some places, such as the small town of Bahama (two hundred people) in Durham County, the only telephone in town was located in a grocery store, and when the store closed, "there is no phone service in or out of this place at night and very poor service in the day time," wrote C. M. Allen, who said that the town had been trying to get residential telephone service for twenty years.[16] O. D. Stallings, who taught at Appalachian State Teachers College in the mountain town of Boone, wrote the governor about the difficulty of keeping watch on his aging father, who lived on the home place in rural, eastern Nash County. "My Dad has lived for over thirty years within one mile of the highway line, and yet I cannot get a telephone message nearer than Spring Hope, which is three miles away," Stallings wrote. He said he had to make a five hundred-mile round trip to check up on his father.[17]

Furthermore, many schools did not have telephones, sometimes with tragic consequences. In 1949, seven children were killed in a school bus wreck near Ferrell's School outside Middlesex in Nash County. The nearest phone was located at least five miles from the school, and area residents signed a petition saying that some of the children's lives might have been saved if doctors and ambulances had been called promptly.[18]

Even when phone service was available, it was often of abysmal quality, which hurt business. Voit Gilmore of W. M. Storey Lumber Company of Southern Pines was one of many businesspeople complaining about service. "The only word for long distance telephone service between Southern Pines and Goldston, Siler City and Asheboro is 'miserable,'" Gilmore wrote. "We can produce evidence to show both our company and lumber companies in those three communities suffer great inconvenience, and actually lose money, as a result of the apparently, inadequate lines joining us. We often spend hours and hours trying to get calls through."[19]

A cabinetmaker who had been waiting for years for a telephone in Kinston said that contractors had to physically visit his shop to solicit his business. A Gibsonville cotton manufacturing executive said that his chief mechanic, responsible for keeping the machines for six hundred employees humming, could not get a telephone installed in his home even though he lived in town, five blocks from a telephone office. Town officials from Boiling Spring said that their community was being held back by telephone service that was so bad it was hardly better than having none at all.[20]

From the beginning of his administration, Scott made telephone expansion a top priority—saying that the state had fewer phones in rural areas than it had thirty years earlier. "I want to see to it that we put telephones in up to 90 percent of the homes seeking them," Scott said during his first month in office. "We have unfortunately a good many small companies who want only the cream of the trade and refused to go to the expense of expanding. I'm speaking frankly, if you people will join me, I'm going to pressure to see to it that they either give this service or give up their franchises."[21]

The North Carolina Grange had been pressing for government action on rural telephones since the 1930s, warning that if private companies didn't start doing a better job of extending rural lines, then it would favor "government ownership." In 1943, Harry Caldwell, Scott's successor as state grange master, and North Carolina governor Melville Broughton, a Grange member, attended the national Grange convention in Grand Rapids, Michigan. They pushed to amend the Rural Electrification Act so that the REA could make loans for telephones as well as electric lines. The North Carolina advocacy—Caldwell was chairman of the national Grange's legislative committee—is credited with playing an important role in Congress's 1949 appropriation of $25 million for REA rural telephone line construction loans.[22]

Despite movement on the national level, telephone improvements stagnated in North Carolina. In January 1950, an impatient Scott stepped up the pressure, telling the state Utilities Commission to use every legal means available to get a telephone in every household. He accused the Utilities Commission of dragging its feet and said that if it did not act soon, "we may have to reorganize again."[23] The governor told the commissioners that they could either get to work or resign.

He then asked representatives of seventy-one private phone companies to Raleigh to explain how they were planning to expand telephone service. Stanley Winborne, the state Utilities Commission chairman, said that most of the companies were doing all they could but lacked capitalization. "The difficulty of getting the stockholders to provide funds for telephone expansion has increased in direct proportion to the rising denunciation of the telephone companies," Winborne explained. "It took $200 million to build roads and you still hear complaints. Give us $50 million and we'll cover the state with telephones."[24]

Scott said that the call for a loan fund was "just alibiing" and that the Utilities Commission was reluctant "to call the telephone companies on the carpet."[25] At the same time, the governor did not wish to push the companies beyond their capacities. "We realize there are many one horse, family affair companies that have neither the means nor the equipment to make substantial improvements or to borrow money," Scott said. "We'll have to go easy with these." But he said that the rights of the companies were not greater than the rights of the citizens, and if a company could not provide services, then the state could take away its franchise.[26] By the end of Scott's term, fifty thousand additional people had received phones, yet only 15 percent of farms had them—far short of the governor's goals.

Four years after leaving the governor's mansion, now a U.S. senator, Scott looked back at the fight to bring electricity to North Carolina's farms with pride, noting that 95 percent of residents had power. But he said that the growth of rural telephones in North Carolina "is a rather sad story by contrast," with merely 17 percent of farmers connected. In 1956, only farmers in Alabama and Mississippi had fewer telephones than their North Carolina counterparts.[27]

LABOR

Scott's jibes at power companies, telephone company executives, and legislators provided good copy for the state's newspapers, although it did not win him any popularity contests with the state's establishment. Nor did Scott's policies on labor and management issues.

It is one of the peculiarities of North Carolina that while it was still heavily rural, it was also the leading industrial state in the South at mid-century—with textile mills, furniture manufacturers, and tobacco factories spread out in towns and hamlets across the state. But its production workers were among the worst paid in the nation. The Tar Heel State has historically had among the least unionized workforces in the country.[28] Like much of the South, most North Carolina governors had favored management and been hostile to labor, in the belief that such policies would attract northern capital and new factories from corporations seeking to cut labor costs.

In 1947, over President Truman's veto, Congress passed the Taft-Hartley Act, which allowed states to pass laws limiting labor unions. North Carolina was one of the states that passed a so-called right-to-work law, which outlawed union or agency shops from requiring new employees at a company with a unionized workforce from having to join the union or pay a fee. Scott was the first—and so far the only—North Carolina governor to call for repeal of the state's right-to-work law, calling it "harsh." A Scott-backed bill to modify the state's right-to-work law was killed in the House Manufacturing and Labor Committee on March 17, 1949, by an 18–14 vote. The bill would have permitted voluntary union shop agreements between employers and labor unions and allowed optional check-off union dues by employers. A minority report brought the measure to the House floor, where it was defeated 59–17. Representative R. L. Harris of Person said that the 1947 right-to-work bill had been sponsored by three members who had served in the South Pacific during World War II and resented wartime strikes by labor unions. "When my son was on the battlefields of France," said Representative "Cousin" Wayland Spruill of Bertie and a longtime Scott foe, "they had a strike [in this country] to defeat our war effort. We've got 'em [labor] by the throat now."[29]

During the 1951 legislature, Scott also tried without success to get the legislature to enact the state's first minimum wage law of seventy-five cents per hour and a forty-hour week with overtime. But the measure met stiff opposition from small businesses and was whittled down to a forty-eight-hour week and a fifty-cent minimum wage. Yet even that was killed in committee after opponents cried "socialism" and "welfare statism."[30] Scott was more successful in convincing the legislature to increase unemployment insurance benefits from a weekly four-dollar minimum and twenty-one-dollar maximum to a weekly scale of six dollars to twenty dollars. Legislators also raised the benefit period from sixteen to twenty weeks.[31]

In the past, North Carolina governors had tended to side with management in labor disputes, sometimes sending in the State Highway Patrol to bust a strike. But Scott took a more even-handed approach. When five hundred workers walked off the job at the Hart Cotton Mill in Tarboro in May 1949, Scott called for arbitration rather than sending in highway patrolmen to break the strike as management requested. The governor twice met with the union and the St. Louis company's management, including once in New York, to try to resolve the dispute. The company complained in a memo that Scott was pro-union, while the union praised his role in the dispute. Eventually, though, Scott called in the patrol after violence broke out. The company's hardline tactics paid off, the strike was halted, and the workers voted against unionizing by a 357–236 vote.

RACE

Scott also set a new tone regarding African Americans. It started with his inauguration when Scott set aside a section for black supporters on the main floor of Memorial Auditorium rather than in the segregated balcony, as was traditional.[32] He had been in office a little more than a week when he chose a North Carolina Dairy Products Association meeting in Winston-Salem to talk about the need for fairer treatment of blacks. "It is time North Carolina stopped dodging the Negro question," Scott said. "I'm going to follow through and see that the minority race has a fair opportunity and gets the training to fit into the industrial and agricultural life of the State. I'm firmly convinced that we've got to go ahead and meet the issue of the minority race. They came here against their will, brought in chains."[33]

In January, Scott met with leaders of the NAACP, who reminded him that black voters had helped him upset Johnson in the Democratic primary. He listened to their goals, which included integrated transportation, the appointment of blacks to boards, and eliminating inequalities in schools.

Such a meeting was unusual among southern governors at the time, and Scott received some angry letters from whites who viewed the NAACP as a radical organization. He also sought funding parity for black and white schools, removed salary differences for employees at the state mental hospitals for black patients, and helped fund ten new buildings at N.C. A&T State University in Greensboro, a historically black college.[34]

Even as Scott moved to be more inclusive regarding black citizens, he simultaneously assured whites that he was committed to maintaining segregation. Responding to one letter from a white constituent, Scott wrote, "My position on this matter is that the Negro should have equal opportunity for economic advancement and certainly no question of social equality is to be considered seriously. As I have said, we should give the Negro opportunity to make a living for himself and family in order that they may become more productive citizens. Even this must be achieved step by step, and you are quite right that any radical departure at this time would defeat the purpose of better relations between the races that we are trying to achieve."[35]

On the last day of the legislative session in April, Scott nominated H. S. Trigg, the president of historically black St. Augustine's College in Raleigh, to the State Board of Education. Uncertain about how the appointment of an African American might be received in the legislature, Scott rushed through the confirmation in one day—bunched together with several other nominations. Representative "Cousin" Wayland Spruill, one of Scott's opponents, moved that a select committee be formed to investigate the qualifications of the nominees, but Scott allies made a motion for approval and pushed the nominations through without debate.

Scott received widespread praise in the black community and some support in the white community from those who thought the inclusion of blacks in government was overdue. But the appointment angered some of Scott's white supporters, such as J. S. Davis of Troy: "I have nothing personal against the colored race but my honest opinion is that we have enough good white men that are capable of filling the offices of our state."[36] Scott replied Davis saying that he appreciated his support and he was sorry that he did not agree. "We have two races living side by side here in our state," Scott explained. "I want to do what I can to promote the kind of helpful relations among the people, and it seemed to me that justice calls for somewhat better representation of the minority race in our public affairs that are closely identified with the well-being of all races." Scott added that Trigg was a moderate on race relations who "has no disposition to hasten change of the established customs with respect to separate education of the races in this State."[37]

In a similar vein, Scott was not willing to push for black voting rights in a state where blacks could vote in the cities but were often prevented from voting in rural areas. Asked by a black reporter if he planned to sponsor any measures during the next legislative session guaranteeing black voting rights, Scott replied, "I think you've got all the laws you need. It's a question of enforcing what we've got." The governor said that in some sections of the state, local sentiment had to change before blacks could freely be permitted to register.[38]

THE SQUIRE OF HAW RIVER

Scott's rough edges—including a slow drawl, a fondness for country expressions, a good sense of humor—created an authentic appeal to country people, but others considered him a bumpkin—especially after the parade of corporate lawyers that preceded him in office. He often wore a rose in his lapel, which became a trademark.

A solidly built man familiar with physical labor, Scott stood five feet, ten and a half inches tall, with black hair and bushy eyebrows. A fighting trim 205 pounds when he took office, his forty-four-inch waist was temporarily under control (he had ballooned to as much as 250 pounds in 1930). An avid eater, as a fourteen-year-old Scott once devoured thirteen apple pies at a wheat-threshing dinner. He smoked up to ten cigars a day, preferring stogies to the plug of Brown Mule or Peach & Honey tobacco that he sometimes chewed. As writer Simmons Fentress put it, society matrons looked around nervously for a cuspidor when the governor entered their home.

"He was rough—and tough; a rough, tough gentleman," said Terry Sanford, a longtime admirer and future governor.[39] Scott once told a hunting buddy, a Burlington newspaper man, that he wanted to urinate off the front porch of the executive mansion as he was used to doing at his farm. The hunting buddy "said he got up one morning and went out and let it fly," recalled A. C. Snow, an editor of the *Raleigh Times*. "He said he felt better after that. He never lost his roots." It is hard to know whether the story is true or merely a brand of Scott's rough, country humor. But the newspaperman did note that there was not much grass growing off Scott's porch in Haw River.[40] If the account is true, however, Scott was at least more circumspect than Georgia governor Eugene Talmadge, who invited the men in rural audiences to "come see me at the mansion. We'll sit on the front porch and piss over the rail on those city bastards."[41]

In a practice he started when he was agriculture commissioner, Scott sometimes lunched at Green's Grill in Garner, where he ordered his beloved chitlins: hog entrails, the staple of poor southerners when no part of the pig could afford to be wasted. They were served with sweet potatoes, hominy, collard greens, and corn bread. Sometimes Scott took others along, and eventually it became the Wake County Chitlins Club, which as of 2018 continues to meet.

To supporters and favored constituents, Scott handed out proclamations declaring a person a "country squire," a sort of North Carolina version of a Kentucky colonel. The proclamation read:

> I, Governor, W. Kerr Scott, note that: He is one of one of the branchhead boys, born and bred in the Tarheel State, who has quit draggin' his feet and is catchin' up on his haulin'; and whereas he has demonstrated that he is a tried and true member of the rougher element and plows out to the end of the row; and whereas, he is versed in both the meaning and the mystery of our significant and proclaimed dates; and whereas he is forward-goin' and has a natural hankerin' for chittlin's, possum and 'taters, lamb fries, potlikker, corn pone, barbecue, and sas'fras tea; I do therefore proclaim him a Country Squire entitled to all the rights and privileges of this estate.[42]

Scott received three hundred thousand letters, and nearly a quarter of a million visitors signed the guest book in the executive mansion. When Scott discovered that there were no Jewish-sounding names among the visitors, he called out to his wife: "Miss Mary, how come no Hebrews have visited the mansion?" Miss Mary replied: "Maybe they are shy." Scott asked his secretary to "to call up the Hadassies and have them come over and visit the mansion so we can have some Hebrews in the books."[43]

Scott brought a Jacksonian view of political spoils to the governorship, just as he did to the agricultural commissioner's job. There was such a sweeping out of Johnson supporters that there might as well have been a change in political party. State employees who had worked for a variety of governors for thirty years lost their jobs, replaced by Scott loyalists. He replaced the state budget director, the commander of the highway patrol, the director of the state parole commission, the director of state purchasing, and so forth. "Virtually every appointive department head in state government, and many in subordinated positions, was given his walking papers by Kerr Scott," wrote James H. Pou Bailey, a conservative columnist and later a Superior Court judge. "That was his way of opening wide the doors.

Whether the man had done a good job in office made little difference. More important was whether he had supported Kerr Scott for governor. No North Carolina governor in 50 years has done so much to make political appointees feel insecure in their position as Kerr Scott."[44]

Some of Scott's appointments blew up in his face. He named C. R. Tony Tolar, a former car dealer and his campaign driver, head of the highway patrol—but then had to fire Tolar after he was charged with speeding and careless and reckless driving.[45] Scott's prison director, Brice Moore, resigned after charges that he used state prisoners to do work at his home. Highway safety director Jeff Eilson left the payroll after questions about juggled expense accounts.

Scott also swept out former appointees to boards and commissions and put in his own supporters. Scott's appointments were more diverse—more rural residents, more women, and a sprinkling of blacks. By the end of 1949, Scott reported that of the 428 appointments he had made, only 20 percent had been reappointments, 15 percent had been women (compared to 7 percent in the past), and 15 posts had been filled by blacks (or 3.5 percent black compared to 1 percent in the past).[46]

Scott was not averse to pulling a few strings for his family. One of his nephews, Ludwig Scott, known as Lud, was denied admission into the first class of the University of North Carolina's new dental school. When the dean of the dental school asked Scott if he could find another $250,000 in his budget for equipment for the dental school, the governor leaned back and said: "Let's see who all is coming to your class. You need to check that list a little better. I think there is a mistake there. My nephew applied and I don't see his name on there. Why don't you check that and we'll talk about those funds a little more?" Lud Scott was admitted, the university got the funds, and the nephew had a successful career as an Alamance County dentist, retiring in 1995.[47]

HOME

Scott returned to Haw River every weekend. Harold Minges, Scott's highway patrol driver, recalled his first trip driving the governor to Haw River. It was a Sunday on the way to church. "He said: 'Minges, I want to stop by the farm first. Can't go Sunday school until I've got a little cow manure on my shoes.'" Most Sundays, though, Scott walked to his brother's farm, and from there the two set off together on a two-mile walk to Hawfields Presbyterian Church, meeting a third brother and neighbors along the way in a scene that seems out of a Norman Rockwell painting or maybe a Frank

Capra movie. "We solved all the world's problems," Ralph recalled. "I heard about almost everybody in North Carolina and Kerr would talk about them along the way."[48] The exchanges between the two brothers became grist for press coverage after Ralph was elected to the state Senate. When a reporter cornered Ralph on Monday to say he heard that Ralph had cussed the governor in church on Sunday, Ralph replied that was a lie: "I cussed him outside of the church."[49] After church and Sunday dinner, Scott sometimes sat under the oak tree in his yard and met with visitors in the afternoon.[50] This kindness wasn't limited to his constituents; Scott once cosigned a $1,000 loan made by the state employees credit union to allow Minges to purchase his first home. "But don't say anything about it," Scott admonished him. "I can't do this often."[51] Scott's governorship was also good for the church. In the early months of his administration, Scott chaired the Hawfields Presbyterian Church committee tasked with raising money for a new community building. After the governor sent out fundraising letters, businessmen from as far away as New York City, Massachusetts, and Florida took an interest in the little country church, allowing him to raise $55,000 (or $576,000 in 2018 dollars).[52]

Scott's idea of relaxation was to grab his single-barrel shotgun (purchased from the Sears catalog in 1908 for $4.12)—later a double-barrel shotgun—his dogs, and a few friends and head out to the hedgerows and honeysuckle, the briars and the brambles, in search of rabbits. He ushered out 1950 by spending two days duck and goose hunting in Dare and Currituck Counties, followed by a Saturday morning rabbit hunting on his farm. Monday, he went quail hunting.[53]

Scott enjoyed college sports, but he couldn't manage to be diplomatic at the UNC–N.C. State football game played in Chapel Hill in 1949. At halftime, he stepped to the microphone during festivities commemorating Greater University Day and announced his support for his alma matter, N.C. State. Then Scott said, "We are rushing the building of a great hospital here." The crowd was silent. "Because we're going to need it to take care of the Carolina players after State College gets through with them." Scott received vigorous cheers from State fans, and boos from Carolina's. According to the *News and Observer*, he got a bigger crowd reaction than did Carolina All-American Charlie "Choo-Choo" Justice.[54] Acting University of North Carolina president Billy Carmichael quipped: "The two most talked-of-men in North Carolina are Choo-Choo Justice and Boo-Boo Scott."[55] Like a Huey Long or a Donald Trump, Scott could command headlines even while doing something as mundane as attending a football game.

6 ★ DR. FRANK AND AFTERMATH

Kerr, just as sure as there is a God in Heaven—and there are one—politics is hell, ain't it?—Dairy farmer who stopped by to see Governor Kerr Scott at his farm to commiserate with him about the problems he was having with the legislature

Although Kerr Scott didn't know it yet, the postwar window for rural progressivism in the South was closing as the threat of racial integration caused a retreat to a safer, more conservative brand of politics, one people thought promised them a greater chance of upholding the color line. As writer and historian John Egerton noted, "A combination of favorable circumstances had opened a narrow window of opportunity through which the South might have reached both internal social reform and external parity with the rest of the nation." Egerton continued, "By 1950, just as racial injustice was beginning to press to the forefront of public consciousness throughout the South, the 'Old Guard' was poised to mount a strong counterattack. In the frenzied atmosphere of cold war anticommunism—just then reaching its peak nationally—the cabal of Southern demagogues succeeded in linking racial equality to 'red menace' in the eyes of their constituents."[1]

Nothing made that clearer than the 1950 North Carolina Senate race.

Following the death of sixty-year-old J. Melville Broughton on the eve of his maiden Senate speech, speculation centered on whom Scott would name to the seat. Much of the speculation centered on traditional party leaders—congressmen, party chairs, and legislative leaders. Scott's list had grown to fifty names when he showed it to Jonathan Daniels, the *News and Observer* editor whom Scott had made the state's Democratic National Commiteeman. When Daniels noted that Frank Porter Graham, president of the University of North Carolina, was missing from the list, Scott paused, relit his cigar, and asked, "Would he take it?" Daniels said that he would ask. Shortly afterward, Scott read the list of potential senators to Miss Mary. When he got to Graham's name, the First Lady said, "You can stop right there. So far as I am concerned, that's it."[2]

Graham was not only the university's president but arguably the South's leading liberal and, as such, a polarizing figure. A native of Fayetteville who grew up the son of a Charlotte schools superintendent, Graham arrived on the Carolina campus in 1905 and immediately became as much a part of the scenery as the Old Well—as senior class president, editor of the *Daily Tar Heel*, and cheerleader. After a stint in the marines during World War I, Graham continued his intellectual journey in Chicago, Washington, and London, obtaining a master's degree at Columbia University and spending a year of study at the London School of Economics, where he met Fabian socialists and Laborites.

Returning to Chapel Hill, Graham became a popular history professor and a gifted fund raiser, traveling across the state promoting the university. When the university's presidency became vacant in 1930, Governor O. Max Gardner convinced him to take the post, and in 1932, Graham became president of the newly created Consolidated University of North Carolina system, with campuses in Chapel Hill, Raleigh, and Greensboro. Graham became legendary thanks in part to his gift for remembering students' names and engaging them in games or in intense, quiet conversations. He and his wife, Marian, invited students to Sunday evening open houses at their home. By the 1940s, the Chapel Hill campus under Graham had become, in the words of writer John Gunther, "a kind of intellectual capital for the whole South."[3] In a South marked by broad-based mediocrity in its colleges and universities, the University of North Carolina stood out as the exception. It was one of the few places where people conducted serious research and published about the South's problems—poverty, education, labor disputes, lynching, the system of tenant farming, and even race. It was where black poet Langston Hughes could be invited for a well-publicized reading and lecture at Gerard Hall in 1931.

If Graham engendered intense loyalty, he also made the veins stand out on some peoples' necks. As the university emerged as an intellectual center, Graham led the fight to protect academic freedom, defending controversial speakers, ending the Jewish quota at the university medical school, and protecting a professor who dined with a prominent black communist. Even more than his defense of academic freedom, Graham's social activism irritated many conservatives. In 1929, he was among three hundred college professors, newspaper editors, lawyers, and others who signed an Industrial Bill of Rights to protect worker rights at a time when labor was making a major push to organize North Carolina cotton mills. As a committed New Dealer, he lent his name to hundreds of liberal groups and

Frank Porter Graham, UNC president, playing horseshoes in 1939.
(Hugh Morton Photos and Films, North Carolina Collection, University of
North Carolina at Chapel Hill Library)

causes, often with little thought about how it might affect his responsibilities as university president. He attended First Presbyterian Church in Chapel Hill, which welcomed black visitors starting in 1945.

In 1938, Graham became the first president of the Southern Conference for Human Welfare (SCHW, 1938–48), a liberal social justice group formed by New Dealers to push for reform in the South. Holding its first meeting in Birmingham with the blessings of President Franklin Roosevelt and with First Lady Eleanor Roosevelt in attendance, the SCHW heard Graham's call to action to improve wages, housing, and health care and for full political participation in the South. Although the SCHW was a broad-based coalition of liberals, it included a number of communists. Despite warnings from friends that he should disassociate himself from the group, Graham refused to desert an organization just because it had, in his words, a "handful of communists."[4]

All of this made Graham a target of conservatives across the country. In June 1947, the House Committee on Un-American Activities issued a report calling the SCHW "perhaps the most deviously camouflaged Communist-front organization."[5] The report cited twelve suspicious groups with which Graham had been associated and said that although Graham was not a communist, he had a habit of lending his name to communist-front organizations.

Despite such attacks from the right, Roosevelt and Truman entrusted Graham with major, sensitive assignments. FDR named him to the War Labor Board to help settle disputes between industry and organized labor during World War II, so that during the war years, Graham commuted between Chapel Hill and Washington. Secretary of State George Marshall appointed him to a three-person United Nations team that negotiated a truce between the Dutch and the anticolonialist forces that led to an independent Indonesia.

Despite declining several overtures, Graham eventually accepted the Senate appointment after Scott and Daniels explained how, as a senator, he could help Truman and Secretary of State Marshall ratify the North Atlantic Treaty Organization (NATO), implement the Marshall Plan, and deal with the cold war, foreign aid, and disarmament.[6] Scott broke the news at a university banquet in Chapel Hill's Lenoir Hall. "While I'm on my feet, I want to make an announcement," Scott said. "The next senator from North Carolina will be Dr. Frank Graham." The crowd of seven hundred greeted the announcement first with stunned silence and then erupted into thunderous applause.[7]

The appointment was a high-risk move—especially for a governor just three months into his administration and facing a hostile, conservative legislature that had not yet passed his legislative program. The move enthralled liberals and cemented his national reputation as a different breed of southern governor, but it eroded his support among his Branchhead Boys political base. Even so, Scott said he was tired of the same old conservative corporate lawyers who usually represented North Carolina in the Senate, and he felt that the state deserved a new kind of voice. He saw Graham as an extension of his brand of politics. "Dr. Graham represents the neglected man," Scott said a few months later. "That is why there is a certain amount of bitterness toward his appointment."[8]

Scott and his supporters had hoped Graham would avoid a serious challenge in the May 1950 Senate primary. Both Senate seats were on the ballot the same year—a rarity—Graham's seat and that of conservative Democrat Clyde Hoey, a political warhorse from the old Shelby Dynasty. Thus, the Scott establishment and organized labor tried to cut a deal with the old-line Democratic organization. They would not run a candidate against Hoey in the Democratic primary as long as Hoey and the machine would support Graham. The deal stuck as far as it went—Hoey did not face any opposition from Scott and his allies, and Hoey voiced support for Graham. But hopes that so polarizing a figure as Graham could dodge a major conservative challenge proved illusory. To defeat someone of Graham's stature, conservatives would need a significant figure of their own, and they found one in Raleigh corporate lawyer Willis Smith. A handsome, distinguished-looking man, the sixty-three-year-old Smith was elected in 1945 as the first North Carolinian to serve as president of the American Bar Association. Smith had served three terms in the state House, culminating with as term as House Speaker from 1931 to 1933. He had nearly run for governor in 1940. He had a blue-chip practice representing many of the state's major banks, textile firms, railroads, insurance companies, and utilities, as well as the medical society.

Filling out the Democratic primary field was former senator Robert "Our Bob" Reynolds of Asheville, a rogue who in the 1930s and 1940s had clowned his way to two terms in the Senate by pretending to be a poor man running against a plutocrat. By contrast, Graham was the very picture of a naive and absent-minded professor, and he knew little about the grubby business of politics as it was practiced in midcentury North Carolina. It fell to Scott to get Graham elected, and in the fall of 1949, the governor began meeting with groups of backers to line up support for Graham. Graham started with some assets: the advantages of incumbency, the backing of the Scott administration, and the behind-the-scenes support of the Truman administration. He also had the support of the Old Well network of Carolina supporters, organized labor, and black voters.

Scott arranged to have supporters such as Clinton businessman Lauch Faircloth and Roy Wilder, a Spring Hope newspaperman, serve as Graham's drivers. (Faircloth said he didn't have any choice but to drive Graham when the governor asked because he had tractors rented to the state as part of the road-building program. When Scott enlisted Faircloth to drive, he pointedly asked Faircloth: "How are your tractors doing?")[9]

The governor sought to convince Jesse Helms—with Graham in the room—to become Graham's publicity man, or what we would call today press secretary, telling him he couldn't make any money in the radio business. But Helms declined, saying that while he liked Graham—and that his wife had often attended Graham's Sunday open houses—he was more philosophically in tune with Smith.

Scott encouraged organized labor to roll up its sleeves. "You haven't got a better liberal in America than the Senator you've got," Scott told 450 labor leaders in Durham. "Don't slip up in the election."[10]

The Truman administration did what it could to help Graham. The president kept close tabs on the race and made sure to send federal pork—awarding the state a surplus U.S. Navy floating dry dock for Wilmington. Jonathan Daniels, although officially neutral as a DNC member, sometimes attended campaign strategy sessions and ensured favorable coverage in the *News and Observer*.

The Smith campaign, by contrast, counted on strong business support and North Carolina's tradition of sending conservatives to Washington. He also had two emerging hot-button issues: reds and race.

The era of the red scare was ushered in when Senator Joseph McCarthy declared in a February 1950 speech in Wheeling, West Virginia, that he knew the names of 205 communists working in the U.S. State Department. People were ready to believe such charges. Eastern Europe and China had fallen to communist control, and American traitors had helped the Soviets steal U.S. atomic secrets. Newspapers were filled with stories about American spy rings, including some involving high-level officials such as Alger Hiss. In short, people were looking for communists under their beds, and that extended to North Carolina. At a University of North Carolina board of trustees meeting in February 1950, one trustee objected to the hiring of a faculty member born in Wisconsin, which he said "is an extremely liberal section" with the "pink tinge of communism." "I don't see why we have to go to the mid-West and the Pacific to get our faculty members," said Mark Lassiter of Snow Hill. "Certainly, there are good people in the South." Apparently, he had not noticed Joe McCarthy's Wisconsin roots. Presiding at the meeting, Scott dismissed the complaint. At the same meeting, the university trustees chose Gordon Gray, the secretary of the army and a conservative, as the president to succeed Graham.[11]

Although never calling Graham a communist, the Smith campaign suggested that Graham had allowed himself to be used by communists. The red-baiting charges spread through Smith's speeches, newspaper advertisements, and leaflets. "I can say to you tonight that I do not now nor have I ever belonged to any subversive organizations and that as United States senator from North Carolina I shall never allow myself to be duped into the use of my name for propaganda or other purposes by those types of organizations," Smith said in Elizabeth City. "The unwary can do just as much harm as the unscrupulous in the days that are at hand."[12] To further discredit Graham, the Smith campaign set up a team of researchers, most notably a young Raleigh attorney named Tom Ellis, to comb through Graham's record. One Smith newspaper ad named twenty "Communist front organizations"—as identified by the House Committee on Un-American Activities—to which Graham had lent his name. They included the Citizens' Committee to Free Earl Browder, the American communist leader; the American Friends of Spanish Democracy; the National Sharecroppers Fund; and the National Council against Conscription. His support for a 1944 dinner honoring the Red Army was also noted.[13] Responding to the attacks, Graham delivered a speech in Dunn in which he declared, "I have never, am not now and never will be a Communist or a Socialist, or a member of any organization known or suspected by me of being controlled by Communists or Socialists."[14]

In the end, red-baiting charges against Graham didn't stick. But race was another matter, and the issue could be traced to the blinding of Sergeant Isaac Woodard, the Goldsboro man coming home from World War II who was grabbed off a bus by a South Carolina lawman. Infuriated by the mistreatment of Woodard and other black GIs, in 1947 Truman had appointed the President's Committee on Civil Rights, which produced the first major government report outlining racial discrimination in the United States. As one of two southerners who served on the committee, Graham became an inviting political target. From that report, Truman recommended a package of civil rights legislation, including the creation of the Fair Employment Practices Commission to prevent discrimination in hiring because of race, color, religion, or national origin. The Senate began debating the FEPC bill on May 8, just weeks before the Senate primary.

Although Graham had signed the report, the two southerners on the committee said that although they favored eliminating segregation, they opposed federal measures forcing states to act. "It [the minority] dissents, however, from the majority's recommendations that the abolishment of segregation be made a requirement until the people of the states involved have themselves abolished the provisions in their state constitutions and laws which now require segregation," the report said. The way to end segregation, the dissenters said, was through education and religious efforts to improve the brotherhood of men.[15]

When he got to the Senate, Graham announced that he would vote against the FEPC bill because he thought that racial integration should be brought about voluntarily as people's attitudes changed. Only three southern senators refused to participate in a filibuster against the bill—Graham, Claude Pepper of Florida, and Estes Kefauver of Tennessee. As a result, Smith tied Graham to FEPC, which if it passed would be the first major civil rights bill of the twentieth century. He accused Graham of supporting FEPC because he had signed the Truman civil rights report and saying that he "looked in vain" for a minority report. Smith asserted that the minority dissent in the report pertained only to education, ignoring the larger dissent in the section marked "general." As the campaign wore on, Smith offered a $100 reward and then a $500 reward (worth about $5,177 in 2018) at rallies to anyone who could produce the minority report. "He, by his own signature, subscribed to the proposed FEPC," Smith said. "Now that he has to go before Tar Heels who are not quite as ultra-liberal as he, he disavows the proposal. He's a little late."[16] Today, any interested citizen could get on the Internet and read the minority dissent for themselves, but that was not true in 1950.

To make certain the race issue translated to the voter on the farm or in the cotton mill, the Smith campaign began using tactics that become infamous. One handbill distributed by Smith supporters pictured black GIs dancing with white English women during World War II. Its caption declared that Graham favored racial mixing. Smith supporters also distributed fifty thousand handbills declaring that Graham had appointed a black man to West Point. Actually, Graham had named LeRoy Jones of Kinston, student body president at St. Augustine's College in Raleigh, as a third alternate, the first southern black nominated for a U.S. military academy—

based on competitive exams. But because the first alternate, a white student, accepted, Jones did not attend.

With the race tightening, Scott abandoned any pretense of neutrality; he hit the campaign trail for Graham and helped him raise money. A "confidential bulletin" went out to the governor's network, imploring them to work for Graham. "Let's stop kidding ourselves. Senator Graham is a member of the team. He was appointed by the Governor, whom we elected to carry out the Go Forward program. A victory for Senator Graham is a victory for Governor Scott. A loss for the Senator would be a severe loss for our governor."[17] This involvement soon made Scott an issue in the campaign, and the political back-and-forth became relentless. The *Durham Sun*, a pro-Smith newspaper, called Scott the "Huey Long of Haw River" and accused him of trying to be North Carolina's little Napoleon. The Know the Truth Committee, affiliated with the Smith campaign, produced a political cartoon showing Graham as a puppet whose strings were being pulled by Scott and Daniels.[18] When, to raise money for Graham, Scott sent two political operatives to Philadelphia, New York, and Washington, D.C., to collect contributions from liquor distillers doing business with the state, they were tailed by private detectives hired by the Smith campaign, which then leaked the story to the press. Scott claimed that all he knew about the affair was that his aides had taken some vacation time. In another fundraising effort, Scott wrote George A. Hamid Sr. in New York, who held the contract for state fair rides, urging him to use his contacts to raise money for Graham.[19] Smith charged Scott with abusing the patronage power of state government to lean on people on behalf of Graham. "Never before has such pressure been brought upon state employees, people who sell to the state and have contracts of one sort or another with the various state departments," Smith charged.[20] Scott said that if state cars or state employees were being used to help Graham, they were being done without his knowledge. But he also said that he appreciated the loyalty of state workers who supported Graham.

In a statewide radio address, Scott made a populist appeal. North Carolina had elected enough corporate lawyers, he said, and the state "needed a man who has devoted his life to the service of others, rather than to building his own personal fortune and tying his loyalty and support to special interests." An amused Smith retorted that if corporate lawyers were so bad, why did Scott urge him to run for governor in 1948? "He apparently thought I would have made a good governor," Smith told a Greenville crowd. "But now he says he's opposed to me because I'm a corporation's lawyer. I was the same lawyer then that I am today." Smith also noted that Scott had appointed him to the state commission for improving justice. Scott confirmed the story, saying that he had urged four or five people to run for governor who turned it down, with Smith being the final person. "I couldn't get any of those to cut loose so I went to see that fellow Kerr Scott," Scott said. "It wasn't my desire to run for governor. A lot of people won't believe that but I didn't want to run. Smith is an able man. He is a smart man or he would [not] be representing those corporations. He's a fine man. He's got a fine wife." Scott added: "At the time I didn't know he was anti-administration—both State and national."[21]

The turnout of nearly 620,000 people for the May 27 primary was the largest in state history. Graham led the primary with 48.9 percent, with Smith receiving 40.5 percent and Reynolds 9.3 percent. It was an impressive showing for the teetotaling Graham (who drank buttermilk to celebrate), and he'd come close to the 50 percent he needed to win outright. Smith initially didn't commit to a runoff, though as he tried to decide, the U.S. Supreme Court handed down decisions on three civil rights cases—involving graduate education and railroad dining cars—that chipped away at segregation.

Even so, Smith initially drafted a telegram conceding the race and gave it to his press aide, Hoover Adams, who disobeyed his boss and pocketed it. Instead, he called a handful of supporters who he hoped might change Smith's mind. Among them was Jesse Helms, the news director of WRAL radio, who bought advertising time and urged people to show up at Smith's house in Raleigh that evening. Several hundred appeared at Smith's Raleigh home, chanting, "We Want Smith," and the next day Smith called for a runoff. In a statewide radio address from Raleigh, Smith called his candidacy an effort to keep "real Southern democracy." His decision to enter the race, Smith said, was based in part on the threat posed by the Supreme Court rulings, which he said had created racial ill-will. He assailed what he called bloc voting—or black voting—for Graham in the primary. "The votes of our Negro voters offer an inviting field to a certain type of politician who had been known in the South since a much earlier generation," Smith said, apparently comparing Graham to a carpetbagger.[22]

The most famous Smith campaign flyer read, "WHITE PEOPLE WAKE UP!" and was distributed by the "Know the Truth Committee":

Do you want Negroes working beside you, your wife and daughters in your mills and factories? Negroes eating beside you in all public eating places? Negroes riding beside you, your wife and your daughters in buses, cabs and trains? Negroes sleeping in the same hotels and rooming houses? Negroes teaching and disciplining your children in school? Negroes sitting with you and your family and public meetings? Negroes going to white schools and white children going to Negro schools? Negroes to occupy the same hospital rooms with you and your wife and daughters? Negroes as your foremen and overseers in the mills? Negroes using your toilet facilities? Frank Graham favors mingling of the races. Vote and help elect Willis Smith Senator. He will uphold the traditions of the South.[23]

Scott stumped across eastern North Carolina's farm country for Graham, moving from crossroads stores to small villages to filling stations and trying to lessen the campaign's racial tension. At Edenton, where about seventy-five Graham workers met with the governor, Scott said: "The good people of this town should rise up in indignation against some of this damnable propaganda they are passing up and down the streets of this town." That morning, the Smith campaign distributed copies of a black newspaper saying that black voter registration had risen to one hundred thousand.[24] In a radio address five days later, Scott said that Graham did not favor the FEPC and had no control over Supreme Court rulings any more than did Smith. "The injection of the race issue into this campaign is an insult to the intelligence of the good people of North Carolina," Scott said.[25]

But racial hysteria filled the air, and Scott was powerless to change that. "The mob mood that was built up in the final days of the campaign was not unlike that preceding a lynching," wrote journalist Samuel Lubell.

In Wilmington a precinct worker telephoned the Graham manager and demanded hysterically, "Come and take all your literature out of my house! My neighbors won't talk to me." Graham stickers came off automobiles as people found it uncomfortable to say they were for him. In Raleigh, an eight-year-old school boy who spoke up for Graham was beaten up as a "nigger lover" by other children. A Durham election official, favorable to Graham, was awakened during the night by the jangling telephone. When his wife answered, she was asked: "How would you like a little stewed nigger for breakfast?" The day before the voting, Graham was scheduled to speak at High Point to some mill workers. His party stopped at a filling station. Five men were sitting around. Introducing himself, Graham offered to shake hands. The men turned their backs. Muttered one, "We're all Willis Smith men here. We'll have nothing to do with nigger lovers here."[26]

On June 24, Smith defeated Graham 51.7 percent to 48.2 percent. In the Manteo ballroom at Raleigh's Sir Walter Hotel, Smith supporters whistled "Dixie." "Tell ole Kerr Scott to go to hell," someone shouted. Kerr Scott took a hard blow, indeed: Graham lost the primary in the farm country of eastern North Carolina, Scott's Branchhead Boy stronghold—the region where Scott's fight for more rural roads, electricity, and telephones was most felt. The same section, however, was home to the state's largest percentage of blacks. Scott's homespun personal popularity was difficult to transfer to a former college president, especially when racial fears were being fanned.[27] Scott made a display of shrugging off the defeat a couple of days after the election. "I've been in a lot of scraps," Scott said. "It's not the first time I've been run over." He later greeted reporters in his shirtsleeves, telling them, "I pulled off my coat just to show you that I had not lost my shirt."[28]

Despite the show of bravado, Scott seemed shaken if not embittered by the racist campaign. He told a group of farmwomen at N.C. State University that they "had been suckered in by propaganda." And to the Roanoke-Chowan Rural Electrification Administration in Rich Square, Scott said, "As long as we base our statewide action in politics on race prejudice or religious prejudice—as long as we work against the rights of the human—how in the world can we convince Russia that the American way of life is right—when we fight each other right here in the state?" Scott even suggested there might be divine retribution for prejudice, noting that the race issue in the Civil War brought on "such misery" afterward; that prejudice against Catholic presidential candidate Al Smith in 1928 was followed by the Great Depression; and that a week after Graham was defeated, the Korean War began.[29] At the annual convention of the state labor federation in Winston-Salem, he criticized white people for their part in the racially charged campaign: "I want you white people to remember this; those of you who spread the most bitter campaign man or woman of North Carolina ever heard. The Negro did not come into this country of his own accord. The white man brought him here." When some black delegates applauded, he said, "I notice you colored brethren clapping pretty hard, but you didn't do your part either. You may be another color, but in this election were just as yellow as the other man"—a reference to low black turnout.[30]

Scott's critics could hardly contain their glee at Graham's loss. Scott had put his reputation and his administration on the line and been rejected.

"Governor Kerr Scott has lost immeasurable influence and prestige," wrote conservative columnist Eula Nixon Greenwood. "He saw fit to drag the governor's office into the political mire and in all probability has buried his political future. Immediately upon becoming governor, he began arraying class against class, the country against the city, the labor force against management. At one point, he urged the Negroes to have 250,000 colored people in the registration books. While he might have thought he was doing the best thing, he at the same time solidified the thoughts and attitudes on the other side of the fence."[31]

Although the Graham defeat did not "bury" Scott as his critics hoped, it left him weakened. Never again would he have the air of political invincibility that had enabled him to upset political favorites—as he did in the 1936 agriculture commissioner's race or the 1948 governor's race—or to masterfully drive his agenda through a hostile legislature. In some ways, the searing experience of the Smith-Graham race appears to have chastened Scott. He seemed a more cautious, reserved political figure afterward—whether in the final two years of his governor's term, in his 1954 Senate race, or his years in the Senate. He never again appointed another black to a major position after Trigg. When asked why, shortly after having left office, Scott said that he had considered "broadened racial representation a mandate" of the 1948 election. But he said that the Smith-Graham race was "rougher" than he had anticipated. "The Graham hate campaign set the state back 25 years," Scott said. "That's when all the Ku Klux stuff got a start in the state."[32] Scott seemed to be implying that he had misjudged the temper of the state. North Carolina's moderate image on race appeared to provide more opportunities for its black citizens only within the confines of the system of segregation, and as the Smith-Graham race showed, any attempt to loosen that system would result in a powerful white backlash.

All across the South, with segregation under attack, whites were retreating on race, and Scott soon followed. When a black reporter from a Pittsburgh newspaper in February 1951 asked Scott why he had not supported more black appointments, the governor curtly replied, "If I were you I never would have asked that question. The appointments have been made faster than members of your race have demonstrated ability to handle them."[33] Of course, there was no evidence of black incompetence. More likely, Scott had been shocked by the raw racial feelings exposed in the Smith-Graham race and was politically recalibrating, now that he was considering challenging Smith in 1954.

Smith campaign aides have denied that Smith had anything to do with the racist ads, blaming them on overzealous county committees. But Smith never publicly denounced the tactics, nor is there any evidence that he took any steps to stop them. This strongly suggests that Smith, the former bar association president and the very pillar of the establishment, comfortable in North Carolina's most important boardrooms and toniest country clubs, acquiesced in some of the most racist tactics ever seen in the state in order to win elective office. When Smith as senator-elect came through a receiving line at a function at the executive mansion, he stuck out his hand to Miss Mary, the First Lady. She looked at his hand for a moment, then at his face and said, "Oh, I couldn't do that," and turned away from him.[34]

Not only did the Smith-Graham race divide many Tar Heels into opposing political camps for a generation, but it changed the course of state and national politics for decades. From the Smith campaign, Jesse Helms and young Raleigh attorney Tom Ellis forged a political friendship that would give rise to the modern Republican Party in North Carolina, create the Christian Right political movement, and help rescue Ronald Reagan's career in 1976.

After the election, Graham turned down several job offers from Truman, eventually moving to New York to take up a new career with the United Nations. He returned to Chapel Hill years later as an elderly widower and died in 1972.

THE LEGISLATIVE SESSION

Scott headed into his second legislation session in 1951 in much changed circumstances. The governor was both politically wounded, and he had run out of new spending money. When Scott became governor the state was flush, having built up reserve funds from the war years. By 1951, however, Scott administered a state with a large debt and no surplus. Demands for appropriations exceeded revenue projections, and for the first time since the Depression, the state had to borrow for expenses in anticipation of taxes.[35]

At war with Korea, the nation faced material shortages. Truman had imposed price and wage controls, which tightened an unstable economy. Moreover, North Carolina governors, then constitutionally limited to one term, generally began to be regarded as lame ducks by their third year. In fact, when former senator William Umstead entered the lobby of the State Capitol in January 1951, he was introduced as "the next governor of North Carolina" by such Scott foes as "Cousin" Wayland Spruill who were counting the days before Scott's exit.

The conservative wing of the Democratic Party saw their chance to embarrass Scott. "He might just as well have been a Republican or something, because he's the one that broke up the machine, as they call it," recalled his brother Ralph Scott.[36] Ralph Scott, an Alamance County commissioner, joined his brother in Raleigh in 1951 as a state senator and moved into the executive mansion, commuting home on weekends with the governor. At the outset of the session, Ralph received a customary letter from Lieutenant Governor Pat Taylor inviting the senator to list the committee assignments he preferred. "And I didn't have any more sense than to tell him that I'd like to be where I could be of service to the Governor," Ralph said. Taylor made him chairman of the Penal Institutions Committee.[37]

In his address to the legislature, Scott argued against retrenchment. "The courageous development of North Carolina through use of the power of state government did not begin with my administration," Scott said. "It will not end with it. We have been fortunate in having governors and legislators who had faith in the people of this state and in the state's resources. What I want to advocate strongly to you now is that there be no halting of the advance—that we move steadily forward, building by plan and with confidence in the future. I am proposing the consolidation of the advance we have made, but not that we dig in for stoppage of the advance."[38] He called for increased salaries for teachers and state employees, expanded health programs, repeal of the right-to-work law, creation of a state minimum wage law, the holding of a statewide referendum on liquor sales favored by the prohibitionists, and funds to create both an arena at the state fairgrounds and a state-sponsored art museum. He also asked for a constitutional amendment to lower the voting age from twenty-one to eighteen.

The 1951 legislature rejected proposal after proposal made by the governor; only 14 percent of his requests were adopted, the worst record of any twentieth-century governor, according to political scientist Thomas Eamon.[39] The legislature blocked his prolabor legislation, killing an effort to establish a minimum wage or repeal or modify the state's right-to-work law. Then, one of Scott's most central issues, road funding—this time for the cities and towns that had been left out of his original $200 million road bond issue—crashed to defeat. Scott had proposed a $9.5 million plan for the state to take over city streets and pay for it by increasing the license fee and adding half a cent to the gas tax. But the legislature rejected his plan, fearing that it would allow Scott to build political support in the cities. Instead, the legislature adopted a plan, known as the Powell Bill, that dedicated a half-cent of the existing tax to urban road construction. This move put municipal streets connecting primary highways under the State High-way Commission but kept other roads under municipal control.

Scott succeeded in pushing through the state's first environmental law, but he was forced to take a half of a loaf. He joined with conservationists to create a State Stream Sanitation Commission, which supervised and controlled waste disposal in North Carolina rivers. The original bill was opposed by industry, which feared it would discourage manufacturers from moving into the state. The final bill changed "commission" to "committee" and placed the body under the State Board of Health. The committee could survey all state water resources; it could also issue regulations and orders to stop pollution, but the measure had been weakened.[40]

Scott succeeded in creating the North Carolina Museum of Art as the first state-supported art museum in the country. The 1947 legislature appropriated $1 million ($11.2 million in 2018 dollars) to create an art gallery, but with the money still unused four years later, some lawmakers wanted it spent for other purposes. In 1951, the Samuel H. Kress Foundation offered to match the state money with another $1 million purchase of Italian Renaissance paintings if enabling legislation could be arranged. Critics said that if the issue was placed before voters, the art museum would not receive the support of 10 percent of the public. But the legislature approved the money on the condition that none of it be used to purchase modern art.

Frustrated by the legislature's inaction on his programs and showing some of his old fire, Scott went on the radio in February to attack a group of lawmakers who called themselves the "hold the liners." "Hold the line against what?" Scott asked.

> Is it against the mental institutions, while 531 mentally disturbed citizens wait to be admitted? Is it against the tuberculosis sanatoriums, while 420 citizens are standing in the shadow of this dreaded killer? Is it against the school for the deaf, where 425 children are crowded into a space adequate for half that number? Is it against our aged and infirm who are dependent upon the welfare department for their daily bread and whose average monthly check amounts to only $22.20, which is less than half the national average for this group? Is it against the hospital program, while seventeen counties in this enlightened state do not have any hospital beds available when sickness strikes their citizens? Is it against merit raises for state employees whose responsibility it is to manage the business of your state government? Are these the things they are holding the line against? Can any group be so callous, so un-

mindful of the past, of the present, and of the future that it would hold the line against the progress of education in our state?

The speech angered some legislators who talked about answering the governor in another broadcast, but tempers cooled.[41]

On a rhetorical roll, Scott at his next news conference referred to the Senate Appropriations Committee as the "Do Nothing for Nobody Club." But Scott's tactics failed to achieve their goal. His 1951 agenda lacked the broad public appeal that caused crowds to turn out to support his plans for rural roads and schools. And, if anything, the legislature's opposition stiffened.

Meanwhile, legal challenges to segregation continued. Although the U.S. Supreme Court's *Brown v. Board* decision on public school segregation was still three years away, southern universities were under pressure from the courts to integrate their graduate programs because there were no equivalent programs at historically black institutions. The University of North Carolina Medical School in April 1951 admitted Edward O. Diggs, a World War II veteran and a premed student at N.C. A&T State University in Greensboro, as its first black student. The University of North Carolina became the first southern college to admit a black student without a court order, although the trustees agreed to integrate only when it became clear that they were likely to lose the legal battle. A few months later, in June 1951, after a two-year-long legal battle handled by future Supreme Court Justice Thurgood Marshall, three black students peacefully enrolled at the University of North Carolina at Chapel Hill law school. Lawmakers were urged to cut off funding to schools that desegregated, but Scott advised against it. "We've got to work with the situation, especially on the graduate level," he said. Nevertheless, the black students suffered frequent harassment and were escorted on campus by the State Highway Patrol.[42]

The grandson of a Klansman, Scott acted decisively when the KKK showed signs of reviving in the state in 1951. The Klan had largely been inactive since the 1920s. But with segregation coming under attack, the KKK began organizing and holding rallies, mainly in the southeastern counties. There were several cases of beatings, and there were threats made against individuals including newspapers that opposed them.[43] Scott warned that North Carolina "is not going to take any foolishness from the Ku Klux Klan" and vowed to use the full police powers of the state to investigate any KKK threats. The governor said he could see little difference between Klansmen and communists. "The Communists threaten to overthrow the government and they [the Klan] want to take the place of government," he said. Reflecting, Scott said that the Reconstruction era KKK was composed of "responsible people" and was centered in Alamance County, his home. "Then it was a question of survival," he said. "Carpetbaggers had invited the Negro race to try to assume a responsibility it wasn't trained for. We had no law and order then, but we got it now. . . . You must know your history well enough to know the difference. . . . My grandfather was arrested and tried in Yanceyville for Klan activity. Some of his old Klan regalia is still stored in my garage in Alamance County."[44]

Scott could take on the Klan without political risk because attitudes had changed. Gone were the days when the KKK was glorified in movies such as *Birth of a Nation*, the 1915 silent film epic based on the novel *The Clansman* by North Carolina writer Thomas Dixon Jr. Playing at Burlington's Paramount Theater in the summer of 1951 was the movie *Storm Warning*, a film featuring an ad of a pretty white woman (Ginger Rogers) being beaten by a masked Klansman. The headline on the ad shouted: "Expose! Expose! Expose! The Shocking Violence of Mob Rule and Hate. Why Are Honest Citizens Afraid to Speak? The Ku Klux Klan Exposed! It could happen to you . . . here in Burlington." The hero of the movie, a prosecutor who stands up to the KKK, was played by actor Ronald Reagan.[45]

THE SCANDALS AND CONTROVERSIES

As the first governor without legal training in decades, and elected with little support from lawyers, Scott struggled with his judicial appointments. Some worked out well, such as his naming of Susie Sharp to superior court judge. She became the first woman chief justice of the state supreme court, meriting conversation as a possible U.S. Supreme Court nominee. But others were less distinguished. When Associate N.C. Supreme Court Justice A. A. F. Seawell died on October 16, 1950, at age eighty-five, Scott named Murray A. James, a little-known lawyer from Wilmington, to the bench. Scott tried to force the state Democratic Executive Committee to make James not only the interim appointment but also the Democratic nominee for the November 7 election. Angry at not having been consulted, the Executive Committee instead designated Jeff Johnson, Frank Graham's campaign manager, as the nominee. James ended up serving one month on the court. Scott named another old friend without bench experience, Itimous Valentine of Nashville, to the Supreme Court after the death of Chief Justice Walter Stacy in 1951. Valentine came in third in the Democratic primary in 1952, handing Scott another embarrassment.

Controversies plagued Scott's final two years in office. People began to notice all the road construction near his farm. The *Greensboro Daily News* published a story in June 1952, complete with a large aerial map, showing how the state had built about fifteen miles of paved highways in a small triangle through or near his property. That included construction of a new four-lane bypass around Graham through Scott's property—U.S. 70, later to become Interstate 40/85. Scott was paid $12,965 (or $124,441 in 2018 dollars) for right-of-way and for crop damages resulting from the taking of 39 acres. The state also built a cattle pass—an eight-foot culvert—under the highway so his cows could travel from one field to another, although according to his son Bob, the cows balked at using the tunnel. (The cattle pass still exists and was later repurposed by Alamance Community College for waterlines to the campus from the Trollingwood area.) The large-scale road construction prompted Nello L. Teer Construction Company of Durham in 1951 to lease 14.1 acres on Scott's Back Creek property to operate as a rock, stone, and gravel quarry. The five-year lease paid Scott a minimum of $2,500 ($25,000 in 2018).

Unapologetic about the preferential treatment for roads near him, Scott said that Hawfields Presbyterian Church had been the main beneficiary. "No, certainly the state at large hasn't any such network of roads as this," Scott said. "I'll say this, if I have stolen a nickel, it was for the church. I did it for the church—and attendance is up 25 percent since my administration opened." He continued, "You know damn well we'd have never have got these roads if I'd waited for some other administration to give 'em to us. The boys in the district said to me that we'd better get 'em now, because when this was over, we were done."[46] Scott did, however, back down in August 1952, when he was scalded for dipping into the highway surplus fund to come up with an extra $750,000 ($7.1 million in 2018 dollars) for Alamance County.[47]

The governor took ironic note of his self-serving in a letter to regional highway commissioner, asking for a road to be paved for Harry Caldwell, the master of the state Grange and one of his oldest friends. "I have known Caldwell for many years and one of his characteristics is that he is very reluctant to urge for anything in which he has a personal interest," Scott wrote. "This is contrary to what many of the rest of us do, including your present governor."[48]

Scott also had few reservations about accepting freebies. One dirt road bordering the Scott property was paved shortly before Scott took office. Governor Cherry had contacted Scott and said he would pave the dirt road in front of his house before Scott took office, so that the new governor wouldn't be criticized for it. Scott agreed, and the highway department built a road and a new bridge across Back Creek. "I never saw a road built that fast," said his son Bob. Scott called it Cherry Lane.[49] He also received free agriculture lime for his farm from the American Limestone Company in Knoxville, Tennessee. How long he had been getting such benefits is not clear, but based on correspondence it seems likely he had been getting deliveries at least since 1944 when he was agriculture commissioner. "For several years, Mr. [Thomas] McCroskey, who was my good friend over a period of many years, complimented me with limestone from your plant for use on my farm," Scott wrote in July 1950. "I, of course, paid the freight charges and sales tax. I always appreciated this kindness very much indeed. I am in need of one carload of lime right away sent to Trollingwood Siding, Haw River, North Carolina. Whether you can feel you make it complimentary or not, I still want the lime. With very best wishes."[50] R. P. Immel, the company's vice president replied: "We are entering an order for shipment to you, one car of our MASCOT agricultural limestone, and will ship this order promptly, as soon as open top cars are available. We are pleased to ship this car, gratis, to such an old friend of long standing, and also because you certainly know good limestone when you see it."[51]

Similarly, when Scott thought he would host the Democratic kickoff to. the 1952 presidential campaign at his Haw River farm, he solicited and received 21.75 tons of nitrogen solution worth $1,141 in the summer of 1952 ($10,744 in 2018 dollars) to make the pastures lush. When the handout was later disclosed, the manufacturer, Allied Chemical and Dye Corporation, said that it staged similar demonstration projects around the country.[52] This was an old habit of Scott's. While serving as agriculture commissioner, for example, he wrote to Merck and Company on official department stationery, asking for a "sample supply" of DDT, the insect control product, "in connection with the operations of my dairy." A Merck executive replied, regretting that the company could send only a one-pound sample "in view of the fact that the entire production is on allocation by the War Production Board."[53] In another ethical lapse, the governor also apparently approached textile giant Burlington Industries, one of the state's largest employers, about the possibility of building a plant on his farmland. J. Spencer Love, Burlington's chairman, thanked Scott for his interest, but it apparently went no further than that.[54]

Some of the controversies were disclosed during Scott's governorship, such as the network of roads and the $750,000 special road fund for Alamance County. During the 1954 Senate campaign, his opponents revealed the quarry deal with Nello Teer and the free fertilizer from Allied Chemical. But some practices, such as his free lime from the American Limestone Company, or his efforts to get Burlington Industries to build a factory on his land, never came to light. Scott had his limits, though. Ben Roney told the story of when Ralph Scott wanted to use a boat owned by the Department of Conservation and Development that was moored in Morehead City. Although the boat had been used by past administrations for political bigshot fishing parties, Kerr told his brother he could not use it. "Kerr, as hard as we worked to win this election, as soon as we get to the trough, you cut off the slop," Ralph replied.[55]

What should we make of Scott's self-dealing? Today, such activity would likely spark the interest of prosecutors. But by the standards of the day, in an era when governors and legislators were more likely to be involved in bribery and kickbacks and other shenanigans, the perks Scott received were regarded as small potatoes. By comparison, E. H. "Boss" Crump of Memphis ruled in Tennessee, Governor Earl K. Long of Louisiana had a flagrant affair with stripper Blaze Starr, and even President Truman had risen as the product of the Pendergast Machine of Kansas City. Campaign finance, ethics, and public disclosure laws were either nonexistent or toothless. The tradition of investigative reporting was weak. Everybody was taking freebies, including newspaper reporters. Even so, while Kerr Scott's freewheeling ways may have been characteristic of the age, the Scott family's continued flouting of campaign and ethics laws would eventually catch up with them: his son threatened with prosecution and his granddaughter going to prison.

THE 1952 CAMPAIGN

Scott felt more time was needed to complete his Go Forward program, and he searched for a friendly successor to carry on his work. But he faced stiff opposition. The gubernatorial candidate of the Democrat's conservative wing, William Umstead, was the teetotaling son of a Methodist minister. Umstead served three terms in the U.S. House before retiring; he also managed Cherry's gubernatorial campaign in 1944 and served as state Democratic Party chairman. Although appointed to the U.S. Senate in 1946, he lost that seat in the 1948 election. Most important, however, Umstead by all accounts despised Scott.

In January 1952, Scott and Miss Mary took a free, two-week Caribbean cruise as guests of Virginia Cruise Lines.[56] In Cartagena, Colombia, Scott met with Capus Waynick, his former campaign manager whom Truman had appointed U.S. ambassador to Colombia, to urge him to run for governor as the alternative to Umstead. Scott argued that Waynick could win, but he was less certain about former superior court judge Hubert Olive of Lexington, the other possible Democratic alternative. Olive, a leading Baptist layman, managed Hoey's 1936 governor's race and was chairman of the State Board of Elections under Cherry. He also had the advantage of being a former state commander of the American Legion at a time following World War II when that group was particularly influential. But Waynick, reluctant to leave his ambassadorial post, turned Scott down.[57] The governor also tried unsuccessfully to convince Dr. Henry Jordan, the Highway Commission chairman and the brother of B. Everett Jordan, the party chairman, to run. But B. Everett Jordan had already pledged to back Umstead.

As a result, Scott supported Olive and arrayed the powers of state government behind his candidacy. But Scott did not campaign for Olive with the fervor that he had campaigned for Graham, nor was he at the height of his power as governor. Even so, Umstead attacked Olive as "Governor Scott's crown prince" and accused Scott of using the powers of state government to back Olive, which he almost certainly did. In response, Scott petulantly fired several members of his administration who backed Umstead over Olive.[58]

Olive tried to gain support by saying that voters were "sick and tired of politicians and lobbyists" like Umstead, who had been a lobbyist for Duke Power Company. Olive also accused Umstead of voting in Congress against rural electrification. But the old populist appeals didn't work this time, and Umstead defeated Olive in the primary, 294,170 to 265,175, with the urban and rural areas dividing between the two candidates. In the fall, Umstead trounced Republican H. F. "Cousin Chub" Seawell, 796,306 to 383,329.

Just as Scott's victory in 1948 represented a broader trend of victories by New Deal–style Democrats in the South, Umstead's 1952 victory solidified the conservative counterswing as white southerners saw segregation threatened. In 1950, Graham and Florida senator Claude Pepper lost their seats to conservative challengers. That same year, conservatives James F. Byrnes of South Carolina and Allan Shivers of Texas were elected governor, followed by Hugh White of Mississippi in 1951 and Robert F. Kennon in Louisiana in 1952.

Scott invited the Democrats to open the party's 1952 presidential campaign on his farm in Haw River, thinking Truman was going to be the nominee. It underscored that Scott—in the days before the Supreme Court's

Brown v. Board decision—had become more of a national Democrat. When Truman chose not to run again, Scott switched his allegiance to Illinois governor Adlai Stevenson at a time when most of the state's political leadership were rallying around southern candidate Senator Richard Russell of Georgia. Among those working on Russell's staff was Jesse Helms, on loan from Smith's Senate staff.

At the National Democratic Convention in Chicago, all but five of North Carolina's thirty-two delegates voted for Russell on the first ballot. Among the Stevenson delegates were Scott and Jonathan Daniels. In an insult to Scott, the delegation chose former governor Cameron Morrison as the delegation chairman—a position that traditionally went to the sitting governor. Two months earlier, at the State Democratic Convention in Raleigh, the presidential election had caused a rift. Party chairman B. Everett Jordan had removed four of Scott's chosen delegates to the national convention without Scott's approval. The convention, controlled by party conservatives, was also prepared to oust Daniels as national committeeman before Daniels—reading the political situation—announced that he would not seek another term. The convention added further insult by naming Scott as a delegate at-large to the national convention, giving him only half a vote. The Democratic conservatives made it obvious that they were back in charge of the party, and they wasted no time in showing their contempt for Scott.

When the state convention at Memorial Auditorium opened, an angry Scott would not sit on the stage but instead sat with his wife on the floor with the Alamance County delegation. Jordan sent an emissary to plead with Scott to join him on stage. But Scott replied, "No, I am going to sit out there and you know why." So Jordan proceeded with the convention without Scott. When they ran into each other a week later, Scott accused Jordan of having "double-crossed me," something which Jordan denied.[59]

In the fall, Scott campaigned for the national ticket, reminding voters of Republican rule during Reconstruction and during the Depression under President Herbert Hoover. "Of course we like Ike in North Carolina," Scott said of Dwight Eisenhower, the GOP nominee for president. "I like the men who milk my cows. They have been trained for it and do a good job. We like Ike as a victorious general, who with the aid of a lot of sergeants, corporals and privates turned back the forces of aggression in Europe. But I can't see him as President of the United States. He has not trained for the job."[60] Scott's advocacy again failed: Stevenson carried the state with 54 percent of the vote—one of only nine states won by Stevenson, all of them in the South. North Carolina delivered the largest number of electoral votes of any state for Stevenson. But Eisenhower performed better in the state than any Republican since Hoover carried North Carolina in 1928. His strong position helped elect Charles Jonas of Lincolnton as the state's first GOP Congressman since 1928.

During his last radio address as governor, in December 1952, Scott's voice became so choked with emotion that the radio audiences could hardly hear his final hundred words. In the recording booth, tears trickled down his face. "I became a candidate because of these two convictions—that rural North Carolina was a land of forgotten people, and what was is bad for two-thirds of the people is bad for all," Scott said. "And now, my friends, as we approach the end of the row that we have been plowing together for the past four years . . . ." His voice trailed off.[61]

Driving a new car given to him by state employees, Scott on January 8, 1953, left the executive mansion for the last time and traveled to Haw River. Shortly after a State Highway Patrol escort left Scott and Miss Mary on the Raleigh outskirts, they pulled over for a basket lunch of sandwiches and fruit prepared by the mansion staff. Realizing that they had forgotten a bottle opener for the soft drinks, they flagged down a passing utility truck, and the driver loaned one he had in his pocket. Soon they were in Haw River. While Miss Mary started unpacking, Scott left with a group of ten hunters to go rabbit hunting. He bagged eight rabbits and said he had no plans for a vacation: "We've got some sawmill work to do. Robert [his youngest son] is getting ready to build a house, and we're going to cut some lumber for it. There are plenty of other jobs right here for me."[62]

7 ★ THE LAST SPITTOON

The poor people of North Carolina have lost the
best friend they ever had. —Kerr Scott's postman

Within days of Frank Porter Graham's defeat in 1950, speculation began that Scott would seek to avenge his loss. Though coy about his postgubernatorial plans, Scott did little to tamp down talk that he would challenge Senator Willis Smith in 1954. Most political insiders assumed that Scott's return to his farm in Haw River was merely for a respite before rejoining the political battles. To help keep his name before the public, Scott began broadcasting a radio program from his farm on WBBB, a five-thousand-watt station in Burlington, just two weeks after he left office. The program, which aired at 6:45 A.M. and was rebroadcast at 1:15 P.M., began with the ringing of an old farm bell. The program had a folksy tone, with Scott telling stories, talking about the importance of the rural church, and commenting on farm problems, the state fair, hog prices, and sometimes developments in Korea.

In the spring of 1953, Terry Sanford stopped by Scott's farmhouse, where he found the former governor in his work clothes and brogans and sat down with him at his kitchen table. Sanford, a thirty-five-year-old Fayetteville attorney, had visited Graham shortly after his defeat and promised "to get even, to rectify that injustice." Sanford, with his close connections to the University of North Carolina, had been more of a Graham man than a Scott man. He had first supported R. Mayne Albright in the 1948 Democratic primary for governor, but switched to Scott during the runoff. Scott subsequently named Sanford to the State Ports Authority.

Several people, including Graham, Capus Waynick, and Scott's brother Ralph, recommended that Scott hire Sanford as his Senate campaign manager. During Sanford's one term in in the state Senate, he had befriended Ralph. Scott's advisers believed that Sanford, with his connections to the

Jaycees, the University of North Carolina, and the World War II veterans, could bring a younger generation of people to Scott's campaign.[1] There were risks for both men. Scott put his career in the hands of much younger man he did not know well, while Sanford, who wanted to be governor, was risking his political career on an antiestablishment candidate. Sanford put his law practice on hold and borrowed $8,500 ($78,855 in 2018 dollars) from First Citizens Bank, part of which he lived on and $5,000 of which he put into the cash-strapped Scott campaign. Sanford said it took him three years to pay back the loan.[2]

Although he was eager to return to politics, Scott would not have the opportunity to avenge Graham's defeat directly. On June 24, 1953, after giving twenty-four speeches in twenty days, Willis Smith suffered a heart attack. Two days later he had a second heart attack and died, three years to the day after his primary victory over Graham. Surprising many, Governor Umstead appointed Alton Lennon, a little-known state legislator from Wilmington, to fill Smith's seat. Lennon, a forty-six-year-old lawyer, had served two terms in the state Senate, where he was part of the conservative "hold the liners" who had opposed Scott's program. "Governor Umstead did not like Kerr Scott at all and probably with some justification on both sides, but he appointed a virtually unknown person in order to make this a race between Umstead and Scott," recalled Sanford. "For that reason, it was a tough challenge."[3] By August 1953, Sanford was busy lining up county chairs for Scott's Senate campaign, and Scott began moving around the state to meet with local political and farm leaders.

Standing in front of a blazing fire at his Haw River home, Scott formally announced his candidacy on February 6, 1954. In his first campaign speech, citing "the bitterness of a recent campaign," Scott proposed a "Code of Ethics for Political Campaigns." He said that the current Senate campaign "should be governed at all times by the rules of decent conduct, fair play and good manners." The code had been written by Sanford for the Young Democrats Club.[4]

Scott started the race with support of farmers, factory workers, organized labor, blacks, liberals, and people whom his administration had helped. Lennon, by contrast, had the backing of Umstead and his administration, the business community, and conservatives. To even the race, Sanford sought to muzzle Scott's sharp-edged tongue and have him deliver scripted speeches. It was one thing to be entertaining but another to win races, Sanford said. As a result, Scott's speeches tended to be filled with talk about farm problems, mainly steering away from controversy. Newspaper columnists complained about the bland, new, disciplined, toned-town Scott. Yet Sanford's makeover was incomplete: Scott often tore up Sanford's speeches ten minutes after he left Raleigh, according to Duke B. Paris, the Alamance County register of deeds and a Scott driver.

Much of the time Scott spent reactivating networks from his old campaigns. Paris remembered one mountain Democrat, a moonshiner, who had been up all night drinking. After being awakened, the moonshiner reassured Scott: "The precinct will be 100 percent for you." As they were leaving, the bootlegger ran after them. "Let's make it 98 percent for you. One hundred percent wouldn't look regular."[5] Early in the campaign, Scott appeared on a Kinston radio program in which he reminisced about his part-time work as a cattle trader, selling and trading bulls and heifers across eastern North Carolina twenty-five years earlier. Scott was in Kinston and wanted to go to a cattle sale at Hargetts Cross Road, twenty-one miles away, but the taxi driver demanded a twenty-one-dollar fare. "So I walked it and saved the money," Scott said. "I walked it in six hours and I'll give a registered Jersey bull calf to anyone who can beat my time." So was born the Great Bull Calf Walk, which on March 3 drew forty entrants, thousands of onlookers, and a flood of free publicity. Paul "Hardrock" Simpson, a Burlington mailman, finished with the best time of under four hours; thirty-nine bulls were given away, with Ralph Scott picking up the cost. Those participating in the walk received certificates making them associate members of the Athletic Order of the Survivors of the Great Bull Calf Walk.[6] "There were thousands of people lining the road and cheering people on," remembered Lauch Faircloth. "I think some of people who won a calf didn't know quite what to do with it." A young Jim Hunt, accompanying his father, was among those in the crowd.[7]

As a committed New Dealer, Scott regularly attacked U.S. Agriculture Secretary Ezra Hart Benson as a free-market proponent seeking to reshape FDR's farm programs. Scott called Benson "the chief apostle and messenger of those forces that would grind the farmer into the dust of economic serfdom." But Scott voiced support for the Eisenhower administration's bipartisan foreign policy, particularly in fighting communism. "Communism, you know," said Scott, "is not really a political or economic philosophy. It actually is a mental and moral disease that abases the dignity of the individual and denies, yes, the very existence of God."[8]

Scott also condemned McCarthy, accusing the Wisconsin Republican of making wild charges of communist influence and using bullying tactics. In a speech to warehousemen, Scott said that no "one-man committee"

The Bull Calf Walk from Kerr Scott's 1954 Senate campaign. In this publicity stunt, participants were awarded a bull calf if they walked twenty-one miles from Kinston to Hargett's Store. (Courtesy of State Archives of North Carolina)

has the right "to brow-beat and debate witnesses. When things like this are tolerated, we are moving in the direction of a police state and the destruction of individual freedoms. This evil practice is in notorious violation of every man's positive right under the Constitution to face his accuser in open court, to be presumed innocent until he is proven guilty, and to trial by due process of law."[9]

Meanwhile, the lesser-known Lennon ran an aggressive challenger's campaign. From the start, he accused Scott of the "demagoguery of a man who sets out to divide and conquer by setting farmers against urbanites."[10] Lennon released his tax returns, which showed that he had earned $6,000 in the previous year ($56,000 in 2018 dollars), and he challenged Scott to do the same. Scott refused, with Sanford later saying he was worried that releasing the tax returns would have been damaging because Scott had paid virtually no taxes in recent years: losses in the farming operation allowed him to offset current income.[11]

The Lennon campaign continued to hammer away at Scott by questioning his integrity. They made an issue of the state roads built around his farm, reminded voters of his firings of state employees, brought up a $75 honorarium he was paid for speaking at East Carolina Teachers College ($698 in 2017 dollars), accused him of using his plane as governor to make a cattle-buying trip to St. Louis, and mentioned the free nitrogen supplied to him for the Democratic rally at his farm. Scott ignored Lennon's jibes, saying that the issues at stake "are too important for any of us to go off on a rabbit hunt at this stage of the national and international crisis and emergency."[12] He did say that charges of 19.5 miles of roads being built around his Haw River farm were false because he had information from a private land surveyor showing that only 3.7 miles of roads had been constructed through or around his farm since 1948—including 1.9 miles built by Governor Cherry shortly before he left office.[13] Overall, however, Scott tried to avoid engaging his lesser-known opponent. Only near the end of the campaign was Scott prompted to compare "this vicious and desperate attack against me" to McCarythism.[14]

Despite the criticisms, an unshakable core of Scott supporters stuck with him, like L. L. Smith, principal of Turkey Elementary School in Sampson County. " You were the man of the hour in 1948," Smith wrote to Scott. "You had the vision and the courage to do what you did for the schools, roads in North Carolina. I remember all too well the condition of the roads around our school. Those conditions have been greatly changed. . . . Roads and schools are not the only things you did for North Carolina. You showed our people a new way of life, you gave us new hope and you renewed our faith in ourselves and our state. You stepped on the toes of the mighty, and you angered the great. You did your job. I supported your campaign in 1948, and I will support it in 1954. With the help of our Dear Blessed Lord you will win."[15]

To shore up support near the end of the campaign, Scott used his son Bob, who had been drafted and was being sent as U.S. Army intelligence officer to Japan, as a campaign prop. The campaign ran a TV commercial featuring Bob in his uniform with army barracks bag in hand. Heading overseas, he boarded an Eastern Airlines plane and waved good-bye at the Piedmont Airlines terminal in Greensboro. In reality, Bob didn't ship out for two weeks, and the event was staged for the cameras.[16]

Publicity was one problem, but funds were another: money worries constantly plagued the Scott campaign. The campaign said it needed to raise $100,000 but managed to raise only $60,000, according to Sanford. The Lennon campaign, one the other hand, could count on the robust business support and help from the Umstead administration. Scott began courting big donors in the spring of 1953. He received contributions from Averill Harriman, a wealthy New York investment banker and a 1952 presidential candidate; members of the National Committee for an Effective Congress, which backed anti-McCarthy candidates; and organized labor. Norman Cousins, editor of the *Saturday Review*, also contributed. Dozens of black agricultural education teachers organized to chip in at least $443 (nearly $4,109 in 2018 dollars) to his campaign.[17]

Money was easy to raise in that era, said Faircloth, because there were fewer disclosure laws. "People could give you a lot of cash and move on and not have to disclose it." Indeed, some of the money Scott raised never showed up on campaign reports, which were largely works of fiction. For example, James M. Johnston, a Washington, D.C., investment banker and coowner of the Washington Senators baseball team, gave $2,000 ($18,544 in 2018 dollars), which was never reported. Sanford wrote a letter to Johnston, which said, "You may have noticed that, after Ben Roney's telephone conversation with you, we did not find it necessary to list your name on the report."[18]

Personal attacks and money troubles concerned the Scott campaign, but a greater threat loomed: another white backlash. The Supreme Court issued its landmark decision on school desegregation, *Brown v. Board of Education*, just two weeks before the May 31 primary. Many white southerners had long dreaded the decision, and it had the potential to dramatically affect the primary.

Scott never appealed to racial prejudice in his campaigns. But neither could any southern politician voice support for the end of segregation and hope to survive at the ballot box. In a carefully worded statement drafted by Sanford, Scott supported segregated schools but avoided the harsh language offered by many southern politicians. "I had hoped that the Supreme Court would reaffirm its own historic decisions approving equal but separate school facilities and services for members of the white and Negro races," Scott said. "I have always been opposed, and I am still opposed to Negro and white children going to school together. It is my belief that most white and Negro citizens of North Carolina agree on this point. . . . I feel certain no candidate would favor the end of segregation, and I am sure they will join me in hope and prayer that we can avoid stirring up fear and bad feeling between races in North Carolina." Scott noted that during his term as governor, 43.3 percent of the new school construction money went for improving black schools, even though black children comprised

29.8 percent of the enrollment. He pledged to support Umstead in developing a response and, if elected, to work with other southern senators "to preserve our traditions."[19]

Two days later, at a campaign rally, Lennon portrayed Scott as soft on segregation, saying that Scott's statement "contradicted every act and word of his public career on the subject. . . . . Candidate Scott and certain of his top political associates and advisors have encouraged the abolition of segregation in our public schools for many years. His statement to the effect that he will fight to preserve southern traditions is double-talk. He did not do so as governor; he would not do so in the United States Senate."[20]

Asked by a reporter earlier in the campaign if he was worried that Lennon would engage in the kind of race-baiting that Smith had four years earlier, Scott smiled and replied: "I'll take care of it son. I'm not as good a Christian as Frank Graham."[21] Sanford too had given a lot of thought about how to handle the race issue if used against Scott. During the 1950 Senate race, Sanford had led the Graham effort in the Cumberland Mills precinct, a tough mill village, located south of Fayetteville. The mill village had voted for Graham despite the racial appeals. Sanford during that campaign kept a small ring-bound notebook in his bedroom bureau to jot down the political lessons he was learning. By the end, Sanford had compiled twenty-five to thirty pages of notes. "I learned one thing," Sanford said. "That is, don't ever let them get off the defensive. Frank Graham let them get off the defensive. He was just so nice and sweet. Well, we . . . gave them blow for blow."[22]

Preparing for racially charged issues late in the campaign, Sanford asked county leaders to contact him if they saw trouble. During the primary's final week, the Scott campaign learned that a bundle of leaflets had been dropped off at a service station in the small eastern town of Columbia. The leaflets were reprinted from an advertisement that had appeared in the *Winston-Salem Journal.* "Vote For W. Kerr Scott," said the ad, which included a photograph of Harold L. Trigg, whom Scott had appointed to the State Board of Education, thereby making him the first black man appointed to a major state post in twentieth-century North Carolina. "The first and only member of our race to serve on the State Board of Education. Kerr Scott increased Negro appointments to official State Boards by more than 300 percent. He has demonstrated his interest in our race and has aided our cause of non-segregation. Vote for W. Kerr Scott for United States Senator, a friend of the Negro." The ad was signed, "J. H. R. Gleaves, President of The Progressive Civic League," a black political organization.[23]

Kerr Scott with his Senate campaign manager, Terry Sanford, in 1954.
(Photo by the News and Observer; *courtesy of State Archives of North Carolina)*

  Sanford engaged in some campaign intrigue to put the Lennon campaign on the defensive. He discovered that the ad had been written and paid for by Winston-Salem mayor Marshall Kurfees, a Lennon backer. Both Kurfees and Gleaves acknowledged its origin, but the Lennon campaign claimed no knowledge of the leaflets. To determine whether the Lennon campaign was the source, Sanford recruited Thomas C. Maupin, a trusted member of the tobacco workers' union of Durham, to pose as a Lennon supporter. When Maupin showed up at Lennon headquarters, he asked for and received information on the location of a print shop where he could pick up a bundle of the leaflets along with instructions to leave them in rural mailboxes and on the front porches of houses in textile-mill towns. After obtaining a pile of the leaflets, Sanford hid Maupin in a Raleigh hotel room with steaks and beer—with a Scott political operative babysitting him like a witness about to testify against the mob—for the final two days of the campaign. Sanford couldn't afford for the press to find out that the leaflets had been obtained under false pretenses. Sanford then leaked the leaflets to Jonathan Daniels at the *News and Observer*, which obliged with a front-page headline the day before the election that read: "Alton Lennon Forces Flood State with 'Phony' Race Issue Leaflets." Sanford, a former FBI agent, called for an FBI investigation, offered a hundred-dollar reward for further information—and sent telegrams to Lennon campaign county managers threatening to sue any of them if they distributed the leaflets.

Sanford's tactics limited the damage, but the leaflets were still a blow to Scott. "I find that where they were distributed they had considerable influence upon the voters," said Zeno Edwards, a dentist in Washington, N.C., and a Scott leader. "For instance, in one box where we had expected to carry by a big majority we carried by one vote. Information discloses that near the voting box was a crossroads store and filling station where beer is sold. Many of the voters stopped at this place to get a beer before voting. I am told that one of these leaflets was either on the beer box or was handed to the voter with the question: You are not going to vote for Scott are you?' I am told that some who had voted before they stopped for a drink expressed regret that they had voted for Scott." But Edwards also said that due to the publicity, the leaflets were not distributed all over the county.[24] In Greene County, Joe Horton said that only two or three leaflets of the four thousand delivered were passed out. "I contacted a member of the Lennon Committee and told him I knew of their plans, and if they were carried out, it would be my duty as the County Solicitor to have warrants issued for all concerned," Horton wrote. He said that five hundred leaflets were found dumped in a pile in Waltonsburg one night.[25] Sanford thought that these tactics made the difference. "We put out that prairie fire out," Sanford said. "We might have gotten our hands a little burned doing it, but we damn well put it out in two days' time. Everything broke just right."[26]

Having started the race as the far better-known candidate, Scott squeaked through the Democratic primary with 312,053 votes (51 percent) to Lennon's 286,703 votes, while five other candidates collectively received 15,875 votes. Lennon waited several days before conceding because of the closeness of the race. "I knew it was going to be a hard one to win," Scott said the day after the election, sitting under his favorite Spanish oak in his front yard where he planned his political campaigns. "That's the reason I had to go over the state to find out whether or not I could win before I announced. Actually, I've been at this one since last July, and that's a lot of traveling." He added that the Senate campaign was a "little rougher" than the one for governor.[27]

Scott ran strongest in eastern North Carolina, his Branchhead Boy stronghold. Lennon did best in the piedmont and western counties where the old-line Democratic county courthouse organizations headed by Umstead had strength. The emerging black vote was crucial for Scott, who carried Forsyth County, the home of Winston-Salem, by 300 votes, thanks to winning the black precincts by 1,362 votes. Scott's victory was sweet revenge for the Smith-Graham campaign of four years earlier. The congratulation rolled in from liberals across the country: from Walter Reuther, president of the CIO (Congress of Industrial Organizations); from former Florida senator Claude Pepper; and from black citizens nationwide. Scott twice sent an aide to Hillsborough to try to convince Graham to stand by his side on election night, but Graham declined.[28]

In a one-party state, Scott easily defeated Republican Paul C. West of Raleigh by a margin of 66 percent 34 percent in the fall Senate race. But Scott could see the day when the increasingly fragile and intellectually incoherent Democratic coalition—of white segregationist farmers, blacks, liberals, and labor—would not hold. Walking across his fields with Burlington newspaperman Howard White one day after the primary, Scott observed: "It is entirely possible that by the way things are going, the South will be Republican in 15 years [1969]."[29] But that was in the future. The midterm elections in 1954 were good for the Democrats and bad for Eisenhower and the Republicans: the Democrats wrested control of both houses of Congress, and Democrats would continue to hold the Senate until 1980 and the House until 1994.

SENATE YEARS

Some twelve hundred people traveled to Washington on November 9, 1954, to watch Scott and former state supreme court justice Sam Ervin Jr. be sworn in as North Carolina's two newest U.S. senators, both of whom filled unexpired terms of deceased senators. Supporters packed the Senate gallery and attended a reception afterward. Senate staff said they could not remember such a large gathering for an oath-taking.

Although Scott and Sam Ervin came from different wings of the Democratic Party, they got along well, with Scott supporting Ervin's reelection effort in 1956. More often than not, the two men voted together. But they emphasized different issues in the Senate. While Ervin focused on national issues, Scott "keeps his sights trained more specifically on matters of direct interest to Tar Heels, such as the Wilkesboro Reservoir, the tobacco program, coastal harbor projects and the like," wrote journalist Tom Wicker. "The former governor is rarely heard on the Senate floor and operates most effectively in the cloakroom and committee conferences." By comparison,

Ervin liked to make speeches and tell stories. "While Sam Ervin worked alone in Washington preparing the eventual southern defense against the civil rights bill, [in the spring of 1957] Kerr Scott was touring through Florida, Georgia, South Carolina, North Carolina and Virginia, hearing the complaints of tobacco farmers and proposing some solutions for them," Wicker wrote.[30]

On his arrival in the Senate, the tobacco-chewing Scott learned that there were no spittoons. The General Service Administration had removed them two years earlier to a Baltimore warehouse, where they had been sold for scrap metal. "This is the most flagrant waste of government money I have seen since I came to Washington," Scott wrote to a North Carolina tobacconist. Scott's search for a spittoon—eventually successful—drew national publicity.[31] Tom Wicker, a *New York Times* columnist, described a Scott-like figure in his novel about a North Carolina senator, *Facing the Lions*: "In his shiny blue serge, his trousers not quite touching the top of his clodhopper shoes, with his southern molasses-drip of a voice rumbling around, a lump in his jaw that anybody looking at him could tell was a chaw of tobacco [Scott] had been the last senator to use the old cuspidors in the chamber—which was a kind of immortality and maybe as good as any other kind."[32]

Despite the tobacco-chewing, many expected that Scott would not be the traditional southern senator. Robert E. Williams, associate editor of the *News and Observer*, wrote that Scott "is regarded as the first out-and-out liberal elected to the Senate from this State in the present century." On race he was viewed as a southern moderate, believing in separate schools, but enhancing the quality of black education. In national politics, Williams wrote, his history suggested that he would "be more of a regular Democrat than a Southern Democrat" and would be largely interested in farm legislation.[33]

In some ways, Scott was a bit of an outsider in the Senate club. After having been an executive in Raleigh, Scott never took to the deliberative pace of the Senate. "He never liked it up there," said his son Bob. "People who have been in the executive branch don't do very well in the legislative branch. . . . It's just a different ball game, a different environment, a different culture. My Dad was far too impatient to get things done. It just irritated him to death to have to sit through those committee hearings."[34] Nor did Scott much care for city life. The Scotts first moved into the Carroll Arms Apartments on C Street on Capitol Hill, where they kept a framed photo of their Haw River farmhouse. They later moved to the stately Westchester Apartments in northwest Washington, where the senator daily, rain or shine, walked 5.2 miles to the Capitol. He left his apartment at 7:00 A.M., walked down Massachusetts Avenue past the Naval Observatory and Embassy Row, across Dupont Circle, and stopped at Thomas Circle for a cup of coffee before continuing down through the skid row district and finally reaching the National Mall.[35] His walking and diet helped Scott trim down to 180 pounds from the 202 pounds he weighed when he took office.[36]

As the only nonlawyer among the southern senators, Scott's interests and committee assignments were shaped by his background as a farmer, governor, and agriculture commissioner. Scott served on three committees, Agriculture, Interior and Insular Affairs, and Public Works, all of which helped dictate his focus on farm and water project issues. Yet no topic interested Scott more than his plan for a world food bank. He had proposed the food bank during the Senate campaign, saying that it would win friends for the United States, fight communism, and provide a way for American farmers to dispose of agricultural surpluses. It was the first piece of legislation he introduced in March 1955. Under Scott's plan, nations participating in the world food bank could borrow food or fiber and repay the loans to the bank when they were able. He called on President Eisenhower and others to negotiate through the United Nations and international channels with friendly foreign nations in setting up a world food bank patterned after the International Bank for Reconstruction and Development.[37]

American agricultural abundance had been used to help needier parts of the world before. In 1954, Congress passed a law authorizing the shipment of American farm surpluses held in government warehouses to the world's hungry. The program would later become known as the Food for Peace program. But the Eisenhower administration never embraced Scott's idea of a world food bank, and soon Scott fired back. "It's obvious the Eisenhower administration is perfectly content in letting surpluses pile up and seeing farmers take less and less from what they grow," Scott in said a July 4, 1955, speech in Carthage.[38] He successfully lobbied to include language in the 1956 Democratic Platform calling for a world food bank. A Senate Foreign Relations subcommittee held hearings on the world food bank, but the State Department rejected the idea. At a meeting of the Economic and Social Council of the United Nations, U.S. representatives said that a world food bank would be too difficult to administer and would interfere with normal trade.

But Scott, the farmer, had planted the seed. South Dakota congressman George McGovern, a fellow rural progressive who served with Scott, picked up the cudgel. McGovern became President John Kennedy's director of the Food for Peace program in 1961. While attending a food conference that year in Rome, he convinced officials to create a United Nations–backed food aid program with U.S. financial backing. Established in 1963, the World Food Programme is the world's largest humanitarian group fighting against hunger. The Rome-based program reaches eighty million people in eighty countries each year. The organization counts McGovern as its founding father and makes no mention of Scott. Scott, however, had prepared the ground.

In another bold move, Scott became one of the first Democrats to criticize Eisenhower after his party took control of Congress in January 1955. Scott's maiden Senate speech was an attack on the "dangerous drift" of President Eisenhower's foreign policy. "No one, I think can question that the American ship of state is meeting heavy weather, and is floundering around," Scott said. "It is pulling first in one direction and then in another in response to contradictory and confusing commandments of a disorganized and undisciplined crew." He called Eisenhower "a master of confusion." In general, leading congressional Democrats avoided attacking Ike, leaving it to backbenchers such as Scott to criticize the popular president. In response to his attack, Scott said he received 530 letters from twenty-one states, 66 percent of whom approved of his comments.[39]

Yet Scott tended to be an internationalist on foreign policy issues, often siding with Eisenhower despite his criticisms of the president. Similarly, although Scott had populist leanings, his votes were not predictable. He broke with many Democratic liberals and voted with conservatives and oil-state lawmakers to restrict the Federal Power Commission from regulating natural gas at the wellhead. After World War II, natural gas had become a primary heating source, replacing coal across the country. Scott said he believed that the absence of regulation would encourage expansion of natural gas facilities in North Carolina and spur new industry. Scott asked Ralph Scott, during a Texas trip, to ascertain if any companies would be interested in building a water terminal and supplying it by barge or tanker with propane gas that could serve the North Carolina market. The natural gas deregulation bill passed Congress, strongly backed by Senate Majority leader Lyndon Johnson, but was vetoed by Eisenhower, in part because there were charges of improper industry lobbying.[40]

With his knowledge of the land, Scott pushed for dam construction for both flood control and providing reservoirs for water supply. North Carolina had been late in developing its rivers, missing out on New Deal money in part because no one had pushed for it. There had been talk of the need for flood control projects in the Cape Fear River basin since at least 1927, because of chronic flooding, especially in Fayetteville. The state had doubled in population since 1900, from two million to four million. Daily water usage had jumped from 200 million gallons to 800 million gallons as people began to live suburban lifestyles with multiple bathrooms, yards to water, and air conditioners to run. More farmers used irrigation, and more industries required water. By the early 1950s, water rationing and shortages were common in such towns and cities as Raleigh, Burlington, and Greensboro.[41] To alleviate the problems, Scott proposed a series of dams via $300 million in projects for flood control, municipal treatment, and improved water supplies and irrigation. Some took years to get approved and funded, but eventually a series of dams were erected: the W. Kerr Scott Dam and Reservoir was built in Wilkes County (1962), Jordan Lake dam and reservoir in Chatham County (1983), and Randleman dam and reservoir in Randolph and Guilford Counties (2010).

Scott continued in the nation's capital to be a spokesman for the small farmer—hardly surprising in a state with more than fifty thousand farmers growing less than five acres of cotton and more than eighty thousand farmers producing less than five acres of tobacco. In particular, Scott criticized Eisenhower's effort to make agriculture more market based, and the new senator proposed a system of "adjusted price supports" for farm commodities patterned along the same lines as the federal income tax. "Under the plan I am proposing," Scott said, "the larger the farmer, the less support he gets from the government."[42] Scott also pushed through significant changes in the federal tobacco program, moving the system of grower controls from one based solely on acres to one based on acres and pounds grown. Scott argued this would result in a better system of supply and demand. Scott's Senate Tobacco Subcommittee held six hearings across the South before Congress enacted reform.

While concentrating on regional issues, Scott kept his national political credentials in order. Scott attended the 1956 Democratic National Convention in Chicago, where the delegation supported former Illinois governor Adlai Stevenson. Scott campaigned across the state, blasting Eisenhower for running a government "by and for millionaires," accusing him of having accepted all sorts of freebies for his Gettysburg farm, and charging that

Senator Kerr Scott at the 1956 Democratic National Convention in Chicago (Hugh Morton Photos and Films, North Carolina Collection, University of North Carolina at Chapel Hill Library)

Eisenhower's brother's bank had been bailed out by an administration program. Rather crudely, Scott put on odds on Eisenhower's chances of survival with heart problems. "While I am not conceding the election to the Republicans, Tricky Dick Nixon has an 80 percent chance of becoming president if the GOP wins next Tuesday," Scott said.[43]

In 1956, Scott's relationship with Governor Luther Hodges, a product of the Democrats' more conservative wing, worsened. Scott and a group that included B. Everett Jordan, Terry Sanford, and former state Highway Commission chairman Henry Jordan met at his brother Ralph's house to get behind Henry Jordan to challenge Hodges for governor in the Democratic primary that year. Ultimately, Henry Jordan decided not to challenge Hodges. But after the election, rumors began that Hodges would challenge Scott when he faced reelection in 1960.[44]

There was tension between the two men when they shared a ride between the National Cathedral and the Tar Heel Club during a North Carolina Day observance in 1957. The First Lady, making small talk, asked if the senator didn't think the stained glass windows were lovely, according to Bill Creech, the club's president, who was driving. "No I don't like them," Scott harrumphed. "I like to be able to spit my tobacco juice out the open window of my church in Haw River."[45]

Stevenson carried the state, but it was the poorest showing by a Democrat since the 1928 election won by Republican Herbert Hoover. (Stevenson won 591,220 to Eisenhower's 576,731 votes.)

CIVIL RIGHTS

For a southern congressman in the 1950s, race, civil rights, and school desegregation overshadowed most other issues. Following the Supreme Court's 1954 *Brown* decision, Scott pledged to join both the South's Southern Bloc in Congress and Governor Umstead in fighting its implementation. But at the same time, Scott was seen by his supporters as a new kind of southern senator, less tied to the old segregationists. This old view, however, would not endure the upheavals to come.

In its follow-up decision on May 31, 1955, the Supreme Court ruled that the schools must desegregate "with all deliberate speed," but left it up to district federal courts to implement the order. North Carolina was the first state in the old Confederacy to implement token integration, with about a dozen black students attending formerly all-white high schools in Greensboro, Charlotte, and Winston-Salem when schools opened in the fall of 1957. All three systems announced their action at the same time to limit objections. Although the students were met with ugly taunts, North Carolina generally received favorable publicity.

Leading up to 1957, white views toward school integration had hardened across North Carolina. In a brief the state submitted to the Supreme Court in the *Brown* case, Assistant Attorney General I. Beverly Lake argued that racial integration could lead to another civil war. In a survey of 198 police chiefs and sheriffs across the state, 191 thought there would be violence that would interfere with the schools. Of 165 school superintendents surveyed, just 7 believed that desegregation could be achieved peacefully.[46] Further, a new segregationist organization created in 1955, the North Carolina Patriots, had 356 charter members and included a number of prominent citizens, including two former state House speakers and a former state party chair.[47]

Tempers flared when five black children—who were being bused eleven miles to a black school in Marion—were denied admission to the all-white elementary school at Old Fort in McDowell County in 1955. A crowd of five hundred whites gathered in the schoolyard to watch as they applied. Highway patrolmen, sheriff's deputies, and deputized volunteer firemen stood by. Albert Joyner, a black man who led the five children, was later beaten before a crowd of twenty-five white men and knocked into the water fountain in the center of town.[48]

In the area around Guilford College, a liberal arts school started by Quakers that had been part of the Underground Railroad, thirty-four white residents petitioned the school board to allow black students to enroll in white schools. Two of the signers, Mr. and Mrs. David Meredith of Guilford College, had dynamite sticks tossed in their driveway.[49] Another signer, George McBride, was fired from his part-time job in a broom factory. "I just don't work with people who sign letters like that," explained his boss, O. W. Gibson. Mr. and Mrs. C. M. Mackie were threatened with a boycott of their furniture store because they signed the petition. At the school under question, a crowd of fifty people surrounded the car of a couple who signed the petition and refused to let them out until police dispersed the crowd.[50]

At about the same time, a commission headed by former House Speaker Thomas Pearsall of Rocky Mount developed a plan offering an escape valve for white parents who did not want to send their children to integrated public schools. The Pearsall Plan included a constitutional amendment to allow local public schools to be closed by a majority vote, with the state providing tuition grants to parents to send their children to private schools if the public schools closed. Voters approved the plan by a 4–1 majority in

September 1956. Both Scott and his former campaign manager, Terry Sanford, endorsed the Pearsall Plan, despite opposition from blacks and some white liberals such as Jonathan Daniels.

A more difficult decision for Scott was whether to sign the Southern Manifesto. Trying to keep members of the southern congressional bloc in line, the leading southern segregationist strategists issued a "Declaration of Constitutional Principles," or what became known as the Southern Manifesto. Signed by 19 of the former Confederacy's 33 senators and 82 of the 106 House members, the manifesto condemned the Supreme Court's "unwarranted exercise" of "naked judicial power" and commended the "motives of the states which have declared the intention to resist forced integration by any lawful means." Senators Strom Thurmond of South Carolina and Harry Byrd of Virginia wrote the manifesto.

According to his aide, Bill Cochrane, Scott telephoned him on the morning the manifesto was released and tried to have his named removed, but the news release had already gone out. Whether that was true or whether Cochrane was later trying to repair Scott's reputation may never be known. There is nothing in the Scott papers to suggest that Scott ever wavered or regretted his decision to sign the manifesto, and Scott subsequently did not hesitate to join with the Southern Bloc in opposing civil rights legislation. It was politically dangerous to oppose the manifesto, as was demonstrated by the fate of the three North Carolina House members who declined to sign it. Democratic voters defeated two, Charles Deane and Thurmond Chatham, in Democratic primaries.

Although Scott voted for the Southern Manifesto, he used his influence to block another Dixiecrat revolt in the Democratic Party during the 1956 presidential elections. The South Carolina Democratic Party, in anticipation of the national Democratic convention, had passed a resolution declaring that the Fourteenth Amendment of the Constitution "does not apply to educational matters or school of any kind" and that the *Brown* decision was "illegal and unconstitutional." South Carolina governor George B. Timmerman Jr. proposed that southern Democrats recess their state conventions and reassemble after the national convention. This would give the southern Democrats the option of backing a third-party candidate if they did not approve of the Democratic presidential nominee or the party platform.

Scott wrote a letter to Timmerman saying, "I have no patience with anything that suggests a third party. The resolution is nothing but Dixiecrat sugar-coating. It is tailor-made for Republicans. They are doing everything they can to split us. We in the South are working day and night to overcome radical coalitions outside the South that have no sympathies for or understanding of the problems we are trying to solve. I am a Southern Democrat, a North Carolina Democrat and I refuse to be split, shaken or 'Shivered.'" In using the word "Shivered," Scott referred to Texas governor Allan Shivers, who in 1952 led a southern revolt that cost Democratic nominee Adlai Stevenson four southern states.[51]

Timmerman replied, "The most charitable thing to be said about him (Scott) is that since he was born in North Carolina, he can't be accused of being a carpetbagger." On the other hand, Scott was praised by Bobby Baker, the right-hand man for Senate Majority leader Lyndon Johnson. "As a South Carolinian, a Southerner, and a Democrat," Baker wrote, "I shall always remain eternally grateful for the masterful job that you did in killing the Dixiecrat boom in its infancy. I know that I speak for many southerners who think likewise. You are man of great courage and vision."[52]

As the battle lines were drawn in the South over integration and civil rights, political moderates found less and less room to operate. Scott became a loyal member of the Southern Bloc when Congress debated the Civil Rights Act of 1957. The act sought to ensure that all Americans could exercise their right to vote. Although black people could exercise their right to vote in cities such as Raleigh, Durham, Greensboro, and Charlotte, they were often barred from voting in rural areas—especially those areas with significant black populations—often through the use of so-called literacy tests. That was what happened to Ernest Ivy, a sixty-two-year-old black minister from Littleton, who was turned down three times in his bid to register to vote in the Democratic primary in 1956. Among the questions he was asked: What is the total membership of the House of Representatives and of the U.S. Senate? What is the full vote of two-thirds of the House and the Senate? How many of the state legislatures must ratify an amendment to make it law? What was the Eighteenth Amendment called? What year was it proclaimed? By what amendment was the Eighteenth Amendment rescinded? On what date every four years is the president of the United States inaugurated, for his first term, second term, third term? Ivy filed suit in federal district court in Raleigh.[53]

The white establishment created other barriers to black constituents, too. During the 1952 election, complaints poured in to the State Board of Elections from black voters who were refused the right to register in such counties as Chatham, Bertie, Harnett, Halifax, Davidson, Warren, and Forsyth. Charlie Britt, the state elections board chairman, referred the complaints back to the county boards of election, where, of course, nothing happened. In Zebulon, a farming town just east of Raleigh, about a hundred black people tried to register for the primary, but the registrar could not be found. Informed of the problem, Governor Scott who wrote a letter to Britt, but nothing came of it.[54]

The 1957 Civil Rights Act created a six-member Civil Rights Commission and established the position of assistant attorney general for civil rights. The key provision gave the federal government new powers to enforce the civil rights of black citizens. Scott denounced the civil rights bill, fought it at every step, and joined the Southern Bloc in trying to dilute it. They fought the measure, filibustered against it, and succeeded in watering it down so that any enforcement would have to be approved by a local federal jury—something white southern juries had proven unlikely to do. It is doubtful that Scott's approach to the bill would have been very different to that of Senator Alton Lennon or Senator Willis Smith. Scott said that the Civil Rights Commission could go around checking up on local election officials, evolving into "sort of a roving election-year Gestapo." He said that the supporters of the bill were more interested in "voting results than voting rights." He called the original legislation "a vicious bill and an unfair bill" designed to win the voters of northern blacks.[55]

During the debate in Washington, Scott criticized the legislation before the Annual Progress Campaign Dinner, an African American dinner held in Roxboro in March 1957. Scott argued for the key measure that weakened the civil rights bill, saying, "The negro as a race has gained nothing if the right to a trial by jury is traded away." He added, "There have been some regrettable incidents in the South in the past two years, but we have been fortunate here in North Carolina. We have avoided outbreaks of violence in spite of the fact that our relations have been strained. Firecrackers have been popping around us, but so far none have gone off under us."[56]

Scott had a history of making controversial speeches, going before business and civic groups to criticize or lecture them. So, while his blunt talk to the black audience was in character, it still had the power to shock. J. W. Jeffries, assistant Negro state agriculture agent at N.C. A&T State University and longtime Scott supporter, had been instrumental in inviting Scott to the event. "To say that the crowd was stunned and flabbergasted is putting it mildly," Jeffries wrote to Scott. "The heat has really been on me. My position right now among our friends in the state is at the Newt Fresh-water level." Jeffries wrote that it was well known that Negro rights had not been protected by white juries for centuries.[57]

The *Carolina Times*, a black-run newspaper in Durham, questioned the wisdom of inviting Scott to speak to a black audience. "His abortive attempt to ram his ideas of civil rights down the throats of Negroes of this state will get nowhere and will only result in making them more determined to struggle on until human dignity has been achieved, even for the humblest citizen of this nation. . . . Senator Scott probably has his mind set on building his fences for his reelection to the U.S. Senate," the editorial continued. "Sometimes in the course of such events, men will sell their souls, but alas, 'what is a man profited, if he shall gain the whole world, and lose his own soul?'"[58]

The nation's first civil rights bill—much watered down—passed the Senate 72–18, with Scott voting against it. The only southerners voting for it were Johnson and Ralph Yarborough of Texas, Al Gore and Estes Kefauver of Tennessee, and George Smathers of Florida. Later, when Eisenhower sent in federal troops to help integrate Central High in Little Rock, Arkansas, Scott denounced it as "the carpetbagger invasion."[59]

Most southern liberals like Scott ran for cover on civil rights, as historian Tony Badger has noted. They included such notables as Senator Lister Hill of Alabama, Senator William Fulbright of Arkansas, Senator John Sparkman of Alabama and Representative Brooks Hays of Arkansas. From the late 1940s to the mid-1950s, Scott's civil rights stance had evolved from being a southern moderate willing to take a few calculated political risks on behalf of his black constituents to becoming just another segregationist little different from most of the southern caucus. Scott began the rightward swing after he took a battering in the racially raw Smith-Graham race, and it had continued apace as the South became racially polarized after the Supreme Court's *Brown* decision. It probably strengthened his political position for his anticipated 1960 reelection campaign, an intention he publicly signaled as early as November 1956. "Incidentally, don't lose a lot of sleep about 1960," wrote Jesse Helms in 1958, who was then executive director of the North Carolina Bankers Association. "I suspect you are going to have more friends than you imagine."[60]

No one suspected that Scott would be the next North Carolina senator to die in office. For an eight-year period, representing North Carolina in the Senate was almost a death sentence: Josiah Bailey died in 1946, Melville Broughton in 1948, Willis Smith in 1953, and Clyde Hoey in 1954. Besides, Scott looked hale and healthy, thanks to his vigorous walking. But Scott was sicker than he appeared. Whether through heredity or a lifetime of country cooking and cigars, Scott suffered from systolic high blood pressure that in 1955 had measured dangerously over 200. Through diet and exercise, he had reduced his weight to 166 pounds by 1956. He was being treated for his high blood pressure with reserpine, an antipsychotic medication then used for high blood pressure, but it is rarely used for that purpose today because of its negative side effects. Scott reported some slight mental confusion, a staggering gait, drooling, stuffiness of the nose, and some difficulty in swallowing, and he told doctors that he needed a whole sidewalk to navigate correctly. A specialist concluded that he was suffering from reserpine poisoning and took him off the medication.[61]

Scott returned to Haw River during the spring 1958 recess, and on Sunday he and his brothers walked to church as usual. On Monday, he began to perspire heavily, and he went to the doctor, who immediately sent him to Alamance County Hospital. Although the first physician's reports of Scott's heart attacks were worrisome, after forty-eight hours the prognosis became more encouraging. Scott told reporters that he would be sent home for three months of bed rest. The chief of medicine at the National Heart Institute, brought in to examine Scott, noted that Eisenhower had recovered from his heart attack.

His death from coronary thrombosis came on April 16, 1958, a day before his sixty-second birthday. Dr. G. Walker Blair said that the cause of death was "a sudden extension of the heart attack. It was just wham. There was no warning, no nothing." An autopsy disclosed that the part of Scott's heart that had been damaged suddenly ruptured, causing instantaneous and painless death. Miss Mary had been in another part of the hospital visiting a sick grandchild when the senator died.[62]

About 7,500 people gathered at the Hawfields Presbyterian Church for Scott's funeral. For two hours, many of the plain country people who had supported his campaigns filed past his open, rose-hung casket. "Most of them were humble, hard-working people who tilled the soil, worked in the factories and made up the bulk of his loyal followers," noted Senator Herman Talmadge of Georgia, who attended the funeral.[63] Ralph Buchanan, Scott's minister, remembers coming across Scott's longtime postman, a Mr. Coble, sitting in his car, tears streaming down his cheeks. "The poor people of North Carolina have lost the best friend they ever had," Coble said.[64]

A convoy of thirty State Highway Patrol cars carried state leaders to the funeral. The congregants sang Scott's favorite hymn, "The Little Brown Church in the Wildwood," and the organ played "How Firm a Foundation." He was buried in the red clay soil of a churchyard almost within sight of his birthplace. Scott would not have been surprised by the size of the crowd. He used to say with a wry half-smile that he'd have a "heckuva big" funeral. "Some of my friends will be there. And there will be a lot of curiosity seekers. And then a whole heap of folks will show up just to make sure the old so-and-so is really dead."[65]

His tombstone read:

William Kerr Scott April 17, 1896–April 16, 1958
Son of Walter and Elisabeth Hughes Scott
Elder in Hawfields Presbyterian Church, 1933–1958
Commissioner of Agriculture of North Carolina, 1937–1948
Governor of North Carolina, 1949–1953
U.S. Senator, 1954–1958
"I have fought a good fight. I have kept the faith." 2 Timothy 4:7

Kerr Scott was part of a post–World War II generation of southern New Dealers who came to power championing the common man, bypassing entrenched courthouse politicians and powerful economic interests, and promising to open up state purses to spend money for better roads, education, and other public services to help a poor area grow. As historian Julian Pleasants noted, Scott's greatest contribution came when he was governor because his Senate career was cut short before he could gain the seniority then necessary to gain influence needed to promote significant legislation.[66] Like other southern liberals of that era, Scott, as scholars such as Badger and Egerton have noted, saw his progress blocked by "the sheer weight of the white commitment to segregation in the South revealed in Mass Resistance."[67]

In spite of his opposition to the Civil Rights Act, Scott was willing to begin to rethink the white-black code that had locked an entire region into a stultifying system of racial separatism. "Senator Scott was a political phenomenon," wrote journalist Harry Golden shortly after his death. "He was the first politician since the Populist days of the 1890s who received the overwhelming votes of both the rural population of a southern state and the Negroes; and to make the story even more fantastic, this Southern farmer also won the enthusiastic support of the textile unions and the intellectuals of the colleges and the newspaper offices. The branch-head boys of the farms, the factory workers, and the Negroes. Quite a story."[68]

"In manner," wrote Greensboro newspaperman William D. Snider, "he was unpretentious and straightforward, a doer more than a talker. In message and manner he proclaimed that the 'bottom layer' should overturn the top, at least for a while. The mud of Haw River still clung to his shoes. . . . Unlike the Deep South's conventional redneck stereotype, his Tar Heel brand of independent ruralism represented decent folk, for the most part. It helped set North Carolina apart in the South. It was chitlins and corn-bread, but it was also light and enlightenment."[69]

But rural progressivism was not done in North Carolina.

8 ★ PASSING THE TORCH

*My dad had a saying that a man could never go to heaven unless he was
a Democrat, a Presbyterian, and owned a Jersey cow. For a long time I
kept a few around here as a safeguard. —Bob Scott, September 18, 1986*

In dying relatively young and unexpectedly, Kerr Scott left no
heir apparent, nor really any organization behind him. For those
wanting to further Kerr Scott's policies, the Squire of Haw River
was simply irreplaceable. His rough-hewn authenticity was
earned from a lifetime working the backroads of North Carolina's
farm country. He could talk with anybody at a country store about
cows, mules, plowing, hunting, brands of tobacco chaw, or the Bible. But
he also was friends and allies with North Carolina's liberal intelligentsia—
such as Frank Porter Graham, Jonathan Daniels, and sociologist Howard
Odum. He had been a New Deal Democrat with close ties to Truman during a time of rising Dixiecrat fever. Organized labor never had a better ally
in the governor's mansion, and before the white backlash against civil
rights, he reached out to blacks more than most southern governors.

The question of who would assume Kerr Scott's mantle as leader of the
Democratic Party's progressive wing would result in decades of competi-
tion, tensions, and colliding ambitions among such Scott admirers as his
son Bob Scott, his Senate campaign manager Terry Sanford, and later Jim
Hunt. Little separated the Scotts, Sanford, and Hunt philosophically, yet
because of personality differences and perceived slights, the antagonisms
would build over the years.

But that would be in the future.

A day after Kerr Scott's funeral, Governor Luther Hodges named B. Everett Jordan of Saxapahaw to the Senate vacancy, infuriating the Scott faction. Jordan had once been a close Scott ally. He had been Scott's chief
fundraiser during his 1948 gubernatorial campaign, and Scott had named
him state Democratic Party chairman. But the two split during Scott's governorship when Jordan, a conservative-leaning, union-busting textile mill

owner, had quietly backed Smith in the 1950 Senate race and Umstead in the 1952 governor's race. Governor Hodges tried to pour salve on the wounds, noting that Jordan was both a Scott neighbor and a first cousin of Miss Mary, Scott's widow. But after the hard-fought battle of 1954, the Scott faction wanted a friend—perhaps even Miss Mary, or Ralph Scott—named to the Senate seat.

Two of Kerr Scott's chief Senate aides, Ben Roney and Roy Wilder, quit in disgust over the Jordan appointment, although a third, Bill Cochrane, stayed and would become a key Jordan aide. "He betrayed Kerr Scott and Kerr Scott considered him more concerned with special interests than with the good of the people," Roney said of Jordan. Sanford also criticized the move, saying that Scott supporters were "deeply offended." He suggested that Hodges appointed Jordan as a seat warmer until Hodges himself could run for the Senate in 1960.

It was hardly a coincidence that Sanford criticized Jordan's appointment, because he was positioning himself as Scott's heir apparent. Sanford became manager of Scott's 1954 Senate campaign with the idea of laying the groundwork for his own run for governor. Statewide campaign managers in the 1950s were prominent figures, often quoted in the press, in an age when television was still in its infancy and campaigns were still grassroots efforts heavily dependent on county volunteers. Not only did Sanford make critical contacts in every county, but he emerged from the Scott campaign as a rising star for his deft handling of the race. Sanford seriously considered challenging Hodges in the 1956 Democratic primary with the encouragement of Scott and his aides, but then thought better of it. He then worked with Scott in trying to convince Henry Jordan, Scott's former Highway Commission chairman, to run against Hodges, but Jordan, after toying with the idea, declined to run.

Sanford then moved to claim the remnants of the Scott organization as his own. He set up a campaign office in Chapel Hill above a drug store with two former Kerr Scott aides, Roney and Wilder, and two secretaries.[1] To help remind people of his Branchhead Boy connections following Kerr Scott's death, Sanford had a plug of Scott's favorite chewing tobacco, Peach & Honey, encased in plastic and distributed around the state. The memento—paid for by fellow Kerr Scott supporter Lauch Faircloth—included the following inscription: "1896 W. Kerr Scott 1958. He plowed to the end of the row; his furrow was deep. Time will not erode his indelible imprint."[2]

Although the Branchhead Boy crowd remained important to Sanford, they were gradually displaced by Sanford's old college friend Bert Bennett.

A hard-driving Winston-Salem oil jobber, Bennett began building a new organization that would dominate progressive Democratic politics in the postwar era. The organization included some of the network of Branch-head Boys. But in an increasingly urbanizing North Carolina, the Sanford coalition also included Jaycees, members of the Young Democrats Clubs, and World War II veterans. Running as a pro-education moderate, Sanford in 1960 defeated I. Beverly Lake, who ran as an ardent segregationist. Gradually Scott loyalists, such as Roney and Wilder, were pushed out of Sanford's inner circle. Instead of serving as Sanford's right-hand man in his administration, Roney was given the lesser—but still important—job of secondary roads officer, where he could hand out political favors in exchange for support for Sanford's programs.[3]

BOB SCOTT

Bob Scott's political initiation took place in the 1960 Sanford campaign. Born when his father was still Alamance County farm agent, Bob initially attended Hawfields Graded School in 1935, a three-room schoolhouse that Kerr had attended and for which the bells had rung when the school bond referendum passed in 1903. The school closed in 1936, and Bob transferred to the new Alexander Wilson Elementary and High School.

Bob had his farm responsibilities, even though farmhands and tenants did the heavy lifting. "This was a family that was pretty well off," remembered Sidney Cecil Johnson, the son of Scott's farm manager who grew up with Bob. "But after school he got out there and worked like everyone else. He didn't back off. He never shirked his duties there."[4] Bob witnessed the transition of farmwork, from mules to tractors, from hand-milking cows to electric milkers, and the first telephones. Even as an old man, Bob recalled with pride his ability to take two teams of mules and back a wagon under a shed. He is less fond of the time workers insisted he try his first chewing tobacco, making him "sick as a dog" and causing him to forswear the habit.

Two beeps of the car horn by Kerr meant that children should pile in for their ride to Hawfields Presbyterian Church. Stragglers walked the more than two miles to the church on their own. During the World War II gas shortage, Bob rode a mule or a horse to church—once thrown when it shied after spotting a tin can in a ditch.[5]

Kerr traveled for his job during much of Bob's childhood, and Bob didn't share his father's interest in hunting. "My mother was the one who really raised me and disciplined me," Bob recalled. "She ran the farm for that matter, because he was gone so much of the time. She managed the em-

*Agriculture Commissioner
Kerr Scott and son Bob in 1938.
(Courtesy of State Archives of
North Carolina)*

ployees on the farm, wrote the checks, paid the bills, kept the books. My knowledge of politics did not come from him."[6]

He entered Duke University in Durham in 1947, hoping to become a country doctor like his uncle Floyd. But he had come from a rural high school with a graduating class of twenty-nine students—twenty girls and nine boys. His high school had offered no chemistry course, and the physics course was taught by the school principal, who wasn't there half the time because of his other duties, according to Scott. "So, I was not prepared for university level—particularly a place like Duke," Bob said. "So, I was lost, man. Even though I was 25 miles from home I might as well have been five thousand miles away. I was flunking chemistry. I was flunking physics. Just barely passing trigonometry. Trying desperately to hang on."[7] While Bob was at Duke in 1948, his father won election as governor. Consumed with trying to stay academically afloat, Bob stayed clear of politics and after the election continued to live in a campus dormitory except for one summer where he lived in the executive mansion.

At the end of his sophomore year, Bob gave up his dream of becoming a doctor and transferred to N.C. State University in Raleigh. At N.C. State, among a host of other activities, Bob joined the Glee Club and participated in several student organizations; he served as secretary of the student government, was a student representative in the Greater University Council, and was a member of the Agriculture Club. Academically, he changed course and studied animal husbandry in preparation for taking over the family farm. Although his father never said anything, Bob said that he always thought that Kerr was happy with the decision, especially since none of the other children had an interest in managing the farm. His sister Mary had married and moved to Ohio, where her husband worked as a research engineer for Goodyear Tire and Rubber Company. His older brother Osborne battled mental illness all his life. His father got Osborne a job working on the Senate Sergeant of Arms staff in Washington from 1954 to 1967. In later years, Bob's wife, Jessie Rae Scott, helped look after Osborne, doing his laundry and making sure he had groceries in his apartment and, later, in his nursing home. Osborne died at age sixty-two in June 1983.

In the sitting room of the executive mansion, Bob proposed to Jessie Rae Osborne in 1951, when he was twenty-two and she was twenty-one. The two had known each other since the fourth grade. When Bob Scott later ran for governor, his campaign biography described Jessie Rae as "a modern Cinderella" story. A mill town girl whose mother had died when she eight, she lived with her family in a mill village near Fayetteville, but the family moved to Swepsonville, another mill village near Haw River, when the mills had closed because of a strike.

Jessie Rae became a pretty, vivacious head cheerleader in high school, and although Jessie Rae and Bob had been high school friends, they were not sweethearts until their senior year because they ran in different crowds. "Our backgrounds were so different," Jessie Rae said. "I don't know if you know what a mill village is like. Robert and his Hawfield friends had a more genteel raising. But we had an aggressive group. And all the best athletes came from our group. To grow up in a mill village and then be marrying the son of the Governor—well, you can see what I mean," she told a reporter.[8]

Their romance bloomed when Bob went off to Duke and Jessie Rae went to the Woman's College, now the University of North Carolina at Greensboro. She had been thinking about college since she was twelve and working part-time as a clerk in the textile mill company store, where the store owner had encouraged her to think beyond high school and offered to assist her.[9] Jessie Rae worked her way through university, serving three meals a day in the dining room all four years, working as a typist for a dietician, and spending the summers in the weaving room of the local textile mills. When one year she found it difficult to find work, Bob loaned her money and signed a promissory note. After she graduated, Bob wanted to tear up the note, but Jessie Rae insisted that she repay it before they got married.[10]

After graduation, Bob moved back to Haw River to manage the farm, to be joined by Jessie Rae after their marriage. The governor did not raise any objections to his son marrying a mill village girl, but it took Miss Mary a while to warm up to Jessie Rae. "My dad was a very democratic type person," Bob said. "I never heard him saying anything. My mother didn't say anything for that matter. She had to adjust a little bit."[11]

They married on September 1, 1951, at the Swepsonville Methodist Church, with Jessie Rae's brother giving her away and the governor serving as the best man. The couple spent their wedding night in the executive mansion, which they had to themselves. When Jessie Rae arrived to live at the Haw River farm, Bob called her "a city girl" and said that she suffered "a culture shock" after her first exposure to rural life.[12] Jessie Rae taught in the public schools for three years and then quit to devote full-time to raising a family—eventually five children.

In July 1953, as the Korean War was winding down, Bob was drafted into the army. He spent two years in the Counterintelligence Corps, receiving top secret clearance, stationed at Fort Jackson in Columbia, S.C., Fort Holabird in Baltimore, Tomioka, Japan, and Fort McPherson in Atlanta. He told his parents that he hated the army but liked intelligence work.[13] After his discharge, he applied for a job with the State Bureau of Investigation (SBI) because he liked police work. Although offered a job, he turned it down because of a requirement that agents work outside their home area and Scott did not want to move.[14]

So, Bob resumed management of a struggling dairy farm, which by the late 1950s had 350 cows on 1,800 acres. Kerr had been plowing the profits into buying more farms and had become financially overextended. By the time of his death, the operation consisted of 2,300 acres. Creditors, such as the Graham Production Credit Association and the Central Carolina Farmers Exchange, were beginning to hound Kerr Scott.

Kerr began looking for ways to produce more income—egg production, selling off farms, raising bullfrogs, surveying for mineral deposits, seeking loan extensions. In July 1957, a financial angel appeared, James M. Johnston, one of the richest men in Washington, D.C., who wrote Kerr a check for $20,000 ($177, 618 in 2018 dollars). It was a no-interest loan that was repaid in two months.[15] Johnston, a cousin of Kerr's who grew up in Orange County, made a fortune in Washington as an investment banker. A co-owner and president of the Washington Senators baseball team, Johnston would also be instrumental in raising money for his cousin Elizabeth Scott Carrington's project of starting a nursing school at the University of North Carolina at Chapel Hill as well as starting the James M. Johnston Scholarships for university students.

When Kerr Scott died in 1958, he left an estate to his widow worth $66,850 ($577,000 in 2018 dollars). He also left $1,000 to his church. On Miss Mary's death, the estate was to be divided among his three children, Osbourne, Mary, and Bob, with Bob getting the home farm, livestock, and tools to continue the farming operation. Bob leased his siblings' share of the land.[16] But Kerr's habit of continuously buying land on credit had created problems. "Dad was executor of the estate," recalled Dr. Charles Scott of his father, Anderson Hughes Scott, a dairy executive. "It took years to get it squared away. Kerr accumulated about 1,500 acres of land. He also had about $500,000 of debt. They sold off some land. They got loans negotiated. Bob was always in debt." (The $500,000 in debt is $4.3 million in 2018 dollars.)[17]

Although Bob spent years taking care of the financial challenges he inherited from his father, it is remarkable how in other ways the son closely hewed to his father's path. First, Bob began making a name for himself in the North Carolina Grange. He had been active in the association from a young age, serving in the youth organizations. In 1955, he chaired the state Grange dairy committee. In 1959, Bob and Jessie Rae were voted one of the five outstanding Young Grange Couples in the nation, earning them a trip to California to collect the award and take the children to Disneyland. That same year, Bob became assistant to the master of the state Grange, and in 1961 he became state master, replacing Harry Caldwell, who had held the post since 1937 and had guided the organization after succeeding Kerr Scott.

During his two years as Grange master, Scott attended more than two hundred meetings across the state, renewing ties his father had made and making new friends. He commuted between his home in Haw River and the Grange office in Greensboro. During the 1963 legislative session, he spent nearly all his time in Raleigh tracking bills of interest to the Grange. Scott used his Grange position to burnish a populist image like his father. He targeted the private power companies, criticizing the state Utilities Commission for its decision to allow Nantahala Power and Light Company to sell its distribution facility to Duke Power. "The whole deal is rotten to the core," Bob said.[18]

Because of his Grange position, Bob Scott waded into a major fight between the rural electric co-ops and the private power companies. In January 1963, Bob became chairman of a new group called North Carolina Consumers' Committee for Low-Cost Power, which was formed to fight the power company efforts to take over service areas annexed into towns or cities. Under the leadership of his father, the Grange had been instrumental in creating the electric co-ops when it worked with the legislature to create the Rural Electrification Authority in 1935. But now private power companies questioned whether the rural co-ops were still needed, saying that they were unfairly competing against private enterprise because they were tax exempt and could borrow capital at 2 percent interest rates. The power companies wanted to place the co-ops under the regulation of the state Utilities Commission and to be able to purchase the co-ops.

Scott made speeches on behalf of the co-ops both in North Carolina and around the country. "The campaign being waged in North Carolina by private power companies is part of a national campaign to destroy the most effective yard stick we have to measure the cost of electricity—the rural electric co-ops," Bob told the annual meeting of the Norfolk Citizens for Democratic Government in April 1963.[19] The legislature blocked the power company effort.

The Grange gave Bob Scott a political launching pad, just as it had his father. As governor years later, following a reception for members of the state Grange in the executive mansion, Bob noted in his diary what the Grange had meant to him. "I have often considered the Grange organization—along with the family name—as one key factor in my success in statewide campaigns," he wrote. "That is, my time as state Grange officer gave me the opportunity to travel about over the state extensively and to visit in many rural communities. This experience provided an excellent base of support that few people realized."[20]

Shortly after his father's death, there were articles in state newspapers speculating that he would follow in his father's footsteps. Bob Scott seemed to be thinking about a political future when, just two months after Kerr's death, he wrote to D. W. Colvard, dean of the N.C. State School of Agriculture and a friend of his father, about the need for "courageous leaders" who will "protect the welfare of the little man" in farming.[21] By 1959, Ben Roney, Kerr's chief political strategist, was sending him notes, praising him for getting around the state and saying that he was following in his father's path.[22]

Terry Sanford included Bob and Jessie Rae in a group of young couples invited to his home in Fayetteville for a cookout as he planned his 1960 campaign, and Bob ended up helping Sanford, particularly working in the Branchhead Boy country of eastern North Carolina, where his father had been so popular. As a reward, Sanford appointed Scott to the state Board of Conservation and Development, a coveted position that oversaw both economic development and the parks. Despite their relationship, the Sanford camp mistrusted Scott and Roney, viewing them skeptically as more interested in advancing Scott's political career than in helping Sanford.

During the 1960 Sanford gubernatorial primary campaign against Lake, Roney, working as a Sanford campaign adviser, decided to take young Bob on a political road trip, providing the next generation with some coaching. "He called me and said, 'Come on, it's time you learned something about politics,'" Scott recalled. "So we went down to Greenville and started there and started down the highway going from Greenville down to Vanceboro. We were sort of assessing the situation for Sanford in that area. We stopped in every country store and fillin' station there was. We'd go in and get us a soft drink and either a pack of nabs or peanuts and a conversation with who was there. Then we'd go to the next place and get a Coca-Cola and some peanuts. . . . That was my first foray into politics."[23]

By late 1962, the question was who would succeed Sanford as governor and carry on the programs of the progressive wing of the party. Most had assumed that Bert Bennett would be the candidate, before he ruled out the race. This set up the first major fissure in the moderate-progressive wing of the Democratic Party. Sanford and Bennett had decided to anoint former federal judge L. Richardson Preyer of Greensboro to be Sanford's Democratic successor. But Roney and other old Scott hands were interested in running the thirty-five-year-old Bob Scott.

The Preyer choice surprised Scott. Sanford had called a meeting of fifty of his most important supporters—called keys—on September 8, 1963, at a Holiday Inn in Greensboro. Bob Scott, one of the Sanford keys, remembers the meeting as being billed as an open search for a gubernatorial candidate, but in fact he said it was "a set up." Sanford and Bennett had already agreed to back Preyer, a Harvard- and Princeton-educated lawyer and scion of a Greensboro Vicks VapoRub fortune. "I'll never forget Terry [Sanford] coming into that meeting," Bob recalled. "I didn't recognize him when he walked in the door. He had on a hat. He never wore a hat. He had on a raincoat with his collar turned up. And he had on glasses. He didn't want anybody to see him come in. He really was in disguise." After someone suggested Preyer's name, Preyer quickly appeared, suggesting that it had been choreographed. "Lauch Faircloth was sitting right behind me," Scott said. "And I turned around to Lauch and said, 'Lauch, what do you think?' Lauch said, 'He will never go over down east.' That was my feeling too."[24]

The next day Preyer announced his candidacy. So did Lake, the segregationist, and former superior court judge Dan Moore of Canton, a corporate lawyer, a favorite of the business community. The Scotts had not been consulted, the Branchhead Boys seemed to be losing their influence, and a factional gap that had been only a crack was beginning to widen.

The opening of dove season each year in early September is a major occasion across the South as hunters take to the fields to shoot the large flocks of swift and darting birds as they come to feed on seeds, corn, pokeberry, and waste grain left on cultivated fields. Kerr Scott had held a traditional dove hunt—part hunt, part political gathering. When he died, the dove hunt was moved to Uncle Ralph's farm. In 1963, hundreds showed up to shoot birds and afterward to dine on a country ham supper with eggs and grits and biscuits served up by Ralph's wife, Hazeleene, and Jessie Rae. Much of the dove hunt political talk centered on where the Branchhead Boys would go in next year's governor's race. Nobody in the race seemed to their liking, so someone suggested Bob. With several political reporters at the hunt, the gossip soon made the state's newspapers.[25]

In October 1963, Scott resigned as master of the state Grange to begin traveling around the state, taking soundings on a possible gubernatorial bid. The move smacked of disloyalty to the Sanford people, since they had already settled on Preyer. Was Bob Scott part of their organization or not?[26]

While finding some encouragement, Scott discovered that Preyer, Moore, and Lake had already lined up most of the campaign workers and money. Some questioned whether, at age thirty-five, he needed more seasoning. W. F. "Bill" Wilson, a county agriculture extension agent from Durham, told Bob that he would be wise to wait four years to run for governor. "I believe you are well known in Grange circles, but you need to become better known throughout the entire state. I think your age would be a handicap."[27]

Scott called a two-minute news conference at Raleigh's Carolina Hotel on January 7, 1964, to announce that although he would not run for governor, he might run for an unspecified office, and he asked his supporters to be patient.[28] Scott then walked down the hall to meet with advisers to figure out what to do next. Scott dismissed the option of following his father's path and running for agriculture commissioner, because agriculture was losing its importance in the state. When he mentioned running for lieutenant governor, Roney dismissed it as "a dead end" where "former legislators are put out to pasture." Scott and his advisers agreed to meet again in a week, and by that time Roney had warmed to the idea of lieutenant governor, saying it might be "a sleeper."[29]

Several days later, Scott announced his candidacy for the Democratic nomination for lieutenant governor. In his announcement, Scott jumped fearlessly into one of the hottest state controversies of the 1960s—calling for the repeal of the University of North Carolina speaker ban. During the last day of the 1963 legislative session, North Carolina became the only state in the nation to pass a law barring certain people from speaking on state campuses: known members of the Communist Party, those who advocated the overthrow of the U.S. or state Constitution, and those who had pleaded the Fifth Amendment in answer to questions about subversive activities.

As in the Smith-Graham race thirteen years earlier, the speaker ban had as much to do with race as it did with communism: the ban had been prompted by growing legislative anger over the civil rights movement. The legislature had already voiced its displeasure in a number of ways. The House had passed a resolution calling for the creation of a new court— a so-called Court of the Union composed of the fifty state chief justices— that would overrule the U.S. Supreme Court. In another pique of anger, the legislature abolished funding for UNC-TV, the university-supported public television network, when they learned that a staff member had participated in a civil rights demonstration. The funding, however, was quickly restored.

But more trouble brewed when protesters tried to integrate the Legislative Building's cafeteria, and outrage flourished as lawmakers were forced to negotiate their way through picket lines as they returned after a day of lawmaking to the Sir Walter Hotel, a downtown hotel where so many of them stayed that it became known as the Third House of the legislature. After one such demonstration on June 20, 1963, angry lawmakers—spotting a white university faculty member—decided to copy a bill that had been introduced but not passed in the Ohio legislature to ban communists from speaking on campus.[30] On the last day of the session, a speaker ban passed by voice vote by both houses one hour after it was introduced—with no hearings or committee consideration. Few knew its contents.

The banned speakers ranged from British geneticist and evolutionary biologist J. B. S. Haldane to American playwright Arthur Miller. The Southern Association of Colleges and Schools threatened to withdraw the university system's accreditation, professors threatened to leave, and academic conferences boycotted the state. But the speaker ban had strong support among conservatives, who equated any opposition as being soft on communism. Jesse Helms, who in 1960 began delivering daily hard-hitting editorials on WRAL-TV, delivered fifty-four editorials in favor of the speaker ban.

In announcing his candidacy, Scott said the speaker ban was "not satisfactory." He continued, "What disturbs me most is that no effort was made to determine the necessity [for the law]. None of the college officials upon whom we depend—must depend—in the proper education of our young people were consulted before enactment. No committee considered it." He said that the law "points a finger of suspicion" at all faculty members, university officers, and trustees.[31]

While Bob Scott attempted to win statewide office, his uncle Ralph was already a powerhouse in Raleigh, and Ralph had been lashing out at the speaker ban, too. "Fidel Castro could speak, because he claims he isn't a Communist," Ralph Scott said in a speech to an American Legion post in September 1963. "Robert E. Lee couldn't speak because he advocated the overthrow of the U.S. Constitution by force. This is the way of the coward. . . . To support this bill is to say that you don't believe in the power of human reason. This kind of legislation is always the last ditch stand of fearful people who are afraid to argue with their enemies."[32]

Senator Ralph Scott of Haw River.
(Photo by Burnie Batchelor Studio; courtesy of State Archives of North Carolina)

Uncle Ralph, as he was widely known, was easy to overlook. In appearance, he resembled an old farmer, with a gravelly voice and a richly accented tongue that could be both startlingly blunt and quick-witted. Born in 1903, seven years after Kerr, Ralph followed his brother to N.C. State University, where he captained the 1923 cross country team that won the state championship. In 1927, Ralph started Melville Dairy, beginning in a little milk house on his brother Henry's farm before eventually building a modern plant in Burlington in 1935. In the early years, Ralph was the only route man, while his new wife, Hazeleene, a former high school classmate, kept the books. He delivered milk seven days a week because homes had no refrigeration facilities to store milk for more than a day. After picking up milk from local farms, he parked his Ford Model A truck in Burlington to save wear and tear and ran across town making his deliveries. Ralph said he never missed a day in six years.

Ralph became a successful businessman, and a competitor of his brother Kerr, who helped found Guilford Dairy in Greensboro. In 1967, Ralph sold Melville Dairy to Guilford Dairy, merging the Scott family enterprises into one organization. He also started a company that made plastic containers and processed aerosol cream, and he served on the corporate boards of an insurance company, a savings and loan, and a textile mill.

Business paid the bills, but politics got Uncle Ralph's blood flowing. He served on the Alamance County commissioners from 1944 to 1950 before being elected to the state Senate in 1950, where he represented Alamance and Orange Counties. Among his major accomplishments was a 1953 law that created a state Milk Commission to prop up the price of milk. Ralph said that the move helped protect small, independent dairy producers from the predatory practices of big manufacturers, but opponents saw it as anticompetitive.

He did not seek reelection in 1956 because of an agreement to rotate the Senate seat with neighboring Orange County. Instead, Ralph tried to join his brother in Washington, seeking to unseat sixth Democratic congressman Carl Durham of Chapel Hill. Ralph began his ill-advised attempt when it was rumored that Durham might not seek another term. Ralph lost a race that had few issues—the first lost for a Scott after a string of victories.

Sanford's 1960 election also coincided with Uncle Ralph's return to the Senate. Scott served as a Sanford political lieutenant both in the campaign and on the Senate floor, with Sanford naming him to the influential Advisory Budget Commission, a now-defunct group that helped draft a joint executive-legislative budget. He served the next fifteen years on the budget commission, including the last six as chair. Some years Scott and key lawmakers assembled the state budget at his house over the weekend.

In 1963, the legislature moved from its cramped headquarters in the Capitol to the new modern Edward Durell Stone–designed Legislative Building—the same architect who designed Washington's Kennedy Center for the Performing Arts. As a high-ranking lawmaker, Ralph earned a prime office with a view of the grounds. When another lawmaker complained about the location of his office, Ralph traded with him for his small, undesirable inside windowless office—the kind assigned to freshmen of the party out of power. Uncle Ralph kept that office the rest of his career.

Such humble gestures and down-to-earth friendliness—combined with his shrewdness, his Scott family pedigree, and his frequent close ties to the governor—made Uncle Ralph a force in the legislature. No matter how high he rose, he never changed his plain-shoe style. An invitation for lunch meant a hot dog in the legislative cafeteria, or for breakfast, it was usually the Farmer's Market for some streak o' lean (fatback with a bit of meat still attached). His frequent use of self-deprecating homespun humor also won him friends or at least made people willing to listen to Ralph. "He always talked as though truth serum coursed through his arteries," wrote journalist Jay Jenkins. "His face was that of a benign bulldog, his gaze was direct, and his voice had a twangy, scratchy quality. And when he talked, nobody had to ask what he meant."[33]

Ralph was devoted to his voters to a fault. When back in his district on weekends, he entertained lines of constituents seeking government jobs, roads that needed paving, paroles, or other government favors. According to his colleagues, Ralph never knew how to say "no" to a constituent. In one instance, Ralph told Sanford that there had been a terrible miscarriage of justice because several young men in Alamance County were serving time for stealing hubcaps, and they really were good boys. Further investigation by the governor's office found that Scott had left out parts of the story. "Indeed he had stolen the hubcaps," remember Tom Lambeth, a Sanford aide. "He had also stolen the wheels and the car." Scott had left out a few details.[34] During this period, Uncle Ralph—moved by the story of a constituent—became the leading legislative champion for the mentally disabled, or what he called "the forgotten children," helping obtain funding for more teaching positions, special centers, and teacher training. Years later, this writer had lunch with Uncle Ralph at a Holiday Inn in Burlington. Ralph had gotten the state to build an access road to the hotel—which had been an issue in a recent campaign. Seated at his table, Ralph resembled a sort of political don, an image enhanced by his gravelly voice. The waitress not only took his order but asked him if he could get a job for her husband in the Department of Natural Resources and Community Development. One patron after another greeted him, and Ralph responded by gesturing with a wave of his right arm and saying, "Hey, how are you doing?"[35]

Now his nephew wanted to join him in Raleigh.

Although Bob Scott entered the Democratic primary for lieutenant governor first, two candidates had informally declared their intentions: House Speaker Clifton Blue and state Senator John Jordan of Raleigh. Both were surprised and unsettled by Bob Scott's entry: Bob had earlier told Blue that he planned to endorse him, while Jordan entered the race with Uncle Ralph's encouragement. In some ways, Scott had broken into the line; North Carolina's lieutenant governors had traditionally been lawmakers like Blue who had worked their way up the legislative ladder. Blue, a newspaper publisher from Aberdeen, was a moderate conservative. A widely liked figure with a disarming speech impediment, he had served in the House from 1946 to 1963, capping his career with the speakership. He had helped push the speaker ban through the legislature, although during the campaign he said he had an open mind about whether it should be repealed. He had also served as head of the North Carolina Press Association.

Bob Scott and John Jordan split the progressive vote in the primary. Scott ran as an opponent of the death penalty and as a supporter for increased spending for the public schools and better roads. He also reminded voters of his family's legacy. "Public service is natural in Bob's family," said one newspaper ad. "Farmer Bob' Scott, his grandfather and for whom he was named, was in the State Senate. He was a pioneer in education and farm programs and stood with Aycock in the fight for public schools. Bob's father, W. Kerr Scott, was Commissioner of Agriculture, Governor and United States Senator."[36]

Overshadowing the lieutenant governor's race was a competitive Democratic primary for governor. Scott, Blue, and Jordan remained neutral in the governor's race, although Scott later acknowledged that his campaign "sort of piggybacked" on Sanford's support because they came out of the same wing of the Democratic Party. Uncle Ralph's vigorous support for Richardson Preyer and his populist digs at Dan Moore complicated matters for Bob Scott. Uncle Ralph portrayed Moore as a politician in the pockets of the highway contractors and "already mortgaged to the special interests and lobbyists." He also derided a Moore TV commercial that used a "high powered New York announcer [actor Mason Adams] . . . who sold so much dog food with the same voice—and with the same kind of sell." Then, introducing Preyer in Waynesville, Uncle Ralph said Moore had been a lobbyist himself, serving as legal counsel for Champion Paper. "These lobbyists are the ones that fought Kerr Scott every inch of the way in the programs he fought so hard for to give the people," Uncle Ralph said.[37]

The repeated attacks on Moore prompted Bob to issue a statement disassociating him from his uncle's remarks and reconfirming his neutrality. "You can tell that Uncle Ralph is a member of the Scott family and speaks his mind on most any matter," Bob Scott said in a statement. "My father used to do that sometimes." In a memo to key campaign leaders, Bob Scott said that he had talked to his uncle and there was no hope in getting him to soften his criticism. "Like most of the Scott clan, he says what he thinks and worries about the consequences later."[38] After the primary, one Bob Scott supporter, Raz Autry, principal of East Montgomery High School in Biscoe, said Uncle Ralph's political attacks on Moore probably cost Scott thousands of votes. "It's hard to do anything with your kinfolks," Autry wrote to Bob Scott. "If Ralph gets on the wrong side again, let us know and we'll kidnap him."[39]

Bob Scott also had to tread carefully because his backers supported different gubernatorial candidates. Take John and Leola Flannery, dairy farmers in Salemburg, Branchhead Boys who helped elect Kerr Scott in 1948. In 1964, John Flannery served as Sampson County manager for Lake's gubernatorial campaign. Uncle Ralph wrote to Flannery in February, saying, "I wish you would do what you could for Robert Scott, Kerr's son who is running for lieutenant governor. I realize that if you are handling one campaign you can't do too much for the second man but where you can help him and not hurt your man, I would greatly appreciate it." In September, Leola Flannery wrote Bob Scott: "John and I are very interested in you. John likes Ralph, your father and of course Bob. John spoke [for] you last spring while he was Lake's campaign manager."[40]

On primary day, Scott led the field with the help of local courthouse machines. He outpolled Blue by 306,992 (44 percent) to 255,424 votes (36 percent), with Jordan receiving 140,277 votes (20 percent). But it fell well short of the 50 percent Scott needed to win the primary outright, and Blue called for a runoff. In calling for a second primary, Blue said that he faced an uphill race, but "many have expressed the feeling that a man who is totally inexperienced in North Carolina legislative background should not be conceded the position by a minority vote."[41]

Blue's decision also related to voting irregularities, such as those that occurred in Madison County, where the mountain machine of the Ponder brothers, Zeno and E. Y., controlled the vote. The Ponders had initially promised to support Jordan in the primary, but that changed after a Scott trip to the mountains. "The Scott people got to him, and with no trouble at all, converted him," Jordan recalled. "But before they had gotten out of town, Zeno calls me and he says, 'John, I'm going to give you a few votes. But I can't give you the county.' Zeno was honest with me." Bob Scott won 4,594 votes in Madison County, an astounding 88 percent. Blue received 315 votes (6 percent), and Jordan received 282 votes (5 percent).[42] But some of those votes looked suspicious to Clyde Norton of Old Fort, who lost the state Senate Democratic primary to Zeno Ponder. He asked for a state Board of Elections investigation. When the state Bureau of Investigation sought to impound the county's poll books, the ledgers mysteriously disappeared—as did the man who had last seen them. The books have never been found. The elections board overturned Ponder's victory because of gross voting irregularities. Blue sought to make an issue of the Madison County anomalies in the runoff, but Scott noted that he had won the primary by 53,000 votes and that Blue himself had benefited from courthouse machines in places such as Buncombe and Durham Counties. Going into the runoff, Blue gained a significant amount of Jordan's white support, whereas Bob Scott picked up the backing of organized labor and some black support that had gone to Jordan in the primary. Echoing his father, Scott also wooed members of the rural electric cooperatives who were engaged in a political battle with the power companies. He proposed freezing the service areas of Duke Power and Carolina Power and Light. He said the private power companies had refused to serve the rural area, but now that the rural electric co-ops had made the areas profitable, the private power companies wanted to go in and take them over. "The power companies have their best chance in years to take over the rural electric cooperatives," Scott wrote in a mailing. "They don't like me, just like they didn't like my father W. Kerr Scott. This is their chance to stop me and stifle the cooperatives."[43]

The governor's race once again overshadowed the lieutenant governor's runoff. In the May primary, Preyer led the field with 37 percent, Moore received 34 percent, and Lake garnered 28 percent. With Preyer short of a majority, Moore called for a runoff. Lake, the ardent segregationist, sealed the runoff when he endorsed and campaigned for Moore, the business conservative. Lake said that Preyer had the support of "all those bloc voters who are captive pawns in the hands of Bobby Kennedy and Martin Luther King; last and least there is that small but noisy clique of professional liberals who are a red and festering sore upon the body of a great university."[44]

Moore won in a landslide with 62 percent of the vote to Preyer's 38 percent. Some interpreted Moore's victory as a rejection of the racial moderation and progressivism of Sanford. "The conservative majority of North

Carolina's people has been a long time getting together as a collective voice," said Helms. "They have too often been lured away from reality by false promises and by cutting wedges driven amidst them. But on Saturday an aroused majority spoke—clearly, militantly and finally. The people are fed up."[45]

The governor's race bled over into the lieutenant governor's race, and although Scott and Blue stayed neutral, there was some general alignment between Blue and Moore and Scott and Preyer based on faction and ideology. Moore's supporters had also encouraged Blue to seek a runoff so that Scott supporters would be too busy to help Preyer. "It is no secret that many leaders of the conservative wing of the Democratic Party had hoped to cut short Scott's political career at its very outset," wrote the *Charlotte Observer*.[46]

More people voted in the second primary—a rarity in Tar Heel politics. Scott squeaked through with 50.9 percent of the vote: he received 371,605 votes to Blue's 356,400. The courthouse machines aided Scott once again, with Madison County delivering a 74 percent vote for Scott—slightly down from the first primary, when the voting records went missing. In Richmond County, a courthouse machine run by Sheriff R. W. Goodman and attorney J. Elsie Webb helped Scott win 53 percent of the vote. Although the margin was not impressive, it was an unexpected victory for Scott. Blue was from a neighboring county and popular in Richmond County, where he had many connections. So you might ask, Webb wrote in a letter to Scott, how did Scott manage to do so well? "It might be well to follow the political philosophy of old Jim Curley, the late Mayor of Boston, when he said, 'If you can say it, don't write it, and if you can nod your head, don't say it," Webb wrote.[47]

Many party progressives disheartened by Moore's victory took solace in Scott's win. But Scott's hometown editor noted the election should not be interpreted as a victory for liberalism. "He knows, among other many other things as a result of his campaign, that he gained support from the conservative, moderate and conservative-progressive divisions of the party, or he would not have won," read an editorial in the *Daily Times-News*. "He knows too, that many of the 'Branch Head Boys,' of his father's day now are solidly with the Lake forces which joined in helping to nominate Dan K. Moore. It is true that the state's so-called big businesses didn't openly endorse him any more than it endorsed his father. Yet he had to have much support from big business to have gained his victory."[48]

In August, both Bob and Ralph attended the Democratic National Convention in Atlantic City. Only Sanford praised President Lyndon Johnson's choice of liberal senator Hubert Humphrey to be his vice presidential running mate, while Moore and Senator Sam Ervin Jr. said his support for civil rights would hurt the ticket in the South. Bob Scott also voiced reservations, saying he would have preferred someone such as Franklin Roosevelt Jr. or California governor Pat Brown. But he put aside his reservations. In September, Scott agreed to become national chairman of Rural Americans for Johnson-Humphrey, describing Republican presidential nominee Barry Goldwater as hostile to the economic needs of the South. "I challenge Senator Goldwater to explain to voters of North Carolina why he opposes price supports for such crops as tobacco, cotton and peanuts, why he seeks elimination of rural electric systems, and why he consistently opposes area redevelopment programs," Bob Scott said.[49]

The Scott remarks were part of a Democratic effort to hold the national ticket in eastern North Carolina, where Goldwater's opposition to civil rights legislation promised to have some appeal. It appeared to hit a nerve. As part of his first southern swing in September, Goldwater made a stop in Raleigh. Such a trip would have been a rarity in the past but was an indication of the growing Republican prospects in the state. Appearing before as many as ten thousand people in front of the Wake County courthouse, Goldwater went after Scott—an unusual move for a presidential candidate to take on the Democratic nominee for lieutenant governor. "Now, there's a fellow here in this state named Bob Scott," Goldwater said. "Now I imagine he's a very decent gentlemanly sort of fellow, but he goes up to Washington and he meets with one James Patton and Clyde Ellis. One heads the socialist farmers group in this country and the other heads every other socialist organization I've ever known of. He rubs a little elbow with Whitewash Lyndon, and then comes back and says some rather peculiar things. He says that I oppose cotton and tobacco and peanuts. I'm probably the most violent advocate of peanut butter that ever lived. Under a dare one day from my youngest son, I actually shaved with peanut butter, and believe it or not, it's not bad except it smells for a few days afterwards." (Patton served as president of the National Farmers Union and Ellis, a former Arkansas congressman, was general manager of the National Rural Electric Cooperative Association.)[50]

Bob Scott did not back down, saying that Goldwater's election would cost North Carolina tobacco farmers $200 million in the first year. "If anything happens to our price support program," Scott said, "the economy of this state will suffer a blow like that of the depression years. Farmers will be selling 25-cent tobacco, 10-cent cotton and free peanuts."[51]

Meanwhile, in campaigning against Dan Moore and fighting the speaker ban, Uncle Ralph had been taking an increasingly risky stance in Alamance County, which was becoming more conservative. His Republican opponent, Richard B. Barnwell, made an issue of the speaker ban. One ad run against Uncle Ralph read, "Within the past week, two Russian spies, caught sending secret data on American launching sites and atomic arms shipments, have been turned loose. Do you want such people using your tax supported colleges and universities? Protect your children against spies and subversion. Alamance County citizens—work to enforce and keep the speaker ban law."[52] In the end, Alamance nearly went for Goldwater and did vote for Republican Robert Gavin in the governor's race over Moore. Uncle Ralph did, however, won reelection to a fifth term in the state Senate by a mere 402 votes. "I'm not a gambler," he told a supporter during the campaign, "but I suppose I'm gambling on this one."[53]

Dan Moore kept an arm's length from the Johnson-Humphrey ticket and became the first North Carolina gubernatorial candidate since 1940 to win the office but trail the president in votes. Bob Scott led the lieutenant governor ticket and defeated Republican Clifford Bell, a sixty-six-year-old retired life insurance agent from Gastonia, with 61 percent of the vote. In the presidential race, Goldwater won five southern states and showed the growing Republican strength in the South, but Johnson carried North Carolina by a 56 percent margin—his strongest showing in the South apart from his home state of Texas. Significantly, LBJ won 61 percent in eastern North Carolina, where Bob Scott had helped make Goldwater's free-market positions on farming a liability.[54]

LIEUTENANT GOVERNOR

The lieutenant governor's office had been vacant since H. Cloyd Philpott of Lexington had died on August 19, 1961, of a heart ailment, just eight months after taking office. Sometimes called the fifth wheel of state government, the lieutenant governor's post paid $2,100 per year, with $3,000 for expenses and with one secretary when the legislature was not in session, for what was a part-time job. Elected independently of the governor, in the sixties the position still had significant legislative powers: the lieutenant governor presided over the Senate and exercised influence through parliamentary maneuvers, naming committees and committee chairs, assigning bills, and serving on the state Board of Education.

Scott continued to commute daily from his Haw River home. Lacking his own agenda, he generally supported Moore, although the two men came from different factions of the party and were never personally close. Scott backed Moore's $300 million road bond issue—the first since the 1949 bond issue pushed through by his father. He also supported a modernization of the state's court system. Yet nothing was more sensitive than the speaker ban. Moore, after consulting with legislative leaders including Scott, decided not to seek immediate repeal of the speaker ban but created a nine-member commission to study the issue. Moore said that although he appreciated the desire for colleges "to be free in the pursuit of truth," there should be tolerance for those who had lost sons or husbands in Vietnam.[55] Bob Scott backed the governor, saying both publicly and privately that the votes were not available in the 1965 session to repeal the speaker ban.

But Uncle Ralph ripped Moore, parting ways with his nephew. "This is the gravest threat to higher education that this state has ever encountered," Ralph Scott said. "I for one fail to see what a study of the situation can produce in a constructive way. We all know what the law does. We know what it can do, namely grind the University down into the dust, taking the proud reputation of our State with it. By our inaction, we do a dishonor to the memory of those leaders in the past who taught us to cherish education and who were not afraid to put principles ahead of politics."[56]

After the study panel came back with a report, the governor called a special session of the legislature in November 1965 that modified the law, returning control of speakers back to individual campus trustees. The *Greensboro Daily News* said that Moore's strategy, no matter how circuitous, worked. "Governor Moore, Lieutenant Governor Scott, Speaker Taylor and the Britt Commission, then, cannot be over praised for bringing this episode down from the realms of bitter debate into the arena of political compromise where it could be effectively resolved. What began in politics had to end in politics; the mere clashing of debate, however pertinent, proved unable to draw the sting. . . . Fundamentally, however, the outcome of the special session is renewed evidence of the capacity of practical statesmanship, under strong leadership, to heal wounds that cannot otherwise be healed."[57]

But the issue continued to generate controversy, with invited communist speakers in 1966 challenging the law by speaking to university students on the Franklin Street sidewalk just a few feet from campus—beyond a stone wall dubbed "Dan K. Moore's Wall." The issue was finally resolved when, on February 19, 1968, a three-judge federal panel struck down the law as unconstitutionally vague.

Ralph Scott, carrying the progressive banner, continued to criticize

Moore's leadership. This drew the ire of Jesse Helms, who called Scott a sore loser. Uncle Ralph, in turn, had little use for Helms. When a woman once asked for his opinion of Helms, he responded: "I told her if she wasn't for nothin' or nobody, he's the man."[58] His uncle's stance prompted Bob Scott, seeking to position himself as a centrist, to defend Moore as a fine leader. "Unfortunately, some folks over the state confuse the two of us since we have the same last name and come from the same neck of the woods," Bob Scott said. "Some say I am jumping on the governor, but they're shooting at the wrong rabbit."[59]

Bob Scott also presided in a special legislative session in January 1966 when North Carolina—responding to the Supreme Court's landmark ruling in *Baker v. Carr*, which established principle of one man, one vote—reluctantly reapportioned how it elected the legislature and Congress. Before the change, the state House had 120 members, with 100 elected from each of the state's one hundred counties and 20 apportioned to the most populous counties. This meant that Tyrell County, with 4,520 people, had the same representation as Wayne County, with 82,059 people. But the Supreme Court required equal representation. In response to a 1965 lawsuit against North Carolina's legislative and congressional plans, the legislature drew new districts. The courts approved the legislative districts but disallowed the congressional districts, which were finally adopted in 1967. The new districts shifted more of an advantage to both urban voters and Republicans.

Bob Scott used the lieutenant governor's office to lay the groundwork for his gubernatorial bid. He gave 203 speeches in 1965 and 245 speeches in 1966, enduring what he called "endless meals of razor-thin roast beef, seventeen green peas, a wad of mashed potatoes, and apple pie the density of lead."[60] Scott largely avoided controversy in the speeches, seeking to emerge as a middle-of-the road candidate acceptable to all factions within the party.

The growing white backlash against racial integration gave Scott reason for caution. The passage by Congress of the Civil Rights Act of 1964 and the Voting Rights Act of 1965, combined with widespread civil rights protests, had intensified white resentment. The tobacco fields of rural eastern North Carolina—Branchhead Boy country—had become the nation's leading recruiting grounds for the Ku Klux Klan.

In October 1965, the House Un-American Activities Committee released a report saying that North Carolina had 112 Ku Klux Klan Klaverns—the largest number in the country. North Carolina officials seemed dumbfounded. Governor Moore said, "I do not concede that we are No. 1. I do not think the Klan membership is anywhere near as large as it is pictured." Bob Scott quipped, "When I first saw the press report, I said to myself that it just confirms the impression I've gotten that the people in North Carolina are a bunch of joiners."[61]

Many didn't realize the extent to which the Klan had organized and grown in recent years. The civil rights–era United Klans of America formed in 1961. Although the KKK received the most attention in Deep South states because of the use of violence there, the organization did indeed grow faster in North Carolina than anywhere else—thanks to a talented organizer named Robert Jones, who became state grand dragon in 1963. By 1964, there were nightly rallies, many held at county fairgrounds with live music, concessions, and souvenirs and raffles. A KKK booth appeared at the state fair in Raleigh. Soon there were between ten thousand and twelve thousand dues-paying members in North Carolina, and by 1964, North Carolina's 192 KKK units exceeded those in Georgia, Alabama, and Mississippi combined. There were not only cross-burning rallies at night but so-called street walks held in towns during the day, where unmasked Klansmen paraded down sidewalks. The Klan burned a six-foot cross on the governor's mansion lawn in 1964, and reports of at least eighty cross burnings crossed Sanford's desk. In 1966, the Klan ran at least thirty candidates for public office; Klan members were elected sheriff and register of deeds in Rowan County.

In June 1966, Scott heard a truck door slam and looked outside to see a six-foot cross burning on his Haw River lawn—an act that made a lasting impression on his children. No one was arrested, and Scott said that he had no idea what prompted the act. Scott dismissed the cross burning as an act "in the same category with anonymous letters, obscene telephone calls and other similar acts. It does not bother me because I consider the kind of person who would do such a thing as this."[62]

Although the vast majority of white North Carolinians supported segregation, the KKK represented only a tiny minority—unlike the Reconstruction era Klan. Political and civic leaders and newspapers regularly denounced the new Klan. When civil rights leaders' homes were bombed, community leaders came together to rebuild or raise money to help them. There were multiple bombings in Charlotte in November 1965 when on a single night the homes of Kelly Alexander, the state president of the NAACP; his brother Fred Alexander, Charlotte's only black councilman; Reginald Hawkins, a black dentist and civil rights activist; and Julius Chambers, a black civil rights attorney were all bombed. "I am opposed to the Ku Klux Klan," said Governor Moore. "It's a sorry organization. It has no place in North Carolina. It stirs up trouble, it stirs up bitterness, it stirs up hate." When the legislature returned to Raleigh the following January, Moore proposed anti-Klan legislation to make it a felony to burn a cross without the property owner's permission or to bomb an individual's home.[63]

While speaking in Edenton in May 1966, civil rights leader the Reverend Martin Luther King Jr. decried what he called "the strange mixture" of the state's reputation for moderation and its fast-growing KKK. Later that summer, at a speech in Raleigh, fifteen hundred Klansmen greeted King in a counterdemonstration. "We've made North Carolina from a moderate state to Klansville USA," declared George Dorsett of Greensboro, the KKK's chaplain at the rally. "We have the greatest Klan state in the country." King wondered how "the state that prides itself on being the most liberal in the South can have the largest marches of the Ku Klux Klan."[64] Eventually, the House Un-American Activities Committee conducted a massive investigation of the Klan that in time sent North Carolina's grand dragon Jones and Robert Shelton, the national grand dragon, to prison on contempt of Congress charges for refusing to turn over KKK records.

The black community, after the initial sit-ins of the early sixties, was organizing, too. On May 5, 1965, Howard Fuller, a social worker, began his new job in Durham. Fuller had been hired to work for Operation Breakthrough, a federally funded antipoverty program. A handsome, charismatic former college basketball star who had grown up in the Milwaukee public housing projects and in Louisiana, Fuller was one of a new breed of social workers—not content just with helping individuals navigate the system but interested in organizing poor people to improve their plight. This type of social work inflamed vested interests from city hall to landlords and from beat cops to congressmen. Fuller later became superintendent of Milwaukee public schools; President George W. Bush would try to hire him as an education adviser; he would be a friend of the Walton retail family of Walmart fame; and in 2014, Republican legislative leaders House Speaker Thom Tillis and Senator Phil Berger would stand beside him at a news conference.

But in the sixties Fuller was one of the most hated and feared black men in North Carolina. He had been hired to work with the poor in Durham, and he had been shocked by what he had found in the Hayti neighborhood: unpaved roads, shotgun shacks, and in some cases no indoor running water. Fuller began working the churches, the barbershops, the res-

During a demonstration in Durham following the death of Martin Luther King Jr. in 1968, Howard Fuller gazes up and spots two white men with rifles on a bank building. They turn out to be police. (Photograph courtesy of Billy E. Barnes)

taurants, and the pool halls, organizing people to fight to get roads paved, street lights installed, businesses to hire blacks, and landlords to fix up housing; they pushed back against urban renewal projects that would destroy black neighborhoods. He didn't see the people he worked with as clients but instead viewed them as brothers and sisters. He hired promising young men out of the black community to be his top organizers, such as Ben Ruffin, who later became a top aide to Governor Jim Hunt and chairman of the University of North Carolina Board of Governors. By 1967, Fuller's territory had expanded to include much of eastern North Carolina. "I had no intention—ever of just helping people learn how to manage oppression," Fuller wrote in his memoirs. "This was a poor people's revolution and we were just getting started."[65]

In July 1967, Fuller and Ruffin were involved in a march of three hundred people in Durham pushing for better play areas, improved housing conditions, and equal opportunities. "Negroes are just fed up with the conditions they live under," Ruffin said. During the march some rocks and bricks were thrown and some windows broken. On a subsequent march, two marchers were superficially wounded by gunfire from a passing car filled by whites. Governor Moore mobilized 350 National Guardsmen to augment police.

The white backlash was immediate, and it was led by fourth district congressman Jim Gardner, a handsome, articulate Rocky Mount native who was also a young man in a hurry. During the early 1960s, Gardner and a partner bought the franchise rights for a hamburger stand in Greenville and quickly built the enterprise into Hardee's, one of the nation's leading fast-food chains. He also became coowner of the Carolina Cougars of the American Basketball Association, the state's first major league professional sports team, and Gardner served briefly as league commissioner.

Gardner left the Democratic Party in 1963 because of what he called its "drift toward socialism" and because of his attraction to Goldwater's presidential campaign. Within months of changing his registration that summer, he became chairman of the Nash County Republican Party. In 1964, the thirty-one-year-old Gardner challenged Democratic congressman Harold Cooley, the powerful chairman of the House Agriculture Committee, who had represented the district since 1934—a district that included large swaths of rural areas heavily dependent on the federal tobacco price support program. Attaching himself to Goldwater's candidacy, Gardner lost the race but won a surprising 48 percent of the vote.

After a stint as state Republican Party chairman, Gardner tried again in 1966, and this time he defeated Cooley, becoming the first Republican elected to Congress in the eastern part of the state in the twentieth century. The Democratic-controlled legislature shifted his home from the fourth district to the second district with conservative Democrat L. H. Fountain, making it a difficult for him to remain in Congress.

Gardner began looking at running for governor, and he quickly made a name for himself as one of the leading national critics of Johnson's anti-poverty programs in general. In particular, he derided the politicization of antipoverty workers. Gardner traveled to Newark, New Jersey, where he placed part of the blame for the national riots on anti-poverty workers.

Closer to home, Gardner charged that the North Carolina Fund had become a "political action machine" and called for an investigation of its "meddling in the affairs of local communities." The North Carolina Fund, created by Governor Sanford, was a nonprofit corporation with a mandate to create experimental projects in education, health, job training, housing, and community development. One of its most prominent programs was Operation Breakthrough. Gardner singled out Fuller for giving "inflammatory speeches in which he advocated the use of black power." He expressed amazement that the fund's leaders countenanced "revolutionary attitudes," and he sent reports to the foundations providing money to the fund as well as asking government officials to examine the fund's tax status.[66]

With rioting in Los Angeles, Detroit, and Newark, the national and state political climates were becoming increasingly polarized. As Scott prepared to run for governor, Sam Ragan, managing editor of the *News and Observer*, convened "a brain trust" for Scott to figure out what should be done about black riots. The group of mainly Research Triangle academics met on May 30, 1967, at the Voyager Inn in Raleigh for dinner and included Abe Holtzman and Bill Toussaint of N.C. State University, Jack Blackburn of Duke University, Juanita Kreps, also of Duke and a future U.S. commerce secretary, Donald Matthews of the University of North Carolina at Chapel Hill, and Greensboro newspaperman Bill Snider. In a three-page memorandum to Ragan, Matthews expressed the confusion among white liberals about what to do. "I think any potential governor must face up to the fact that the civil disorders now wracking Detroit and—to a lesser extent, Durham—are going to get worse in the future and will become more common in this state. What should he do or say about these violent episodes? This is a difficult question to handle, since we really don't know their meaning, causes or significance." Matthews argued that Scott should make a clear distinction between lawful protests and lawless riots and that he should set up a study commission of social scientists to study the cause and cures of the violence before the outbreaks occurred.[67]

Scott responded by moving to the political right in preparation for facing Gardner in 1968. "When I was getting to run for governor, I was labeled a liberal," Scott recalled years later. "I was identified with the Terry Sanford–Kerr Scott wing of the party, not the conservative wing. This was a time when things were in turmoil in our society and law and order was the code word of that day. I felt and Ben [Roney] agreed strongly that I needed to break that image that I was a liberal. One of the first things I did was I went down to [Harnett] County, right in the heart of the Klan Country, and spoke to a civic club down there. I carried with me a lieutenant colonel of the Highway Patrol named Edwin Guy. But I gave the damnedest law and order speech you ever saw."[68]

Scott traveled to Dunn, a Harnett County town on November 14, 1967, to give a tough law and order speech to several civic groups. The Scott campaign calculated everything about the speech: the place, the timing, and even his driver. Just two years earlier, in May 1965, six thousand people attended a KKK rally in Dunn where the special guests were three of the four Alabama Klansmen accused of murdering Viola Liuzzo, a white Michigan civil rights volunteer, as she drove to Selma after a march.[69] Well publicized in advance, the Scott speech was heavily covered by the state's news media.

The Dunn speech also came less than two weeks after a riot in Winston-Salem in which four hundred National Guardsmen and helmeted police battled rioters for four days after a black man, James Eller, died after being struck on the head by a policeman with a blackjack. Thirty-four people were injured, including seven policemen, during the disturbances. There were 192 arrests and fifty-five fires, as police, firemen, and National Guard came under sniper fire.[70] In his speech, Scott decried events in Winston-Salem, "when bands of lawless youths burned buildings, looted stores and endangered life. Somehow it has become accepted in some quarters that the end justifies the means and that it is right to burn cities, shoot innocent people, destroy public and private property, and steal what is not theirs." He also criticized the March on the Pentagon, held the previous month to protest the Vietnam War and made famous by Norman Mailer's book *Armies of the Night*. Scott said, "50,000 howling mobsters bent on destruction and obscenities, engaged a U.S. Army contingent of 6,000 men and literally scores of U.S. Marshals in a two-day battle. . . . The rest of the world was aghast at this polishing of the Ugly American image. But surely, there must have been joy in Hippie-land. The courts, at all levels, must share the blame for this kind of lawlessness. They have perverted the constitutional right to petition for redress of wrongs by extending this right to license sit-ins, lie-ins, love-ins, study-ins, campus sit-ins, and engage in rioting, looting and arson. Some misguided erstwhile leaders call such acts civil disobedience. I call it law-breaking—bordering on sedition."

Scott also criticized academic institutions for their relationships with the black power movement. First, he blasted the University of North Carolina at Chapel Hill for hiring Howard Fuller as a part-time lecturer. "I believe it to be a glaring lack of such academic responsibility when a college or university employs a faculty member—fulltime or part-time—who is widely believed to be an advocate of black power," he said. After the speech, Scott told reporters that Fuller should be fired. He also attacked a "black power forum" held at the University of North Carolina at Greensboro in November that was sponsored by the National Student Association. "I believe it wrong for a college or university campus to be used as a forum of black power advocates—where they make such statements as 'No black person should be fighting in Vietnam.'"[71]

Afterward, Bob Scott received some of the worst press reviews of his political career. The *Charlotte Observer* said Scott had "invaded segregationist country" and told them what they wanted to hear.

Both the tone and content of what was billed as a major position paper Tuesday suggested that the heir of progressive W. Kerr Scott has reached one or both of these conclusions in the formulation of his strategy: Most of the more liberal Democrats and Negroes belong to Scott because they won't have anywhere else to go in next spring's primary. He has kissed them off as inconsequential factors in the election and decided to direct his pitch to ultra-conservatives and the racist-minded among us. Those of us who remember the late W. Kerr Scott admired him for his courage in saying the right things about issues in all parts of the state. In the case of his particular speech, we cannot apply the old adage, "Like father, like son."[72]

The *Greensboro Daily News* wrote:

It is obvious that the 1968 election, from the White House to the local precinct, will be among the most turbulent and divisive in American history. It is an ugly frustrating time for all Americans, fighting as they are an unwanted war in faraway Asia while they sense an ominous disruption of their own social fabric that cries for attention. It would be understandable if Scott was underdog or if he came from the Lake wing of the Democratic Party. But the fact is that Mr. Scott is neither an underdog nor a Lake protégé, and that makes his self-indulgent speech at Dunn all the more remarkable. He is in fact acknowledged to enjoy perhaps the most commanding lead a candidate for governor has enjoyed in recent decades. . . . Bob Scott ought to be using his commanding position to talk sense to the people of North Carolina, not whetting mobbism.[73]

Scott did win plaudits in some quarters. "In every possible way," said Jesse Helms, "it was excellent." He suggested that Scott had become wiser since the days when he "was a member of Lyndon Johnson's campaign team in 1964 when Mr. Johnson was lining up a tidal wave of bloc votes that inundated Barry Goldwater."[74]

Helms later remarked, "It may well be that Mr. Scott won the election that evening."[75]

9 ★ 1968

That would be like separating ham hocks and collard greens or biscuits and red-eye gravy. It just can't be done. We haven't got politics out of the church yet, let alone government. —Bob Scott on his opponent's proposal to remove politics from government, News and Observer, *October 15, 1968*

Twenty years after his father had run for governor, Bob Scott faced a much-changed political geography. In 1948, North Carolina was part of the Solid South—where elections were determined in the Democratic primary, where Republicans were largely inconsequential, and where black voters were still a minority mainly controlled by white politicians. By 1968, North Carolina had become a two-party state with a rapidly expanding Republican Party and an impatient black community flexing its growing political muscle.

But political geography wasn't the only difference between 1948 and 1968: whereas Kerr Scott had started his gubernatorial campaign as the outside challenger, his son began as the insider favorite. Bob Scott spent four years as lieutenant governor cultivating an image as a moderate and assembling a coalition that cut across Democratic Party factional lines—from white rural segregationists to moderate downtown bankers to black political leaders. "Kerr was a rebel against the establishment," said Uncle Ralph. "Robert had a much easier time getting into the governor's mansion." The closest thing to a Kerr Scott–type rebel going up against the establishment in the 1960s, Uncle Ralph said, was Lake, the two-time segregationist candidate.[1] Interestingly, Scott faced his most difficult challenge in the fall election against the Republican candidate Gardner, not in the Democratic primary when he ran against conservative former party chairman J. Melville Broughton Jr. and Reginald Hawkins, the state's first serious African American gubernatorial candidate. The 1968 North Carolina gubernatorial election would be one of the last gasps of the conservative wing of the Democratic Party before it morphed into the Republican Party.

But the 1948 and 1968 elections did share some similarities. In both years, the southern Democrats were saddled with an unpopular presidential nominee—Harry Truman in 1948 and Hubert Humphrey in 1968. And in both years, independent Dixiecrat-type presidential efforts tapped into the white backlash against civil rights—Strom Thurmond in 1948 and George Wallace in 1968.

In part to mitigate election losses related to white backlash, Scott stumped under the moderate image he cultivated as lieutenant governor. On the campaign trail, he called for the creation of a kindergarten program, raising teacher salaries to the national average, increasing state employee salaries by 10 percent, improving substandard housing, upgrading vocational education, and raising per capita income. He wanted to "let some fresh air into the carpeted, paneled offices in the ivory tower of the Highway Building."[2] But much of the campaign focused on law-and-order issues—and played to white conservatives—as racial unrest grew, antiwar protests spread on the college campuses, and the push for school integration caused white resentment. Scott championed the freedom of choice plan, which allowed parents to choose the schools to which they would send their children—and which had left North Carolina's schools still largely segregated in 1968. He also opposed the proposed Fair Housing Act of 1968, which banned discrimination of the rental or sale of housing by race, saying, "The North Carolina way has worked and will continue to do so." When asked about race, Scott replied, "My policy toward the Negro is this: They are citizens of North Carolina, no more and no less."[3]

Although Scott ran as a law-and-order candidate, he tempered his remarks by saying that the state needed to tackle the problems of inadequate housing and a lack of jobs that helped breed crime and violence. He called for establishing a department of urban affairs and housing to help address the problems of the urban areas. "There is much to be done on the preventive side of the problem of maintaining law and order," Scott said. "We need to give close attention to the ills of our society. While maintaining law and order, we should get to the root causes of the ills."[4]

While Scott did his best to sure up his political right, a Scott was still a Scott—and therefore not to be trusted by what remained of the Democratic Party's Old Guard. His conservative primary challenger, Broughton, was a forty-six-year-old Raleigh attorney who shared certain similarities with Scott: both were sons of a former governor and U.S. senator. The younger Broughton had been chairman of the Highway Commission under Hodges. Ever since Moore had appointed him state Democratic chairman in 1964, there had been speculation of a Scott-Broughton primary. But while credentialed, Broughton seemed a reluctant candidate, a shy and an awkward

The 1968 gubernatorial candidates. From left, Reginald Hawkins, J. Melville Broughton, Bob Scott, John W. Stickley, and Jim Gardner. (Hugh Morton Photographs and Films, North Carolina Collection, University of North Carolina at Chapel Hill Library)

man who found small talk with voters difficult and made an "an awful candidate," according to his consultant Grady Jeffreys.[5] But more importantly, the conservative wing of the Democratic Party was shrinking as conservatives shifted to the Republican Party. By 1970, Broughton himself would become a Republican.

If Broughton were to win the nomination, he would have to be the aggressor, raising doubts about the front-runner. To do so, Broughton campaigned with Lake, now a state supreme court justice, at his side, and cast Scott as a liberal.[6] "I am a moderate-conservative," Broughton said. "Unlike my two liberal opponents, I do not believe in change just for the sake of change. . . . I believe we can have progress without taxing ourselves into the poor house [if] we maintain the sound principles of fiscal responsibility and integrity that have guided our state for many years. I believe our cities should not have to fear the torch every summer, I believe that businessmen should not have to worry about their stores and businesses being burned and looted by criminals. I believe that white and black can live together in harmony if we rid ourselves once and for all of the small minority who preach and practice lawlessness."[7]

If Broughton represented the Democratic Party's past, Reginald Hawkins, a forty-four-year-old dentist, minister, and civil rights activist from Charlotte, represented its future. During the 1950s and 1960s, Hawkins had been an aggressive organizer for improving the plight of black people. He founded the Mecklenburg Organization for Political Affairs (MOPA) and led picketing and boycotts to break down segregation. He took on the Charlotte school system, the state's white doctors and dentists, the YMCA, segregated hotels and restaurants, election officials, county health departments, and even leaders of antipoverty programs. His house was one of those belonging to four civil rights leaders that were firebombed in Charlotte on November 22, 1965. The bomb meant for Hawkins's house hit a tree branch and failed to do much damage. Hawkins emerged from his home with a rifle, but his wife dissuaded him from shooting the getaway car.[8]

By 1968, blacks had begun winning office across the country—mainly mayoral races such as Carl Stokes in Cleveland and Richard Hatcher in Gary, Indiana. Although a black governor in the United States was still years in the future, Hawkins hoped to use his candidacy to broaden black voter registration following Congress's passage of the Voting Rights Act of 1965. At the beginning of the primary, North Carolina had 277,000 registered black voters, composing about 15 percent of the Democratic electorate. Hawkins estimated that 200,000 would vote for him, giving him enough votes to swing the election in a runoff and play a similar role to Lake in the 1964 Democratic primary gubernatorial primary. To create excitement around his candidacy, Hawkins used his slogan, "tel-a-negro," to denote his poor people's strategy of campaigning in the streets. He called himself "the ink in the milk" of the primary.[9] Yet he suffered from a lack of campaign funds and also from charges that he had mishandled money in his dental practice. In that instance, the state board of dental examiners charged Hawkins with malpractice for his work for Project Head Start children in Charlotte in 1966. He was accused of not completing needed work. He later blamed his conviction—after the primary—on "racial bigots" out to get him.[10]

A statewide internal Scott-funded survey in February 1968 by pollster John F. Kraft found Scott with 48 percent of the vote, Broughton with 14 percent, Hawkins with 10 percent, and 28 percent uncertain. Scott's middle-of-the-road strategy seemed to be working: both Moore (70 percent) and Scott (71 percent) had high approval ratings, although people had a hard time articulating why they liked him. Scott had his most reliable support in rural areas (68 percent approval), but he polled poorly in the cities (35 percent approval) and among newcomers to the state (27 percent)—all of which suggested that he continued to benefit from his father's Branchhead Boy appeal.[11] "Scott represented the rural interests," said Lauch Faircloth, a Scott supporter, said. "You have to realize there were still hundreds of thousands of farmers. They were beginning to exit pretty fast. But at that point North Carolina was still the king of small farmers. Scott could only do it because of his heritage. His father was so closely related to roads. Bob Scott was a good candidate. He had what is known, as the Marine Corps uses the term, command presence. He made a good speech. At that point, Bob was big and strong and very impressive, big deep voice, spoke well. Bob was confident."[12] Scott was also by far the most experienced candidate, and he had majority, but not overwhelming, support among African Americans.

Voters would choose their next governor in an increasingly polarized environment. The Vietnam War continued to drag on, with American troop levels reaching their highest deployment and casualty levels in 1968 and with the Viet Cong's Tet offensive in January raising new doubts about the progress of the war. The war created restiveness on college campuses, where many students were both opposed to the war and worried about the military draft. Protesters greeted recruiters for Dow Chemical, the manufacturer of Napalm, used by the U.S. military in Vietnam, when they arrived at Duke University and the University of North Carolina at Chapel Hill in February and March. In Chapel Hill, fifteen people were arrested when they tried to block the Dow recruiters.[13] In April, three hundred students at Fayetteville State Teachers College took over the administration building for two days to protest poor conditions at the historically black campus. This mirrored the national situation. Between January and June, there were 221 significant demonstrations involving nearly forty thousand students at 101 colleges.[14]

The upheaval was not limited to the college campuses. Most North Carolina secondary and elementary schools had undergone only token racial integration in 1968, and tempers were rising as school officials faced new pressure from the federal government, the courts, and lawsuits. Scott criticized boycotts conducted by black students in Wadesboro, Hillsborough, and Edenton to oppose poor conditions in their schools, the slow speed of integration, or the unequal treatment black schools were receiving under desegregation plans.[15]

North Carolina's black communities were tinder boxes, too. Paul Wellstone, a graduate student at the University of North Carolina and a future U.S. senator from Minnesota, interviewed 175 black residents in Durham in 1968. Unemployment in the black neighborhoods stood at 18 percent compared to a national rate of 3.5 percent, and 85 percent of the families were living under poverty conditions. Wellstone described those he interviewed as "frustrated, resentful and willing to resort to violence to achieve the social and political change which they hope will improve their lives."[16] A twenty-six-year-old woman told him, "I am sick and tired of talking and getting nothing accomplished. The black has got to get out here in the street and show the white man that he is not going to take it anymore. Only by taking to the streets can we make the white man wake up."[17]

In March, civil rights leader Martin Luther King Jr. announced that he would spend April 4 touring the state and campaigning for Hawkins. But King canceled the North Carolina trip to return to Memphis to support striking garbage workers. On April 4, King was assassinated. As in the rest of the country, King's murder tripped an explosion of pent-up anger in the black community, with fire bombings, arson, looting, and sniper fire across the state.[18] Forty-eight North Carolina towns and cities were in "a state of crisis," according to a report prepared for the governor. In eight cities, Governor Moore sent in the highway patrol to help overwhelmed local police restore order. In six of those cities, 4,300 National Guard soldiers were dispatched—1,300 in Raleigh, 1,000 in Greensboro, 800 in Wilmington, 600 in Wilson, 500 in Durham, and 100 in Goldsboro. There were 1,791 arrests and 151 fires.[19]

After the riots, Broughton took a hard line and said that if he were governor he would have arrested the "hoodlums." He said that police had the right to shoot looters and rioters, and he proposed a special session of the legislature to strengthen antiriot and anticrime laws, something Moore declined to do.[20] Scott praised Moore's handling of the crisis. "We don't have licenses to steal in North Carolina," Scott said. "As governor I will make every effort to protect life and property, both public and private."[21] For his part, Hawkins said that the prime responsibility of law enforcement was to protect people, not property: "Our enemy is persistent and pervasive racism and poverty created by the leadership of our state, against which the riots are an anguished and self-wounding protest."[22]

Scott fell short of winning a majority (48.8 percent) in the May primary as Broughton managed to partially close the gap (32.3 percent) and Hawkins made major inroads (18.7 percent) with his support in the black community. Despite being a flawed candidate, Hawkins's ability to gain 18 percent changed the political game. It showed not only the growing strength of the black electorate but their willingness to support an African American candidate. "Dr. Hawkins has altered gubernatorial politics in North Carolina," Vernon E. Jordan, the head of the Southern Regional Council and a future adviser to presidents, said two years later in a Raleigh speech. "His candidacy was a new phenomenon and it had made a difference in the political strategies in the state."[23]

Broughton faced the decision whether to call for a runoff. Late in the campaign, he had brought into his campaign Tom Ellis, a Raleigh attorney and conservative hard-liner who had worked in Willis Smith's 1950 Senate campaign and would later become a key strategist for Jesse Helms. Ellis helped draft an election night statement with strong racial overtones. Others in the Broughton camp urged a more moderate course and questioned whether he should in fact call for a runoff.[24]

While still weighing a decision early on election night, Broughton lashed out at Scott: "We know who has sought the votes of the militant minorities. We know who has appealed to the persons of goodwill of all races. We belong to the latter group. . . . Mel Broughton would rather not be governor at all than to owe his victory to militant pressure groups." But he stopped short of calling for a runoff.[25] The election night statement prompted fears of a racially divisive runoff that would split the party for the fall. Scott thought that Broughton's statement was "very vicious" and "smacked of racism" but held his tongue. Behind the scenes, Moore privately urged Broughton, his former state party chairman, not to call for a second primary. The Scott campaign also pressured Broughton through county party chairs and Broughton fund raisers. Two conservative Democrats friendly to Scott, Raleigh banker Lewis "Snow" Holding and Superior Court Judge Pou Bailey, also met privately with Broughton.[26]

Through a series of negotiations between the principles and their key supporters, Scott agreed to hold a series of joint fund raisers aimed at helping Broughton retire his $148,000 campaign debt as well as his own $50,000 campaign debt and at finding a place for his supporters in his campaign and administration. For the first time since 1940 that there would be no gubernatorial runoff—a reflection that the real action had shifted to the general election. Broughton was among Scott's first visitors as governor, bringing with him a list of key backers that Broughton hoped would be appointed to boards and commissions. Scott also appointed Moore to the state supreme court.[27]

Helms, among others, viewed Broughton's endorsement of Scott with skepticism. His friend and poker buddy Tom Ellis had been preparing for a bare-knuckles, racially loaded runoff. Now nothing. Helms called Broughton's decision "curious": "Throughout the campaign, he emphatically drew a line between what he has called the liberalism of Robert Scott and his own declared philosophies of government. He made clear, at that early Sunday morning hour that the candidates, and their supporters on both sides, were clearly identifiable by present associations and past activities. And he declared, amid the cheers of his supporters, that he would rather not be governor at all than to owe his election to those who he said would have an improper influence and an undesired effect on the best interests of the state."[28]

REPUBLICANS

While Scott captured the Democratic primary, Gardner reinvented the state Republican Party by patching together the traditional western Republicans and suburbanites and joining them with disaffected rural white Democrats who were angered by the civil rights movement, the growing social programs of Lyndon Johnson's Great Society program, the counterculture, and the protests against the Vietnam War.

Before 1964, Republicans nominated their candidates in a convention, but Gardner faced the first GOP gubernatorial primary in North Carolina. His major opponent was Jack Stickley, a sixty-five-year-old textile manufacturer making his first run for political office. Stickley had the backing of the state's two Republican congressmen, Charles Jonas and Jim Broyhill, state GOP chairman Jim Holshouser, and former GOP gubernatorial candidate Robert Gavin. The demographics favored Stickley: 50 percent of the GOP's registration was in the piedmont, 35 percent was in the west, and only 15 percent was in Gardner's base, the east. But none of that mattered. A Democratic poll conducted in November 1967 found Gardner, a rising political star in his party, leading Stickley by a 40 to 13 percent margin with 47 percent undecided.

Kraft, the Democratic pollster, in a memo to Scott wrote that Gardner spelled potential trouble for the Democrats. "Gardner strikes people as new, progressive, active and a change. These are the kind of qualities that could persuade a Democrat to vote for Gardner rather than the Democrat Scott, who he has heard of, but not much. Scott must not relax and figure that because Gardner is so far behind a year before the election, Scott doesn't have to push himself."[29]

Both Gardner and Stickley commended Moore for his handling of the violence following King's assassination. Gardner expressed "outrage that this country has to deal with the a second front at home against rioters and beatniks when its fighting men are risking death overseas." He said those who engage in looting or destruction of property "should be met with massive force if necessary to stop the riots." He said that the problems in the ghettos had been greatly exaggerated and that civil rights leaders need to talk more about responsibilities of their race. "They must meet us half way," Gardner asserted.[30]

When not talking about law and order, Gardner took some surprisingly progressive positions. He called for creating a statewide kindergarten, gradually raising teacher salaries to the national average, lowering the voting age from twenty-one to eighteen, offering more job security for teachers, and establishing new community colleges. Even on labor unions, he did not take a hard line. Gardner said that in plants where the majority of employees voted for a union, the nonunion workers ought to make a pro rata contribution to the cost of union representation at the bargaining table. Stickley accused him of playing both sides of the right-to-work issue.[31] Gardner beat Stickley by a 3–1 margin.

PRESIDENTIAL RACE

As the two parties were choosing their gubernatorial nominees, two Frank Porter Graham followers—Terry Sanford and Allard Lowenstein—were headed in different directions in the 1968 presidential race.

Four years out of governor's mansion, Sanford was looking to move into national politics. He had considered challenging conservative Senator Sam Ervin Jr. in a Democratic primary in 1968 but decided against it, saying it would be too divisive.[32] Instead, Sanford met in the White House on March 31, 1968, with Johnson's top political advisers and agreed to manage the president's reelection campaign. That evening, Sanford flew back to North Carolina only to learn that LBJ had gone on national television and shocked the country by announcing that he would not seek reelection.

It is unlikely that Johnson would have made his announcement had it not been for the work of two former University of North Carolina students, Lowenstein and Curtis Gans, both sons of New York City area immigrants, who had met in 1957 in Chapel Hill. Gans was an undergraduate while Lowenstein, an older army veteran, was a graduate student counselor for the athletics department. Both were active in liberal causes. Gans aided the student lunch counter sit-ins, provided strategy and cash for bail, and helped place expelled students in other colleges. Lowenstein ran Gans's campaign to be editor of the *Daily Tar Heel*, the student newspaper. Lowenstein also became a Senate aide to Graham, worked as an assistant to Eleanor Roosevelt, became president of the National Student Association, worked in the dangerous voter registration campaigns in Mississippi, and became involved in a wide variety of other liberal causes.

As the Vietnam War dragged on, both Lowenstein and Gans looked for ways to bring political pressure to end it. In April 1967, the two young men began what became known as the Dump Johnson movement, which they ran out of Gans's Capitol Hill townhouse. Gans and Lowenstein traveled to forty-eight states in three months, organizing and concentrating their efforts on the early primary states of Minnesota, New Hampshire, and Wisconsin, as well as New York and California.

They first tried unsuccessfully to recruit New York senator Robert F. Kennedy before convincing Minnesota senator Eugene McCarthy to run. On March 12, McCarthy received 42.2 percent of the vote in the New Hampshire. LBJ, stunned by the strong showing and looking at poor polling numbers in upcoming states such as Wisconsin, announced on March 31 that he would not seek reelection.[33]

The Democratic Party was in disarray as summer approached. McCarthy's antiwar candidacy had prompted Robert Kennedy to join the fray, splitting the antiwar vote. Kennedy's assassination in Los Angeles on June 6, 1968, on the same evening he won the California primary, unnerved the party. A few days later, two thousand people attended the state Democratic convention in Raleigh, where the delegates chose Moore as the favorite-son candidate in a move widely seen as an effort to hold the state's delegates for Vice President Hubert Humphrey, the establishment candidate. Then Reginald Hawkins led a walkout of about 200 delegates to protest the defeat of a resolution requiring that 25 percent of the delegates to the national convention be African American. Of the 131-member delegation, only 8—or 6 percent—were black. Hawkins and his supporters took the challenge to the Democratic National Committee's Credentials Committee in Chicago in a nationally televised hearing, but the committee voted to seat the regular delegation without further review.[34]

In Chicago, Scott, now the Democratic nominee, did everything he could to keep his head down, avoiding association with Humphrey or with the street violence that unfolded before TV audiences between antiwar protesters and Mayor Richard Daley's Chicago police. Scott seconded the nomination for president of Moore, who became North Carolina's first favorite-son candidate. On the first ballot, all fifty-nine of North Carolina's votes went to Moore. On the final ballot, twelve North Carolina delegates stuck with Moore, including Scott, allowing him to say that he never voted to nominate Humphrey.[35]

Sanford hoped to be named Humphrey's vice presidential running mate. A four-page analysis of Sanford's worth as vice presidential choice was circulated to selected leaders, and a Sanford headquarters was set up in Chicago's Blackstone Hotel. But Humphrey chose Maine senator Edmund Muskie as his running mate. The episode left hard feelings among the Sanford people when Scott expressed a lack of enthusiasm for Sanford as a vice presidential pick. Scott said that he had "no strong feelings one way or another on the subject," adding that he thought the pro-Sanford movement was coming from outside North Carolina.[36] Meanwhile, Scott gave Humphrey a tepid endorsement, not even mentioning his name. "This is a pledge that every candidate running for office has to sign," Scott said of his endorsement of the ticket. "I signed it. I will honor that pledge."[37]

Sanford got over his disappointment. When Humphrey called him, Sanford agreed to manage a campaign that appeared to be in shambles after the disastrous, strife-torn Chicago convention. Sanford and a few of his top advisers, including Bert Bennett, moved to Washington to take charge of the Citizens for Humphrey-Muskie Committee. This helped Sanford to make key contacts across the country for a future presidential bid, just as managing Kerr Scott's 1954 Senate campaign had enabled him to build a future organization to run for governor.

In early August, the Republicans convened in Miami Beach, where former vice president Richard M. Nixon was heavily favored to capture the nomination over New York governor Nelson Rockefeller. Gardner headed a delegation, although officially uncommitted, that was expected to vote unanimously for Nixon. In January, Gardner, along with thirty-six other House members, had urged Nixon to enter the presidential race, and in March they endorsed him.[38] But Ronald Reagan, in his second year as California governor, had been traveling around the country, exploring a potential presidential bid. As governor, Reagan won cheers on the right with his crackdown on student protesters at Berkeley and his spending cuts on education, health, and social programs. Reagan, with his ringing speech for Goldwater in 1964, had made a strong impression among southern conservatives.

A week before the convention, Reagan appeared in Winston-Salem at a fundraiser for Gardner, where he met with many delegates to the GOP convention—his fourth fundraiser for Gardner. Not only was Gardner impressed by Reagan and his views, but a pro-Reagan push was part of a southern effort to strengthen its bargaining position with Nixon on civil rights. The opening day of the convention, Reagan announced his candidacy, and Gardner switched his allegiance from Nixon to Reagan. Gardner seconded Reagan's nomination and led the North Carolina delegation to vote 16 to 9 in favor of Reagan over Nixon.[39] In the end, the convention nominated Nixon, a Duke University law school graduate, with 692 votes—just 25 more than he needed to be nominated on the first ballot. Rockefeller came in second with 277 votes, and Reagan third with 182. It would take two more tries for Reagan to finally win the nomination in 1980.

Credit Gardner with seeing the future of the Republican Party and the conservative movement. But in the short run, it caused him major problems and quite possibly cost him the gubernatorial election. Gardner's candidate-hopping made him seem opportunistic, which alienated many traditional Republicans located in the state's GOP piedmont and western heartlands. "That really came back and bit me in Mecklenburg County among Republicans," Gardner recalled. "I would run into situations, where I would go out and give a speech and there would be a Nixon man in that area and he would have a Bob Scott for Governor button on."[40]

THE GENERAL ELECTION

Scott opened the general election season in August with internal polls showing him leading Gardner by a 48 to 37 percent margin, with 15 percent undecided. Kraft, the Scott pollster, warned that Gardner "could become a real threat."[41]

The presidential race presented a political landmine for the gubernatorial candidates—mainly because of former Alabama governor George Wallace, who had gained national attention as the die-hard segregationist who stood in the schoolhouse door trying to block the desegregation of the University of Alabama. Ineligible to seek reelection in 1966, Wallace convinced Alabama voters to elect his wife, Lurleen, as the state's chief executive. With the rise of black militancy and the spread of race riots, Wallace in 1967 launched a presidential campaign on the American Independent

Party ticket, picking up support both in the South and among working-class whites in the North.

In North Carolina in August, the presidential contest was a three-cornered hat with Nixon at 29 percent, Wallace at 27 percent, Humphrey at 26 percent, and 18 percent uncertain, according to Scott's internal polls. Both Scott and Gardner needed Wallace voters to win. For Scott that meant wooing many of the old Branchhead Boys and their children who were now backing Wallace. But Gardner needed Wallace supporters just as much, because he was counting on a strong showing in the tobacco country of eastern North Carolina, a Wallace stronghold. According to the polling, the Wallacites were split between Scott (43 percent) and Gardner (46 percent).[42]

In August, the Scott campaign mailed four to five thousand three-sheet flyers to Wallace supporters across the state. The literature included a quotation from Gardner: "I don't see where anyone voting for Wallace is accomplishing anything." A cartoon from the *Greensboro Daily News* on the back of one sheet depicted a farm truck bouncing along the road with two stickers: one reading "Wallace for President" and other reading "Scott for Governor." Other sheets included Scott's positions on law and order and school integration. On the campaign trail, Scott did little to discourage support from Wallacites. Stopping at the Onslow County courthouse, Bucky Bynum asked Scott: "I'm a George Wallace man and I can't vote for both of you, can I?" Replied Scott, "Yes you can. I'm not running against him."[43]

While Scott courted Wallace voters, he kept his distance from Humphrey. When the vice president campaigned in Charlotte, Miss Mary was the only Scott to welcome him in the state with a telegram. That prompted a *News and Observer* editorial comparing Scott to a mugwump. "The mugwump is that bird of politics who perches on the fence, mug one side and wump on the other, unable to decide where to light. This is Bob Scott's position in the presidential race."[44]

Gardner at least showed up when Nixon appeared at a rally at Greensboro Coliseum on October 16, although he was treated frostily—Nixon heaped praise on the local congressional candidate, not Gardner, and Gardner did not introduce the GOP presidential nominee.[45] Returning to Wallace country the next day in the eastern town of Burgaw, Gardner said: "I don't disagree with Mr. Wallace on anything he says." In the Burgaw speech, Gardner said, "That's [Wallace] the best thing I've got going for me. I am like George Wallace in every respect."[46] The Wallace praise continued as the Gardner campaign printed and distributed "Gardner-

Wallace" bumper stickers. They also distributed literature showing Democrats Ed Muskie and Hubert Humphrey with blacks. One showed Muskie and his wife with three white children and one black child. It read: "Meet the Muskies."[47] In response, the Wallace camp issued a statement that both campaigns were trying to ride Wallace's coattails but that Wallace was supporting neither candidate.[48]

The Nixon camp, meanwhile, was doing everything it could to convince conservatives to vote for Nixon. In 1948, Strom Thurmond began his third-party Dixiecrat presidential run in North Carolina to protest Truman's civil rights policies. Twenty years later, the Nixon campaign sent Thurmond into eastern North Carolina to rally conservatives for the Republican ticket. In New Bern, Thurmond said that a vote "for the third-party candidate would mean a vote for Humphrey," never mentioning Wallace by name. As to Humphrey, Thurmond said, "I think he is a socialist at heart."[49]

Wooing Wallace supporters engendered risks for both candidates: Gardner alienated some Nixon backers, and Scott angered some liberals, particularly the state's three hundred thousand registered African American voters. Black leaders complained privately that Scott wasn't reaching out to former Hawkins supporters after the primary and that this could cost him black support. Then Hawkins withheld his endorsement of Scott and openly hinted that he might back Gardner. Golden Frinks, the state coordinator for the Southern Christian Leadership Conference (SCLC), the civil rights organization of Martin Luther King Jr., offered to back Gardner to show his displeasure with Scott's cozying up to Wallace. Gardner rejected both offers, saying that Frinks's overture was a ploy cooked up by the Scott organization to link him to black voters. He said that he wanted the support of "decent, law-abiding citizens, but I don't want the support of any militant groups, particularly groups led by Golden Frinks."[50]

Scott did what he could to cater to the political right, with tough talk about maintaining law and order. He also visited a Georgia army base to witness antiriot training, and he accused Wake Opportunities, Inc., Raleigh's main antipoverty program, of asking for salary kickbacks from its employees to purchase weapons and turning black culture classes into meetings meant to incite violence. He offered no proof, saying that he wanted to protect the confidentiality of his informant. An investigation by the State Bureau of Investigation found no violations of the law or misuse of money. Scott simply shrugged and said that the SBI had "cleared up some points I felt should have been cleared up." An investigation by the national Office of Economic Opportunity also found no wrongdoing. But

Scott got the headlines he had desired. Eugene Toton, the executive director of Wake Opportunities, resigned in May 1969, saying that Scott's baseless attacks had crippled his effectiveness.[51]

Even so, Scott's opponents tried to tag him as an integrationist. The "Committee for Truth" ran a full-page ad in the *News and Observer*, suggesting that Scott had not done enough to fight school integration. The headline read, "WHERE WAS BOB SCOTT WHEN HEW GAINED CONTROL OF OUR SCHOOLS?"[52] The Scott forces were playing the same game. A pro-Scott group, called "Committee for Truth in Government," distributed a flyer that asserted: "IF JIM GARDNER HAD BEEN ON THE JOB; Freedom of Choice—Instead of Federal Desegregation Guidelines—Could Be The Law of the Land." The flyer said that thirty-six school systems in North Carolina now operated under federal court order or had been placed on deferred status by the Department of Health, Education, and Welfare (HEW). It said that North Carolina's delegation, minus one—Jim Gardner, who was absent—voted to curb HEW power.[53] By the end of the campaign, the N.C. Council on Human Relations criticized both Scott and Gardner for their emphasis on law and order, saying they were ignoring justice.[54]

But along with his law-and-order talk, Scott tempered his remarks. "Racism has no place in North Carolina," he said. "There will be no forgotten people in North Carolina. Under my administration, we're not going to divide our party by geography, race or any other way."[55]

Gardner had hoped to run against Lyndon Johnson and the Great Society—his two favorite targets as a congressman. But LBJ had foiled that plan by not running for reelection. Instead, Gardner did his best to tie Scott to Humphrey and to Sanford. Gardner noted that Scott had worked for Sanford in his 1960 governor's race and been named by Sanford to three state commissions. "In 1964," Gardner declared, "my opponent was the handpicked candidate of the Sanford-Bennett liberal wing of the Democrat Party. After the 1964 primary, my opponent was named Chairman of Rural Americans for Johnson-Humphrey. Now he claims to be for Governor Moore—period. Three weeks ago, Scott praised Sanford as a good vice presidential candidate, saying he had many nationwide contacts in education fields."[56]

Gardner ran a modern campaign, relying on a crisp, Kennedyesque speaking style, public relations experts, TV advertising, and his background as a rising business tycoon. Jim Gardner portrayed himself as a change agent who would end years of Democratic rule, bringing a new professionalism to state government. "It is time that our government is no longer run by professional politicians, political hacks, and party retreads," Gardner said. "I am not a politician and that is precisely why I ask for your support."[57] But Scott said that this was asking the impossible. "That would be like separating ham hocks and collard greens or biscuits and red eye gravy," Scott said. "It just can't be done. We haven't got politics out of the church yet, let alone government."[58] As the folksy son of a governor, Scott provided a reasonably good foil as a symbol of old-time Democratic politics that spoke more of the farm and country stores and less of the corporate boardrooms. "The Scott style of campaigning has been strongly built on personal contact," wrote Jack Childs, a *News and Observer* writer. "If he has secret weapon, it's his father's image. 'You don't have to tell a Scott from Haw River about roads,' he says and the audiences applaud."[59]

Bob Scott's campaign operated in an anything-goes era, even though state campaign finance laws had been on the books since 1933 and, among other things, banned corporate contributions. But the laws were widely regarded as a sham, with violation a misdemeanor—not that there had ever been a prosecution. Secretary of State Thad Eure, the supposed regulator, mainly sent letters asking candidates to send in reports. Scott and his campaign were no exception to the loose laws: they accepted numerous offers from businesses, particularly the free use of company planes, helicopters, and pilots. There were so many free flight offers that the Scott campaign had a state map showing the location of all the planes available to them at each airport. State senator John J. Burney Jr., a Wilmington attorney, gave the Scott campaign a telephone credit card and a gasoline credit card. In August, campaign manager Roy Sowers sent out a memo to key supporters asking them to contact "car dealers, gasoline dealers, department stores, soft drink and beer distributors, furniture and appliance dealers, etc.," and ask them to donate billboard space for which the Scott campaign would provide the billboard posters. Scott didn't even pay for his campaign polls; those were commissioned by the Tar Heel Electric Membership Association in Raleigh and passed along to Ben Roney.[60] When a newspaper pointed out that Scott had taken more than $4,000 in donations from a Franklin campaign breakfast but not reported it, Attorney General Robert Morgan shrugged his shoulders. "I think it's probably common knowledge that the Corrupt Practices Act has been loosely enforced and complied with in past years by all the candidates, all the way from the courthouse on up," Morgan said.[61]

Most acknowledged that the campaign reports—when eventually filed—showed only a fraction of the contributions and expenditures. Corporations paid handsome bonuses to executives, who in turn made contributions to candidates. Companies put secretaries, aides, and public relations assistants to work on campaigns. Company credit cards, automobiles, airplanes, and business equipment were put at the candidate's disposal to buy gasoline and meals and rent hotel rooms. None of this ever showed up on campaign reports. At the time, insiders estimated that the 1968 campaign for governor probably cost Bob Scott and Jim Gardner more than $600,000 each—far more than what was reported.[62] "We were still dealing with big cash money in Scott's campaign," said Lauch Faircloth, a major Scott fund raiser, recalling the days when contributions arrived as cash in brown paper bags. "At that point, big blocks of cash money were floating around."[63] Gardner agreed that politics was a wide-open affair back in 1968. "That was the way politics operated back in those days," Gardner said. He recalled getting a call from an unnamed banker who asked him to swing by the office at 8:00 P.M.—presumably so that no one could see him—to give his campaign $1,000 in $100 bills ($7,171 in 2018 dollars), all off the books. Gardner said that the banker, a Democrat, wanted Gardner to win but didn't wish to alienate the Democrats in control.[64]

Gardner was one of the first candidates in North Carolina to campaign against the news media—something that would become a common tactic among conservatives in future years. He often excluded reporters from events, calling them "left-wing rags" and "the liberal pro-Democratic press." He sometimes left traveling reporters stranded at airports and rallies without transportation and often refused to disclose his campaign plans. "We're going to pave the street all the way to the governor's mansion with every one of them," Gardner said. All of the state's larger newspapers endorsed Scott.[65]

Although the race was closer than the Scott campaign would have preferred, internal polling continued to show him with an eleven-point lead in mid-October.[66] Near the end of the campaign, the racial cues became more explicit. Scott showed reporters one unsigned handbill that featured a photograph of Humphrey kissing a black girl with the caption "sloppy kiss." Another handout showed a photograph of Scott with Reginald Hawkins; Mel Broughton had been cropped out.[67] Meanwhile, Scott's courting of Wallace voters continued to cause him problems in the black community. Several prominent activists such as Howard Fuller and Golden Frinks advised African Americans to sit out the gubernatorial election. Hawkins did not endorse in the governor's race until October 30 and then did not mention Scott's name, saying that he backed the entire Democratic ticket "from the White House to the courthouse." Scott downplayed the endorsement, saying that Hawkins was just living up to his commitment as a Democratic candidate to support his party's nominee. Gardner responded by saying: "Under my administration this state is not going to be controlled by the blacks, the radicals, nor the white liberals, but will be controlled and run for the benefit of all the people of this state."[68]

Whereas Scott downplayed the Hawkins endorsement, he made sure that everyone knew about another semi-endorsement. A few days before the election, Scott received the blessing of the Reverend Billy Graham, the famous evangelist whom *Time* magazine had once dubbed "the Pope of Protestant America." Graham, a North Carolina native, was closer to Nixon than any other political figure—a decades-long friendship that began when North Carolina senator Clyde Hoey introduced the two in 1952 in Washington.[69] Scott had first met Graham years earlier during his father's administration when the evangelist was in Raleigh to lead a prayer breakfast. Graham had spent the previous night as a guest in the executive mansion, and that morning, Bob Scott had stumbled into an upstairs family room and found Graham kneeling in prayer before going down to speak.[70]

In the fall of 1968, Graham invited Bob Scott to tea at the Biltmore Country Club, where Graham told reporters that he had voted early and had split his ticket. He swung a golf club that he noted had been given to him by his friend Nixon. He would not say how he split his ticket, but he said that reporters could guess. "I am determined not to get involved in local politics or endorse any political candidate," Graham said. "But I do have a great warm spot in my heart for the Scott family. I asked Bob to come up and see me when he could. When he said he could come today, I asked him to have tea with me here at the country club." Graham noted that Kerr had invited him to make his headquarters at the governor's mansion before his crusade at Reynolds Coliseum in 1951. "He did me a number of personal favors," Graham said. "I never asked for anything that he didn't turn heaven and earth to do it."[71] By comparison, Graham had called Gardner two or three times before he endorsed Reagan to ask that he stick with Nixon, and Graham had requested permission to address the North Carolina delegation at Miami Beach. Graham met with part of the delegation.[72] Several weeks after the election, Graham would write to Bob Scott and congratulate him on his "magnificent race" and victory. "I believe you have all the moral and spiritual attributes to make a great governor," Graham said.[73]

Despite Graham's support, the election was close, and election night uncertainty increased when the Associated Press's computers, which had been keeping a running tabulation of the votes, crashed at 11:00 P.M. Scott went home to his farm to be awakened by a telephone call at 5:00 A.M. that informed him he had won. "Well," said Jessie Rae, "now that you've won, what are you going to do with it?"[74]

Scott had held on despite a conservative tide that swept 13 Republican gubernatorial candidates into office in twenty-one races across the country, and saw the North Carolina GOP pick up a record four congressional seats. With the closest margin by any Democratic gubernatorial candidate in the twentieth century to that date, Scott polled 821,233 votes to Gardner's 737,075 votes, or 52.7 percent to Gardner's 47.3 percent. Scott won sixty-seven counties, gaining every region including eastern North Carolina and every major urban county; Gardner won thirty-three counties, running best in traditional Republican strongholds in the west. And although Scott won thirty-six of the forty-three eastern counties, Gardner with 43 percent of the eastern vote performed much better than previous Republicans. But Gardner did not do as well as expected in the piedmont, where traditional Republicans were alienated by his flirtation with Wallace.

In the presidential race, thousands of white voters left the Democratic ticket to vote for Wallace, but Wallace's party had no candidate for governor. As a result, Scott was able to hold enough of the Branchhead Boys because of the family name, because he distanced himself from the national ticket, and because of his law-and-order stance. Although African Americans and white liberals were lukewarm about Scott, they had no other place to go, and they provided support, but less than they gave to Humphrey.

Some pundits believed that Bob Scott was the only Democrat who could have held the governorship for the Democrats. "He was a fortunate choice because of the popularity of George Wallace in the state," wrote reporter Jay Jenkins. "Thousands of citizens who supported Wallace were the 'Branchhead Boys' who had flocked to Kerr Scott's banner in 1948. As the election returns demonstrated, the Wallacites also gave stout backing to Scott. If the historic allegiance to the Scott name had not been present, Gardner could have copped the prize."[75] Jesse Helms correctly saw Gardner's close vote as a sign of a coming sea change in North Carolina politics. "So conservatism, which was the bedrock upon which the state Democratic Party in North Carolina was years ago built originally, is on the rise again in our state," Helms said. "The people are simply beginning to return to what they have subconsciously believed all along."[76] Reflecting in later years, Gardner said he believed that he would have been elected governor if the country had experienced a two-man presidential race. But he said his support of Wallace had badly damaged him in Charlotte and elsewhere, although he did not regret backing Reagan.[77]

Scott won in different ways from his father. In Mecklenburg County, Bob Scott garnered the support of the business community and black neighborhoods but lost the blue-collar neighborhoods where Kerr Scott commanded allegiance. Scott also won "near unanimous support" from the state's bankers.[78]

In 1968, North Carolina Republicans doubled their number of congressional seats from 2 to 4. They captured 12 of 50 state Senate seats and 29 of 120 state House seats, the highest totals since the 1928 landslide by Republican Herbert Hoover over Democrat Al Smith. Democratic senator Sam Ervin Jr., a conservative who had been a leading strategist for the segregationist forces in Washington, won. No Democratic senator has won reelection in North Carolina since. In one notable race, Henry Frye, a Greensboro attorney, became the first black person elected to the state House in the twentieth century.

In the presidential contest, 1968 signaled the crackup of the Democratic Party in North Carolina. Nixon, the first Republican to carry the state since Hoover in 1928, received 39.5 percent of the votes and carried fifty of one hundred counties. Wallace ran second with 31.3 percent and forty counties, while Humphrey ran third with 29.2 percent and ten counties. Nor was this defection some sort of temporary phenomenon. Except for Jimmy Carter's election in 1976, Republican presidential candidates would carry the state in the next nine presidential elections—a string that did not end until 2008, when the state went for Democrat Barack Obama.

Wallace did particularly well in eastern North Carolina, the heart of Branchhead Boy Country, where he won thirty-one of the forty-three counties. He also carried Scott's home of Alamance County. Between 1964 to 1968, the Democratic presidential vote in the east had dropped from 61 percent to 32 percent. This was a sea change.[79] Eastern North Carolina—Kerr Scott's Branchhead Boys—had supported various levels of rural progressivism meant to help rural people improve their lives. They had backed the Farmers' Alliance and the Populists of the 1800s. They had supported the Grange and Franklin Roosevelt's New Deal. They had backed Kerr Scott and Harry Truman. But in 1968, they split their ticket and largely supported George Wallace and Richard Nixon as part of the political backlash against racial integration, the riots, calls for black power, and divisions over the Vietnam War. One could see the hinges of history moving.

*I believe it is time to destroy the myth that tobacco
is king in North Carolina. —Governor Bob Scott*

Robert W. Scott took the oath of office on January 3, 1969, on a raw, cold, gray day twenty years after his father had been sworn in as governor. He began the day with a communion service at Hawfields Presbyterian Church and a visit to his father's nearby grave. Because Scott's election had been widely expected, the day did not draw the same kind of Jacksonian excitement, passion, and crowds of country people as had his father's inaugural. Indeed, Bob Scott represented a link to the past— the last governor to wear a top hat and carry a walking stick to his inaugural. He also wore a red rose in his lapel to honor his father. Although more of an establishment figure and less of a provocateur than Kerr Scott, he sought to convey the same sort of forward motion. "Let the timid, the faint-hearted, the foot-draggers, the do-nothings be forewarned: We are going to make progress in this administration," Scott said in his inaugural address at Raleigh's Memorial Auditorium.[1]

Scott noted that these were troubled times—and Scott would soon feel the full brunt of the social upheaval. Even as he was being sworn in, a dozen demonstrators from rural Hyde County were present, protesting the closing of two black schools as part of desegregation. "There will be no toleration of extremists who seek only to divide our people—whether they take to the streets, whether they act unseen, whether they throw rocks and firebombs, or whether they burn crosses in the dark of night," Scott said. "We will work for the day—yes, we will live for the day—when every man walks in the dignity and is mindful that he is regarded for his individual worth and that alone."[2]

The inaugural included both new and old North Carolina. Scott had placed newly elected Representative Henry Frye, the state's first black

Bob Scott and Jessie Rae and children gather at church in Haw River on inauguration day in January 1969. (Photo by Edward J. McCauley; North Carolina Collection, University of North Carolina at Chapel Hill Library)

elected state legislator of the century, on the inaugural committee—an honor that gave the freshman representative a highway patrol chauffeur and a place on the inaugural reviewing stand. Jessie Rae Scott sent a note to Shirley Frye, the new lawmaker's wife, inviting her to lunch at the executive mansion. But three rows in front of the Fryes on the reviewing stand sat Chief Justice R. Hunt Parker. As a National Guard unit from Halifax County passed by, Parker leaned over to Lieutenant Governor Pat Taylor Jr., whom he had just sworn in, and said, "Here are some real men. Their grand-fathers fought at Appomattox and Gettysburg. Not a nigger in the crowd."[3]

After the inaugural, Bob Scott and Miss Mary posed for photogra-phers in front of the official portrait of Kerr Scott in the Capitol. The Scotts were the second father-son gubernatorial combination following Richard Dobbs Spaight Sr. and Jr., who were chief executives in the late eighteenth and early nineteenth centuries. At age thirty-nine, Scott was North Carolina's youngest governor since Zebulon Vance took office at age thirty-two in 1862. A physically imposing man at six feet, one inch in height and weighing 245 pounds, Scott had gained 20 pounds after giving up cigarettes during the campaign. He had not given up his cigars, which he smoked during the inaugural parade. The cigars along with his recently fashionably grown sideburns led an acquaintance to say that he "looked like a riverboat gambler."

"Well," Scott quipped, "you've got to be kind of a con man in this business anyway."[4]

Scott became governor of a state that had become more affluent in the postwar years yet trailed the nation because too many people still scratched out a living on marginal farms or worked in low-wage textile and furniture plants. Despite the economic recruiting activity under Governor Luther Hodges and Governor Terry Sanford's efforts to turn the state—in the words of *National Geographic* magazine—into "a Dixie Dynamo," North Carolina was still poor, ranked forty-first in the nation in per capita income. The state's income was only half that of New York and fully one-third below the national average.[5] One study placed North Carolina forty-seventh among the states (including the District of Columbia) in the quality of life available to its citizens, a rating virtually unchanged from a study in the 1930s, when the state ranked forty-third.[6]

Clearly, North Carolina's Sun Belt growth had yet to occur. Although the state had grown from four million to five million since Kerr Scott's administration, the percentage of the growth rate (5.5 percent) trailed the southern average (7.7 percent).[7] As a result, small towns and rural areas still dominated the Tar Heel State; more North Carolinians lived in nonurban areas than any other state in the South.[8] These statistics were borne out in popular culture, too: in 1968, the *Andy Griffith Show* had just ended its eight-year run on CBS with its kindly portrayal of small-town life in the fictional North Carolina town of Mayberry. For farmer Bob Scott, the Mayberry model worked just fine. "I hope that our population growth continues to slow down," he said. "North Carolina does not need its cities to become gigantic overpopulated, urban jungles."[9]

Unlike his father, Scott did not face a hostile legislature. The Democrats controlled the General Assembly, although Republicans had their strongest representation since Herbert Hoover's 1928 landslide. Republicans held

12 of the 50 Senate seats and 29 of the 120 House seats. Even with the legislature largely on his side, Scott proposed a moderately forward-looking program, though not as far-reaching as that of his father: a sort of rural progressivism-lite. He recommended starting a statewide kindergarten program, expanding vocational education, increasing salary by 10 percent for teachers and state employees, enhancing the community college system, enabling legislation to start a state zoo, establishing a state-sponsored low-income housing program, and, like his father, funding a stepped-up road-building program. To finance his agenda, Scott proposed a five-cent-per-pack sales tax on cigarettes, a two-cent-per-gallon gas tax hike, and a $21 million increase in automobile license fees—a total of $97 million in new taxes.[10]

His recommendation to raise the cigarette tax challenged a Tar Heel sacred cow. Called "the golden leaf," tobacco was embedded in the state's economy and culture. North Carolina both grew the most tobacco and manufactured the most cigarettes of any state. Tobacco provided work for two hundred thousand Tar Heel families, employed thirty thousand factory workers, and had been a leading export since colonial times. Some of the state's major universities, foundations, and hospitals had been founded by tobacco money. Everything from political rallies to formal dances were held in cavernous, sweet-smelling tobacco warehouses. Money from the cigarette manufacturers greased the state's political machinery. In short, tobacco meant to North Carolina what automobiles were to Detroit or oil to Texas.

Scott needed the revenue from the cigarette tax to finance the creation of a statewide kindergarten program. North Carolina was one of only three states in the country that did not offer kindergarten as part of its public school system, although about one third of the state's five-year-olds attended private kindergartens.[11] During the campaign, Scott had followed political convention and opposed levying such a tax. Now he ate his words. "I am man enough to stand before you today to say I have found it necessary to change my earlier opinion," Scott told the legislature. "I believe it is time to destroy the myth that tobacco is king in North Carolina. Income from livestock and poultry already exceeds that of tobacco. True, it's very important to our economy and will be for as long as man wants to enjoy a smoke. But tobacco must not dominate our thinking to the detriment of our progress."[12]

Although Scott was the first farmer to serve as governor since his father, the leaders of the N.C. Farm Bureau, the traditional representative of tobacco interests, had not backed him in the primary or the general election. Scott's farm support tended to come from the State Grange, the second largest farm organization, which was less tied to tobacco and more connected to piedmont dairy and livestock farming. To one complaining eastern North Carolina tobacco farmer, Scott wrote: "The tobacco companies, who make the real money off tobacco did not support me politically. The leadership of the main farm organization did not support me. Many eastern North Carolina farmers voted for Gardner. I carried more votes from the cities than I did from the rural areas, percentage-wise in many precincts."[13]

The legislature provided money to begin phasing in kindergartens, with the first eight kindergarten programs opening on December 1, 1969, with 320 children. There were seventy-four pilot programs by the end of Scott's term. But kindergartens would not expand statewide until the administration of his successor, much to Scott's frustration.

The gas tax plan grew out of a blue-ribbon report issued by the departing Moore administration, which warned that the state was falling behind on road construction and called for more revenue. The report recommended a three-cent-per-gallon motor fuels tax increase, which provided Scott with political cover.[14] Scott said that the gas tax and license fees would raise more revenue than the $200 million bond issue pushed through by his father in 1949—although it would not buy as much concrete because of inflation.[15] The gas station operators and oil jobbers opposed his gas tax hike. Republican lawmakers joined the opposition, leading Scott to angrily say that they had "prostituted" themselves on the issue.

By June, Scott's tax bill had run into so much trouble that the House voted to send it back to committee by 59–51.[16] "The taxpayers . . . are in revolt," declared TV commentator Jesse Helms. "The long-accepted theory of tax and spend and spend and tax, has run its course. The political uprising of last week had all the raucous clamor of some badly bedraggled economic chickens coming home to roost."[17]

On the verge of losing his tax hike, Scott borrowed a page from his father's bond tour and hit the campaign trail. Scott took a five-city helicopter circuit to argue that the money would improve roads, start a kindergarten system, provide occupational or career training in the middle schools, offer free transportation for handicapped children, and open new community college or technical institute campuses in Roxboro, Smithfield, and Hendersonville.[18] Scott recalled campaigning with his father for the road bonds in 1949. "Just as 20 years ago the people rose up and supported his program," Scott said in Greenville, "I'm confident the people today will support this one."[19]

Uncle Ralph, the chairman of the Senate Finance Committee, shepherded the tax package through the Senate. Opponents accused him of rushing the bill through without adequate debate and the governor with dangling "sugar plums" in front of legislators. Scott and his chief political operative Ben Roney were certainly dangling patronage and roads in front of lawmakers. "Some of these groups are giving me a rough time," Scott wrote in his diary. "But some of these legislators are going to learn who has financial authority over roads and other plums that go in their district. Some are asking for all kinds of appropriations but vote against any tax to pay for their projects. That's political hypocrisy and a few can't stand heat in the kitchen."[20]

As was the practice with most governors, Scott waited until the end of the legislative session to make most of his appointments for judgeships, boards, and commissions, using those appointments as leverage to help get his program through the legislature. Scott appointed House Speaker Earl Vaughn to the state court of appeals.

A compromise crafted by lawmakers saved Scott's tax package. Instead of Scott's proposed five-cent-per-pack cigarette tax, they countered with a package that included a two-cent-per-pack cigarette tax and a one-cent-per-bottle tax on soft drinks—also a first for the state. The anti-tobacco-tax forces thought that Scott would reject the deal because his campaign manager and party chairman, James Johnson, owned a Coca-Cola bottling company in Charlotte and had lined up bottlers to contribute to Scott's campaign. Scott surprised everyone by agreeing to the deal. "I lost a dear friend, Jimmy Johnson," Scott later recalled. "The soft drink people never forgave me for yielding. But I wanted the $99 million for the public-school kindergarten program."[21]

North Carolina still had the lowest cigarette tax in the country—a half-cent lower than Virginia and Kentucky, sister tobacco states. But the gas tax increase gave North Carolina the highest gas tax in the country, although Scott said that was misleading because other states supplemented their road budgets with tolls and through property taxes.[22] The package included other tax increases as well, including an additional penny an ounce for whiskey and one and a half cents per bottle of beer, a two-and-a-half-cent sales tax hike on motor vehicles, motorboats, and airplanes, and an increase on the rate at which building and loan associations were taxed. The 1969 session proved to be the longest in North Carolina history to date, and it raised the most taxes ever—$197 million.[23] "Governor Bob Scott won an impressive victory in obtaining enactment of his legislative program with few significant changes," wrote Claude Sitton, editor of the *News and Observer*. "But the cost of that victory in terms of his own popularity, the future of his administration and the future of the Democratic Party is great." Sitton found fault in Scott's "intemperate attack" on Democrats who opposed to his tax program and in his blaming Republicans for opposition when Democrats controlled the legislature. "Given the outcome of this legislative session, no one can question Scott's courage," Sitton wrote. "No one can question his candor and firmness. The manner in which he exercises them is another matter. There are many of his friends who hope that in the months left to him in the governor's chair he will keep in mind Theodore Roosevelt's admonition to 'walk softly.'"[24]

Republicans attempted to make Scott pay a political price for the tax hikes, turning taxes into a major issue during the 1970 midterm legislative elections. They tried unsuccessfully to repeal the taxes in the 1971 session: the House voted for repeal 70–42, but a Senate committee killed the measure. Even with the new taxes, North Carolina still was fiscally conservative. In 1972, it ranked forty-first per capita among the states in state and local taxes and forty-eighth per capita in state and local debt.[25] In a personal victory, though, aided by the gas tax hike, Scott paved 4,200 miles of secondary roads, the farm-to-market roads that had been so important to Kerr.[26]

THE RURAL PROGRESSIVE

Scott's rural progressivism surfaced on other issues such as housing, capital punishment, the minimum wage, teacher pay, and later the environment. Scott had promised during the campaign to address the problem of four hundred thousand North Carolinians living in substandard housing. He had been moved by such stories as a High Point couple awakened by the cries of their six-month-old twin daughters being bitten by rats. As governor, he asked the legislature to appropriate $500,000 to launch the nation's first state housing corporation to promote and finance the construction of single-family dwellings for low-income families. Declaring that the issue of low-income housing had been ignored, Scott said that he hoped to eliminate the state's housing problems over the next seventeen to twenty years. His plan called for the creation of a North Carolina housing authority empowered to issue tax-exempt bonds up to $200 million. "It is time that housing become the public's business and the state . . . should enter the field," Scott said.[27] The North Carolina Housing Corporation had difficulty getting off the ground because of legal challenges, but it put the issue on the table. In 1973, the legislature created its successor, the North Carolina Finance Agency, which by 2017 had financed more than 255,000 affordable houses and apartments totaling $19.2 billion.

Scott became the first North Carolina governor to call for an end to the death penalty. North Carolina had not used its gas chambers since October 27, 1961, and death penalty foes urged him to make his private opposition known when a bill banning capital punishment was being considered in the legislature. Scott at first demurred, but by March, he had decided to go public. "I feel the time has come to abolish capital punishment," Scott said. "I am conscious of the arguments on both sides of the issue and there is something to be said for each viewpoint. However, my position reflects a personal conviction."[28] Despite the governor's support, the House defeated bills to repeal the death penalty in the House by 68–38 in 1969, and again in 1971 by 65–46. Scott took comfort when the U.S. Supreme Court ruled on June 29, 1972, declaring capital punishment, as currently employed, unconstitutional.[29]

Scott demonstrated his rural progressivism in other areas as well. He pushed through the 1971 legislature a law raising the minimum wage from $1.25 per hour to $1.60 per hour (or $9.86 in 2018 dollars), phasing in the increase over two years. That is higher in relative dollars than the state minimum wage in 2018 of $7.25.

Scott's governorship also coincided with the rise of the environmental movement, fueled by oil slicks off the coast of Santa Barbara, California, and dead fish in Lake Erie. Scott marked the first Earth Day on April 22, 1970, with a speech, led a losing fight for the state to buy the privately owned Bald Head Island to keep it from being developed, and voiced "great concern" over the U.S. Army's proposed shipment of nerve gas through North Carolina to be dumped off the Florida coast. In April 1971, Scott gave the first environmental speech to a joint session of the North Carolina legislature. Noting "a groundswell of public concern for the environment," Scott outlined twenty-four conservation recommendations, the centerpiece of which was the State Environmental Policy Act (SEPA), which mandated the environmental review of state-funded projects. "This act establishes for the first time an environmental policy for North Carolina," Scott told the legislature. "This measure will require that all state agencies give consideration to the environmental values, aspects and consequences of their decisions."[30] Besides speaking to the joint session, Scott flew around the state pushing his agenda in speeches, declaring 1971 the year of the environment.

Decades later, in 2015, a conservative Republican legislature sharply curtailed SEPA—nearly gutted, in the view of environmentalists—by exempting from review all state projects under $10 million that affect less than ten acres.

MIDTERM POLITICS

Rocked by social unrest and seeking to capitalize on the Scott tax hikes, the Republicans focused on North Carolina during the 1970 midterm elections. Both President Richard Nixon and Vice President Spiro Agnew stumped in the state, seeking to pick up both GOP congressional and legislative seats by separating white voters from their Democratic moorings. Scott, as the titular head of the state Democratic Party, sought to keep that from happening.

Campaigning before fifteen thousand people in a cold rain in Asheville, President Nixon railed against court-ordered busing. "I believe that a child—and I don't care whether he is a white child or a black child or what his background is—is better off going to that school closest to his home, his neighborhood school," Nixon said. "I do not favor for that reason—and Congress has so stated, and I support that proposition—the use of busing solely to achieve racial balance."[31]

A few days later, Scott campaigned in the mountain town of Valdese, blaming the GOP for rising unemployment and low economic growth. He said that there were 10,700 fewer doffers, weavers, knitters, spinners, loom fixers, and other textile workers in North Carolina than a year earlier. "I wonder if Mr. Nixon really has any idea of what it is like to be poor, to be out of work with no job opening in sight?" Scott asked. "I wonder if maybe he has been on Wall Street and in Key Biscayne and in sunny San Clemente California for so long that he has no conception of what life is like for someone on the thin edge of poverty?"[32]

As the administration's chief attack dog, Agnew became known for his alliterative criticisms of "nattering nabobs of negativism" and "pusillanimous pussyfooters." Speaking to a group of Democratic women before Agnew made an appearance in Raleigh, Jessie Rae Scott said, "Personally, I'd rather spend time contemplating the construction of my belly button than try to figure out what he is trying to say." But she tried her own hand at alliteration, calling Agnew "a bagpiper of bombastic, but boomeranging barb," "that effusive enunciator of elephantine elocutions," and "that discombobulating disciple of debilitating dichotomy."[33] Agnew had kind words for "the charming First Lady of the state," saying that he could use her as a speech writer in his campaign.[34]

When it came to the midterm elections, the Nixon-Agnew sally had little effect, nor did the GOP's first coordinated, statewide campaign designed to capitalize on Scott's tax increases. The state's congressional delegation held its 7–4 Democratic majority, and the Democrats picked up five seats in the state Senate and eight seats in the state House. Scott had campaigned across the state for Democratic candidates and cut TV ads, and the midterms were seen by observers as a political validation for Scott. An elated Scott wrote in his diary: "I consider this a personal victory since most Republicans in N.C. were campaigning against my Administration and my programs."[35] Ralph Scott, however, had a close shave. As chairman of the Senate Finance Committee who had ramrodded the governor's finance package through the Senate, he had been targeted by Republicans. Uncle Ralph shrugged off his fourteen-vote margin—thirteen after a recount. "I got twelve more votes than I needed," he said.

SCOTT LIFE IN THE MANSION

Bob and Jessie Rae Scott moved into the executive mansion with five young children: twins Mary and Meg, age twelve, in junior high; Susan, eleven, and Kerr, ten, in grade school; and Jan, five, starting kindergarten. Duke, the family basset hound, came along, too. Because of security and tensions of the era, the children were driven to public schools in a chauffeured patrol car. The children hated that, and Scott arranged for the patrolmen to use an unmarked car, dress in plainclothes, and park a block away from the school so that the children could walk the rest of the way.[36]

In Raleigh, Scott continued to revel in his rural roots. Following a tradition started by his father, he invited friends to the mansion for possum dinners (the possums had been caught by a mansion employee and stored in a refrigerator), along with barbecued spareribs, black-eyed peas, collard greens, bean soup with pig's tails, corn bread, and persimmon pudding—all washed down with wine, champagne, and homemade peach brandy. Scott also hosted a chitlins dinner complete with finger bowls. After formal dinners at the mansion, Scott would sometimes retire with his military aides to cigars and moonshine supplied weekly by one of his highway patrol trooper bodyguards from a Wilkes County bootlegger.[37]

Scott had a sense of playfulness about him. Charles Craven, a columnist for the *News and Observer*, regularly wrote about a group of charac-

Governor Bob Scott conversing with young men in a general store in Watauga County. (Hugh Morton Photographs and Films, North Carolina Collection, University of North Carolina at Chapel Hill Library)

ters who hung out at a Raleigh pool hall. One day Scott—sporty in a pair of sunglasses and puffing on a cigar—drove over in his state limousine. He picked up Craven and his buddies and took them to the mansion. Scott shot pool with the likes of Bankshot Fraley, Rexy Rexy, Handicap Mudwell, and Skeeter Stockman and then played some poker. When Rexy Rexy dealt the governor a straight flush, Scott quipped: "That kind of thing could get you a judgeship."[38]

Scott may not have been the populist of his father, but he brought a common-man approach to Raleigh. In his spare time, he often played cards or golf with his highway patrol or SBI security detail, rather than with the state's major business executives or with legislators. In many ways he treated his security detail like family. He bought them Christmas presents. He attended the wedding in Mount Airy for a patrolman assigned to protect him. To celebrate the birthday of his patrol driver, Lieutenant Wayne Keeter, he drove to the patrolman's home—with Keeter sitting in the back seat of the limo—to cook chili beans. "I would rather—much rather—spend my leisure hours with them than to be at a cocktail party or dinner," Scott wrote in his diary.[39]

Scott befriended his barber, Earl McLamb, who had a shop on Raleigh's

Hillsborough Street, and gave his security detail the slip to breakfast with McLamb at his Garner home and then hit the golf links; sometimes Scott invited him over to the mansion at the end of the day for a piece of coconut cake or to shoot pool. Their children sometimes played together. Near the end of his administration, he invited McLamb and his wife, Doris, Jessie Rae's hairdresser, to be part of a small group that traveled to New York City with Scott when he had his official portrait painted by Daniel Greene. "Bob could be whatever he wanted to be," McLamb said. "He could deal with the high class, or the middle class or the low class. He could fit in wherever he wanted to."[40]

Scott's small democratic inclinations were also evident when it came to the debutante ball. The Scotts turned down a request for the traditional debutante tea in the mansion, despite a personal plea by George Ragsdale, Moore's former legal aide, whose wife headed the ball effort. Scott told a news conference, "Frankly, last year they were insulting to the First Family of North Carolina." He said matchbooks were passed out bearing the inscription "Burn Scott Up." He also complained that the debutantes had called him a farm boy and made comments about Jessie Rae having been brought up in a mill village.[41] "JRS and I feel very strongly that this is a private group, highly selective and mainly for the girls in Raleigh and eastern N.C. towns," Scott wrote in his diary. "So, in our effort to cut down on this type of function being held at the Mansion, and using up our time, JRS & I just decided not to fulfill their request to use the Mansion this year."[42]

Scott always carried with him a sense of being an outsider whose boots still carried the aroma of cow manure. "I was a farm boy from Haw River," Scott said.

> What did I know about it—about government, about politics and all of that? All of a sudden I became lieutenant governor. I came out of nowhere. I was never accepted by the quote establishment—that is to say the shakers and the movers behind the scenes, the business community. Because I didn't move in their circles. I wasn't a member of the country club set. I'm not bitter about that at all. In fact, I kind of consider it a plus. I didn't belong to a city club or a country club or anything like that. Secondly, I've always felt I identified with the less affluent or the middle class. I have always been socially conscious. Is that the right phrase?[43]

That farm boy from Haw River would be thrown into a cauldron of social unrest that would have tested the political agility of a far more seasoned chief executive.

11 ★ FIRE IN THE STREETS

Now I know you think the governor is a son-of-a-bitch. But I want to tell you something. There's a lot of folks that think you all are sons-of-bitches, too.
—*Uncle Ralph Scott to University of North Carolina protesters*

Even as Bob Scott lobbied for his legislative program, he often found himself consumed by rising social tensions across the state. Despite North Carolina's reputation for moderation in civil rights and other matters, in the late sixties and early seventies, the Tar Heel State would, in the words of one observer, "lead the South with the number and intensity of its Northern-style confrontations in the streets and on the campuses."[1] During his first six months in office, Scott called out the National Guard nine times to deal with civil unrest.[2]

The state's college campuses were roiled both by black student activism and by protests against the Vietnam War. North Carolina's secondary and elementary school system underwent full-scale racial integration. And years of suppressed black anger spilled out onto the streets. There were building takeovers, marches, fire bombings, and riots. Extreme and violence-prone voices gained new followings. Many of the leading protest figures of the turbulent era would be drawn to North Carolina, including Ralph Abernathy, Andrew Young, Stokely Carmichael, Jane Fonda, Dick Gregory, Rennie Davis, and Joan Baez.

The national black student movement began on historically black college campuses. With eleven such schools, North Carolina, more than any other state for much of the decade, had become a center of black student activism, witnessing the start of the lunch counter sit-in movement in Greensboro in 1960, the formation of the Student Nonviolent Coordinating Committee in Raleigh that same year, and the creation of the Congress for the Unity of Black Students in Raleigh in 1968. By the late sixties, black students had moved beyond the campaign for racial integration and were pushing for a greater voice on campus. Although still a small minority on traditionally white campuses, they had reached a critical mass in numbers that could have some influence. "Black activism exploded in the spring of 1969," wrote historian Martha Biondi. "It was the high-water mark of the black student movement, with militant actions and mass confrontations at campuses across the country, most notably at the University of California, Berkeley; Cornell University; Harvard University; Rutgers University; and Howard University."[3] The image of black activism had also changed. The sit-in movement had featured neatly dressed black students abused by white rednecks. Now the black activists often wore sunglasses and dashikis; they raised their arms in black power salutes. Many whites saw all of this as threatening.

Scott's first test occurred at the predominantly white, elite Duke University in Durham. On February 13, 1969, about sixty black students, members of the Duke Afro American Society, seized the registrar's office in the Allen Administration Building and labeled it the Malcolm X. School of Liberation. They demanded among other things the abolition of Scholastic Aptitude Tests for black student admissions and the creation of a black studies curriculum, a black student union, and a black dorm. The students barricaded themselves in and threatened to burn records if police were called to the scene.

There had been prior warnings of trouble. Two days earlier, black students had marched with comedian and activist Dick Gregory to the home of Duke president Douglas Knight to discuss their grievances. He had invited them inside, and they had talked for two hours. Caught by surprise at a breakfast meeting in New York City when the takeover occurred, Knight chartered a plane and returned to campus by 11:00 A.M. After failing to convince the students to leave, Knight called in the police, in part because of intelligence about Klan activity. "I was getting reports of men in pickup trucks, shotguns in the window racks, driving slowly around the outer perimeter of the West Campus, watching, waiting for the dark," Knight later recalled.[4]

At 3:30 P.M. the provost read a statement ordering the students to leave the administration building within one hour or face legal ramifications. Arriving on the scene in the afternoon from out of town, the black activist Howard Fuller, who had ties to some of the protest leaders, helped convince the students to leave by a side door before the deadline.[5] As night fell, a crowd of white student supporters grew to two thousand. Scott ordered the highway patrol onto campus to reinforce city and campus police, and he mobilized 965 National Guardsmen at an armory two miles from campus.[6]

What set off the violence that night is in dispute. Durham police chief W. W. Pleasants said that the melee began after several thrown objects hit policemen, who responded with tear gas. But a report by a U.S. Army Counter Intelligence unit, which had agents on the scene, said, "When the crowd of spectators saw the police entering the building, derogatory remarks were shouted at the police by individuals in the crowd. The police responded by spraying tear gas at the crowd."[7]

About 150 policemen—half Durham police and half highway patrol—began moving out the students, using tear gas and billy clubs, with students responding with taunts of "Fascists" and "Nazis." The students heaved back the tear gas canisters, rocks, buckets, and pieces of wood with nails. They tried to overturn a police car. In the end, twenty-one students were injured, and five were arrested.

Knight told the student newspaper that he had been advised by Scott adviser Ben Roney to call in the police. "If one university gives in to a set of demands like this, we're afraid that within 24 hours all of them will be in trouble," Knight said he was told.[8] Roney, the old Kerr Scott hand and Bob Scott's chief political strategist, pushed the young governor in a conservative direction during the social turbulence. "He was very close to me, and I relied on him, perhaps more than I should have," Scott said years later. "I didn't do everything he recommended I do. Ben was a hard nose. During that turbulent period he was a law and order man. He had the Eastern North Carolina conservative flavor."[9]

The governor stayed in close contact with the Duke situation, not leaving his office until 10:00 P.M. that evening. Scott praised Knight for acting in a "fair and firm" manner. "I commended him for his actions because, in a sense, he has set the tone for our actions in similar potential situations on other campuses," Scott said.[10] In a letter to Scott, Knight expressed his "deep appreciation for the full, prompt and forthright cooperation which you extended to Duke University." He called it a "tremendously painful decision" to call in the police for which he was severely criticized. But Knight said his decision resulted in only three hours of disruption instead of days of siege that had occurred on other campuses.[11]

The campus, however, still faced turmoil. Two days after the takeover, about a thousand students marched on Knight's house. Knight agreed to form a task force, which eventually produced the first black studies program at a southern university. A university hearing committee found forty-eight students who had occupied the building guilty of violating university regulations. The defendants were sentenced to one year of probation.

In March, two nights of marches in downtown Durham involved about 400 to 600 students from Duke and North Carolina Central University, a historically black campus in Durham. Some of the Central students marching back to campus began throwing rocks, breaking twenty-five plate-glass business windows, damaging buses, and roughing up two newsmen. The next day Scott ordered 660 National Guardsmen to Durham to keep order; more than 150 demonstrators were arrested for curfew violations.[12]

After receiving personal threats, Knight began packing a pistol in his dressing gown when he made his 1:00 A.M. tour of his grounds with a campus security guard whom he had posted at his home.[13] Having lost the confidence of his trustees, Knight resigned in late March and took a job as vice president for educational development with the RCA Corporation. He never returned to a college post. Later in the year, Duke trustees hired former governor Terry Sanford as the university's new president.

The Duke episode left some state officials feeling that they needed to be more severe. "I think it is long past the time when action should be taken to deal with revolutionaries, the flag burners, the black organizations, and the other organizations supporting lawlessness in this country and let them know we are not going to let them destroy America," Charles T. Bowers, adjutant general of the National Guard wrote to Charles Wade, vice president of R. J. Reynolds Tobacco Company in Winston-Salem and chairman of Duke's board of trustees. "If the policy of petting and appeasing is continued, their demands will continue to grow until complete takeover is accomplished and chaos will rule in this great country of ours."[14]

Just ten days after the takeover of the Duke administration building, the cafeteria workers at the University of North Carolina at Chapel Hill went on strike. On Sunday, February 23, Lenoir Dining Hall food workers set up their counters as usual. But when the doors opened, sixteen workers led by Mary Smith walked out from behind their counters, sat down at the cafeteria tables, and didn't budge. On Monday, nearly a hundred dining hall employees didn't show up for work.

So began a monthlong labor struggle that had major racial overtones and divided the campus. The workers had several demands, especially to raise their salary from $1.60 per hour to $1.80 per hour, end split shifts, and drop the requirement that they pay for meals they didn't eat. The university attempted to carry on food service with supervisors and by hiring students.

Like most southern universities in 1969, the campus at Chapel Hill was a study in racial contrasts: an overwhelmingly white student body (only 1.5 percent of its students were black) was served by a mostly black non-academic workforce of food workers, maids, and janitors. The first black professor was hired in 1966. Organizing themselves into a group called the Black Student Movement, University of North Carolina students not only pushed for academic changes such as an Afro-American studies program but also allied themselves with the black workers.

As at Duke, the issue had been building for months. In December 1968, the Black Student Movement issued twenty-three demands that included eliminating racial bias from admissions policies and the firing of two white administrators. In March, a group of 250 white students had briefly occupied the ground floor of the administration building in solidarity with black students before dispersing.[15]

To support the striking cafeteria workers, black students began first by picketing Lenoir Hall and handing out leaflets. Then they escalated their tactics, entering the cafeteria on March 4 and taking places in line to slow down service. Next, they sat one to a table with glasses of water—a move that led to shouting and shoving matches and some minor injuries. According to some accounts, some white students, including football players, attacked students supporting the strike. In response, the university shut down the cafeteria.

After the violence, University of North Carolina president William C. Friday became more involved. He met with Chancellor Carlyle Sitterson and planned to reopen Lenoir Hall. But the university wasn't acting fast enough for Governor Scott, who summoned Friday and Sitterson to Raleigh and demanded that the cafeteria be opened immediately. After what was described as "a violent argument," Scott insisted the cafeteria be opened for breakfast the next morning, and he dispatched highway patrolmen to enforce his order. Both Friday and Sitterson opposed the use of outside police force, with Sitterson describing the action as "astonishing."[16]

"Called Dr. Friday and Chancellor Sitterson and told them to open the cafeteria in the morning," Scott wrote in his diary that night. "Would back them up with the guard and Highway Patrol. They didn't want to do it (it seemed) but I was getting tired of the delay. I know the great majority of the people in the state back me on this. Many calls and telegrams coming in to congratulate and pledge support. Folks are fed up with it."[17]

On March 7, about one hundred highway patrolmen took up positions around Lenoir Hall to enforce the cafeteria opening and help break the twelve-day-old strike. In the same hall twenty years earlier, Kerr Scott had announced the appointment of Frank Graham to the Senate. There were no arrests, although several stink bombs were planted in the dining area during the lunch hour and one picketer sustained minor injuries after being hit by a delivery truck that did not slow down when it approached the picketers.[18] Scott had already mobilized the National Guard because of the violence in Durham and had 603 soldiers on standby.[19] The use of police force created an uproar on campus and drew opposition from many students and faculty, but Scott's conservative law-and-order tactics received broad backing from citizens across the state.

As an alternative to Lenoir Hall dining hall, the Black Student Movement set up what they called a "Soul Food" cafeteria for two weeks in Manning Hall, an abandoned classroom building. Citing health and safety concerns as well as rumors of weapons in the building, on March 13, Scott sent a hundred troopers to empty the building. At Howard Fuller's urging, the students left the building, avoiding a confrontation.[20] "Tough decision today—to order state troopers to clear Manning Hall," Scott wrote in his diary. "Fortunately, no confrontation was held. But I didn't know that when the decision was made. Early this A.M. I told Dr. Clayburn Jones of the UNC Administration that 'I am sick and tired of the Administration dragging its feet' in dealing with the militants. Thus, I feel they at last knew I meant it when I said I wanted that building cleared. . . . Guess a lot of people think I am a red-necked, right-winger, who is irresponsible and immature. But I feel I am right and I know the people are behind me."[21]

March 13, 1969, may have been the height of the student activism confronting Scott. On that day, the governor sent 100 state troopers to Chapel Hill to clear Manning Hall; 660 guardsmen were on their second night of curfew duty in Durham; and police exchanged gunfire after a rally on behalf of striking cafeteria workers at N.C. A&T State University in Greensboro.

The next day, March 14, Scott met behind closed doors with the University of North Carolina's executive committee and told them that he would not allow demonstrators to disrupt university operations. He said that law enforcement officers needed no permission from college administrators to enter a campus and enforce criminal laws. "The people of North Carolina elected me to be governor of North Carolina—not a university president," Scott said in remarks made public in April. But he said that no part of state government—including the colleges—should "buckle under violence or the threat of violence." He added, "Your administrators may take the view that making concessions delaying confrontations gives hope, at least of avoiding probable riots, property damage and even bloodshed. This, in my opinion, is a forlorn hope. There will be trouble either way. In my opinion, the power of the state should be used in an effort to stamp out the work of these offenders before their efforts attract more attention and more followers and take on greater and more dangerous proportions." Scott continued, "It may be that your president and some of your administrative officers, may not be willing to take positive action in an effort to end or impede the destructive progress now being made by those who like to be called only 'demonstrators.' Some folks are hard to move—and sometimes it's hard to get folks to move—but as far as I am concerned, as governor of this state, the hour of decision is at hand."[22]

In a speech at a Democratic Party fundraiser in Greenville, S.C., on March 24, Scott portrayed himself as a defender of the core values of western civilization. "Unless we are willing to face up to the mood of violence creeping across our college campuses," Scott said, "we will merely preside over the liquidation of excellence in higher education. Institutions in North Carolina have been targeted as a testing ground for the entire region."[23]

Scott's hard-line stance won him wide applause across the state, with letters pouring in from not only his rural followers but from business leaders. Among them was Shearon Harris, president of Carolina Power and Light in Raleigh: "Last Saturday morning the other three members of my golf foursome were thoughtful and responsible business leaders. A considerable amount of conversation during our round related to your recent action to preserve order on the campuses of state institutions of higher learning. Our group was unanimous in our enthusiastic commendation for your clear, swift and resolute action. I have had a number of other conversations in which the same sentiments were expressed. It is my firm belief that you have not only taken the wise and proper course but that a very large majority of the citizens of our State admired your strong leadership."[24] Scott won repeated plaudits from Jesse Helms. "Governor Robert Scott, bless him, continues to stand undaunted in his apparent determination that the campuses of state-owned colleges and universities in North Carolina shall not be surrendered to the arrogant absurdities of a loud minority of faculty and student hotheads. The Governor, and perhaps the people of the state, should count the blessing that this is one of those rare circumstances wherein a leader can at once do the right thing and the popular thing. It has not really been necessary that the Governor explain his actions to the people. They have understood, and they have been grateful."[25]

Sending in the troopers had political benefits, providing Scott with political capital to pass his legislative agenda. A national poll conducted for *Newsweek* magazine found that 84 percent of respondents felt that college demonstrators had been treated too leniently as opposed to 11 percent who did not. Eighty-five percent of those surveyed said black militants were being treated too leniently. Another 59 percent thought that the danger of racial violence was increasing, while 26 percent disagreed.[26]

Scott received some liberal blowback from people such as Josef Perry of Chapel Hill, who said that the Chapel Hill police were capable of handling the situation and that Scott had intentionally inflamed the situation by sending in the troopers. "A really responsible governor would not send in troops just to titillate the 'branchhead boys' in opposition to hippies, militant black students, intellectuals and liberals or deprived workers trying to make a decent living in dignity—the last group being the crucial ones really involved," Perry wrote.[27] The Chapel Hill chapter of the American Association of University Professors declared, "The presence of state policemen on our campus today is an ugly sight. We believe that the local machinery of justice is capable of handling the few and minor disorders (which we also regret) which have occurred to date." The group called for the withdrawal of the state police and their replacement by qualified mediators.[28]

As Scott brandished his law-and-order credentials, he showed more flexibility behind the scenes in resolving the strike. The intermediary was Uncle Ralph. If the campus confrontation had shades of Berkeley and Columbia, it also had its own unique small-town, southern flavor. Uncle Ralph had been tipped off that the strike leader, Mary Smith, had been born in the Alamance County community of Pleasant Grove and had been delivered by his brother, Dr. Floyd Scott. Smith said she didn't know whether to trust the governor. "Well, you know the Scotts, and the Scott family ain't never lied to you," Ralph told her.[29]

Ralph met with the governor at his home in Haw River and at church and told him the workers had real grievances; then he set up a meeting between the strikers and the governor. The meeting, scheduled for fifteen minutes, ran for an hour, broke for a Scott lunchtime appointment, and then resumed. Ralph promised a pay increase for all six thousand low-wage workers—including the cafeteria employees—that would go into effect July 1, and the governor signed off on the deal, giving them the pay raise ninety days earlier. Representing the workers was civil rights lawyer Julius Chambers, who had already helped negotiate the outlines of the settlement with university officials. Bob Scott later conceded that the negotiations came pretty close to collective bargaining with public employees, illegal under North Carolina law.[30]

Uncle Ralph also met with the protesters, pulled into a meeting by chance as he was walking across campus to attend a parley with the medical school dean. "Now I know you think the governor is a son-of-a-bitch," Ralph told a room packed with students. "But I want to tell you something. There's a lot of folks that think you all are sons-of-bitches, too," Ralph said, prompting deep laughter in the room. The students said they didn't like the highway troopers being there. Ralph responded: "You quit tearing up my stuff and the troops will leave. That's your trouble."[31] Uncle Ralph later said that his nephew had no choice but to send in the highway patrol. "For a man working out here in the filling station or working in these mills who never had a chance to go to Chapel Hill to school, but he knows that he's helping for that, and you've got to keep that in the back of your head too," Ralph said.[32]

The disruptions at Duke and UNC–Chapel Hill, North Carolina's two prestigious college campuses, were just the opening acts for what would be a spring of demonstrations, riots, and activism that would threaten the state's social fabric. A state official could be pardoned for thinking that the state's campuses were under siege.

A mass student demonstration took place at the University of North Carolina at Greensboro on behalf of striking cafeteria workers. Fifteen non-academic workers seeking better working conditions for campus maids were arrested after taking over the chancellor's office at N.C. State University. Scott dispatched the State Highway Patrol to East Carolina University in Greenville during a cafeteria strike, and an SBI bodyguard was provided for the chancellor. At the University of North Carolina at Charlotte, protesting students replaced the U.S. and North Carolina flags with a black nationalist flag. The president of Fayetteville State University, Rudolph Jones, announced his resignation "for personal and health reasons," shortly after student boycotts, demonstrations, and demands. At Belmont Abbey College, seven black students took over the science building to press their demands.

The protests spilled beyond the campuses and onto the streets. By 1969, black people could measure visible progress. But in eastern North Carolina—the area with the state's largest black population—progress had lagged when it came to school integration, voter registration, and the election of black elected officials. The Southern Christian Leadership Conference pressured Bob Scott on a range of issues. The list of grievances included the closing of two black schools in coastal Hyde County as part of desegregation. The SCLC wanted more black judges, more black highway patrolmen, a state civil rights bill, more black highway workers, total desegregation of the schools, and a new trial for Marie Hill, a seventeen-year-old Rocky Mount girl who had been sentenced to the gas chamber for her role in killing a shopkeeper during a robbery.

In April, SCLC civil rights protesters threatened to set up a tent city in downtown Raleigh, creating several days of chaos. A group of 600 protesters marched on the Capitol, prompting Scott to mobilize 450 National Guardsmen at a nearby armory.[33] The governor met with a small group of the protest leaders for more than an hour, which he wrote in his diary went well. But he told Raleigh's mayor that he was opposed to another "Resurrection City," the shantytown on the National Mall put up by the Poor People's Campaign, viewing it as counterproductive. "What these civil rights people fail to realize is that those of us who are willing to correct some of the injustices (and there are some) can do it easier and quicker if we are allowed to handle it quietly," Scott wrote in his diary. "But I can't even tell them this fact because they will surely tell it to the press. Then the public becomes aroused. I know these folks are impatient and they feel like they have waited long enough. But they make it awfully hard on those who want to help."[34]

In the ensuing days, marchers began what they called jail-ins, tying up downtown traffic and harassing shoppers. One day, nine were arrested on a street corner. The next day, nine more. The following day, fifteen protesters were arrested for blocking the entrance to the Legislative Building. The civil disobedience spilled over into a few cases of violence, with a Raleigh warehouse destroyed, a nearby office gutted, and three more fires set by Molotov cocktails.[35]

Golden Frinks, a flamboyant and fearless former nightclub operator, truck driver, and army sergeant, led the state SCLC. He began civil rights demonstrations in Edenton in 1956 and became a force across the eastern part of the state. Frinks claimed to have been jailed eighty-seven times for his civil rights activities.[36] For his role in the Raleigh disorders, Frinks was sentenced to a year in prison. In September, Scott ordered an SBI investigation of Frinks for his role in the Hyde County school boycott, but the probe found no illegal activity, and nothing came of it.[37]

On May 8, five young black men erected a tent on the executive mansion grounds. When they refused an order by a highway patrolman to take it down, they were arrested. Among them was G. K. Butterfield, a twenty-two-year-old U.S. Army soldier home on leave whom Frinks had asked to participate. Butterfield later become a state supreme court justice and chairman of the national Congressional Black Caucus. "Some civil rights workers pitched a tent on the Mansion grounds last nite & were arrested,"

Scott wrote in his diary. He emphasized his earlier perspective on the Raleigh demonstrations: "What these folks don't seem to understand is that this kind of thing only hurts their cause. They are forcing me to take a harder line against them."[38] But things were far tenser in Winston-Salem, where Scott ordered 150 National Guardsmen to the city to restore order after two nights of unrest in which businesses were vandalized and firemen came under sniper fire.[39]

Racial tensions were running so high that the smallest incident could mean trouble. At Walter Williams High School in Burlington, cheerleader tryouts lit the fuse when four African American girls failed to make the squad. Several fights broke out, and on May 16, the situation escalated quickly: from a walkout to a march on the school administration building, then to fire bombings, the ransacking of school administrative offices, and the shooting death of a fifteen-year-old junior high school student by police while she allegedly looted a small grocery store. Scott ordered 502 National Guardsmen, four armored personnel carriers, and four armored vehicles into Burlington. There were 250 arrests.[40] "Big trouble in Burlington tonight," Scott wrote in his diary. "Jesse Rae, Kerr and Jan are at the farm and I had planned to join them, but security officers advised [me] to stay here in Raleigh. I suggested to Jessie Rae by phone that she return to the Mansion for security reasons, but she refused. Therefore, we had to put a couple of patrolmen around the house at Haw River. Jessie Rae doesn't believe anyone would actually do harm. She is not aware of the threatening phone calls and letters nor that some of these militants get 'hoped up' [sic] on dope. Then they are likely to do physical harm. It's difficult to know how much to let such events dictate our private life."[41]

With events beginning to spin out of control, Scott and his security detail took threats against the governor seriously. During a meeting of the Consolidated University of North Carolina trustees in Charlotte on May 26, Scott slipped out through the kitchen and a back door after a local TV station received an anonymous threat of a possible bomb and gunfire. Scott was whisked away in a plain car while a trooper drove the governor's limousine as a decoy. "Police intelligence say 3 Black Panthers from out-of-state came to Greensboro this afternoon," Scott wrote in his diary two days later. "Object—to 'get' the Governor. One has a record of mental trouble. Security will be stepped up considerably as long as they are here, especially during 4 university commencement exercises this weekend. Should I tell Jessie Rae?"[42]

The most troublesome episode of the spring occurred at N.C. A&T State University in Greensboro, one of the nation's largest historically black campuses with 2,200 students. By the spring of 1969, the mood on campus had been radicalized. First, campus violence had erupted the previous spring following the King assassination. Then, in December 1968, black radical Stokely Carmichael told students that he had stayed home and cleaned his gun rather than vote during the recent election. He urged "every black to get guns to protect himself and his family." In February 1969, 200 students took over the Dudley Administration Building, pressing their demands for more involvement in school decisions. Finally, in March violence broke out when students supported a cafeteria workers' strike. A student and a by-stander, both black, were wounded by gunshots; a family of white motorists and a nearby convenience store owner were beaten. A subsequent police raid that month surprised half a dozen students making Molotov cocktails, according to an FBI report.

In short, the campus was on edge, and all it took was a student council election at nearby all-black Dudley High School for it to explode. The students elected Claude Barnes, a student activist, to be president, but a faculty-student committee disqualified him because of his political views. The decision led to picketing and a student boycott, then escalated to rock throwing and police clearing the area with tear gas, which spread through residential neighborhoods. As the situation worsened, Scott first ordered in 50 highway patrolmen and 735 National Guard troops. At the same time as the high school fracas, the founding convention of a new national black student group, the Student Organization for Black Organization, was being held at N.C. A&T State University. Nelson Johnson, a Greensboro activist, stood on a table and urged the college students to support the Dudley students, an act that was later labeled an "incitement to riot" and landed him in jail.[43]

The crisis shifted to the N.C. A&T State University campus, where the situation continued to deteriorate. Willie Grimes, a nonactivist twenty-year-old student from Winterville, was shot dead in the back of the head while crawling on the ground. Students and militants blamed the police, but officials found that he had been killed a .32 caliber bullet of the type not used by law enforcement. His death remains unsolved. A white truck driver was pulled from his car and beaten before being rescued by black cafeteria workers. Police and National Guard began returning sniper fire. In the early morning hours, two Greensboro police officers and three auxiliary officers were hit by gunfire from the area of the Student Union and Kerr Scott Hall, a men's dormitory. Chancellor Lewis Dowdy announced that the campus would close.

After the police were wounded, a teleconference was held at Greensboro police headquarters with Attorney General Robert Morgan, SBI director Charles Dunn, Greensboro police chief Paul Calhoun, and Colonel Arthur J. Bouchard of the North Carolina National Guard—with Scott on the line in Raleigh. Around midnight, the governor decided to clear Kerr Scott Hall, Cooper Hall, and the Student Union at 6:30 A.M.[44] At the appointed hour on May 29, five hundred National Guard troops began forming in the darkness on the southwest corner of Scott Hall to prepare for a military assault on an American college dormitory. Four armored personnel carriers accompanied them, as did a helicopter to lay down a tear gas barrage and an L-19 Bird Dog military observation plane of the type often used in ground assaults in Vietnam.

Kerr Scott Hall had a special history. Kerr Scott had obtained the $2 million to build the residential hall for 1,100 students in 1949, at the time the largest state appropriation in the school's history. Not only had Scott been grateful for black support during his 1948 gubernatorial campaign, but there were marked family connections to the school, with his brother Henry serving on the N.C. A&T State University board of trustees from 1943 to 1962. The dormitory's residents were equally notable: Henry Frye, who would become the state's first black state Supreme Court justice, had lived there. So had future presidential candidate the Reverend Jesse Jackson and NFL Hall of Famer Elvin Bethea. The four students who had planned the historic Greensboro lunch counter sit-ins had lived in Kerr Scott Hall. Today, the original window and frame of Room 2128 is part of a replica of that room on display in the International Civil Rights Center and Museum in Greensboro.

The military assault was a product of faulty police intelligence and miscommunication. A police informant had said that there were two hundred to three hundred guns in Kerr Scott Hall, plenty of ammunition, and a first-aid station set up on the first floor, according to an FBI report. None of that turned out to be true. Police also reported seeing as many as twenty individuals firing down from the dormitory roof, the FBI said.[45]

Chancellor Dowdy was informed at 6:30 A.M. that Kerr Scott Hall was about to be stormed. At 6:45 A.M., a police major ordered the students to evacuate, although it is not clear how many heard the order. Their campus counselor, following the chancellor's instructions, told them that they were under strict orders to stay in their rooms. At 7:00 A.M. the helicopter and plane dropped tear gas and smoke over the men's dormitory while one group of soldiers laid down a heavy screen of tear gas. Other soldiers ran to an outside staircase and raced to the roof, working their way down, room by room. In many cases, the soldiers went down the residence hall with their guns blazing; they shot the locks off more than eighty doors. A survey in the governor's file afterward found twenty-seven rooms damaged by gunfire in Kerr Scott Hall and seventeen rooms in Cooper Hall, which the soldiers took next.[46]

Some two hundred students were taken into protective custody and released that afternoon—with no charges or arrests—to university officials. One National Guardsman was slightly wounded, but it was not clear if his injury was from sniper or friendly fire. "No sleep at all last night because of riots at A&T University," Scott wrote in his diary. "Was on the phone all night with law enforcement and city officials in Greensboro. It was tragic that the University had to be closed. Even more tragic was the loss of life. But our intelligence was correct—there were firearms in the dormitories. I feel that the Nat. Guard was a little too rough when they went into the dorms—that is, they shot off too many locks and maybe did more damage than necessary. But then, it was a military operation. Thank God no one was killed in the actual sweep of the campus—it was a miracle. . . . No sleep for 42 hours. I'm tired."[47] Actually, it was not a miracle because the students were not armed. Police initially reported having found nine high-powered rifles but later retracted that statement. Only two were operable, and the rest were dummy guns used by the ROTC.

The North Carolina Advisory Committee sent a scathing report of the state's handling of the N.C. A&T State University crisis to the U.S. Civil Rights Commission. The group, chaired by King Virgil Cheek Jr., president of Shaw University in Raleigh, included Julius Chambers, a civil rights lawyer and future chancellor of N.C. Central University. The report said that the A&T students, who were either sleeping or packing, were given no chance to leave. There was no reason, the report said, that the troops could not have used keys to open the doors. "It is difficult to justify the lawlessness and the disorder in which this operation was executed," the commission report said. "It appears that those persons responsible for restoring law and order to the campus engaged in a disruptive and unprofessional exercise, destroying property and endangering their own lives and the lives of innocent students in the dormitories."[48] Scott backed the adjutant general's decision not to appear before a fact-finding committee of the Civil Rights Commission. Scott said that the report "probably was not in the depth it should have been and was not as balanced as it should have been."[49]

Years after he left office, Scott said that the N.C. A&T State University decision was "if not the most, one of most difficult" decisions of his governorship. "That was a tense, very tense situation," Scott said. "I was on the phone all night, open line to people on the scene. And it was just ripe for violence, for somebody to be killed. . . . Am I making the right decision to use military force? What if somebody did get killed or hurt? . . . It's much like a law enforcement officer judging how long you are going to talk and try diplomacy?"[50]

A decade later, when a *Greensboro Daily News* reporter visited the dorm for a story, he found the red brick of Kerr Scott Hall still pockmarked with sixty bullet holes—something you would expect to see on a college campus in a banana republic rather than in the United States. Behind the Dudley Administration Building, a granite marker read, "In Loving Memory of William Grimes, May 22, 1969." Kerr Scott Hall was razed July 11, 2004.[51]

During a visit to N.C. A&T State University in February 1971, Scott asked the chancellor to set up a private meeting with student leaders. But the meeting, attended by the governor, Dowdy, Representative Henry Frye, and four student leaders, including the student body president and editor of the student newspaper, went poorly. One of the students refused to shake Scott's proffered hand. "The students are naturally hostile to the establishment and they are hostile to the whites and to me as governor," Scott wrote in his diary. He wrote that it was doubtful that his visit did much good. "They are separatists. And they don't have much use for Bob Scott as an individual—I can tell you that."[52]

Scott was handling one civil disturbance after another while at the same time trying to guide his program through the legislature. "It's difficult to concentrate on what needs to be done on governmental matters when so much attention must be given to civil disorders," Scott wrote in his diary in May. "They are almost getting to be routine."[53]

By May 1969, fourteen bills had been introduced in the legislature dealing with riots and civil or campus unrest, mostly increasing criminal penalties, revoking scholarships, making it illegal to seize a campus building, and making it easier to expel a student.[54] Senator Edward Griffin, D-Franklin, spoke for many lawmakers when he said that he was "sick and tired of hippies with their long hair, beards and sandals on our campuses." Uncle Ralph introduced the only prostudent legislation—an unsuccessful effort to get student representation on the boards of trustees of state-supported schools.[55]

Some constituents wrote to the governor proposing radical remedies—shuttering historically black campuses, arresting Howard Fuller, and urging greater use of the army. "The situation in Greensboro is a disgrace and I think you should have told us you would see that our schools and state-supported colleges would not be disrupted by the revolutionaries this fall," wrote Betty Crouch of Lenoir. "I would say keep a standing army ready, with tanks and ammunition and use it if necessary."[56]

In fact, police, military, and civil authorities were mobilizing in unprecedented ways to deal with the unrest. During the first six months of 1969, the State Highway Patrol transformed itself from an agency designed to keep the roads safe to a part-time peacekeeping force. During that period, they spent 40,498 hours investigating accidents and 23,151 hours involved in civil disturbances.[57] In August, Scott announced the formation of a fifty-man highway patrol riot squad and declared, "Force will be met with overpowering force each time it is necessary." Although Scott described the action as a law-and-order move, it also meant that a highly trained group of officers could be moved quickly into a tense situation to help defuse the crisis. During the coming months of racially loaded street confrontations, there were few police shootings of demonstrators of the type that would plague many communities across the United States in the twenty-first century.[58]

The SBI meanwhile operated its intelligence-gathering unit and kept tabs on everything from campus groups to labor organizations to civil rights groups. The SBI began conducting intelligence-gathering operations at least as early as 1953 on such groups as the KKK. The SBI also infiltrated such groups as the Student Nonviolent Coordinating Committee and Students for a Democratic Society, using both agents and paid informers.[59] After his election as attorney general in 1974, Rufus Edmisten, a former aide to civil-libertarian-minded Senator Sam Ervin Jr., ordered an end to the SBI surveillance. Edmisten said that the files were filled with hearsay, which he deemed "pure garbage," and ordered the practice stopped. "It infuriated me because the SBI was not set up to do that," Edmisten said. "They had virtually a whole room devoted to it—thousands of files on people. I told them to destroy those files."[60]

Unknown to the public, the U.S. Army had been spying in North Carolina. The army had a six-member Raleigh Field Office, Region II of the Military Intelligence Group, from which plainclothes undercover agents spied on protesters around the state.[61] Responding to the Detroit riots of 1967, President Lyndon Johnson had ordered the Defense Department to assume a larger role in handling the administration's civil disturbance strategy. The army repatriated thousands of intelligence officers who had been serving abroad to begin gathering information on U.S. citizens. An intelligence clearinghouse operated out of Fort Holabird, Maryland—where Bob Scott was once stationed—known as CONUS, where it collected a vast amount of information a wide variety of groups and individuals, including civil rights groups and public officials.

The secret domestic spying program became undone when an army captain named Christopher Pyle blew the whistle in an article in *Washington Monthly*. Senator Ervin, chairman of the Constitutional Rights Subcommittee, who despised left-wing radicals but revered the Constitution, ordered hearings on the army spying. He called the surveillance program "a violation of the First Amendment rights of our entire nation."[62] David Murray, Scott's point man on civil disturbances, downplayed the importance of the army's intelligence gathering, saying that most of the information they provided was out of date.[63]

The FBI's activities went far beyond watching. As part of its COINTELPRO, an acronym for Counterintelligence Program, the FBI operated a secret effort of covert and illegal operations aimed at surveilling, infiltrating, discrediting, and disrupting domestic political activity. In earlier years, COINTELPRO had directed its efforts against the Communist Party, the civil rights movement, and the KKK. In the late sixties, at the direction of FBI director J. Edgar Hoover, COINTELPRO turned its attention to left-wing campus groups. In North Carolina, the FBI particularly focused on so-called New Left groups such as the Southern Strategic Organizing Committee at Duke University and Davidson College and a chapter of Students for a Democratic Society at UNC–Chapel Hill. The FBI kept its program secret. "It is believed that any action designed to expose or disrupt activists of these groups must be such that there will be no indication that the Federal Government is behind this action," read a May 31, 1968, memo from the Charlotte FBI office to Hoover. "Even a New Left group on a college campus has the advantage of wrapping itself in the cloak of academic freedom. It is believed that many students, while sympathetic or not to these groups, would strongly resent any so-called government interference into any activities on campus."[64] Among other things, the FBI memo suggested writing fictitious, anonymous letters tying the New Left groups to communists. The FBI engaged in a range of other activities designed to disrupt left-wing students in North Carolina, according to FBI memos made public through the Freedom of Information Act.

The FBI also went hunting for government loans, scholarships, and grants to left-wing students at Duke and the University of North Carolina and sought to have them cut off. "The Charlotte Office is currently conducting investigations on several new leftists who are students at the University of North Carolina, Chapel Hill and Duke University, Durham to determine if they have a loan, scholarship or grant which is being paid from U.S. Government funds," said one FBI memo. If found, the memo continued, the information "will be submitted for dissemination with end in view of having the financial aid terminated." The FBI contacted immigration officials and prevented one foreign-born doctoral student at Duke—dubbed "a dangerous radical"—who was traveling abroad during the summer from reentering the country. When the FBI found a woman student radical living in a Durham house with several men, they planned to send a letter to her parents letting them know of their daughter's "immoral conduct." When one student got into an unspecified dispute with a shop owner, the FBI urged the shop owner to go the police, thereby making it difficult for the student to finish his education at Duke.[65]

The FBI's campaign was discovered in 1971 when a radical group broke into an FBI field office in Media, Pennsylvania, and stole more than a thousand top secret dossiers. The group mailed copies to leading newspapers and several members of Congress. The files revealed that the FBI had engaged in massive domestic surveillance of nonviolent, lawful political dissent.[66] A Senate committee investigating the FBI's COINTELPRO effort, called the Church Committee, which included Senator Robert Morgan of North Carolina, criticized the surveillance, saying that "many of the tactics employed by the FBI were indisputably degrading to a free society."[67]

Bob Scott wasn't under surveillance, but he did get more personal security. In 1969, a brick and iron wall was erected around the grounds of the executive mansion. Although the wall had been approved earlier, Morgan, then attorney general, urged Scott to build the wall "as fast as possible." "My greatest concern is the intelligence reports I have received pertaining to the extremist groups operating in our state with their stated objectives of mayhem, arson and murder, including your assassination," Morgan said in a memo.[68] This wasn't enough for Scott's protectors. In March 1969, the Secret Service sent a team to Raleigh to train the SBI to better protect the governor—the first time a state had ever made such a request.[69]

Scott's hard line on protesters won plaudits from most white constituents, but he got different reviews from the black community. In May, Howard Lee was elected mayor of Chapel Hill, the first black man to become mayor of a white-majority southern city since Reconstruction. Attending a conference of black elected officials in Washington, D.C., in September, Lee was asked about North Carolina's attitude about accepting federal funds. "You can't expect a southern state like North Carolina, which has a southern Democratic, bigoted governor who refused to appoint one black person to a major commission to aggressively pursue federal funds to help towns such as Chapel Hill," Lee replied. Unknown to Lee, a reporter heard his remarks, and the mayor's comments were headlines the next day. Lee, who saw his fledgling political career pass before his eyes, issued an apology, calling his comments "unwarranted and ill considered." He sent a telegram apologizing to the governor.

Scott was livid. The governor wrote in his diary that night that he had spent the day at a University of North Carolina executive committee meeting arguing that they should hire Lee as a lecturer, even though many on the committee opposed the move. Scott recorded that he argued if Lee wasn't hired, it would hand an issue to campus militants. "And then, tonight, I heard on the 11 pm news that Howard Lee while in Washington D.C. called me publicly a Southern Bigot. God! It sure doesn't sound like a Mayor who wants to get help from the Governor from the state for his town. A little statement from a little man."[70] As usual, Uncle Ralph served as peacemaker. He visited Lee and assured him that once he got to know the governor, he would understand that Scott was not a bigot. He later set up a meeting between the two. Ralph Scott supported Lee in 1976 when he unsuccessfully sought the Democratic nomination for lieutenant governor against conservative House Speaker Jimmy Green. Bob Scott, on the other hand, worked as a paid Green campaign consultant.

No one represented the black establishment more than Asa T. Spaulding, president of North Carolina Mutual Life Insurance, the world's largest black-owned insurance company, and Durham County's first black county commissioner. In the safety of a colloquium at Harvard University in November 1969, Spaulding suggested that black people were moving toward rebellion and many whites were heading toward creeping fascism. "Unless there is a drastic change in racial attitudes in this country, as well as acceptance of the concept of the fatherhood of God and the brotherhood of man and acting accordingly, men may cry peace; but there will be no peace," Spaulding said. "Nor any law and order for years to come short of large scale massacres, if not genocide."[71]

Although Scott angered many in the black community with his law-and-order posture, he also made efforts to reach out. In August 1969, he named Clifton Johnson, a Charlotte prosecutor, as the state's first black district court judge, and in November 1971, he named Sammie Chess of High Point the state's first black superior court judge.[72] Scott also appointed former professional football player John Baker Jr., thirty-six, the son of a veteran Raleigh police officer, as the first black member of the State Board of Paroles. "The time has come," Scott said, "to repudiate forever the notion of many that southern prisons have become cesspools of human waste simply because the majority of their inmates are black, poor or the less fortunate in life."[73] A few months later, Scott dined at the home of John and Juanita Baker, head of the state's women's prison. "If anyone had told me 4 or 5 years ago that I would be accepting a dinner invitation (especially as Governor) in the home of a black family, I would have laughed," Scott wrote in his diary. "How times have changed—and for the better." Scott later spoke at the Baker's church and had the Bakers back to the executive mansion for dinner.[74] In a community-minded move, Scott also approved a $300,000 planning grant for Soul City, a largely federally funded New City project in the Warren County area being pushed by the Nixon administration. Scott wrote in his diary that the project had "a 50 percent chance of being successful" and that if it failed, he would be "severely criticized." But he said, "We must be innovative and try new ideas." The project later came under heavy criticism, but Scott was not the target.[75]

Scott also granted clemency to five black Benson youths who had each been sentenced to twelve years in prison for setting fire to a Ku Klux Klan meeting hall after KKK members had driven through a black neighborhood brandishing firearms. The fire had been quickly extinguished, causing only $100 in property damage. The harsh sentence drew international attention, and the governor received hundreds of letters from as far away as Saipan and Morocco. Scott granted the youths clemency after they had served only two months, saying that their sentences had been too severe.[76]

Despite high-profile black appointments and overtures at supporting the black community, the North Carolina Human Relations Council criticized the Scott administration for hiring minorities more slowly than his predecessor, Dan Moore. The report said the Scott administration's minority hiring policy "seems to be one of drift rather than one of clear purpose." It found that the percentage of black workers in state government had declined 0.1 percent to 17 percent since a similar survey in 1968. (The state's black population was 21 percent.) The report also found that his record in appointing minorities to boards and commissions was no better than his administration's hiring record. Near the end of his term, Scott ordered all state agencies to aggressively recruit blacks and other minorities, sending them all a six-page affirmative action plan. But critics charged that it was too little, too late.[77]

RADICAL VOICES

North Carolina, with its history as a moderate Upper South state—a little bit of Alabama and a touch of Berkeley and Harlem—was one of the few places that supported an active Klan and a Black Panther Party. Right-wing white supremacists and left-wing campus radicals made for an unstable political brew.

The FBI campaign of harassment and prosecution had broken much of the power of the North Carolina Klan that had made it the largest in the country in the midsixties. But although reduced in numbers, the Klan had hardly disappeared. In 1969, there were still 118 units in North Carolina with 2,800 members, according to the SBI. The black protests in 1969 may have revived the Klan, for that spring and summer KKK rallies were scheduled in Lexington, Smithfield, Reidsville, Goldsboro, Stedman, Faison, Englehard, Stanfield, Rocky Mount, and Oxford.[78] Not far from Raleigh, on U.S. 70, one of the major highways leading from the state capital into eastern North Carolina, a billboard read: "Join & Support The United Klans Of America, Inc. Help Fight Communism and Integration. Smithfield is KKKK [sic] Country."[79] In another instance, a Florida woman traveling through the state wrote to Scott expressing shock at a billboard off Interstate 95 near Dunn that declared, "This is Klan Country." Scott replied with, "I hope that your impression of North Carolina will not be dictated by a single objectionable billboard. I believe we are a State of generous, tolerant people. I do hope you will visit us again; and if you spend any time in our state I believe you will agree with my assessment of our people generally."[80]

Billboards weren't the only source of trouble in rural areas. Racial tensions in Hyde County over school integration led to a gun battle in the rural crossroads of Middletown on July 4, 1969. A sniper fired two shots into a carload of black people as they passed a KKK meeting in Middletown; luckily, no one was hurt. The car's passengers told the sheriff, but he seemed unconcerned. Thirty minutes later, more than one hundred black citizens, many of them well armed, surrounded the Klan hall—resulting in a confrontation with about eighty Klansmen. State troopers hurried to the scene to form a line between the two groups, and the standoff lasted two hours. Despite the crowd, a cross was burned; as soon as it was lit, a shot was fired and a ten-minute gun battle ensued, with the Klan using high-powered rifles and automatic weapons and the black people using hunting rifles and shotguns. "It was like war," a stunned police officer told a reporter. Despite the gunfire, there were no serious injuries, although a bullet grazed a twelve-year-old and buckshot wounded several police officers. The police arrested seventeen Klansmen and seven black people. Everyone pled guilty to misdemeanors, received suspended sentences, and faced a fine of $1,000 each plus court costs.[81]

It was no longer just white vigilante groups like the Klan who cultivated a menacing profile by toting guns. Black radical groups were also arming themselves, and North Carolina had some of the most active Black Panther Party chapters in the South. Formed in Oakland, California, by Huey Newton and Bobby Seale in 1966, the Black Panther Party sought a "radical restructuring of the system."[82] The group became highly controversial because its members carried firearms and became involved in shootouts with police. After Stokely Carmichael, the honorary prime minister of the Black Panther Party, visited N.C. A&T State University in December 1968, Panther chapters sprang up in Greensboro, Winston-Salem, and Charlotte. The Panthers ran programs to help the poor, but they were also involved in gun battles with law enforcement in Winston-Salem and High Point.

KENT STATE

With the opening of fall classes in 1969, the intensity of campus activism waned, particularly among the black students. Opposition to the Vietnam War continued, however. In October during the anti–Vietnam War moratorium, peaceful marches and rallies occurred at thirty-seven of the state's seventy-four college campuses.[83] That spring, on April 27, 1970, David Murray, a Scott aide, wrote a memo suggesting that the student body presidents and newly elected editors of the campus newspapers be invited to meet with the governor in Raleigh for coffee to open up communications. "Up to now, we have had a good year on the campuses," Murray wrote. Scott signed off on the idea, but advised that they wait until after the May 30 primary.[84]

Three days later, on April 30, President Nixon ordered the invasion of Cambodia by U.S. troops, which widened the Vietnam War. The announcement sparked demonstrations on campuses across the country, and when National Guard troops killed four protesting students at Kent State University in Ohio, the campuses exploded. About 900 colleges were forced to close because of student strikes, and more than four million students at nearly 1,350 campuses demonstrated. Protestors exploded 169 bombs, and 35,000 National Guardsmen were called to quell riots on 21 campuses.[85]

After the Cambodian invasion, Scott had sent a telegram to Nixon offering his "strong support behind your decision regarding essential military action in Cambodia."[86] North Carolina campuses were soon in turmoil. The students knew of Scott's telegram, but they were primarily opposing Nixon and U.S. policy. At Duke University and the University of North Carolina at Chapel Hill, thousands of students marched through campus, shouting, "On strike, shut it down," and in some cases blocking public streets. At N.C. State University, thousands attended a convocation at the brickyard.

On May 8, an estimated 4,500 students from nine North Carolina campuses marched down Hillsborough Street from N.C. State to the Capitol—a journey that began with a four-hundred-car motorcade from Chapel Hill. Years later, Scott recalled: "One of the things permanently stamped on my memory is looking out the governor's office up Hillsborough Street one day and here comes just curb to curb, linked arm and arm, as far as you could see, students marching on the Capitol. . . . The next thing I know, I looked out there and they were burning me in effigy."[87] Scott put six hundred highway patrolmen on alert but did not call them out.[88] "They [the students] also asked if I would [use] troops and if I would authorize the use of ammunition by National Guard troops," Scott wrote in his diary. "My answer to both questions was 'yes, if the conditions warranted.' They may not have liked my answer, but at least it was honest and frank."[89] Publicly, he commended the marchers for the peaceful protest, but he declined to retract his telegram of support to Nixon. The governor agreed to meet with a student delegation and to pass on their concerns during a White House meeting with governors the following week.

After the march, Scott received many letters, most of them backing his support for Nixon's decision to invade Cambodia and calling on him to punish students who boycotted classes and to fire any teachers or administrators who let them get away with it. "Thousands of citizens salute your endorsement of president's Cambodian policy," said a telegram from Louis N. Howard of New Bern. "I hope you will not allow the communist-inspired students to force retraction. I proudly supported both your father and you."[90] Brad Strickland of Wendell sent a telegram saying: "Mr. Scott please do not let the North Carolina state college demonstrations make you [rescind] your telegram to President Nixon. Please stand your ground and if necessary give North Carolina state university give them some of the medicine that Kent State got in Ohio—please double the dose."[91]

But there were other opinions as well, such as the one written by Mrs. Evon Ray of Waynesville. "I had a son killed in Vietnam on Dec. 3 of 1969 and it seemed a terrible waste of young lives. I have another son who is ready to go in Service as soon as he receives his notice. The graveyard in our town is full of young boys that have been killed in Vietnam. What can you do to save our young men of North Carolina? Will you please help if you can?" Scott wrote her back: "I have deep feeling of sympathy for you and other mothers who have lost their sons in Vietnam. Each day I pray that this conflict can be brought to an end so that additional sacrifices will not be necessary."[92]

Jesse Helms in his broadcasts put the heat on the governor, insisting that as ex officio chairman of the university's board of trustees, Scott should demand a list of professors who granted class "amnesty" to students and a list of all students who took advantage of it.[93] But Claude Sitton, editor of the *News and Observer*, commended officials for their handling of the crisis. "North Carolinians owe thanks to the men of moderation who stood in the breach during the campus crisis over Cambodia," Sitton wrote. "No student at a state university was denied his right to an education. No building was seized and none was destroyed. No troops were called. No gunshots were fired. None was killed. But it could have been different had it not been for the leadership of Governor Bob Scott, President Bill Friday and the chancellors of the Consolidated University of North Carolina."[94]

The generation gap and the rupture over Vietnam had important consequences for the Democratic Party, splitting the party into prowar and antiwar factions and leading to what would later be described as the culture wars. The conflict would last for a generation. For his part, by the end of his administration, Scott began to sour on the war. In June 1972, Scott called Vietnam "one of the greatest tragedies of American history. . . . We have reaped a tragic harvest of death and destruction and upheaval to learn a very basic lesson. We cannot impose upon Oriental people our ideals, our concepts and our culture."[95]

For all the unrest that Vietnam caused on his home state turf, Scott faced an even more difficult problem than campus turmoil and urban riots—one that affected every little hamlet in the state—racial integration of the schools.

12 ★ BUSING

One of the most disturbing of all possibilities is that these problems
will erode the base of public support for our public schools.
God forbid that this would ever happen. —Governor Bob Scott

lthough the Supreme Court outlawed segregation in its landmark 1954 *Brown v. Board* decision, most North Carolina children still attended segregated schools when Bob Scott became governor fifteen years later— a decision made during the father's time but left to the son to deal with the consequences.

Even more than the campus and urban violence, school integration dealt a hammer blow to rural progressivism and caused many of the Branchhead Boys and their children to back more conservative politicians who promised to protect them against outside forces of change.

Just as Kerr Scott's constituent mail was dominated by people asking for government assistance in getting roads, electricity, and telephones, Bob Scott's correspondence came to be monopolized by people asking that their schools be left alone by what they saw as a malevolent impersonal, big government.

Although North Carolina did not engage in massive resistance as did other southern states, it just as effectively maintained segregation with its Pearsall Plan, which required civil rights advocates to sue each school district individually. Federal pressure, however, grew. The passage of the landmark 1964 Civil Rights Act opened a second phase of school integration. Title VI prohibited discrimination in any federally funded program, and since virtually all public schools received federal funds, the federal government had a lever to pressure school districts to desegregate.[1] But there were few compliance checks of the so-called Freedom of Choice plans adopted by most school districts, in which any black or white students could attend the school of their choice if they could get there on their own. In 1966, the U.S. Department of Health Education and Welfare (HEW) issued a second set of guidelines requiring school systems using Freedom of Choice plans to achieve specific progress toward desegregation.[2] Then, in 1968, HEW abandoned its acceptance of Freedom of Choice plans. It adopted a set of guidelines requiring the end of segregated systems by the fall of 1968 or 1969—with the Nixon administration later allowing some schools to desegregate by 1970. By the time Scott took office, 28 percent of North Carolina's black children attended desegregated schools, up from 16.5 percent from the previous academic year. North Carolina had moved from the bottom among southern states in desegregated schools to near the top.[3]

As Scott entered the governorship, he faced an angry white backlash against school integration, especially from rural eastern counties with large black populations. Many of these were the Branchhead Boys or their children, and they suddenly found their school boards—under federal pressure—requiring their children to attend black majority schools, something for which they were culturally unprepared. They wanted their governor to do something about it.

One letter came from Mrs. Robert G. Ferrell of Maysville, a black majority town of 912 in Jones County, where the schools were integrated in the fall of 1968. She had a first-grader and a third-grader in the public schools. Her first-grader was in a class with a black teacher, twenty black children, three white boys, and her daughter. "I could not and never will expose my child to such an arrangement," she wrote Scott. "Would you or anyone else? There are 18 white children and over 100 negroes out there. I took my 2 children and enrolled [them] in private school." She wrote that the private school was twelve miles away. It cost seventy dollars a month, and her husband earned only ninety dollars per week working in the log woods. "I guess with the help of God they may get through with the 1st and 3rd grade but that will probably be all they do get," she wrote. "Many people are just keeping them at home. I have an uncle who is keeping five at home. It is so pitiful. So please sitting up there in the Governor's Mansion, I know you are busy, but think of us in Maysville, North Carolina sacrificing to send our children to school. The negroes are getting the education and the welfare checks. If you reads this, thank you for listening and please try to help us, or write back saying you agree or disagree. I am not against negroes in any way, but I am for opportunities for my children."[4] Many other parents were sending their children to private school: in 1962, North Carolina had 135 private schools; by 1969, there were 1,974, with an estimated 30 to 40 new private schools opening in the fall of 1969.[5]

The backlash to school integration became so harsh that the 1969 legislature created separate public school systems in the eastern towns of Scotland Neck and Warrenton in effort to separate the white and black school populations. The U.S. Justice Department and the NAACP filed lawsuits, claiming that the new districts created "white islands" to avoid desegregation, and federal courts declared the districts unconstitutional.[6]

Officials were expecting more trouble with the opening of 1969–70 school year as the rate of integration quickened, and from the opening school bell, there were difficulties.[7] In some localities, white parents simply kept their children at home. In Wilson, only 5 of the 123 white pupils assigned to Barnes Elementary School (192 black children) showed up on the first day of school; many of the white students attended Wilson Christian School at a local church. In Kinston, only 11 of the 80 white students assigned to Adkin Senior High School showed up.[8] In New Bern, white parents staged a protest outside a previously black school where their children had been assigned. In Columbus County, parents of 300 Lumbee Indian students threatened to boycott and return them to an all-Indian school because they questioned the adequacy of the new school. Fights broke out regularly and often were serious enough to bring in police, and the State Highway Patrol and sometimes the SBI were called into such communities as Asheville, Rocky Mount, Sanford, and Greenville.

Letters from anguished white parents poured in to the governor, and one could almost visibly see the Branchhead Boy support for the Scotts and the Democrats peeling away as white families expressed disappointment with Scott's inability to preserve the old segregated schools. Mrs. Mack Webb of Elm City (population 1,201) in Wilson County wrote that her six-year-old daughter was one of only six whites in a black majority class. "My 6-year old girl is in a class of 6 white children and the rest colored and in the sight of God they are as good as she, but when a 6-year old child does no[t know] his name, if in 6 years he hasn't learned his name, then he should be in a class with his kind. [How] About bringing you[r] little Girls to Gardners school and let them sit with my first grader so she will have a white friend or send me $600.00 dollars and I will place my children in a private school w[h]ere they can be taught."[9]

Scott received letters from students such as seventh-grader Edith Craft of Norlina, who talked about the difficulty of attending previously all-black North Warren Junior High School.

The other day I was in the way of a colored girl and she said "get out of the way white bitch." It's also rather hard to ignore the colored boys when you're continuously asked for your phone number and whistled at and asked many other questions. I suppose now you'll refer [us] to a private school. Well, I have an answer for that too. My father died three years ago. That left Mama and us 3 girls to run a farm. Which is rather hard work if you have ever tried it. Three girls to a private school is rather expensive now isn't it? Maybe you would like to come down and see all of this. Our school is open to the public and I would be delighted to show you or anyone else who would like to come.

Scott wrote in reply that he too believed a school should be for education, and not for rowdiness, and that she should talk to her principal. That brought a reproof from the seventh-grader, who wrote: "I really don't think my principal could get us back in white schools and stop all this unnecessary segregation [integration] but I really do think you could and that's why I wrote you in the first place."[10]

Some letters were overtly racist, but many were from people just trying to deal with a situation they had never imagined. Mrs. A. C. Smith of Lillington wrote to Scott about her seven-year-old son, Jeffrey, one of five white students attending formerly black Shawtown Elementary with seventeen black children.

When we realized that he had to go school there he was instructed to be friendly with the other children if he could, but as different incidents happened, we told him not even to look at trouble makers and maybe they would let him alone. He himself is no angel, this I know. . . . Finally, one day last week, he said to me, "mother, why do the colored children dislike me? I have tried being nice to them or leave them alone?" What can you say that a 7-year old will understand without making him think you are against them all? We have taught him that God sees a person's heart and never sees his skin color. He has grown up with that belief.

She wrote that her daughter was finishing Lillington High School and was considering going to work rather than to college so that she could send her brother to private school. "I think every child withdrawn from public school is like removing a brick from the foundation of something very big and very important," she wrote. Scott replied: "I share this concern for I have five children in the public schools. It seems very difficult to accept the rulings of the Supreme Court and I don't suppose it will change much until the make-up of the court is changed. For the life of me I cannot understand some of the reasoning behind some of the federal district court rulings. The ruling in the Charlotte-Mecklenburg case is one of the most sweeping in the nation."[11]

All five of the Scott children attended public schools, both in Alamance County and in Wake County. When their youngest child, Jan, was assigned to Murphey Elementary School with a student body that was 61 percent black in 1971, the Scotts tried to get her transferred without success. "I am terribly disappointed, as is she, but we cannot make objection, because of the turmoil so many parents are in over our new busing system," Jessie Rae Scott wrote in her diary.[12] The First Lady expressed alarm when she showed up with her daughter on the first day of school at Murphey, located a couple of blocks from the executive mansion. "Schools began today—I went with Jan to Murphy [sic]—I wonder what their racial balance is—I could see nothing but a corridor filled with black children and black teachers—my resentment flared stronger than my conscience would like to admit for my feeling is that all should be educated equally," she wrote in her diary. "We are different tho', and my concern lies with Jan not really establishing any close friendships there for this is important to her. The people of Wake County and in other places in N.C. are seething over the busing situation. My sympathies are with them. We just pray there will be no violence."[13] But Jessie Rae was in a different mood at the end of the school year, as she noted in her diary: "When I returned to the Mansion, Jan's class was waiting for me to present a gift. One of the little black girls made the presentation. So sweet. They said it was in appreciation of all I had done for their class. This was a lovely moment."[14]

Not all responded in kind. Just as he had seen the hand of communist conspiracy in the college campus turmoil, Jesse Helms now saw dark conspiracies afoot in the daily disruptions in the schools. "This is precisely in line with the forecasts last spring by congressional investigators who had intercepted plans for revolution in the United States," he told his television audience. "Thus the country warned months ago that subversive elements had become satisfied that their strategy for continuous disruption of college campuses was far enough along to expand their agitation into high schools, and thence into elementary schools."[15]

BUSING

The eyes of the state—and the nation—were on the Supreme Court on October 12, 1970, when it heard arguments in the case that would determine whether school districts were required to use busing to racially balance their schools. Black parents had brought the case of *Swann v. Charlotte-*

Mecklenburg because the state's largest school district remained largely segregated under the school system's Freedom of Choice plan.

Integrating schools in major cities such as Charlotte, Greensboro, Winston-Salem, Durham, and Raleigh proved difficult without busing because housing patterns remained segregated, and Scott—like most southern politicians—opposed federal open housing legislation designed to prevent discrimination in the sale and rental of housing. But even with open housing laws, discrimination remained. When black families tried to integrate a white neighborhood, they often met with violence or threats. That is what happened when Horace B. Caple, a black drama professor at Shaw University, moved with his family into the previously all-white Rollingwood neighborhood in East Raleigh, just three miles from Scott's office in the Capitol. Caple moved out of his house after three weeks, saying that he feared for his life, that he was hung in effigy, and that taps were played one Saturday morning. An all-white jury acquitted Caple's white neighbor of racial intimidation under the 1968 Open Housing Act. According to court testimony, the neighbor shouted at Caple, "If you come down to my yard, I'm going to kill you. If you come out into the street I'm going to kill you. If you leave your house I'm going to kill you." When a Raleigh detective asked the neighbor about the testimony, the neighbor replied, "How would you like it if a nigger moved into your neighborhood?" Other neighbors were hardly more welcoming. Another neighbor circulated a letter in that section urging everyone to ignore the Caples. Even the neighbor's lawyer argued to the jury, "Honestly, search your conscience, and ask yourself, wouldn't you be afraid if a colored man moved into your neighborhood lowering the value of your house?"[16]

An anguished Caple wrote in 1969 to Scott,

> Sir, I implore you, who pays for the physical and mental damage done to my family and me, the chronic depression, the anxiety and fears and anguish that we bear? How do I explain this to my children and how do I rectify the damage in their mental growth that their father's manhood and dignity as a human being have been stripped away by white extremism? What is the impression of my children and of America's children to be of America? What is my impression and that of my wife's to be of America, and what is the impression of millions of other black and white Americans to be of America? How do we equate the American dream? Where is the dream, the hope and love for my land, and your land, our children's land and our children's promise for a future?

There is no indication in the records that the governor replied to Caple's letter.[17]

Bringing the Charlotte suit was Julius Chambers, the young black Charlotte attorney who would eventually become one of the nation's premier civil rights attorneys—and pay a price for his advocacy. Extremists bombed his house and his law office in Charlotte, as well as his car in New Bern; even his father, a Mt. Gilead auto mechanic, had his garage twice burned down. As a high school student in Mt. Gilead, the young Chambers had ridden a bus nearly an hour each way past his hometown whites-only high school to Montgomery County's only black, and markedly inferior, high school. Now he petitioned the federal courts to use busing as a remedy to integrate the schools.

U.S. District Court Judge James B. McMillan, a Harvard-educated native of rural Robeson County, ruled that widespread busing was the only remedy to achieve racial integration. On the subject of busing, McMillan declared, "When racial segregation was required by law, nobody evoked the neighborhood school theory to permit black children to attend white schools close to where they lived. The values of the theory somehow were not recognized before 1965."[18]

Although the governor was one of the defendants in the Charlotte busing case, that was mere legal formality. More important was Scott's role as the state's chief executive and the tone he set for the state. On the day the U.S. Supreme Court heard the appeal, Scott issued a proclamation declaring October 12 as a day of "earnest hope" that the high court "will render decisions which will preserve for us the great values of both public education and individual liberty."[19] But compared to his fellow southern governors, and although a moderate who repeatedly said he opposed court-ordered busing, Scott did not intend to defy the courts. "I think it does destroy neighborhood schools and harm the children involved by taking them out of their environment and moving them to a strange environment," Scott said.

Nobody seems to want it. The blacks don't want it—they're often the ones picked up and taken away from their neighborhoods—the whites don't want it; teachers don't want it. But because of the court desegregation rulings we must accept it. But for the governor to go around the state and say we're not going to do this or that is not unlike a loud-mouthed kid running around the school yard saying he's not going to do what the principal says. For the governor or any other government officials to say they are going to defy the federal government is sheer folly. This was settled by the Civil War . . . reaffirmed by federal troops removing the governor of Alabama from the school house door.[20]

With other southern governors such as Florida's Claude Kirk and Louisiana's John McKeithen vowing to oppose busing in any form, Scott wrote in his diary that his call for cooperation with the court orders "may have been one of the most important in my administration in view of what other Southern governors are saying."[21] Scott was not entirely at ease with the antibusing position. In his diary he asked for understanding from future generations. "When historians or researchers read this after my death, no doubt all this fuss about integration, busing of students, etc. will seem rather ridiculous!" Scott wrote. "But our statements and actions must be understood within the context of the times we live in. And a good writer and historian will do that!"[22]

Scott won praise from newspapers such as the *Raleigh Times*, which wrote that "Scott may well have set the mood that will prevail in North Carolina. Certainly he has provided a sensible example and that is far more mature and realistic than the ones being set by some of his fellow governors."[23] The governor also received an appreciative note from Judge McMillan. "Thank you! That took guts—and is an act of real leadership at a time when local leaders need to be encouraged to come out of their caves and get on with a job they find distasteful. Since I'm now technically non-partisan and inhibited by judicial ethics from even talking about pending cases, I can't say all of this publicly—but I can let you know my appreciation to you."[24]

The busing issue caused Jesse Helms to sour on Scott. Helms criticized the stance of both Scott and South Carolina governor Robert McNair, who also called for compliance with the law. "The two governors chose the side of the oppressors. . . . They may be Captain Courageous in the eyes of a network television commentator," Helms said. "But to parents of school children in their own states, they more nearly resemble a brace of faint-hearted Neville Chamberlains, simply seeking peace in their time. As history has repeatedly proved, such non-leadership is the road to disaster."[25]

Similarly, most of the letters Scott received were antibusing and criticized Scott for not being vocal in his opposition. Betty Vance Cain of Kernersville called Scott "a chicken governor" for not standing up to federal judges. "Bob, enjoy these 4 years in the mansion because I feel sure at the end of these 4 years you'll have to return to Haw River and go back to shoveling cow manure, where you should have stayed. And if you want a job you really qualify to start a chicken farm. I am a concerned mother of three boys. Proud of my state of NC but not its governor. God Bless George Wallace at least he's got back bone enough to stand up for his people of his state."[26]

Faced with a strong backlash and with Republicans increasingly raising the issue, Scott did some political backfilling. He proposed enforcing a 1969 state law that no public funds could be used for involuntary busing. He wrote a blatantly political letter to President Nixon, reminding him of his opposition to busing during the campaign. He also traveled to Washington to underline his support for an amendment offered by Mississippi senator John Stennis, which passed the Senate, requiring that school desegregation efforts be applied uniformly in the North and the South.[27]

On April 20, 1971, the Supreme Court ruled unanimously in *Swann v. Charlotte-Mecklenburg* that the courts had the power to order busing to achieve a racial balance. The case was viewed as the most important ruling involving the schools and desegregation since the *Brown* decision in 1954. Chambers said that the NAACP Legal Defense and Education Fund asked the federal courts to order similar plans for Raleigh, Greensboro, Winston-Salem, and other school systems.[28]

Opposition to court-ordered busing was not limited to North Carolina, as resistance in Boston and other cities soon made clear. A Harris Survey taken in March 1972 found that the American people opposed busing to achieve a racial balance by 73 percent to 20 percent.[29]

Scott, meanwhile, tried to calm the waters. In March 1971, he convened a small group of education leaders for a Sunday night meeting at the executive mansion to discuss ways to ways to reduce or avert further violence. Craig Phillips, the elected state superintendent of public instruction, who entered office the same time as Scott, assembled a biracial team of two veteran educators, Gene Causby, a white man, and Dudley Flood, a black man, and sent them to trouble spots to help with desegregation. Scott quietly provided the team with unmarked cars and other assistance. "He could not be public," Flood said. "They would have chased him out on a rail if he had said some of things in public that I had personally heard him say. But there was never a time, when I thought he was vacillating or waffling on the issues." Flood also said, "Jessie Rae was a tremendous influence on him. . . . [She] was the most liberal person during that period, much more than the public knew. If all else failed, we would get to Jessie Rae to do some pillow talk. Bob Scott was a tremendous asset in helping move the integration issue along."[30]

The 1970–71 school year may have been the nadir—a nightmare for school authorities, teachers, students, and parents—as full-scale integration finally occurred in many schools across North Carolina. At the end of the academic year, Scott called it "dark days" for public education.[31] During 1970, the North Carolina Human Relations Council counted 137 racial incidents in North Carolina, most related to the schools. There were countless walkouts and boycotts, assaults, attempted bombings, fights, bomb threats, actual fire bombings, stabbings, and rocks thrown. "Practically no section of the state has been free from at least a little trouble," said one SBI official. The problems often began over the selection of cheerleaders, a mascot, or the singing of "Dixie." In some communities—probably about 5 percent—schools dropped activities such as proms, student clubs, or student government to avoid friction. Athletic events were some of the most frequent battlefields. School officials in Greensboro discussed the possibility of eliminating sports after several fights, and they did erect eight-foot-high fences to separate fans of opposing schools.[32]

Black leaders had pushed for school integration for years, but African Americans now paid a heavy price. Across the South, school integration meant the closing of black schools and loss of jobs for black teachers and principals. North Carolina lost 3,051 black teachers by 1972, second only to Texas. The corps of black principals was particularly hard hit: the number of black elementary school principals fell from 620 to 170 between 1963 and 1970, while the number of black high school principals fell from 209 to 3 between 1963 and 1973.[33] There was wide anger in the black community about the way integration was implemented. It was almost always black schools that were closed and black students who were bused—a one-way process in which black students were asked to give up their values, traditions, and customs to assimilate into white schools, including foods, words, music, ideas, and values. They felt "rejected, insulted, dehumanized and humiliated," according to a report by the Good Neighbors Council. Often they were not given a chance to participate equally in student government, as cheerleaders, and in school clubs.[34]

Scott hoped that 1971–72 would be a better school year—it could hardly have been worse. "Public education in North Carolina was caught up in a churning whirlwind of change—sudden change, massive change," Scott said in a talk opening schools in Alamance County before the start of the 1971 academic year. "Many schools were plagued by unrest, tension, hostility, fear, disturbances, disruptions, hooliganisms, violence and destruction. At times, it seemed that the very foundations of our school system were cracking and that the public support the schools had plunged to a dangerously low ebb." He urged teachers, parents, and students to make the 1971–72 school year "a better year than we dreamed possible. A peaceful year. A year marked by mutual respect and understanding."[35]

But it quickly became apparent that 1971–72 would be another difficult academic year, with walkouts, bomb threats, and fights. Scott convened the Citizens Task Force on the Schools in December 1971 to examine the unrest. The governor told the group, "Here and elsewhere, many students live in fear of assault or insult by fellow students. Undisciplined elements disrupt proceedings, engage in physical attacks and intimidation, extort money from students, and generally flag their noses at duly-constituted school authority. Some students, we are told, skip school rather than expose themselves to the uncertain dangers of a hostile terrain. Depending on the severity of the situation, maybe this is an exercise in common sense in some instances." "Still," Scott said, "I think you will agree that self-preservation should not be one of the concerns of a child at school. The existence of such an atmosphere is disturbing. It is wrong. It must be corrected. It cannot help but adversely affect the climate of learning and, quite possibly, the quality of learning. One of the most disturbing of all possibilities is that these problems will erode the base of public support for our public schools. God forbid that this would ever happen. But it is entirely possible unless some of the present conditions and problems are brought under control or eradicated."[36] In May 1972, the task force recommended state funding to allow every school district to hire a public information officer, creation of a student task force for each local school unit, more minority representation on local school boards, adoption by each school unit of its own written uniform code of regulations governing student conduct, and other changes.[37]

EASTERN NORTH CAROLINA

Although school integration often served as the flash point, racial tensions were evident everywhere, particularly in eastern North Carolina, the heart of flue-cured tobacco country and the section of the state that most resembled the Deep South. The civil rights movement had largely bypassed the coastal plains area, the region with the state's largest black population, and frustrations were building over the pace of racial segregation, voter registration, the hiring of blacks, and the provision of public services.

In the early 1970s, civil rights leaders, displaying a new level of assertiveness, were ready to take their case to the streets—men such as Golden

Frinks, field secretary of the SCLC; Ben Chavis and the Reverend Leon White of the United Church of Christ's Commission for Racial Justice; and Howard Fuller, among many others. Violence erupted in small towns across eastern North Carolina, sometimes sparked by school integration, other times by other racially explosive incidents. While the violence did not attract national headlines of a Watts or Detroit or Newark, it produced the same white backlash. Consider:

- Henderson: Scott dispatched 360 National Guardsmen and 61 state troopers in November 1970 to the town located forty-one miles north of Raleigh after rioting broke out in a dispute centering on the reopening of a segregated school because of overcrowding. Fire trucks were ordered to stop responding to fires in black neighborhoods after coming under sniper fire. Several buildings were burned, and flames from fire bombings were visible six miles away. Officials cut off electrical power and telephone service to black residential neighborhoods for three days.
- Warrenton: Scott sent in 28 highway patrolmen to restore order after protests regarding demands for a black principal, resumption of a junior-senior prom, and a black studies program were ignored in November 1970. After a student march failed to disperse, students were gassed, and Frank Ballance, a local lawyer, was clubbed bloody. Ballance and Eva Clayton, both future members of Congress, were among those who complained that 36 high school girls were arrested, maced, strip-searched several times, and given a vaginal exam before being sent to Women's Prison in Raleigh by the local sheriff's office.
- Oxford: In a small town located thirty-seven miles north of Raleigh near the Virginia border, a murder provided the kindling. Scott sent in the highway patrol and then the National Guard as the town literally exploded after a twenty-three-year-old black veteran named Henry Marrow was murdered by whites for allegedly insulting a white woman on May 1, 1970. More than forty firebombs were thrown, and the *News and Observer* described one block of downtown as resembling "Berlin following the Allied bombing raids of World War II.[38]
- Roxboro: Scott ordered in 50 highway patrol troopers in June 1969 after a week of racial unrest in which 2 police officers were injured by a shotgun blast and the firebombing of a grocery store.
- Wilmington: Scott dispatched 50 highway patrolmen and then 675 national guardsmen in February 1971 into the port city to restore order that that grew out of school boycott by black students but soon erupted into

snipers, the firebombing of Mike's Grocery, a roaming white vigilante group, and eventually the murder of two Pinkerton guards at a school.

More than a year after the disturbances in March 1972, twenty-four-year-old civil rights leader Benjamin Chavis and nine others, mainly high school students, were charged with firebombing and conspiracy. They would be known as the Wilmington Ten. They had been identified by three witnesses of shaky veracity who were given special treatment by the prosecution. After the trial, all three recanted their testimony—although some recanted their recantation.

The Wilmington Ten were given a total of 282 years in prison, with Chavis given twenty-nine to thirty-four years: long sentences for the burning of a grocery. The case drew national and international attention, becoming one of the most famous legal cases in North Carolina history—one that would have long legs.

After intense pressure from both sides, Democratic governor Jim Hunt went on statewide television in January 1978 to announce that he was reducing the sentences of the Wilmington Ten but would not extend a pardon. In 1980 the Fourth U.S. Circuit Court overturned the convictions on the grounds that the prosecution failed to disclose exculpatory evidence to the defense. On December 31, 2012, shortly before she left office, Democratic governor Bev Perdue issued pardons for the Wilmington Ten.

Any of the episodes would have loomed large in most gubernatorial administrations. Two of the events, the Wilmington and Oxford episodes, resulted in books. The black protesters—and in some cases rioters—were often met with extreme white hostility: roaming vigilantes in Wilmington, strip searches of teenage girls in Warrenton, or turning off the electricity to the black part of town in Henderson. The hostility toward the black community extended to the law enforcement and justice systems. Perhaps most memorably, District Court Judge Johnny Walker of Wilmington remarked to reporters: "Maybe we should have brought in Lieutenant Calley to go in there and clear the place up." At the time, William Calley was being tried for the murder of 102 unarmed civilians in the Vietnamese village of My Lai.[39]

Officials usually prosecuted black leaders to the full extent of the law, and these young protest leaders, some of whom were beaten or arrested, would later emerge as the next generation's leaders. Howard Fuller became superintendent of Milwaukee public schools; Ben Ruffin became chairman of the University of North Carolina Board of Governors; Milton "Toby" Fitch became House Majority leader and a Superior Court judge;

G. K. Butterfield became a state supreme court justice and chairman of the Congressional Black Caucus; Benjamin Chavis became executive director of the national NAACP; Eva Clayton became a member of Congress; and Frank Ballance became a state senator and a congressman.

By 1972, the social unrest began to subside. In his final year in office, Scott called out the National Guard only once: sending 235 troops to Concord after rioting following the shooting of a twenty-three-year-old black man by a white grocery store owner.[40] But overall, the civil unrest dominated Scott's term as governor, detracted from his ability to focus on his agenda, and helped undo the rural progressive political support that his father and his grandfather had helped build. "I feel in looking back twenty-five to thirty years ago, the real story of our administration will probably be never told or recorded because it didn't happen," Scott said in 2005. By that, he meant a story in which the cities did not explode and riots did not happen. "We spent an enormous amount of time and energy trying to put out the fires, both figuratively and literally," Scott said.

Scott said he was satisfied that he prevented things from getting worse by opening communications. But he did not downplay the societal rift. "I recall a story told by my dad in 1954 I guess it was," Scott said. "He was campaigning for the United States Senate. When the [*Brown*] decision was handed down he was down in southeastern North Carolina when some reporter who had heard it and said, the decision has been handed down: 'What have you got to say about it?' My dad said, 'Well, it took them a hundred years to decide that we were wrong. They ought to give us fifty years to get it worked out.' I have thought about that a lot. It took fifty years and I'm not sure it's fully worked out yet."[41]

13 ★ REFORM, CONTROVERSY, AND BACKLASH

God help me from my friends; my enemies I can take care of.
—*Governor Bob Scott, writing in his diary*

In the first half of the twentieth century, a college education in North Carolina was mostly for the chosen few—the sons and daughters of the elite, the gifted, and the determined strivers. But after World War II, when the GI Bill of Rights made college affordable for the middle class, that began to change. In 1930, there were 18,929 students enrolled in North Carolina's colleges and universities. By the time Kerr Scott became governor, that number had more than doubled to 44,742. The postwar baby boom exploded those numbers so that by 1970, 140,485 students crowded into North Carolina public and private colleges.[1]

The state's higher education system had grown like kudzu. North Carolina had consolidated its three major campuses in 1931—the university at Chapel Hill, N.C. State University, and Woman's College in Greensboro, later renamed the University of North Carolina at Greensboro—into the Consolidated University of North Carolina, the first system of its type in the nation. In 1955, Governor Luther Hodges and the legislature created a State Board of Higher Education to better coordinate the other state-supported campuses—mainly former teacher training schools and historically black campuses—which were all vying for the river of baby boomers seeking a college education. But the board was never very effective and became less so as the legislature chipped away at its powers. By 1970, the Consolidated University of North Carolina system included six campuses, with the nine remaining state-supported campuses coordinated by the state board.

This led to a legislative free-for-all. Individual campuses became increasingly aggressive in lobbying the legislature, seeking new degree-granting programs and new buildings. Lawmakers often measured their own effectiveness by their ability to deliver for their regional campus. The leading educational entrepreneur of the era was East Carolina University chancellor Leo Jenkins, a former marine from New Jersey, who helped build ECU into a major regional campus. His successful push to build a medical school at ECU—opposed by UNC and most of the major newspapers—consumed more than a decade. (Scott sided with ECU in taking steps to build the medical school.)

Having taken on tobacco, one of North Carolina's sacred cows, in the first half of his term, Scott decided to undertake the reorganization of higher education as his political swan song. In doing so, Scott started what he later described somewhat melodramatically as "a civil war in higher education."[2]

Scott expressed concern about the increasing political infighting among the schools for the state's limited tax dollars. "The log rolling, the gilding of the lily, the rivalry and the distrust within the higher education system can only worsen if it is not given immediate attention," Scott said in a speech to a press association in Wilmington. "If allowed to continue, it could rip the system apart." He said that the fighting among three leading educators, UNC president William C. Friday, Jenkins, and Cameron West, the director of the State Board of Higher Education, resembled "kids. It's comical. It's vicious. They've got an intelligence system that's unbelievable. Bill Friday, Leo Jenkins, Cam West . . . they're like kids. It's sickening. It really is."[3]

Scott, an N.C. State graduate, came to the debate with a deeply ingrained skepticism about Chapel Hill as the institution of the state's elite. His clash with UNC leaders over their handling of the cafeteria strike had made things worse. "I think one problem, at least in the past, has been that the University of North Carolina at Chapel Hill has been too much of a 'closed shop' attitude," Scott wrote to George Watts Hill, a Durham banker and major UNC backer. "This may have been all right a number of years ago, when the majority of the state's civic, social, professional, and government leaders were University of North Carolina alumni. Not so today."[4]

In November 1970, Scott met at the executive mansion with Friday and West to broach the idea of a reorganization and, to his surprise, found Friday receptive to the idea.[5] Friday, who had been president of the Chapel Hill campus since 1956, was one of the most widely respected figures in American higher education. Despite Friday's openness, he and Scott would come to circle each other during the reorganization fight. Scott sought a complete overhaul of the 1931 Consolidated University structure, whereas Friday desired changes that kept the state's institutions under UNC control and maintained the one-hundred-member board of trustees. "Bob Scott and Bill Friday were polar personalities," historian William A. Link wrote. "Scott was impulsive, drawn to political conflict, spontaneous in his reactions, and willing to alienate his opponents by political overstatement. Friday, in contrast, was temperamentally cautious, eager for support from all quarters, averse to open conflict, and sensitive to public opinion. Scott believed in confrontation, Friday in accommodation."[6]

In January 1971, Scott created a committee headed by former state senator Lindsay Warren of Goldsboro to study the governance structure. In May, the group released a report recommending the creation of a board of regents to govern the entire system, with each of the sixteen campuses having its own board of trustees. As part of the plan, the Consolidated University and the State Board of Higher Education would be merged under a single chancellor.

Scott began a vigorous lobbying effort to win support for the reorganization during the legislative session. He addressed the legislature on May 25, saying that public higher education had been "proceeding with all sail and no rudder."[7] The governor advocated a plan that diminished the power of the Chapel Hill campus. The plan proposed a new thirty-two-member board composed of fifteen members from the consolidated university, fifteen from the regional universities, and two from the State Board of Higher Education. It meant that members from the consolidated university could be outvoted, and it drew strong opposition from many University of North Carolina allies who feared that the restructuring would reduce the importance of the state's research universities, including its flagship at Chapel Hill. Using hardball tactics, Scott suggested budgetary reprisals in the legislature if the consolidated university fought his restructuring plan; he also implied that he had a lot of leverage to make political trades. "I've got a lot of Green Stamps over there," Scott told the executive committee of the UNC–Chapel Hill trustees in May. "Shoeboxes full of Green Stamps."[8]

The Scott reorganization bill was introduced late in the session, and University of North Carolina supporters blocked any action before adjournment on July 21. Lawmakers agreed to return to Raleigh in mid-October in special session to debate further and vote on reorganization. During the summer and fall, both sides furiously worked the issue. Scott directed much of the battle personally. He lined up endorsements and promised plum jobs, and one can only guess at how many roads were promised.[9] Opponents of restructuring offered an alternative plan that called for the strengthening of the State Board of Higher Education, opening the doors for other institutions to enter the Consolidated University of North Carolina system, and placing a moratorium on all new doctoral programs until July 1973.

During a few days in October, the legislature debated, argued, voted, and reconsidered the issue before passing the reorganization on October 31. The governor's plan passed the House by a 55–51 margin and called for a thirty-two-member board of governors to run the university system. University of North Carolina backers felt that it put them in a minority position, but an effort to have the bill reconsidered resulted in a 53–53 tie and was defeated when House Speaker Philip P. Godwin Sr. cast the deciding vote against it.

What happened next was remarkable, if not unprecedented. After the bill passed in the special session on Friday, many lawmakers headed home. But the bill had not been formally enrolled, nor the special session adjourned. Scott got wind Friday night that UNC forces intended to employ a rarely used parliamentary maneuver to bring the bill back to the House floor Saturday morning. Scott and aides desperately worked the phones Friday until midnight attempting to get lawmakers to return to Raleigh. Scott wrote personal notes to thirty House members, staying up until 4:00 A.M. and rising again at 6:30 A.M.; he delivered coffee and sandwiches to his team in the legislature. One House member, Charlie Phillips of Guilford County, was sick in bed, and Scott offered him an ambulance to return to Raleigh. A highway patrolman stopped another legislator trying to leave town and told him to return to Raleigh to see the governor. State senator Hargrove "Skipper" Bowles of Greensboro, vacationing at Martha's Vineyard, returned by private plane.[10]

By Saturday morning, the pro-UNC forces won a vote to reconsider by a 55–54 margin. With that, the Scott forces agreed to renegotiate, and the new University of Carolina Board of Governors included sixteen trustees from the Consolidated University of North Carolina and sixteen from the regional universities. That meant that the consolidated university forces could not be outvoted. The new board had almost complete planning, program, and budget control. Though the reorganization was a signature victory for Scott, he was outmaneuvered at the end and forced to accept a board with the UNC contingent still holding the strongest voice because they could not be outvoted.

"Say what you will about Governor Robert Scott: That he was heavy-handed, abrasive, abusive," wrote the *Chapel Hill Weekly*. "That he dangled political plunder more openly and more cynically than any North Carolina

Governor in recent history. That he blundered and stumbled, wheeled and dealt, roared and purred, threatened and wheedled—to the bewilderment of the opposition and often to the consternation of his friends. You can say all of that about Bob Scott and his relentless drive to reorganize higher education. All of it is true. . . . But then you have to concede that he took on the University of North Carolina and its thousands of loyal alumni in a deadly struggle—something no other governor has dared to do—and virtually staked his place in history on the outcome."[11] His opponents were less impressed. "If I'd had as many roads and political appointments as Governor Scott had, it would have been like pushing biddies in the creek," said state senator John Burney of Wilmington, a leading opponent of the Scott reorganization. "It wouldn't even have been a ball game."[12]

Scott still had more reorganizing to do. He was part of a new generation of southern moderate governors that included Democrats Dale Bumpers of Arkansas, Reubin Askew of Florida, Jimmy Carter of Georgia, and John West of South Carolina and Republicans Winfield Dunn of Tennessee, Linwood Holton of Virginia, and Jim Holshouser of North Carolina, who succeeded Scott. As historian Numan Bartley has noted, they tended to be pro-business moderates who "stressed centralized government, business-like management, state planning, and the delegation of decision making to experts. Virtually all the southern chief executives undertook government reorganization."[13]

In December 1970, Scott appointed a fifty-member group called the State Government Reorganization Committee to reorganize and modernize state government. The panel found that there were 317 administrative units, most of them reporting directly to the governor. The number of state employees had grown from 14,732 in 1945 to 61,217 by 1969. "The house of our state government . . . has become bulky and misshapen," Scott told the legislature. "It has produced overlapping, wasted motion, and inefficiency." Scott said he believed that $50 million could be saved if the reorganization was put into effect.[14]

The voters approved a constitutional amendment in November 1970. It required the reduction of the number of state administrative departments to not more than twenty-five by 1975. That included the eleven independently elected departments established under the state constitution as well as seven other major departments formed by mergers and consolidations. Old departments such as Conservation and Development were divided into the Commerce Department and the Department of Natural Resources and Economic Resources. The Highway Commission became the Department of Transportation, and so forth. The basic organization of state government was set for the foreseeable future.

At Scott's urging, the 1971 legislature also created the North Carolina Council on State Goals and Policy to help recommend long-term policies for the state.

LAME DUCK

After the higher education reorganization fight, Scott increasingly resembled a lame duck and not a happy one, dealing with personal grief and aggravated by a number of controversies and minor scandals that tarnished his administration's final months. His mother, Miss Mary, died at age seventy-four on April 23, 1972, following several days of steep decline in the hospital after battling pneumonia. On top of that, during the last half of his administration Scott suffered a drip-drip of embarrassments that centered on political cronyism and detracted from his efforts to portray himself as a modernizing reformer.

While attending a dinner party in 1971, the governor was informed that John Lockamy, his assistant commissioner of motor vehicles, had been caught driving drunk. Scott told the highway patrol to handle it routinely, and Lockamy was charged. Previously, Ben Roney, his chief political adviser, had been convicted in 1969 of drunk driving and received a six-month suspended sentence. In 1971, Roney was convicted of a misdemeanor charge of hit-and-run driving. Then in June 1972, Scott accepted the resignation of two highway commissioners, Arthur Tripp and E. J. Whitmere, for conflicts of interest involving the sale of highway material to the state by either their companies or companies owned by close relatives. "God help me from my friends; my enemies I can take care of," Scott wrote in his diary.[15] There were cries of favoritism or worse when a Democratic Party official found $500 in his mailbox with a request that an inmate get favorable parole treatment. The official, executive director Charles Barbour, had treated the money as a campaign contribution. The Wake County solicitor later found no evidence of criminal wrongdoing, and the Democratic Party returned the $500. But the Scott administration received another black eye.[16]

Scott used the political patronage system, whether rewarding key legislative allies with judgeships or handing out state legal work to lawyers or making appointments to key boards and commissions. Critics accused Scott—as they had his father—of being overzealous in getting road paving projects for Alamance County. Like his father, Scott's instinct was to brazen it out when it was disclosed that he spent $4.3 million in highway surplus money to pave more than one hundred miles in his home county of Alamance, an amount that dwarfed all other counties. "I have no apology to make whatsoever," Scott said after the *News and Observer* reported his largesse. "Most of these needs I am personally familiar with since I have traveled these roads myself. . . . I am proud of every substandard bridge improved, every bad curve removed, every home, church volunteer department or business served." He later told a radio reporter, "There is nothing improper about it. This kind of thing has been done by governors in the past. *The News and Observer* is after me because I told them to go to hell. Frankly, I think they have gone."[17] Paving country roads in Alamance County was a Scott family preoccupation. At a roast for Ralph Scott held in Burlington in 1974, Lieutenant Governor Jim Hunt quipped, "It's good to be here in Asphalt County. I know you folks slip up and call it Alamance County, but I like to tell it like it is."[18]

Although most of the major North Carolina newspapers leaned Democratic and had supported him in his 1968 campaign, Scott had a stormy relationship with them—alternately courting and feuding with them. He had the editorial staff of the *Greensboro Daily News* to the executive mansion for dinner. Reporters covering him and their spouses were invited for drinks at the mansion and dinner at the Frog and Nightgown nightclub in Raleigh's Cameron Village section. He also had his favorites. Scott appointed Woodrow Price, the managing editor of the *News and Observer* who had covered his father, as chairman of the State Ports Authority.[19]

But more often he feuded with the news media. In the late 1960s and the late 1970s, the news media had begun practicing a more aggressive brand of journalism, and Scott pined for the older-style reporters and resented any sort of investigation as a personal attack. In particular, Scott clashed with the *News and Observer*. He likely remembered the days when the paper was led by Jonathan Daniels, an ally of his father, or by Josephus Daniels, a friend of his grandfather Farmer Bob, and resented the sharper investigative edge under new editor Claude Sitton, who came to the newspaper in 1967 from the *New York Times*, and its hard-nosed investigative reporter Pat Stith. Scott complained in his journal of the paper's "character assassination." He had several run-ins with Franks Daniels Jr., a top executive with the paper. Spotting him at a plant dedication in Wake Forest, Scott said that the company should put some money in research and development to come up with a product "that would cause the newspaper to self-destruct whenever the percentage of the half-truths they print gets above 50 percent that now seems to be the company policy."

"Later, Frank told me he thought it was a clever statement," Scott wrote in his diary. "I replied, 'I meant every damned word of it.' He replied, 'I know you did.' He started to extend his hand for a handshake, but I gave him a look of disgust, turned away and walked off."[20]

1972 ELECTIONS

Unlike his father, Bob Scott did not attempt to name his successor. Early in the campaign, he declared his neutrality, although he privately hoped that Attorney General Robert Morgan would run. Morgan ran for the U.S. Senate in 1974 instead.[21]

The two main gubernatorial candidates were Lieutenant Governor Pat Taylor, a country lawyer from Anson County who had the backing of many lawmakers, and state Senator Skipper Bowles, a wealthy businessman from Greensboro who had served in Sanford's administration. Taylor, a Scott ally, had helped him pass his legislative program. There were also two lesser candidates, Reginald Hawkins, making a second run, and labor leader Wilbur Hobby, who ran on the slogan "Keep the big boys honest."

Scott was caught in the middle. Bowles charged that key Scott aides, such as Ben Roney, were helping Taylor. Taylor complained that Scott wasn't assisting him and had tried to dissuade him from calling for a run-off. Scott did not back a candidate but noted in his diary that he had voted for Taylor.

Bowles, using a well-financed and modern TV-driven campaign, led the first primary by 45 to 37 percent margin over Taylor and won in a run-off by a 54 to 46 percent margin. Scott wrote in his diary that he was surprised by the Bowles victory but thought either man would make a good governor. The governor was also taken aback by the upset of U.S. senator B. Everett Jordan by Congressman Nick Galifianakis. Jordan, his mother's cousin, had been appointed to his father's Senate seat, much to the chagrin of his father's backers. Bob Scott voted for Jordan, the chairman of the Senate Rules Committee.

The Democratic primary saw the emergence of a new Democratic power—a thirty-two-year-old lawyer from Wilson whose career Scott had nurtured. In October 1969, Scott appointed Hunt chairman of a sixty-member commission to study the state Democratic Party—a distinguished group that included former governors and party chairs. The lives of the Hunts and the Scotts had been intertwined in rural progressivism for decades, particularly through their activity in the state Grange movement. James B. Hunt Sr., a dairy farmer and federal soil conservation agent in

Rock Ridge in rural Wilson County and his wife, Elsie, a public school teacher, were rural progressives who were friends and allies of Kerr Scott and strong supporters of Frank Porter Graham. Kerr Scott appointed Elsie Hunt to the State Board of Health in 1949, the first woman to serve on the board. The Hunts were charter members of the Rock Ridge Grange, created in 1944. Hunt Sr. became master of the Wilson County Pomona Grange and had also served as unpaid Grange organizer, helping start five or six Grange units in eastern North Carolina. Elsie Hunt served as state director of the Junior Grange and in 1968 was named the Grange's "woman of the year." The two Hunt boys were Grange babies, taken by their parents to Grange meetings and placed on a table to sleep through sessions. The boys were active in the Junior Grange and later the Grange Youth. Young Jim Hunt took to Grange work, which helped him develop his abilities as a leader, presider, and public speaker. In 1948, he won the National Junior Grange Essay Contest and a trip to the national convention in Atlantic City, New Jersey. Serving as North Carolina Youth Grange president, Hunt met his future wife through the Grange in 1955 at a Grange Youth Conference in Hamilton, Ohio.[22]

Hunt was already an accomplished Democratic operative when Scott appointed him to head the Democratic commission. He had chaired the state Young Democrats Club, served as an assistant to the party chairman, where he had written the party's precinct organizational manual, had organized the college campuses for Terry Sanford's gubernatorial campaign, and had worked in Washington as college director of the Democratic National Committee during the Kennedy administration.

Although he shared the same roots as Scott, Hunt was climbing the political tree along a different branch. His chief political sponsor was the Sanford organization and most particularly Winston-Salem oil jobber Bert Bennett. With Bennett's backing, Hunt sought the Democratic nomination for lieutenant governor in 1972. Hunt's leading competitor was Roy Sowers Jr., a member of Scott's cabinet as well as Scott's 1968 general election campaign manager. Hunt visited Scott to express his concern that Sowers would use his public post to help his campaign, but Scott assured him that would not happen. However, it seemed clear that some Scott allies, including Ben Roney, were helping Sowers.[23]

After Hunt led the first primary over Sowers in a five-member field by 44 percent to 23 percent, Sowers decided not to seek a runoff. That summer Scott attended a reception for Hunt and viewed him favorably. "I sure hope he wins," Scott wrote in his diary. "Jim will make a good Lt. Governor and later (in four or eight years a good governor). Jim is smart, articulate, politically savvy, good-looking, and up with the times."[24]

But the fracture in the Scott/Sanford-Bennett wing of the party was becoming more evident. Not only was there the Hunt-Sowers primary, but Scott and Sanford were circling each other in presidential politics. Scott was an early supporter of Edmund Muskie, the Maine senator and 1968 Democratic vice presidential nominee who was the early front-runner in the 1972 Democratic presidential primary. The governor brought Muskie to the state, hosted two fund raisers for him, and agreed to become his state chairman. Complicating matters was Sanford's presidential ambition. In September 1971, Sanford visited the executive mansion, where he cooked steaks on the patio and told Scott that he was considering running for president in 1972. Scott told him that he didn't think he had a chance. Already committed to Muskie, Scott thought that Sanford was merely laying the groundwork for a presidential run in 1976 even after he announced.[25]

In February 1972, Scott campaigned in the conservative Florida Panhandle for Muskie, hoping to cut off some of former Alabama governor George Wallace's support. Trying again, Sanford visited Scott once more and asked the governor to at least use his influence to convince Muskie to bypass the North Carolina primary. Sanford wanted a one-on-one primary with Wallace, pitting New South versus Old South governors. But Scott was not moved. Sanford then sought to call in his political chits. In a handwritten April 2, 1972, letter marked "PERSONAL AND CONFIDENTIAL AND FOR HIS EYES ONLY," Sanford made a plea to Scott that carried across Tar Heel generations. The letter was so sensitive that Scott placed it in his diary so that it could be opened only after his death.

In the "Dear Robert" letter, Sanford pleaded with the governor to maneuver Muskie out of the North Carolina primary. "I need for you to figure out some way to help me," Sanford wrote. "It will not help Ed Muskie to run third and it will not help me to run second and it would not help North Carolina for Wallace to run first. I think you can make some points for Bob Scott—I hope so—in a dignified, acceptable, appreciated way—with my friends . . . It can be done. Just how, I will not try to spell out, but you can figure a way—a way that will serve all these purposes.

"I helped your father in 1954 because I wanted to. I believed in him. I wanted him to win. I saw considerable personal and political risks involved and most of my close friends advised against it. I took those risks because I believe it should be done. I did not see any merit, let alone honor, in seeking favor with Governor Umstead and the 'Establishment.' I wanted to help Kerr Scott and if it did hurt me 'to hell with it.' It turned out all right and I have never regretted it, and I have continued to take political risks, including the most recent laying it all on the line in the presidential primary. In that [Scott] campaign we had little organization, no money, no staff we could pay and the Governor and his organization working against us. (It is ironic that when I ran for governor I had the Governor against me.) I left my law practice. I was not in a firm. I simply lost the income by not being there. I borrowed $8,500 from the 1st Citizens Bank during the campaign, part of which I lived on and $5,000 of which I put in the campaign in the early hard days. It took me nearly three years to pay it all back. I not only have not regretted it—it has been a tremendous source of inner pride for me. When I ran, you helped me. When you ran for Lt. Governor, I helped you, especially by personally (at least I think so) turning some significant blocs to you in the second primary. As you built up for your candidacy for Governor I kept the Bert Bennett influence (considerable and not at all inclined towards you) from developing opposition, and finally, as I always assumed you and Ben (Roney) would put them in your camp. I take no credit. I did what I wanted to do for a friend, a son of a dear friend, and for the State. Now, Bob, it is just that damn simple. I need your help. And you can help me without hurting yourself (and probably will help yourself)."[26]

Scott continued to support Muskie publicly, but Muskie's campaign began to falter. On April 27, after Muskie withdrew his candidacy, Scott threw his support to Sanford.[27]

That set up a showdown between Sanford and Wallace, or what the *News and Observer* called "the Dixie Classic." Wallace made court-ordered busing a vital issue, saying that he was against the "ludicrous and asinine busing of the little school children" and that he favored "freedom of choice." He also campaigned for tax reform, against the remoteness of government, and against urban disorders. Sanford ran on his record as governor and called for ending tax loopholes for the wealthy, putting price controls on all foods, increasing Social Security benefits by 25 percent, advocating equal rights for women, and establishing national health insurance. Claude Sitton, editor of the *News and Observer*, wrote, "It would have been no contest without the busing issue."[28]

Wallace handed Sanford a decisive and humiliating defeat, winning 50.3 percent of the vote compared to 34.3 percent for Sanford and 7.5 percent for Congresswoman Shirley Chisholm of Brooklyn, the first African

American to make a serious presidential bid. Just nine days after winning the North Carolina primary, a gunman shot Wallace in Laurel, Maryland, leaving him paralyzed for life.

Scott led the North Carolina delegation to the National Democratic Convention in Miami Beach, while most of the leading Tar Heel Democratic candidates stayed away for fear of being tied to an unpopular Democratic ticket headed by South Dakota senator George McGovern.

Scott, meanwhile, faced a potential scandal that he suspected was related to the presidential campaign. On December 28, 1971, two officials with the Internal Revenue Service's office in North Carolina visited Scott to inform him that they were investigating the expenditures of his 1968 campaign for governor. They told the governor that they found instances where business firms paid some of his campaign bills and charged them as business expenses. A month later, the story of the IRS investigation broke in the *News and Observer* based on an anonymous source. The newspaper reported that the corporate contributions were made through Scott's campaign advertising agency, Charles Crone Associates of Raleigh, whose firm was awarded the state advertising contract. Roy Wilder Jr., an account executive with Crone Associates, was a longtime personal and political friend of the Scott family who had served on Kerr Scott's Senate staff. "This practice has been going on for years, but the IRS has decided to crack down," Scott wrote in his diary. "In all fairness, however, I do feel that investigations should be made into the campaign contributions of Republican candidates & other Democrats as well as me. The IRS should not single me out. Was the investigation politically motivated? I don't know and never will. But the fact that I first hear about it not long after stating that I was supporting Ed Muskie for President and that the investigation intensified after I announced that I would be State Chairman for Muskie, is a peculiar coincidence of timing."[29]

Although Scott could not have known it when it when he voiced his suspicions, the Nixon White House and the president's reelection committee had engaged in a raft of dirty tricks to sabotage Muskie's campaign, viewing him as their most dangerous Democratic opponent. The Nixon White House also abused the IRS, using it as a tool to harass political opponents—a tactic cited in the impeachment proceedings against Nixon. Although it is possible the IRS investigation of the Scott campaign was part of the Watergate scandal, it cannot be said with certainty. The IRS to this day refuses to release any records pertaining to the investigation.

In August 1972, the IRS regional counsel in Atlanta recommended that thirteen people be indicted, including state representative John Church, the state Democratic chairman, Crone, and most of the top people in Scott's 1968 gubernatorial campaign. Scott rushed to the defense of his friends, asserting that they had done nothing wrong and suggesting that the Nixon administration—which was under suspicion for Nixon's own handling of campaign finances—had wrongly tried to tar his associates. "Silence can be golden yes, but it can also be yellow," Scott said. "I cannot sit idly by and watch stain being brushed on a group of fine North Carolinians whose only 'crime' seems to be their choice of political party labels. I cannot sit idly by while these individuals who have not been charged with anything and conceivably never will be, are being nailed to a political cross."[30] Scott asked the U.S. Justice Department to investigate the IRS leaks, but it took no action. In March 1973, however, the Justice Department announced that it would not seek indictments against the thirteen men investigated by the IRS.

In August, Scott agreed to become state chairman for—the only southern governor to back—McGovern. He said that his father had supported Senator Adlai Stevenson in 1952, and it had not harmed his bid to win a Senate seat two years later. "Although I do not have any enthusiasm for McGovern," Scott wrote in his diary, "I see no choice but to support him openly and fully. I also feel that it will do no harm politically."[31] Scott was one of the few Tar Heel office holders who spoke up for the unpopular McGovern. Yet how hard Scott worked for the ticket is debatable. Although he made a few campaign appearances that fall, he also took an official trip to Japan, went elk hunting in Idaho, and had plenty of time for golf and fishing.

In part because of white backlash against busing, a Republican tidal wave was developing, not only in the presidential contest but in statewide elections as well. In the GOP primary, Jim Holshouser, the GOP House leader and a former state party chairman, upset Jim Gardner, in part because of resentment over Gardner's flirtation with Wallace four years earlier. Holshouser, a moderate mountain Republican, had benefited from divisions left from the Democratic primary. Holshouser hesitated to make busing an issue, in part because his wife, Pat, did not want to stir up racial feelings. But his media consultant, Roger Ailes, who was Nixon's chief media consultant in 1968 and who later founded Fox News, had a face-to-face with his candidate, telling him that the election could turn on antibusing sentiment. "I have no fucking idea if busing will work or not," Ailes recalled telling Holshouser.

I haven't seen any data on it. I don't know the issue. I don't know if it is a good thing or a bad one. But here is what I do know. If you don't do an antibusing spot on TV, you'll lose the election. Now if I were you I would do the fucking spot, win the election, and then once you're in office, do whatever you think is right. Or, you cannot do the fucking spot, make your wife feel better, and not be governor, in which case you won't be able to do anything about the issue one way or the other. But that's not my problem. I'm going to cash my check before Election Day and be back on a plane for New York before the votes are counted. You have to live here. It's your life and your decision.[32]

Holshouser ran an antibusing ad.

Jesse Helms had no qualms about using the busing issue. After delivering 2,761 editorials for WRAL-TV, Helms changed his registration to Republican and entered the U.S. Senate race.[33] Helms tied his campaign closely to Richard Nixon and ran on the slogan "He's one of us," which could be taken several ways—that Helms thought like most North Carolinians or that he was from native stock or that Galifianakis was a Greek American. Helms, the one-timer admirer of Kerr Scott, assumed the role of George Wallace and Jim Gardner as the voice of working-class resentment against busing, campus protesters, black demonstrations, and street crime. Helms had been voicing similar concerns for years on WRAL, anticipating the rise of right-wing talk radio and Fox News a generation later.

Kerr Scott had exploited rural southerners' wariness of the political cliques running Raleigh, not to mention the big bankers and utility companies. Helms, by contrast, was always an ally of big business, having served as director of the state bankers' association and positioning himself as the self-styled champion of free enterprise and untrammeled capitalism. But, because the Branchhead Boy vote had been drifting away from rural progressivism—through I. Beverly Lake Sr.'s gubernatorial campaigns, through George Wallace and Richard Nixon's presidential campaigns, and now through Helms's Senate race—Helms shifted the rural populism to wariness of a big federal government, federal judges, and college professors and college students from privileged backgrounds. Helms won by a 54 to 46 percent margin.

In the presidential race, Nixon won the state with 69.5 percent of the vote, compared with the 39.5 percent plurality he had won in 1968. In eastern North Carolina—the scene of months of racial strife—Nixon won 69 percent; against Kennedy, he had won only 31 percent of the region.[34] The

Republican sweep did not surprise Scott. "History was made yesterday!" Scott wrote in his diary. "The first Republican governor elected since 1896. Also a Republican U.S. Senator! I was not surprised at this, because one could see the change in the last 10 days but I was surprised at the margin of victory for Helms for the Senate and somewhat for Holshouser. The presidential race was about what I anticipated. Frankly, I was not displeased that Jim Holshouser won. Although I dislike losing to the Republicans, it was a feeling of satisfaction to see Bowles beaten. Jim did not criticize me personally; Bowles did. Jim was not cocky and overconfident; Bowles was. Bowles never once asked me or my staff for support. He felt he was unbeatable and could win without my support."[35]

SCOTT LEAVES OFFICE

The *Charlotte News* and the *Charlotte Observer*, in assessing the Scott administration, said that his "achievements [were] overshadowed by blatant politics" and that gubernatorial decisions were often besmirched by "pettiness." The newspapers characterized the administration as having "unswerving loyalty to old-style politics" and called Scott a "vigorous champion of the spoils system." The Charlotte papers also said that Scott's programs had "not paid off in reaching the daily lives of the people." In focusing on government management, Scott's policies "are the kinds of change that a political theorist might have undertaken, not a dairy farmer and son of a Populist governor. The people programs that Governor Scott wanted the state to provide never got off the ground. . . . He initiated a state kindergarten program, but on a scale so small it underscored the enormous needs waiting to be met. His proposal for meeting North Carolina's housing deficiencies has yet to show even the promise of results."[36]

The *News and Observer*, despite Scott's feud with the Raleigh paper, provided a kinder assessment. The paper cited three major accomplishments. It called the restructuring of higher education "a remarkable achievement." It also praised his reorganization of state government and his leadership in creating the North Carolina Council on State Goals and Policies. "They are more notable than the mistakes in judgment or the instances of cronyism that sometimes marked his appointments. Bob Scott has left some commendable and enduring marks of good government on North Carolina."[37]

Looking back on his administration decades after he left office, Scott considered that he had been a generalist. If he had focused on one area, he might have been known as a roads governor or an education governor or an environmental governor. "We were all constrained by the times we lived; mine being those turbulent times," Scott said. "I often wonder what we could have gotten done if we could have devoted all of our energies and attention on the more positive things."[38]

Kerr Scott had a clear legacy of fighting to improve the lives of rural North Carolina, but his son Bob's legacy is far murkier. That Bob wanted to follow in his father's footsteps seems obvious, but the state had changed by the late sixties—less rural, less poor, more Republican, and more torn by societal dissent, whether civil rights, Vietnam, or the counterculture.

Bob Scott did inherit some of his father's little-man instincts, but he was also a product of the cultural conservatism of rural midcentury North Carolina. Scott, with a less fixed ideology or goals than his father, tried to straddle the state and nation's growing political divide with mixed results. Yet Bob Scott was smoother than his father. "Like the younger generation of Longs of Louisiana and Talmadges of Georgia, he reflected the gray flannel suit, post–World War II generation," wrote journalist William Snider. But he was also not as gifted a politician, nor was as he as a beloved figure.[39]

14 ★ END OF AN ERA

This is our home. These are our friends. These people
will come to our funerals. —Bob Scott on Haw River

On January 5, 1973, Bob Scott became the first North Carolina governor in the century to turn state government over to a Republican. Scott wrote in his diary that he felt relief, "almost comic relief," but that he didn't appreciate the partisanship of Jim Holshouser's inaugural speech, "the part where he implied that my administration was full of cronyism and the roads built by the Highway Department were solely on the basis of politics. I did not care for that at all."[1]

A young former governor at age forty-three, Scott could look forward to two decades of work before retirement. Unlike his father, he was not eyeing a run for higher political office. Lacking a law degree, Scott could not look forward to being snapped up by law firms as a rainmaker or appointed to the bench. Making money from the dairy farm was increasingly difficult.

By January 8, Scott was worried about a drive shaft snapping on the cows' forage box because the silage that had been loaded the day before froze in the eleven-degree weather. He also had a tanker milk truck's brakes freeze and lock and two large tractors were needed to straighten out the problem. He checked forty-two cows for pregnancy and breeding problems.[2]

But it wasn't all reality check. In the month after he left office, the Scotts took a vacation to St. Martin and Puerto Rico. That September, Holshouser invited him along on a three-week trade mission trip to the Soviet Union, Poland, Romania, and Yugoslavia.[3]

Scott did not have to rely on his farm income for long. Scott commuted part-time to work as executive vice president for the North Carolina Agribusiness Council, located in a suburban office park in Raleigh. He resigned from the agribusiness council in 1975 and joined a lobbying firm, called the Governmental Relations and Assistance Group, that he had created with

Governor Bob Scott on the farm. (Courtesy of State Archives of North Carolina)

former lieutenant governor Pat Taylor and with Charles Barbour, former executive director of the state Democratic Party. He would also form a political consulting firm.[4]

He toyed with the idea of running for lieutenant governor in 1976, but instead helped his wife, Jessie Rae, make her debut as a candidate. Although she had spent much of her life raising her children, Jessie Rae Scott had been active in her husband's career. Her political opportunity came when Democratic labor commissioner W. C. "Billy" Creel died of a heart attack in 1975 and Holshouser appointed Republican Avery Nye to replace him. Jessie Rae was the best known of four candidates for the Democratic nomination the following year. She positioned herself as a conservative, business-friendly Democrat—a divergence from the family's rural progressivist history. The North Carolina Department of Labor ran the federal Occupational Safety and Health Administration (OSHA) under an agreement with the U.S. Department of Labor. The agency, created in 1971 during the Nixon administration, was designed to protect worker safety. But OSHA came under fierce attack from such conservatives as Ronald Reagan for being too intrusive in the workplace. Jessie Rae Scott, the daughter of mill workers, seemed to agree with the Reagan critique, saying, "Individuals, small businesses and industries are overwhelmed by the burden of governmental regulations and forms to fill out. What is needed is not more government, but better government."[5] Not surprisingly, one of her opponents, Raleigh attorney John Brooks, thirty-nine, won the endorsement of the state AFL-CIO president Wilbur Hobby.

Jessie Rae Scott led the first primary with 37 percent, and Brooks finished second with 33 percent. Because Scott did not win a majority, Brooks called for a runoff. The former First Lady criticized Brooks as someone too cozy with organized labor, but Brooks easily handled that volley by noting that Kerr Scott, Ralph Scott, and her husband had all won election with union support. In the runoff, Brooks scraped by Scott by a 51 to 49 percent margin. No woman had ever come as close to winning a statewide nonjudicial office.

Although Jessie Rae Scott never ran for elective office again, she remained politically involved. After losing the primary, Scott became state coordinator for Jimmy Carter's presidential campaign that fall. She also championed state ratification of the Equal Rights Amendment (ERA) for women—first as honorary cochair, with her husband, of a pro-ERA steering committee and then as chief lobbyist. The ERA had been ratified by thirty-four states but needed passage in four additional states to become part of the Constitution, and North Carolina became one of the major battlegrounds. The ERA passed in the state House 61–55 in 1977 but lost in the state Senate by a 2-vote margin. In 1979, it never made it out of committee.

With the election of Jimmy Carter, a fellow southerner, to the White House, Bob Scott was in line for a federal patronage job. Carter appointed him as federal cochairman of the Appalachian Regional Commission, a Kennedy era program designed to help the economically struggling mountain areas of twelve states that stretched from New York to Alabama. For Scott, the $52,500 per year post ($216,000 in 2018 dollars) meant moving to Washington, D.C. Like his father, Scott never cottoned to Washington, and during his two years working in the nation's capital he made fifty-eight weekend trips back to Haw River and spent as much as time as he could traveling in Appalachia. For one thing, Scott missed the clout he wielded as governor. "You could just pick up the phone and reasonably expect certain things to happen," Scott said of his governorship. "It was different in Washington. Up there, you could pick up five phones, and nothing happened. That just wasn't for me." There was also friction between Scott and the staff, who felt he spent too much time away from his Washington office.[6]

When an opening occurred in 1978 for the presidency of North Carolina's fifty-eight-campus community college system, Scott went to see Hunt, who was already preparing for his reelection campaign, about becoming the new leader. Hunt gave him the green light to apply to the State Board of Education, over which he had considerable influence through his appointees. But whatever was said, promised, or implied became a matter of dispute. Hunt said he told that Scott he was qualified and that he should go through the selection process. Scott interpreted Hunt's remarks as an endorsement, which Hunt said was not the case. "I knew he had the qualifications," Hunt later recalled. "But I also knew that the board wanted to have a thorough-going search for the best person they could find. I didn't think it was right for me to pre-empt them and tell them what they ought to do."[7] In various interviews, Scott told a different version. Scott said he never met with Hunt, but had legislative allies talk to Hunt to get assurances. And Scott insisted that Hunt actively opposed his presidency, making calls to board members.[8]

The search committee unanimously recommended Larry Blake, a Montana native who headed a community college in British Columbia. The State Board of Education approved him, 8–2, and Blake stayed until 1982. Scott felt betrayed and believed that Hunt or his associates didn't want to give him a platform because they saw him as a political threat in a Democratic primary when Hunt ran for reelection.[9]

CHALLENGE AGAINST HUNT

In 1979, Scott began laying the groundwork for his ill-fated and ill-considered Democratic primary challenge against Hunt. The challenge seemed motivated by personal considerations—Scott's anger over his rejection of the community college post, a feeling that Hunt had not treated him fairly, and a sense that a protégé had double-crossed him.

While the Scott-Hunt relationship was a deep, multigenerational one that went back to their parents, that relationship had frayed over the years into mutual distrust and dislike. It had the feel of a long-simmering factional feud. Hunt may have started life as a Kerr Scott admirer, but he rose in politics as part of the Sanford-Bennett organization.

The discord reached back to the 1960 gubernatorial campaign, when the Sanford people thought that Bob Scott was more interested in helping himself than electing Sanford. Scott stewed when Sanford did not invite him to the executive mansion. Friction continued in 1964, when Scott thought that Sanford and Bert Bennett had blocked his gubernatorial ambitions. In 1969, Scott appointed a highway commissioner to Bennett's area over Bennett's strong objections. And Bennett and Hunt were suspicious that Scott and his aides were quietly aiding Sowers in the 1972 Democratic primary for lieutenant governor. In the governor's race that year, the Scott crowd tended to be for Pat Taylor, while the Bennett-Sanford-Hunt organization gravitated more toward Skipper Bowles, a former Sanford aide. Finally, Scott had only reluctantly and half-heartedly supported Sanford's presidential ambitions.

Those who had encouraged him to run, Scott soon learned, were being polite. Scott had not kept his old political organization alive. In fact, many of the Democratic workers and financiers who once helped him had gravitated to the Hunt organization—a now potent political operation.[10] There were about five hundred so-called Hunt keys or political leaders spread across the state and a network of thirty-five thousand volunteers.[11]

Scott didn't conduct a poll before entering the race, and when he finally commissioned a survey midcampaign, it showed him being swamped by Hunt. It was too late, a mistake he later acknowledged. He also found that Hunt had vacuumed up all the Democratic money, leaving little for his own campaign.[12] "I knew halfway through that campaign that I didn't stand a prayer," Scott said.[13] Funding challenges had an impact on campaign style, too. Hunt ran a modern media campaign, while Scott, relying on the old pro Ben Roney—who had learned his courthouse-style politics in the 1940s and 1950s—put his emphasis on traditional grassroots organizing. The Scotts ran just one TV ad, relying on less expensive radio.[14] To make matters worse, Scott did not have any compelling issues since he and Hunt were products of the same wing of the Democratic Party. In announcing his candidacy, Scott said that he wanted to repeal the constitutional amendment, pushed through by Hunt, that allowed governors to serve two consecutive terms—a flip-flop from his earlier position. Scott explained that Hunt's use of the governor's office had caused him to change his mind, but for many, including newspapers and Hunt's campaign, it seemed like political opportunism on Scott's part.[15]

Once in the campaign, Scott appeared to be a candidate in search of a rationale. He did engage in a little populism, proposing that members of the state utilities commission be elected by the voters, and he called for a ceiling on the salaries of power company executives that could be paid with ratepayer money.[16] Swinging to his right, he proposed making state government more efficient and limiting its growth, capping property taxes, banning the sale of farmland to foreigners, and emphasizing the upgrade of the current highway system rather than building super highways.[17] In summing up his campaign pitch, Scott said: "As we come to the last day of the primary campaign, it is important that Democrats in North Carolina decide how they will vote in the governor's race, basing that decision on what is best for our state instead of reacting to the million-dollar media efforts of the Hunt machine. As governor, I will clean up the utility controversy by letting the people elect the utility commissioners who determine our energy future. I will stop wasteful spending of big government and consider every tax dollar to be sacred. . . . I am seeking only one term as governor, and I will make decisions based on what is right instead of my political future."[18]

Hunt won the primary by a 70 to 29 percent margin—a humiliating defeat for Scott, who mainly did well in black precincts. In the fall, Hunt won 62 percent against Republican state Senator I. Beverly Lake Jr., the son of the segregationist gubernatorial candidate.

Bob wasn't the only Scott who lost a political race in 1980. Uncle Ralph had increasingly been at political risk as the farmers and textile workers of Alamance County shifted their allegiance to the Republican Party. In 1980, seventy-six-year-old Ralph Scott was challenged by Republican Cary Allred, a thirty-three-year-old pharmaceutical salesman whom Scott had defeated two years earlier. Allred criticized Scott for helping a Holiday Inn get an access road in Burlington, charging that it was a conflict of interest because Scott held stock in the company that owned the national hotel chain. It didn't help that Ralph Scott had had a heart attack in 1977. (Returning to the Senate after a heart attack, Ralph said, "Hell is just as crowded as Central Prison. I can't get in.")[19] He had also passed out during a school board meeting, which prompted someone to call an ambulance.

On a fence-mending foray, Hunt joined about four hundred Democrats at a unity rally at Bob Scott's farm that fall. Hunt called the Scott farm "hallowed Democratic soil. By just standing on it, you're going to be a better Democrat." Bob Scott, who didn't speak, stood on the edge of the crowd and talked trash with his Alamance County friends. "You believe all that junk?" Scott asked one Democrat. "He's carrying on like he believes all that." The Scott-Hunt rift never healed. "I guess he carried it to the end," Hunt said.[20]

A Republican tide swept through Branchhead Boy country and Alamance County that November; it helped elect Ronald Reagan president, and it retired Uncle Ralph. The change was fueled in part by a new wave of activism by religious conservatives who had a different interpretation of the gospel and were more concerned about social issues. The Scotts had always closely allied themselves with the rural church, making religious uplift an important component of their rural progressivism. An active churchman, Uncle Ralph had strong religious beliefs that had animated his political views on helping the poor and the handicapped. But Allred attacked Scott for his vote for the ERA and for tax-funded abortions. When voters attended church across Scott's Senate district on November 2, they were blanketed by flyers in their windshields from conservative groups endorsing the GOP ticket.[21] Just days before the voting, Senator Jesse Helms campaigned in Burlington at rally attended by 250 at the National Guard Armory. Citing his father's faith in God, Helms criticized the National Council of Churches for "promoting Marxist philosophy" while advocating the return of voluntary prayer to the public schools. "When America stops being good, America will stop being great," Helms said.[22]

In the end, Allred defeated Uncle Ralph, 58 percent to 42 percent. It was the end of an era. Years later, among the hundreds who would attend Ralph Scott's funeral on April 5, 1989, were four former governors, university presidents, state supreme court justices, lobbyists, and lawmakers. Terry Sanford called Ralph Scott "the conscience of the legislature." Former Senator Robert Morgan said that he had as much influence "as any single individual ever in the state, including governors."[23] The epitaph on Ralph Scott's gravestone read, "A champion for those who had no champion."[24]

After his loss to Hunt, Bob Scott joined with Ben Roney to form a public affairs consulting company in Raleigh. Scott sold his dairy farming operation in July 1982, a heart-breaking decision but one that he described as inevitable. The farm had not made money since the late sixties, and he had continued the operation for sentimental reasons, subsidizing it with his salaried income or by selling off land. By the 1980s, suburbanization had overtaken what had once been isolated farm country. Interstate 85 had been widened from four lanes to six lanes, Alamance Community College now adjoined the Scott farm, and residential subdivisions with names such as Governor's Green, Mill Creek, and Hawfields Crossing were now planted across the rolling countryside. There were few farmers left in the area, and none of Bob Scott's children were interested in trying to hang on. In 2016, a Walmart warehouse was built on Scott land, with the result that Governor Scott Road finally got paved.

Scott sold his herd of 175 cows to his cousin P. W. "Slick" Scott, who ran a large Orange County dairy. Bob Scott kept the land, but his cousin owned the cows and the dairy equipment and leased the grazing pasture. "It was a hard decision to make," Scott recalled. "The Scotts have been farming that land since the 1700s. We've been in the dairy business since the 1920s. We've been milking cows in that place for 64 years, twice a day, seven days a week—Christmas, New Year and Yom Kippur, too. But times change. I can't stay in the dairy business just because my daddy and granddaddy did. . . . I decided there was just no need to keep pouring money down that rat hole. I was not being fair to my children. That's their money, too."[25]

The Scotts kept the farm operation going for as long as they did, in part, by selling land. At one point the family farm had totaled 2,200 acres, but by 2005 it was down to 23 acres.[26] In 1995, he and Jessie Rae built a modern home in the woods at Melville Farms. Daughter Meg and her family moved into their older house.[27]

The Scott farm was listed on the National Register of Historic Places in 1988. It was proposed to make it a state historic site celebrating North Carolina's rural heritage because it was the birthplace of two governors. The Scott family proposed giving the state 18.6 acres, including the Kerr Scott house, the barn, and eleven other buildings, in 2000. But the state Department of Archives and History estimated that the project would cost up to $15.5 million to restore, with annual operating costs of as much as $325,000, and the project never gained the necessary political support.[28]

Faced with growing suburbanization, the need to raise money for retirement, and other financial pressures, Scott sold most of his farm to developers. The new two-hundred-acre development, called Old Fields, kept the old Scott dairy, silo, and Kerr Scott home to provide atmosphere. But the fields were subdivided into residential streets with such names as Old Fields Boulevard, Stanchin Street, Single Tree Circle, Jersey Street, and Barn Owl Avenue.

Although Scott failed to win the community college presidency on his first try, he had better luck on his second attempt after Blake left the post in 1982. By then, control of the community college system had shifted from the State Board of Education to a newly created State Board of Community Colleges. The idea of community college system had been discussed for years, and community college as an ethos dovetailed with the Scott political philosophy. Kerr Scott in his inaugural address in 1949 had called for the creation of "a system of junior colleges with facilities for affording vocational education."[29] The first industrial education center—the forerunner of the community college system—opened in Burlington near the Scott home in 1957, the same year that Hodges began his aggressive industrial development program. When the community college system was established in 1963 under Sanford, it had eight thousand students.[30] Later, as governor, Bob Scott called the system "this university for the working man."[31] There was once again some opposition to Scott's appointment, from the *News and Observer*, among others. But Scott won the appointment in a unanimous vote. The board was looking for someone to raise the visibility and the political clout of the community college system so that it could compete for state money with the public school system and with the university system.

In 1983 Scott became president of a fifty-eight-campus community college system—the third largest in the country, serving the equivalent of six hundred thousand students. It had a diverse mandate, from training skilled workers for the state's growing high-tech industries to performing as a junior college system to teaching reading and writing in a state with the third highest illiteracy rate in the country. Operating out of a state building located just across from the street from the Capitol, Scott sought to strengthen vocational and technical training needed by business and industry and reduce illiteracy. North Carolina's workforce literacy rate ranked forty-eighth in the nation, ahead of only Kentucky and South Carolina. "Business people are complaining," Scott said. "Illiteracy is like a cancer. It's unseen and hidden, yet it's just eating at the underbelly of the state—socially and economically." A campaign was begun in August 1984 by the community college system to involve business people, educators, clergy, and civil leaders in identifying adults who were too embarrassed or proud to seek help.[32]

Scott retired from the post in 1995.

MEG SCOTT PHIPPS

Meg Scott Phipps was the only Bob Scott child drawn to the twin family businesses of politics and farming. Her sister Susan became a Christian medical missionary in the African country of Chad and, eventually, a leader in a worldwide missionary organization based in Singapore. Jan became a public health administrator with the National Centers for Disease Control, and Mary operated a convenience store across from Hawfields Presbyterian Church. Kerr fought mental illness much of his life.

A twelve-year-old twin when her father moved into the executive mansion, Meg was drawn to political talk with her parents and Uncle Ralph. She earned an undergraduate degree at Wake Forest University, a law degree from Campbell University, and an agricultural law degree from the University of Arkansas. She was the only Scott offspring to work in her father's

1980 gubernatorial campaign, taking off a semester from law school, showing both an aptitude and a joy in politics. "It's just like the carpenter who grows up to be a carpenter because that is what his dad was," Phipps said. "It's what you know. Your parents are comfortable making speeches, so I am comfortable making speeches. The best absolute thing I like is meeting people—it's almost as simple as that."[33]

Phipps and her husband with their two children lived on the Scott farm in Haw River, from which she commuted daily to Raleigh, where she worked as an administrative law judge. She ran unsuccessfully for the state House in 1992. With veteran agriculture commissioner Jim Graham considering retirement in 2000, she began laying plans to succeed him. Graham was a Branchhead Boy appointed by Kerr Scott to run the state fair and elevated by Sanford to the commissioner's job. Bob Scott seemed torn by the idea of another generation of Scotts entering the fray—both eager for another campaign and warning his daughter of the "meanness" of politics. Jessie Rae Scott had even more reservations. "Our daughter, Meg, continues to prepare for a race for Commissioner of Agriculture in case Graham does not choose to run again," Bob Scott wrote to a friend in 1999. "It's frustrating to her (and me) to try to run under those circumstances. I have to stay in the background of course, less it be perceived that I am 'running her' to perpetuate the family name in politics. Truth is, Jessie Rae and I prefer that she not run for anything in today's acrimonious climate."[34] And yet, Bob Scott, the old political warrior, plunged in providing guidance, and fundraising for his daughter's campaign. He begged off helping other candidates, saying that he would be "focusing on her campaign, including fundraising."[35] The former governor was at Phipps's campaign headquarters most days and sat in on some key job interviews.[36]

North Carolina is one of only twelve states—largely in the South—where voters elect their agriculture commissioner. In most states, governors appoint the top agricultural official. In the past, one needed only the backing of the Democratic organization to win. But with the decline of political organizations, candidates now must raise money themselves. For agencies such as agriculture, that means raising money from businesses they regulate or from those seeking state contracts or from the candidates and their friends and families. To run a $1 million campaign, Phipps's father and husband lent the campaign $518,000, mainly through mortgaging the farm. She also raised $546,00 in contributions, much of it from the carnival industry.

With the support of women, blacks, and remnants of her family's rural network, Phipps captured the Democratic primary on May 2, 2000, winning 44 percent of the vote. Tobacco lobbyist Graham Boyd followed with 27 percent, former Hunt administration official Norris Tolson with 17 percent, and motivational speaker and carnival figure Bobby McLamb of Raleigh with 13 percent.[37]

In the fall, she faced Republican Steve Troxler. She had a large lead early in the polls, but with GOP presidential candidate George W. Bush running strongly, the race tightened. Both ran on similar platforms, promising to be a champion for small farmers, to stabilize the state's sagging tobacco industry, to fight new environmental regulations on agricultural enterprises, and to limit the Department of Agriculture's role as a regulatory agency. She defeated Troxler 51 percent to 49 percent.

At first, there were visions of a return to past glory. "I'll wager that your Dad is sitting up there on Cloud Nine using his bragging rights about Granddaughter Meg's campaign for the job he held so many years," Senator Jesse Helms wrote to Bob Scott early in the campaign.[38] Some saw her as a natural politician who was destined to be governor someday, although Phipps said that she never harbored such ambitions. But all of that became irrelevant. Even as she took the oath of office on a Bible that had belonged to her great-grandfather Farmer Bob, the seeds of Phipps's downfall had already been planted.

One of the chief responsibilities of the agriculture commissioner is running the North Carolina State Fair, a ten-day amusement park and agricultural exposition held annually in Raleigh. The fair, started in 1853, is one of the nation's largest, drawing nearly a million people annually to take part in the extravaganza of midway rides, farm exhibits, daredevil racing stunts, crafts, baking and flower-growing contests, country crooners, and artery-clogging food stands. Since 1948, Strates Shows of Orlando, Florida, had brought their sixty railroad cars and thirty-four trucks into Raleigh to unload their rides, fun houses, concessions, freak shows, and games of chance.[39]

During the campaign, Phipps—without criticizing Graham—said that she wanted to end the Agriculture Department's cozy relationship with Strates and put the fair-ride business out to bid. This set off intense interest in the carnival business and turned on a spigot of campaign donations from the industry—some of it in cash. One of Strates's biggest rivals was Amusements of America Inc., a New Jersey carnival company founded by the five Vivona brothers in the 1940s, which sought to gain influence in the 2000 agriculture commissioner's race. Their ally in North Carolina was

*Meg Scott Phipps, state agriculture commissioner and daughter of Bob Scott.
(Photo courtesy of the* News and Observer *and State Archives of North Carolina)*

Norman Chambliss, owner of the Rocky Mount Fair Inc., where the Vivona brothers had provided rides for years. The New Jersey company paid Chambliss $50,000 to help them get the inside track to the fair business. (Chambliss's grandfather had tangled with Kerr Scott.) Chambliss backed McLamb, a former carnival talent agent and one of the Democratic primary candidates, and obtained a $75,000 loan from Amusement of America. Chambliss then laundered the money, wrote a check to the Rocky Mount Fair, and issued a personal loan to McLamb, who in turn loaned his campaign $75,000. Such corporate contributions are illegal under state law.

The Vivona brothers, putting their money behind a candidate who won only 13 percent of the vote, clearly had a lot to learn about North Carolina politics. On election night, McLamb offered to support Phipps, and in return he received a promise to help pay off his campaign loans—which is how she allowed herself to be pulled into the scandal. McLamb also promised to help Phipps raise money from the carnival industry.

The series of campaign violations that followed caused even one of Phipps's own attorneys to call it "surprising and stupefying."[40] Various carnival companies made large amounts of illegal cash contributions; the Phipps campaign made illicit contributions to retire McLamb's campaign debt; campaign finance disclosure laws were routinely violated. Overall, Phipps accepted at least $285,000 from carnival industry sources—including Amusements of America, which won the contract, and even more from Strates, which lost out.

When first reporters and then government investigators began snooping around, Phipps and her campaign aides repeatedly lied about it in a coverup. As the investigation intensified, Phipps pleaded ignorance of campaign finance laws—despite being an attorney, an administrative law judge, and a member of a prominent political family. Yet there didn't seem to be any attempt by Phipps to enrich herself—she was trying to retire a $518,000 campaign debt after having mortgaged the farm as well as a $100,000 campaign debt for McLamb. But regardless of motive, Phipps got in deeper and deeper as the investigations became more serious. The newspaper stories were soon followed by subpoenas from the State Board of Elections and then finally by SBI and FBI agents as part of a state-federal probe. People wanting to do business with the state have always financed state politics. But prosecutors argued that Phipps and her aides had crossed a very fine line, and they hauled Phipps & Co. before a grand jury that charged them with extortion.

It is possible that part of Phipps's problems could be laid at the feet of her father, who rose in politics in the pre-Watergate age, when unre-ported campaign cash delivered in brown paper bags was accepted with a wink and a nod. Those who participated in politics in that era say that Bob Scott was never very scrupulous about where he got his campaign money. Evidence of those practices surfaced from time to time in the Phipps inquiry. Linda Saunders, the Phipps campaign treasurer, testified before the elections board that she didn't know she was breaking the law. She testified that she really didn't have a boss in the campaign, but she sometimes turned to Bob Scott with questions. "He learned very quickly that things weren't done like they used to be," Saunders said.[41] She also said Scott passed on stacks of $1,000 bills—totaling $19,000—to the campaign and told Saunders to record the cash illegally as contributions under made-up names. Saunders falsely attributed the money to family members, including her mother, uncle, stepfather, and grandmother.[42] "I would submit to you that Meg's troubles came out of Governor Scott," said Brad Crone, the Phipps campaign consultant. "The premise was that he was working under 1968 rules. I think Governor Scott probably persuaded Meg to take the [carnival industry] cash money and use that."[43]

On June 6, 2003, Phipps resigned and was replaced by interim commissioner Britt Cobb. In October, a Wake County jury of nine women and three men deliberated five hours before convicting Phipps on four felony counts: lying under oath to the State Board of Elections, encouraging an aide to lie to the board, covering up her campaign's misdeeds, and conspiring with an aide to hide her crimes from investigators. Her father watched as his daughter was led away by three deputies. Phipps's jaw moved almost imperceptibly as she looked at the jury. Her family and friends gathered in a circle and began to cry. Reporters shouted questions at Bob Scott. The former governor, leaning on a cane and wound tight with raw emotion, charged up to one reporter and silently backed her into a wall, then walked away laughing.[44]

Phipps still faced federal charges. She pled guilty to three of thirty federal charges after she said that federal prosecutors threatened to seek indictments against her father, who was in declining health, and her husband. "I had to plead guilty then," she said. After she plead guilty and received jail time on the federal charges, the state court passed sentence but allowed the jail time to run concurrently with the federal sentence. She said she made her plea with her fingers crossed behind her back.[45]

In the end, Phipps was sentenced to forty-eight months in federal prison and fined $25,000 with a supervised release term of two years. "That's the message for those whose political instincts are to look to the Scott legacy for inspiration: 'No more, Hoss,'" wrote newspaper columnist Dennis Rogers. "The bad old days when campaign cash came in brown paper bags and was accompanied by a wink and a handshake are gone. On this warm and blustery late winter's day, a federal judge sent the darling of her clan to prison for playing modern-day politics by old-timey rules."[46]

Looking back sixteen years after the campaign, Phipps seemed to have little understanding about what happened to her. She said that she always told the truth as best she understood it, and she believed that her conviction on perjury represented a miscarriage of justice. "But my biggest mistake was not paying attention," she said. "I honestly don't know that much was done wrong. . . . Even to this day, I rely on the trustworthiness of people. My legal mistake, I didn't read the election rules that said you can't take any cash. Maybe that is because I grew up in the political day where you had the political basket and that was perfectly alright."[47] Phipps said that she believed she was the victim of a political prosecution—just as her father was targeted by the Nixon administration during Watergate. She noted that Democrats had accused the George W. Bush–era Justice Department, at the urging of Karl Rove, of targeting Democratic office-holders and firing those prosecutors who were insufficiently aggressive in going after Democrats.

In all, eight people either went to prison or pleaded guilty as part of the Phipps investigation, including McLamb, Saunders, and two other Agriculture Department aides, as well as Chambliss, Morris Vivona, and a third fair industry official.

Phipps was assigned to Alderson Federal Prison Camp, a minimum security facility in West Virginia, the nation's oldest federal prison for women. Sometimes called Camp Cupcake by the news media because there is no barbed wire on the fences, it mainly houses nonviolent white-collar criminals. Phipps stayed most of her time in a dormitory that held 120 women, and all her personal belongings had to fit in a three-by-five-foot locker. She got a slot helping women with their GED programs and teaching English as a second language. "Although we have beautiful tree-covered space, I live, work, eat, sleep, teach, exercise and pray with the 1,100 women behind the fence: the homeless, the poor, the addicts, thieves, bankers, PhDs, lawyers, and doctors," she said in an interview with Carroll Leggett. "It was like a college campus or small town with 1,100 women there. Everyone had a job to go to each day and freedom to go pretty much where they pleased," she said. She may have been the prison's most high-profile inmate until she was joined by Martha Stewart, the businesswoman and television personality who served five months for stock fraud.

Her family members, including her father, frequently made the four-hour drive to the prison. Phipps credited her family and friends with helping her get through her ordeal. She began sending Christmas letters to her friends. In her last Christmas letter sent from prison she wrote, "Even though I'm in prison, I am blessed to have my health, my family's health and the love of my family and friends. I refused to be angry or bitter about my situation. I won't let myself be disgraced when I have this amazing grace. I have dined with presidents and prisoners, prosecutors and prostitutes, preachers and a princess. I have shared meals in ball gowns and in ball caps, on china and in chains. Everybody holds his/her fork the same. I would venture too that everyone ultimately wants the same thing—to be healthy and happy, loved and respected. Thanks to you, I feel all of that. Christmas 2006."[48]

On April 23, 2007, Meg Phipps was driven home to Haw River by her husband, Robert. She had made a short visit on a weekend pass several weeks earlier to attend the funeral of her brother, Kerr. Phipps did not have to go a halfway house. Her church, Hawfields Presbyterian, offered her a job as director of Christian education starting on her return. She could leave home only for work-related matters and was monitored electronically with an ankle bracelet for six months.[49] The night she returned home, a local florist made yellow ribbons and went from house to house on Cherry Lane Road, asking people to tie them to their mailboxes.[50] After working three years for her church, Phipps taught women's studies at Alamance Community College and pursued advanced degrees at UNC-Greensboro. She later worked as an administrator for assisted living communities in Mebane and Chapel Hill before retiring with her husband to Lake Lure in 2017.

Phipps has talked with calm and grace about her experiences, including her indictment and imprisonment, saying that it was far harder on her family than on herself. In an interview, she became emotional only when describing how the Haw River community accepted her back in its fold. "What stands out is the safe haven," Phipps said. "These people will always be here for me."[51]

Yet time was taking its toll on the Scott clan. The last of the Kerr Scott generation—the fourteen surviving children of Farmer Bob—passed away when Agnes Scott Haesler died at age ninety-five in 2003 in Twin Lakes. Bob Scott died on January 23, 2009, at age seventy-nine, at Hospice Palliative Care Center of Alamance County, twenty-one months after Phipps returned home. In his final years, he was on oxygen twenty-four hours a day as he slowly declined. He was laid to rest at a service at Hawfields Presbyterian Church—just as were his father, Kerr, and his grandfather Farmer Bob before him. The mourners sang the hymn "Faith of Our Fathers." On his gravestone across from the church, Bob Scott listed "Farmer, Educator, Public Servant. Elder in Hawfields Presbyterian Church. Lt. Governor of North Carolina, 1965–1968. Governor of North Carolina, 1969–1972. President of N.C. Community Colleges, 1983–1994." His choices for the headstone mirrored his father's; Kerr listed the offices he held and that he was an elder in the Hawfields Presbyterian Church. He also included this inscription from 2 Timothy 4.7: "I have Fought A Good Fight . . . I have Kept the Faith." Bob's tombstone reads: "He also Fought A Good Fight And Kept The Faith."

Jessie Rae Scott died at Hillcrest Convalescent Center in Durham on December 26, 2010, aged eighty-one, nearly two years after her husband's passing. On July 17, 2009, she fell at a friend's house and sustained a traumatic brain injury from which she never recovered, and she was unable to communicate as her children kept vigil.

Decades earlier, Kerr Scott had died suddenly, so he had not prepared any remarks to be read at his funeral. But according to those who knew him best, he never forgot the story of the ex-slave who cast the deciding vote to build the local school. "The six-year old Kerr never for the rest of his life, forgot the meaning of the bell which rang all night long proclaiming the family and community victory for local taxes for a public school in Haw River Township," remembered Frank Porter Graham, a UNC president and senator. "The bell was to keep ringing in his mind not only for the school for the Scott children but also for schools for all the children, roads for all the people and more excellence in the colleges for all the aspiring youths of North Carolina."[52]

Kerr's brother Ralph, on the other hand, had time to prepare remarks for his pastor to read at his 1989 funeral. In thanking his friends and neighbors, Ralph singled out an unnamed black tenant farmer whose brave vote in 1903 had caused the Hawfields school bond referendum to pass and all the church and farm bells to ring in a celebration of a small step toward progress.

Kerr Scott never forgot. Neither had Uncle Ralph.[53]

CONCLUSION

The Kerr Scott home at Haw River is a modest structure for having housed North Carolina's leading political family—a 1919 bungalow that started life as a Civil War–era log home. But it is fitting, given North Carolina's history as a state of poor farmers and, later, struggling textile workers. The Scott home place also perfectly fits the family's brand of politics, rural progressivism that helped set North Carolina on a more moderate course than the rest of the South.

Decades before the great Sun Belt migration that helped transform the Tar Heel State, and well before today's urbanization, the Scotts offered a different type of rural politics than is often portrayed in the modern media. The rural progressivism grew out of the needs of farmers who were among the poorest in the country and well into the twentieth century were still living in terrible rural isolation without such modern amenities as paved roads, electricity, telephones, medical service, and decent schools.

The Scotts were involved in several farmer movements that helped push the political parties to respond to the cries of the countryside. Farmer Bob was active in the Farmers' Alliance and Industrial Union in the 1880s, which later morphed into the Populist Party. Kerr and Bob headed the Grange, which came into its own during the Great Depression of the 1930s. The two movements prodded the state to modernize: expanding the university system, blacktopping rural roads, building new schools and ports, and championing rural electrification. Rural progressivism also steered the North Carolina Democratic Party away from the Dixiecrat mold and reconnected it with the national party of Franklin Roosevelt, Harry Truman, Lyndon Johnson, and others.

The Scotts and the rural progressives were not the sole creators of modern North Carolina politics. When Kerr Scott was elected governor in 1948, the state had already had a half century of moderate, probusiness leadership that had overseen the state's industrialization, the elevation of the University of North Carolina into a top university, and the construction of a major urban road system. So the rural progressives were not replacing reactionaries—far from it. But the traditional Democratic organization had arguably become increasingly moribund and less risk-taking since its earlier days under Governors Cameron Morrison and O. Max Gardner in the 1920s and early 1930s.

Kerr Scott was, in the view of historian Anthony Badger, the most liberal North Carolina governor in North Carolina history. "Scott was one of the last North Carolina politicians to be proud of the adjective liberal," Badger wrote.[1]

The Scotts practiced a bottom-up politics, literally leaving their plows or tractors to run for office. Their agendas were not crafted by pollsters, nor were they the product of focus groups. Rather, the Scotts came to their projects and policies out of the genuine desire for people to have a better life. The family was also culturally attuned to rural America, from church-going to gun-owning and the hard work of farm labor. Every weekend they could, they returned to Haw River to mingle with their neighbors. Such connectivity partially insulated the Scotts from racial politics and in later years from some of the social issues like the ERA and abortion.

When Kerr Scott was elected governor in 1948, the country had just emerged from the Great Depression and had successfully mobilized during World War II. There was a greater willingness to believe in the efficacy of government, yet rural people did not have to be convinced of the need for better rural services. People such as Sam Peele, a rural letter carrier from Hamlet, could see with their own eyes the results of Kerr Scott's Go Forward program. "When I voted for you for governor, I thought you would make a good governor, but I never dreamed you would put over a program like you have," Peele wrote to Scott in 1951. "I am a rural mail carrier and have been traveling over 54 miles of rough dusty roads every day serving about two thousand people and burning lots of gasoline, but now I am glad to say I have 36 miles of good black top roads and they really drive good. I want to say that you in my estimation, you are the greatest governor North Carolina has ever had. To the people who needed lights, telephones, good roads and anything for the betterment of North Carolina you have been a Miracle of Divine Grace. You are in a class to yourself, to try to describe you is like to try to describe forked lightening which can be seen running in every direction and always producing results."[2]

Politically, Kerr Scott was an important influence on a younger generation of moderate to progressive North Carolina Democrats, the most important of which were Terry Sanford and Jim Hunt. This enabled elements of the rural progressivism to continue in North Carolina into the twenty-first century with the election of Democratic governors from rural eastern towns that were at the heart of Branchhead Boy country—Bev Perdue from New Bern, Mike Easley from Rocky Mount, and Roy Cooper from Nashville.

Although North Carolina has received considerable national publicity for the rightward turn of its politics since 2010, the Tar Heel State voted Democratic longer than most any other southern state. North Carolina's twenty-year run of Democratic governors from 1993 to 2013 was the longest east of the Mississippi. Only in the states of Oregon and Washington did Democrats have longer gubernatorial runs. During the past one hundred years, only Hawaii has elected more Democratic governors than North Carolina.

But Kerr Scott and his allies had difficulty holding together a biracial coalition that included white farmers and urban blacks. Time and again, conservative opponents of rural progressivism wielded racial supremacy or separatism as a political cudgel. In particular, the white supremacy campaigns of 1898 and 1900 were used to break Populist and Republican control of the state. Later, Kerr Scott was politically damaged by the 1950 Senate race in which his handpicked senator, Frank Porter Graham, was defeated in a race-baiting contest.

The passage of the civil rights bills in 1964 and 1965, the riots following the assassination of Martin Luther King Jr., the direct-action protests in town after town by civil rights activists, and the federal mandates for school integration caused a massive white backlash against the Democratic Party. Many white voters fled to George Wallace, Jesse Helms, Richard Nixon, Ronald Reagan, and later Donald Trump. But the backlash was not just in North Carolina. Political scientists Doug McAdam and Karina Kloos have argued that the two driving forces in American politics since 1960 are the civil rights movement and "the counter movement." Since 1968, approximately two-thirds of white voters in America have voted Republican, regardless of the candidates.[3]

Although race has been a powerful issue, it is not the only reason why many rural voters moved from Kerr Scott to Jesse Helms as the political voice of the "little man." Powerful cultural currents also were in play: the polarization over the Vietnam War; the counterculture of sex, drugs, and rock and roll; and later a backlash over rapid societal changes involving the role of women in society, abortion, homosexuality, and, more recently, transgender rights. Kerr Scott could quote the Bible as well as most politicians, sided with antiliquor preachers, and always asserted that one of his chief goals was the uplift of the rural church. But starting in the 1970s with the rise of the religious right, many of the social issues split spiritually minded people. Being active in your church was no longer enough. During the 1970s, Uncle Ralph, a longtime Presbyterian Church leader, was cornered by opponents of the Equal Rights Amendment. "I thought I knew all about this thing [ERA] until I was asked yesterday if I was saved and been born again," he recalled. "I told them, it depends on who's judging. If I was judging, I was saved. If they [ERA opponents] was judging, I was going to hell."[4]

North Carolina's changing politics also reflect the shifting economy. The state had more than three hundred thousand farms in 1935, but by 2016 that number had declined to about fifty thousand. Many of the remaining farms are no longer small, struggling operations but sophisticated corporate agribusinesses. Many tobacco farmers, once dependent on the New Deal–era federal tobacco price-support program, now grow their leaf in the free market following the 2004 congressional passage of the tobacco buyout. Though not a rich state, North Carolina can no longer be called "a poor man's paradise." Per capita income in North Carolina in 1929, when the Grange movement took hold, was 47 percent of the national average. As of 2016, North Carolina's per capita income was 86 percent of the national average. With fewer people living on isolated subsistence farms and more people living in fast-growing suburban subdivisions, it is hardly surprising that there was less demand for energetic government.[5]

The Democrats mostly retained control of the legislature until the 2010 election, when a Tea Party movement helped sweep Republicans to victory, and subsequent GOP control of redistricting has helped solidify those gains. The sons and daughters—and grandsons and granddaughters—of many of the Branchhead Boys now tend to vote Republican. The reddest parts of the state are the rural and small-town areas where the Scotts ran strongest, while the bluest areas are the metropolitan areas. Many of the descendants of the Branchhead Boys voted for George Wallace, Richard Nixon, Jesse Helms, and Donald Trump.

But in many ways, things have not changed since the Scotts were in office. Rural North Carolina may now have paved roads, electricity, and telephones, but it is the area of the state with the highest unemployment, the lowest education attainment, and a myriad of other problems. In reality, North Carolina is still much more rural than the rest of the nation (66 percent urban versus the U.S. average of 80 urban percent), and it is still divided into two states—just as it was in the 1930s when Kerr Scott began his political climb. The metropolitan areas are among the fastest-growing areas in the nation, while rural North Carolinians have seen agriculture decline and textile and furniture plants shutter their gates, all while watching their population shrink and age. In recent years, nearly half of the state's one hundred counties have lost population, all in rural areas. Many of the Branchhead Boy regions of eastern North Carolina have poverty rates exceeding 20 percent.

The rural areas may no longer need their roads blacktopped or electric or telephone lines strung, but they need lots of help from government for new roads, utilities, the Internet, good schools, job training, and other infrastructure needs. Yet these areas now tend to be represented by free-market adherents. Many of the descendants of the Branchhead Boys favor the Jesse Helms brand of antigovernment populism that has become a signature of the southern Republican Party: cutting taxes, fighting for gun rights, opposing abortion and gay rights. In short, the rural Republicans have all but abandoned the rural progressivism of their forefathers, who advocated devoting more government efforts to help rural areas. So far, that gambit does not seem to be working, as North Carolina's rural areas fall further and further behind and the urban areas—which need the least government intervention—quickly expand. "Government was perceived then as being the solution to a lot of problems," Bob Scott said near the end of his life, reflecting on his father's era. "Today, unfortunately, it's perceived as being the problem." Even so, the Branchhead Boy legacy can still be seen in North Carolina; it is one reason why North Carolina is the most culturally southern state that is regarded as a battleground in recent presidential contests. (Virginia's politics are dominated by the Washington suburbs, and Florida's politics have been influenced by a huge in-state migration.)

Today, Haw River is part of the Interstate 85 megalopolis that stretches from Raleigh to Atlanta. It is no longer the isolated rural community that launched Kerr Scott's political career. Yet each day, thousands of motorists drive over Kerr Scott's cattle tunnel under Interstate 85—a reminder of North Carolina's not-so-distant past.

ACKNOWLEDGMENTS

I would like to thank the staff of the State Archives, where most of the Scott records are kept. You cannot find a more professional, more knowledgeable, or friendlier group than Doug Brown, Vann Evans, Josh Hager, Alison Thurman, Matthew Crain, Colleen Griffiths, and Gay Bradley. They made my months of research a pleasure. I would also like to thank Kim Anderson of the audiovisual section for her vast knowledge of the state's photographic history.

Peggy Boswell, curator of the Scott Family Collection at Alamance Community College, was immensely helpful in making available the resources of the facilities as well as in pointing out some valuable resources and oral histories.

Historian H. G. Jones is a Tar Heel treasure. A longtime friend of the Scott family who at one point thought about writing a Scott biography, he selflessly lent me Scott materials. Dr. Jones also was instrumental in ensuring that the Scott papers were housed in one location in the State Archives and encouraged Bob Scott to keep a diary. North Carolina history owes Dr. Jones a debt. I am also in debt to the folks at UNC Libraries, especially Jason Tomberlin, head of research for special collections.

I would like to thank Lamara Hackett for her research. And I would like to thank the *News and Observer*, particularly John Drescher, for allowing me the flexible work schedule necessary for me to conduct the years of research. The *N&O* has always been supportive of my history work.

The University of North Carolina Press has been supportive of the project from the very beginning, starting with David Perry before his retirement and later with Mark Simpson-Vos and Lucas Church, Andrew Winters, and Cate Hodorowicz, who guided the project through to completion. I am grateful for the wise advice of several readers, some known to me, such as Tom Eamon.

I would like to thank the gracious cooperation of the Scott family, from early interviews, before I knew I was working on a book, with Bob and Ralph Scott, to later interviews with Meg Scott Phipps, Dr. Charles Scott, and Dr. Samuel Scott. Although I hope that this book is an honest appraisal of the Scott family and their era—warts and all—the Scotts are still at the end of the day a remarkable family.

It would have been difficult to write this book without the work of some talented historians and writers: Julian Pleasants on Kerr Scott and the 1950 Senate race, Carole Troxler on Alamance County, Bill Link on the University of North Carolina, Howard Covington and Marion Ellis on Terry Sanford, Herbert Turner on the Scotts, Tony Badger and John Egerton on the midcentury South, Tim Tyson on the 1970s, and so forth.

North Carolina has also been blessed with a talented group of journalists who will compare favorably with any state who charted the careers of the Scotts. If I start listing them, I will leave out important names. But some went on to become national stars during the golden age of journalism.

Last, I would like to thank my wife, Margot, who has often been a history widow, patiently forgoing weekend trips and holidays so that I can work on my book, and kindly reading and offering suggestions.

NOTES

ABBREVIATIONS

DTN	*Daily Times News* (Burlington)
N&O	*News and Observer* (Raleigh)
RSP	Ralph Scott Papers, North Carolina Division of Archives and History, Raleigh
RWS	Robert W. Scott
RWSFP	Robert W. Scott Family Papers, North Carolina Division of Archives and History, Raleigh
SFC-ACC	The Scott Family Collection, Alamance Community College, Haw River, N.C.
SOHP	Southern Oral History Program, Southern Historical Collection, University of North Carolina at Chapel Hill
WKS	W. Kerr Scott
WKSP	W. Kerr Scott Papers, North Carolina Division of Archives and History, Raleigh

INTRODUCTION

1. Woodrow Price, "Liberal Democratic Party Urged Governor Scott," *N&O*, September 17, 1949.

2. C. C. Burns to WKS, July 22, 1949, Box 43, WKSP.

3. Harry Golden to WKS, April 26, 1951, Box 117, WKSP.

4. Jesse Helms to WKS, September 16, 1949, Box 34, WKSP.

CHAPTER 1

1. Turner, *Church in the Old Fields*, 182–83; A. Howard White, "The Editor's Desk," *Daily Times-News*, May 21, 1966; "Victories for Local Taxation, Telegrams Bring the News to Gov. Aycock and State Supt Joyner," *Morning Post* (Raleigh), May 6, 1903; *Greensboro Patriot*, April 8, 1903; Speck, *Gentleman from Haw River*, 6; Fitzgerald, *Remembering a Champion*, 7.

2. WKS, radio talk, February 16, 1953, Box 9, WKSP.

3. WKS, "The Rural Church," *Christian Observer*, June 24, 1942, Box 4.1, WKSP.

4. Bureau of the Census, *Eighth Census, 1860*, Slave Schedules; Troxler, *Shuttle and Plow*, 222.

5. Turner, *Scott Family of Hawfields*, 113.

6. Ibid., 115.

7. Ibid., 123.

8. Woodward, *Origins of the New South*, 191.

9. Ibid., 203, 235.

10. Lefler and Newsome, *North Carolina*, 513–14.

11. McMath, *Populist Vanguard*, 150.

12. Fitzgerald, *Recollections*.

13. Ibid.

14. Ibid.

15. Speck, *Gentleman from Haw River*, 90.

16. Fitzgerald, *Recollections*.

17. Ibid.

18. Charles Scott interview; Turner, *Church in the Old Fields*, 128.

19. Application for induction into the Field Artillery for men of draft age, WKS Papers, Box 185; WKS, breakfast meeting with senators, reprinted in *Congressional Record*, June 27, 1955, Box 179.

20. Betty Loudermilk, printed remembrances of W. Kerr Scott, May 1960, Box 184 WKSP.

21. Discharge papers, April 25, 1919, Box 185, WKSP.

22. *Agricultural Review*, May 1, 1958, Box 188, WKSP.

23. "The Life of Mary White Scott," 1970, Box 184, WKSP.

24. Fitzgerald, *Recollections*.

25. Legal document, Alamance County Register of Deeds, Graham Courthouse, October 17, 1921; Clarence Poe, "Friendly Talks from Hilltop Farm," *Progressive Farmer*, January 16, 1926.

26. Nellie B. Picken, "Four Sons of Alamance County and Famed 'Farmer Bob' Develop the Work in Which Their Father Pioneered," *Durham Herald Sun*, February 11, 1940; The Commissioner's Record, Co-operate, April 18, 1948, Box 184, WKSP; State Historic Feasibility Report, N.C. Division of Archives and History, Raleigh.

27. Scott application to Teachers and State Employees Retirement System of N.C., SFC-ACC.

28. Sanford address for the presentation of the portrait of WKS, May 7, 1959, Box 10, WKSP.

29. Clarence Poe, "What Do You Think of Governor Scott's Six-Point Program for Helping Farm Folks?," *Progressive Farmer*, February 1949, Box 4.2, WKSP.

30. Charles Scott interview.

31. Howard White, "Strategy of Kerr Scott Could Follow Established Pattern," *DTN*, December 9, 1953.

CHAPTER 2

1. Hobbs, *North Carolina*, 115–17.

2. Ibid., 123–24.

3. Badger, *North Carolina and the New Deal*, 2.

4. Noblin and Humphries, *Hold High the Torch*, 5, 101.

5. Hunt interview.

6. Noblin and Humphries, *Hold High the Torch*, 10.

7. "Grange Memorial to Sen. Scott Dedicated," *DTN*, October 16, 1958.

8. *Annual Progress Report of Rural Electrification in North Carolina*, REA of North Carolina, Box 31, WKSP.

9. "The Next Step for N.C.," *DTN*, April 12, 1933.

10. AP, "Ready to Extend Lines for Rural Electrification," *Robesonian*, April 1, 1935.

11. *Annual Progress Report of Rural Electrification in North Carolina*.

12. Annual Progress Report of Rural Electrification in North Carolina, REA, July 1, 1950, Box 71, WKSP.

13. Editorial, "Relief or Revolt," *N&O*, March 13, 1931.

14. AP, "Call for Economy of No New Taxes," *Robesonian*, March 6, 1933.

15. WKS letter, "The Pet Milk Company," *DTN*, April 18, 1931.

16. RWS interview, December 16, 1998; C. W. Pegram to Ned Wood, November 27, 1946, Box 2, WKSP.

17. "This Contest Interests," *Statesville Record and Landmark*, January 15, 1931.

18. Corbitt, *Public Addresses, Letters and Papers of William Kerr Scott*, xvi.

19. Scott form on Teachers and State Employees Retirement System of N.C., SFC-ACC.

20. Badger, *North Carolina and the New Deal*, 2.

21. Under the Dome, *N&O*, November 8, 1935; "Scott Denies He's Spite Candidate," *N&O*, May 31, 1936.

22. Coon, "Kerr Scott," 7; *N&O*, November 8, 1935, April 9, 20, 1936; *Greensboro Daily News*, April 27, 1949; Puryear, *Democratic Party Dissension*.

23. WKS statement, April 25, 1936, Box 1, 2008, SFC-ACC.

24. "Native Son Launches Campaign for Commissioner of Agriculture in Opening Address Last Night," *DTN*, April 25, 1936.

25. "Candidate Scott Aides His Hand in Milking," n.p., n.d., SFC-ACC.

26. Christensen, *Paradox of Tar Heel Politics*, 96–99.

27. "A New Commissioner of Agriculture," *DTN*, June 9, 1936.

28. "W. Kerr Is Down Home behind the Mules to Plow," *DTN*, June 22, 1936.

29. AP, "Kerr Scott Records Largest Majority, Eure Biggest Vote," *Robesonian*, November 16, 1936.

30. Hobbs, *North Carolina*, 90.

31. Noel Yancey, "Agriculture Commissioner Plans Program," *Raleigh Times*, January 7, 1937; Yancey, "Scott Promised Changes and They Were Fulfilled," *Raleigh Times*, May 1936.

32. "Increased Activities in the Agriculture Department," 1939, Box 4.2 WKSP; WKS on WPTF, September 29, 1939, Box 9.18, WKSP.

33. "Graham Contends Scott Made False Statements," *N&O*, April 9, 1940.

34. State Board of Elections, Certification of General Elections, N.C. Manuals.

35. Furman interview.

36. Kid Brewer, "Tramps and Chitlins," *Sandhills Citizen*, Box 189, WKSP.

37. RWS interview, December 16, 1998; WKS to Jim Doggett, Box 27, RSP.

38. RWS interview, September 22, 2005.

39. Coon, "Kerr Scott," 9; Corbitt, *Public Addresses, Letters and Papers of William Kerr Scott*, xv.

40. Billinger, *Nazi POWs in the Tar Heel State*.

41. Fitzgerald, *Remembering a Champion*, 133.

42. Charles Blackburn, "Mobilizing for Health," *Our State Magazine*, January 2009.

43. Editorial, *Salisbury Post*, October 1, 1947; editorial, *Durham Herald*, October 2, 1947.

44. WKS to W. E. McNeill of Jefferson, May 6, 1943, Box 1, 2008, SFC-ACC.

CHAPTER 3

1. Key, *Southern Politics*, 211.

2. George Haskett, "Machines and Parasites," reprinted in *DTN*, March 25, 1948.

3. Faircloth interview.

4. Gunther, *Inside U.S.A.*, 718.

5. RWS interview with author, December 16, 1998; Lauch Faircloth interview with author; "Scott Outlines Campaign Aims," *N&O*, February 25, 1948; "Scott Trades Verbal Blows with His Foe," *Gastonia Gazette*, June 24, 1948.

6. Royall to WKS, November 28, 1947, Box 3, WKSP; *N&O*, May 23, 25, 1950.

7. "W. Kerr Scott to Announce within Week Whether or Not He Will Enter the Democratic Campaign for Governor," *DTN*, January 21, 1948; Marjorie Hunter, "Scott Seeks Governorship, to Quit Agriculture Post," *N&O*, February 7, 1948.

8. Coon, *"Kerr Scott."*

9. Faircloth interview.

10. RWS interview, September 22, 2005.

11. "An Agricultural Program for North Carolina," March 1948, N.C. State College of Agriculture and Engineering, Box 1, WKSP; "Rural Health and Medical Services in North Carolina," C. Horace Hamilton, head of the Department of Rural Sociology, N.C. Agriculture Experiment Station, State College Station, August 1950, Box 95, WKSP.

12. Jay Jenkins, Ralph Scott Profile, 1978, Box 26, RSP.

13. "Scott Outlines Campaign Aims."

14. *N&O*, June 14, 1948.

15. "Cherry to Allot Surplus for Farm Road Building," *N&O*, February 13, 1948.

16. UP, "Scott and Johnson Vie for Votes," *Statesville Record and Landmark*, June 10, 1948.

17. UP, "Scott Demands State-Wide Liquor Referendum," *Statesville Daily Record*, April 14, 1948.

18. Pleasants, *Political Career of W. Kerr Scott*, 64.

19. William A. Shires, "An $88 Million Legacy from Gov. Kerr Scott," *Greensboro Record*, July 29, 1966.

20. Bulla, *Textiles and Politics*, 22.

21. Pleasants, *Political Career of W. Kerr Scott*, 45–46.

22. Corbitt, *Public Addresses, Letters and Papers of William Kerr Scott*, 48.

23. "Jesse Helms and Senator at Odds in Many Matters Get Together," *DTN*, February 13, 1957.

24. AP, "Scott Says Voters Ask Own Choice," *DTN*, June 10, 1948.

25. "Scott Trades Verbal Blows with His Foe," *Gastonia Gazette*, June 24, 1948.

26. AP, "Johnson Hits at 'Machine' in Radio Talk," *DTN*, June 24, 1948.

27. "Scott Answers Johnson Attack," *N&O*, May 14, 1948; "Johnson Raps Scott Record," *N&O*, June 19, 1948.

28. *N&O*, June 22, 1948.

29. Lynn Nisbett, "Around Capital Square," *DTN*, June 29, 1948.

30. Myers, "Resonant Ripples in a Global Pond."

31. McCullough, *Truman*, 588.

32. Margaret Kernodle, "Southern Group Organizes Drive," *N&O*, March 6, 1948.

33. Marjorie Hunter, "Democrats Given Free Range at Democratic Convention," *N&O*, May 21, 1948.

34. Eamon, *Making of a Southern Democracy*, 21.

35. Pleasants, *Political Career of W. Kerr Scott*, 67–68.

36. Pietrusza, *1948*, 238.

37. Christensen, *Paradox of Tar Heel Politics*, 129.

38. Nelson Warren, "Thurmond Civil Rights," *DTN*, October 5, 1945.

39. Covington and Ellis, *Terry Sanford*, 97.

40. Pietrusza, *1948*, 99.

41. Simmons Fentress, "Wallace Appearances Bring Shows of Tomatoes, Eggs," *N&O*, August 31, 1948; John N. Popham, "President Assails Wallace Egging, Missiles Thrown Again in the South," *New York Times*, September 1, 1948; Covington and Ellis, *Terry Sanford*; Culver and Hyde, *American Dreamer*, 494.

42. Culver and Hyde, *American Dreamer*, 495.

43. Haynes and Klehr, *Venona*; Romerstein and Breindel, *Venona Secrets*.

44. Pietrusza, *1948*, 67.

45. Ibid., 289.

46. Capus Waynick oral history interview by Bill Finger, February 4, 1974, SOHP.

47. Ibid.; "Democrats Rally and Honor W. Kerr Scott," *DTN*, September 25, 1948.

48. Lyle Edwards, "Crowd Wanted to Applaud but Couldn't Get the Cue," *Gastonia Gazette*, October 20, 1948.

49. "Scott Is Versatile," *DTN*, October 20, 1948.

50. Matthews, *North Carolina Votes*.

51. Pietrusza, *1948*, 394.

52. R. Mayne Albright, "O. Max Gardner and the Shelby Dynasty," *The State* (Columbia, S.C.), August 1983.

CHAPTER 4

1. Speck, *Gentleman from Haw River*, 32.

2. Advertisement, *N&O*, January 2, 1949.

3. U.S. Census Bureau, "Urban and Rural Population, 1900–1990."

4. WKS, "North Carolina's Agricultural Problems," February 4, 1949, WKSP, ; Corbitt, *Public Addresses, Letters and Papers of William Kerr Scott*, 337.

5. Jay Jenkins, "A Red Rose for Kerr Scott," *Charlotte Observer*, April 17, 1965.

6. AP, "Scott Demands Phones, Power for Rural Areas," *Robesonian*, December 16, 1948.

7. C. A. McKnight, "Liberal Governor's Coups Awe Carolina Assembly," *Charlotte News*, April 9, 1949.

8. Senator Henry Shelton, remarks at dedication of Kerr Scott Building at fairgrounds, October 23, 1974, Box 27, RSP.

9. Jack Childs, "Assembly Veterans Recalls Days of the First Scott," *N&O*, February 3, 1969.

10. Coon, "Kerr Scott," 31–32; *Charlotte Observer*, January 1, 1949; *Durham Sun*, January 6, 1949.

11. Eamon, *Making of a Southern Democracy*, 23.

12. Ibid., 69.

13. Turner, *Paving Tobacco Road*, 1, 3–4.

14. Ibid., 60–61.

15. WKS to J. H. Harris of Marion, February 1, 1946, Box 4.1, WKSP.

16. Coon, "Kerr Scott," 34.

17. Faircloth interview.

18. Corbitt, *Public Addresses, Letters, and Papers of William Kerr Scott*, 22–23.

19. W. H. Rogers, administrative assistant for the State Highway and Public Works Commission, to WKS, memorandum, December 3, 1948, Box 27, RSP.

20. UP, "Better Business Pushed by Scott," *Statesville Daily Record*, May 13, 1948.

21. D. Reeves Noland to WKS, March 3, 1949, Box 15, WKSP.

22. Charles D. Thorne to WKS, November 10, 1949, Box 16, WKSP.

23. Finley L. German to WKS, October 1, 1948, Box 14, WKSP.

24. Mrs. William H. Wood to WKS, January 20, 1946, and undated follow-up, Box 4.1, WKSP.

25. Jim Chaney, "Governor Says That Clique Trying to Kill His Program," *N&O*, March 26, 1949.

26. Corbitt, *Public Addresses, Letters, and Papers of William Kerr Scott*, 98–99.

27. Jim Chaney, "Scott Says Third House Running General Assembly," *N&O*, April 6, 1949.

28. Dan Hodges, "Scott Asks Bonds Passage," *N&O*, June 2, 1949.

29. "Proposals for North Carolina Education," Box 22, WKSP.

30. Report to the People, The Administration of W. Kerr Scott, 1949–53, , RWS Campaign, 1968 papers, Box 2, WKSP.

31. Jim Chaney, "Record Breaking Throng Backs Governor Scott's Program for Schools," *N&O*, March 4, 1949.

32. Coon, "Kerr Scott," 61; John Marshall, executive secretary of Better Schools and Roads, Inc., to WKS, May 15, 1949, Box 7, WKSP.

33. Ralph Scott oral history interview with Jack Bass in Burlington, Dec. 20, 1973, SOHP.

34. Wilder interview.

35. *N&O*, May 17, 1949.

36. Jim Chaney, "Outside Groups Rapped by Scott," *N&O*, May 21, 1949.

37. Ibid.

38. "Candidate Scott Was Right," *Charlotte News*, June 3, 1949. Undated clipping, Scott scrapbook, no box, WKSP.

39. Jim Chaney, "Scott Sparked Bonds Campaign," *N&O*, June 5, 1949.

40. C. A. Dillon to WKS, January 2, 1952, Box 112, WKSP.

41. UP, "Scott Again Assails Civic Organizations," *Statesville Record and Landmark*, June 11, 1949.

42. "Congressman Thurmond Chatham Raps Governor for Civic Club Attacks," *DTN*, September 12, 1949.

43. Hoke Norris, "Is Scott Another Andrew Jackson?," Undated, but probably 1949. Box 186, WKSP.

44. *Better Roads Magazine*, June 1949, Box 26, WKSP.

45. Jim Chaney, "State Makes Big Purchase of New High Machinery," *N&O*, August 20, 1949.

46. "Scott Road Program Cited as an Example for Nation," *N&O*, February 5, 1956, Box 181, WKSP.

47. Turner, *Paving Tobacco Road*, 69–70.

48. Otis Banks, executive secretary of N.C. State Highway Employees Association, to WKS, December 3, 1951, Box 91, WKSP; Turner, *Paving Tobacco Road*, 69.

49. Hunt interview, April 1, 2003.

50. James H. Pou Bailey, "Road and Politics," editorial, *Charlotte Observer*, August 1, 1951.

51. Chester Davis, "A Progress Report, North Carolina Roadways," September 1950, Box 59, WKSP.

52. *North Carolina Roadways*, January–February 1953, publication of State Highway Department, Box 192, WKSP.

53. Jim Chaney, "State's Rural Progress Noted following Scott Road Program," *N&O*, January 19, 1956, Box 181, WKSP.

54. Jim Chaney, "Tar Heel Road-Building Pace Tops Nation," *N&O*, August 13, 1950.

55. Simmons Fentress, "Scott Roads Taking a Heavy Toll," *N&O*, December 12, 1954, Box 180, WKSP.

56. Faircloth interview.

57. Turner, *Paving Tobacco Road*, 53.

58. WKS, speech dedicating the port on September 18, 1952, in Corbitt, *Public Addresses, Letters and Papers of William Kerr Scott*, 297; "Plans for Ports Moving Forward," *N&O*, April 5, 1949.

59. James Free, "State Gets 50-Year Lease on Ship Yard at Wilmington," *N&O*, November 17, 1949.

60. Lt. Gov. Robert W. Scott Papers, Campaign Materials, 1968 files, Box 2, RWSFP.

61. U.S. Army Corps of Engineers, Navigation Data Center, *U.S. Waterway System*, 5–6: "Leading U.S. Ports in 2016" (table).

62. State budget director D. C. Coltrane to WKS, August 5, 1950, Box 51, WKSP.

CHAPTER 5

1. *Annual Progress Report of Rural Electrification in North Carolina*, REA of North Carolina, Box 31, WKSP.

2. WKS, speech in Rockwell, October 9, 1952, in Corbitt, *Public Addresses, Letters and Papers of William Kerr Scott*, 306.

3. Woodrow Price, "Utilities Expansion Asked in Scott's Surprise Talk," *N&O*, July 20, 1949.

4. "Low Voltage Sutton," *Robesonian*, November 8, 1950.

5. Copy of toast, May 16, 1980, Box 27, RSP.

6. Corbitt, *Public Addresses, Letters and Papers of William Kerr Scott*, 382–83; "Scott Tells Utility Body to Speed Rural Program," *N&O*, July 14, 1949.

7. Corbitt, *Public Addresses, Letters and Papers of William Kerr Scott*, 127.

8. Herman Minnema to WKS, September 3, 1949, Box 16, WKSP.

9. Betty Lowdermilk, W. Kerr Scott, May 1960, Box 184, WKSP.

10. Corbitt, *Public Addresses, Letters, and Papers of William Kerr Scott*, 43–44.

11. Annual Progress Report of Rural Electrification in North Carolina, 1952, Rural Electrification Authority of North Carolina, July 1, 1952, Box 129, WKSP.

12. Harry Golden, commentary, reprinted in *Greensboro Daily News*, August 1, 1954.

13. U.S. Census of Agriculture, House Committee Report, March 9, 1949, Box 49, WKSP.

14. R. H. Holden to WKS, November 29, 1950, and WKS to Holden, December 1, 1950, Box 78, WKSP.

15. Mrs. Frank Terrell to WKS, January 15, 1949, Box 43, WKSP.

16. C. M. Allen to WKS, January 17, 1949, Box 43, WKSP.

17. O. D. Stallings to WKS, July 21, 1949, Box 43, WKSP.

18. "Governor Urges Phone Campaign," *N&O*, January 28, 1950.

19. Voit Gilmore to WKS, January 4, 1951, Box 78, WKSP.

20. J. F. Everett to Carolina and Telegraph, October 26, 1951, Box 105, WKSP; D. M. Davidson Jr. to WKS, May 3, 1950, Box 105, WKSP; Felix Hamrick to WKS, March 14, 1950, Box 105, WKSP.

21. "Scott Pledges Negro Program," *N&O*, January 15, 1949, Box 36, WKSP.

22. Noblin and Humphries, *Hold High the Torch*. 43.

23. "Governor Urges Phone Campaign," *N&O*, January 28, 1950.

24. Jim Chaney, "Utilities Men Answer Scott," *N&O*, February 16, 1950.

25. Woodrow Price, "Just Alibis, Governor Says of State Utilities Chiefs," *N&O*, February 22, 1950.

26. "Governor Urges Phone Campaign."

27. Corbitt, *Public Addresses, Letters, and Papers of William Kerr Scott*, 382.

28. WKS, speech to Tarheel Electric Association, Raleigh, September 18, 1956, Box 70, WKSP.

29. Hobbs, *North Carolina*, 98–99.

30. Dan Hodges, "Governor Scott Rebuffed on Requested Labor Bill," *N&O*, March 18, 1949.

31. Dan Hodges, "House Ignores Scott Plea, Rejects Labor Law Revision," *N&O*, April 2, 1949.

32. Coon, "Kerr Scott," 86, 47, 55–56; Corbitt, *Public Addresses, Letters and Papers of William Kerr Scott*, 385–86.

33. "Scott Pledges Negro Program," *N&O*, January 15, 1949.

34. Annual Report of F. D. Bluford, North Carolina A&T State University, May 16, 1951, WKSP.

35. WKS to Mrs. R. L. Welsh, January 31, 1949, Box 26, WKSP.

36. J. S. Davis to WKS, April 28, 1949, Box 10, WKSP.

37. WKS to Davis, May 19, 1949, Box 10, WKSP.

38. AP, "State Investigates Reports of Teachers' Pay Kickbacks," *Gastonia Gazette*, March 11, 1950.

39. Sanford address for the presentation of the portrait of WKS, May 7, 1959, RWS Private Collection, Box 10, RWSFP.

40. Snow interview.

41. Bartley, *New South*, 161.

42. Box 114, WKSP.

43. North Carolina Department of Cultural Resources, *Kerr Scott Farm, Haw River, North*, 8; Covington and Ellis, *Sanford*, 113.

44. James H. Pou Bailey, "Raleigh Round-Up," *Robesonian*, July 10, 1954.

45. "Tolar Submits Resignation, Next Move up to Governor," *N&O*, April 13, 1950.

46. Corbitt, *Public Addresses, Letters, and Papers of William Kerr Scott*, 383.

47. Dr. Charles Scott interview.

48. Speck, *Gentleman from Haw River*, 30.

49. Fitzgerald, *Remembering a Champion*, 34.

50. Furman interview.

51. Harold Minges to Dr. Floyd Scott, April 29, 1958, Newspapers, Misc. Files, SFC-ACC.

52. Box 4.1, WKSP.

53. WKS, news release, December 29, 1950, Box 70, WKSP.

54. Simmons Andrews, "Governor Gets Mixed Ovation," *N&O*, September 25, 1949.

55. "Not Strictly News," *Greensboro Record*, October 1, 1949.

CHAPTER 6

1. Egerton, *Speaking against the Day*, 340.

2. Ashby, *Frank Porter Graham*, 243.

3. Gunther, *Inside U.S.A.*, 654.

4. Egerton, *Speaking against the Day*, 295–96.

5. Ashby, *Frank Porter Graham*, 233.

6. Ibid., 244.

7. Jim Chaney, "Scott in Surprise Action Names Graham to Senate," *N&O*, March 23, 1949.

8. "North Carolina's Farmer-Governor," September 1949, Box 4.2, WKSP.

9. Faircloth interview.

10. UP, "Scott Makes Bid for Union Votes," *Statesville Record and Landmark*, January 19, 1950.

11. "Red Query Posed to UNC Trustees," *N&O*, February 7, 1950.

12. AP, "Graham Hit in Talk by Smith," *Greensboro Daily News*, March 23, 1950.

13. "Frank Graham's Undisclosed Record," advertisement sponsored by the Read-the-Record Committee Smith, Wake Co. Headquarters, *N&O*, May 22, 1950.

14. "Graham Cites His Opposition to Communism, Socialism," *N&O*, March 25, 1950.

15. President's Committee on Civil Rights, *To Secure These Rights*, 167.

16. "Candidate Smith Assails Graham for His Failure to Follow the Lead of Hoey in Senate," *Charlotte Observer*, June 21, 1950.

17. Ben Roney Papers, North Carolina Division of Archives and History, Raleigh.

18. Pleasants and Burns, *Frank Porter Graham*, 119.

19. Ibid., 172.

20. "Wilmington Hears Smith," *N&O*, May 13, 1950.

21. "Smith Says Scott Asked Him to Run," *N&O*, May 23, 1950; "A Good Lawyer Scott Says," *N&O*, May 25, 1950.

22. AP, "Smith Assails Bloc Voting by Negroes," *Greensboro Daily News*, June 14, 1950.

23. Lubell, *Future of American Politics*, 109.

24. Arthur Johnsey, "Scott Stumps for Graham," *Greensboro Daily News*, June 16, 1950.

25. WKS, radio address, June 20, 1950, Box 4.2, WKSP.

26. Lubell, *Future of American Politics*, 110.

27. Pleasants, *Political Career of W. Kerr Scott*, 180.

28. Christensen, *Paradox of Tar Heel Politics*, 147.

29. Lynn Nisbett, "Governor Scott Declines in Prestige and Influence," *Gastonia Gazette*, August 29, 1950; Roy Parker Jr., "4,000 Hear Scott in Rich Square," *N&O*, August 10, 1950.

30. AP, "Governor Scores Prejudice in Speech to AFL Members," *N&O*, August 15, 1950.

31. Eula Nixon Greenwood, "The Raleigh Roundup," *Robesonian*, June 28, 1950.

32. A. A. Morisey, "Ex Governor Discusses Race Issue," *Winston-Salem Journal and Sentinel*, January 25, 1953.

33. AP, "Scott Says Negro Appointees Must Show Abilities," *Greensboro Daily News*, February 28, 1951.

34. Ehle, *Dr. Frank*, 191.

35. Coon, "Kerr Scott," 66; *Raleigh Times*, January 3, 1951; *N&O*, January 24, 1951.

36. Ralph Scott oral history interview by Jacquelyn Hall and Bill Finger, April 22, 1974, Southern Oral History Program, Southern Historical Society, UNC–Chapel Hill.

37. A. Howard White, "Earthy Outspoken Maverick," *DTN*, June 26, 1965.

38. Corbitt, *Public Addresses, Letters, and Papers of William Kerr Scott*, 38.

39. Eamon, *Making of Southern Democracy*, 36.

40. Coon, "Kerr Scott," 85.

41. Corbitt, *Public Addresses, Letters, and Papers of William Kerr Scott*, 219–20.

42. UP, "Scott Points to State Law on Education," *DTN*, March 27, 1951.

43. WKS to W. T. Fullwood Jr., November 27, 1951, Box 96, WKSP.

44. Ibid.

45. *DTN*, July 17, 1951.

46. "Roads on Scott Farm Paved," *Greensboro Daily News*, June 12, Box 4.2, WKSP.

47. Woodrow Price, "Governor Rescinds Action Giving Alamance $750,000," *N&O*, August 27, 1952.

48. WKS to James Barnwell, February 8, 1952, Box 119, WKSP.

49. RWS interview, September 22, 2005.

50. WKS to American Limestone Company, July 31, 1950, RWS Private Collection, Correspondence, Papers, Clippings, 1948–1950, RWSFP.

51. R. P. Immel to WKS, August 3, 1950, RWS Private Collection, Correspondence, Papers, Clippings, 1948–1950, RWSFP.

52. Box 4.2, WKSP.

53. WKS to Merck and Company, May 1, 1945, and K. L. Ader to WKS, May 17, 1945, Box 1, WKSP.

54. J. Spencer Love to WKS, September 22, 1950, Box 73.

55. Roney interview.

56. Ally Dillard, president of Virginia Cruise Lines, to WKS, September 27, 1951, WKSP.

57. Waynick oral history interview.

58. "Coltrane May Thumb Nose at Governor," *Greensboro Daily News*, June 11, 1952.

59. Covington and Ellis, *Terry Sanford*, 115–16; Woodrow Price, "State Delegates to Go Unpledged; Rebuffed, Governor 'Takes Back Seat,'" *N&O*, May 23, 1952; Under the Dome, *N&O*, May 30, 1952.

60. Corbitt, *Public Addresses, Letters and Papers of William Kerr Scott*, 312.

61. Ibid., 327.

62. Howard White, "It's Private Citizen Scott Now," *N&O*, January 9, 1953.

CHAPTER 7

1. Covington and Ellis, *Terry Sanford*, 128.

2. Terry Sanford to RWS, April 2, 1972, in RWS Diary, RWS Private Papers, RWSFP.

3. Sanford interview, Transcript of UNC TV interview with Sanford, "Biographical Conservations with Terry Sanford," taped in 1997 and aired in May 1998. In possession of author.

4. WKS, speech at Chapel Hill, February 10, 1954, Box 9.18, WKSP.

5. George Steen, "Paris Recalls the Way It Was," *DTN*, May 20, 1976.

6. WKS, campaign news release, May 1, 1954, Box 9.16, RWSFP.

7. Faircloth interview; Hunt interview, April 14, 2016.

8. WKS, speech at Aycock High School, Vance County, April 15, 1954, Box 9.18, WKSP; and WKS, speech at State College, April 16, 1954, Box 9.18, WKSP.

9. WKS, speech to the N.C. and S.C. Warehouse Association in Charlotte, March 5, 1954, Box 9.18, WKSP.

10. "Scott Branded as Demagogue as Lennon Fires Opening Shot," *Durham Morning Herald*, February 10, 1954.

11. Covington and Ellis, *Terry Sanford*, 132.

12. Ibid.

13. WKS, speech, May 26, 1954, Box 9.18, WKSP.

14. Ibid.

15. L. L. Smith to WKS, April 27, 1954, Box 9.12, WKSP.

16. Robert Walker Scott oral history interview by Karl Campbell, September 18, 1986, SOHP, 15.

17. Jay Jenkins, "The Plowboy Seeks Seat in the Senate," February 7, 1954, Box 9.15, WKSP; S. B. Simmons to WKS, August 16, 1954, Box 9.16, WKSP; Norman Cousins to Jonathan Daniels, May 28, 1954, Box 9.15, WKSP.

18. Faircloth interview; Sanford to Johnston, July 3, 1954, Box 9.15, WKSP.

19. WKS, statement on Supreme Court decision, May 17, 1954, Box 9.14, WKSP.

20. "Down in Iredell," *Statesville Record and Landmark*, May 19, 1954.

21. Golden, *Right Time*, 273.

22. Sanford oral history interview.

23. Copy of leaflet, Box 9.16, WKSP.

24. Zeno Edwards to Sanford, June 2, 1954, Box 9.16, WKSP.

25. Joe Horton to Sanford, memorandum, Box 9.16, WKSP.

26. Sanford interview, 63.

27. Howard White, "Scott Reserves Celebration until Victory Is Definite," *DTN*, May 31, 1954.

28. Ehle, *Dr. Frank*, 194.

29. "Shifting Political Sentiment Challenges Southern Democrats," *DTN*, November 8, 1969.

30. Tom Wicker, "Scott, Ervin Appear Well-Matched," *Winston-Salem Journal and Sentinel*, September 8, 1957, Box 181, WKSP.

31. Journal Bureau, "Scott Shocked to Find Capitol Has No Spittoons," *Winston-Salem Journal*, n.d., Box 4.2, WKSP.

32. Wicker, *Facing the Lions*, 49.

33. Robert E. Williams, "North Carolina's Next Senator Is a Farming Expert," *N&O*, n.d.

34. RWS interview, December 16, 1998.

35. Tom Wicker, "Keeping Up with Kerr Scott: It's Tough on a Man's Feet," *Winston-Salem Journal and Sentinel*, June 2, 1957.

36. Frank Van Der Linden, "The Kerr Scotts Are Keeping Their Down-on-the-Farm Ways," *Charlotte Observer*, June 24, 1955, Box 181, WKSP.

37. WKS, news release, March 29, 1955, Box 178, WKSP.

38. AP, "Kerr Scott Tears into Eisenhower," *Daily Independent* (Kannapolis), July 5, 1955.

39. Thomas L. Stokes, "Back Benchers Rising Up in Senate," *N&O*, April 30, 1955; William H. Stringer, "Washington Scene, President's Responsibility," *Christian Science Monitor*, April 25, 1955; *Congressional Record*, April 1, 1955, Box 179,WKSP.

40. "Kerr Scott Explains Vote on Natural Gas," *Durham Labor Journal*, March 29, 1956, Box 181, WKSP; Roney to Ralph Scott, September 29, 1955, Box 27, RSP.

41. Chester Davis, "Entire State Faces Worsening Water Problem," *Winston-Salem Journal and Sentinel*, November 28, 1954, Box 179, WKSP.

42. WKS, news release, November 29, 1955, Box 178, WKSP.

43. AP, "Ike Won't Live 4 Years—Scott," *N&O*, October 31, 1956.

44. Fitzgerald, *Remembering a Champion*, 97.

45. Creech interview.

46. Drescher, *Triumph of Goodwill*, 41–42.

47. "Amongst Patriots, Traces of Reaction," *Durham Morning Herald*, August 28, 1955, Box 179, WKSP.

48. Ibid.

49. Graham Jones, "Under the Surface, Increasing Tension," *Durham Morning Herald*, September 4, 1955; Fred McGee, "Over in Guilford, Tangible Evidence," *Durham Morning Herald*, September 11, 1955, Box 179, WKSP.

50. WKS, statement, June 13, 1956, Box 178, WKSP.

51. Graham Jones, "After Hot Words, a Cold Shoulder," *Durham Morning Herald*, June 17, 1956.

52. Bobby Baker to WKS, June 21, 1956, Box 71, WKSP.

53. Graham Jones, "To the Winner, a Primary Vote," *Durham Morning Herald*, June 24, 1956, Box 179, WKSP.

54. Charlie Britt to Raymond Maxwell, May 7, 1951, Box 116, WKSP.

55. WKS statement, "Washington Report," July 31, 1956, Box 177, WKSP; AP, "Sen. Scott Declares CR Fight Really Scrap for City Votes," *Durham Morning Sun*, August 8, 1957.

56. WKS, press release, March 18, 1957, Box 178, WKSP.

57. J. W. Jeffries to WKS, March 26, 1957, 74, WKSP.

58. Louis Austin, editorial, *Carolina Times*, March 23, 1957.

59. Graham Jones, "'Carpetbagger Invasion,' Says Scott," *Durham Morning Herald*, Box 181, WKSP.

60. Jesse Helms to WKS, January 20, 1958, Box 177, WKSP.

61. Dr. W. M. Nicholson of Duke Hospital to Dr. Samuel Floyd Scott of Burlington, February 20, 1956, SFC-ACC.

62. Charles Clay, "Senator W. Kerr Scott Is Dead," *N&O*, April 17, 1958.

63. U.S. Congress, *William Kerr Scott: Memorial Address*.

64. Ralph Buchanan to Sen. Julian Allsbrook, May 12, 1971, Box 27, RSP.

65. Marjorie Hunter, "Squire of Haw River Laid to Rest," *Winston-Salem Journal*, April 19, 1958. .

66. Pleasants, *Political Career of W. Kerr Scott*.

67. Badger, *New South/New Deal*, 70.

68. Harry Golden, "Senator W. Kerr Scott," *Carolina Israelite*, May–June 1958.

69. William D. Snider, "Last Tribute to Ralph Scott of Haw River," *Greensboro News and Record*, April 16, 1989.

CHAPTER 8

1. Covington, *Terry Sanford*, 194–95.

2. Bob Hoffman to Bob Scott, June 1969, RWS General Correspondence, 1969, Box 53; Faircloth interview.

3. Covington, *Terry Sanford*, 269.

4. Johnson oral history interview.

5. RWS interview, December 16, 1998.

6. Ibid.

7. RWS oral history interview.

8. Marion Gregory, "Move to Mansion Will Be Honeymoon Repeat," *N&O*, November 10, 1968.

9. Bob Scott interview, Biographical Conversations with Bob Scott, UNC-TV, aired April 2004.

10. Gregory, "Move to Mansion Will Be Honeymoon Repeat."

11. RWS interview, September 22, 2005.

12. Ibid.

13. FBI background check files and RWS to parents, July 14, 1954, RWS Private Collection, Box 1.

14. RWS oral history interview; Scott interview with UNC-TV.

15. James M. Johnston to WKS, July 1, 1957, RWS Private Collection, Farm Correspondence, Johnston letter to WKS acknowledging repayment, September 16, 1957, RWSFP.

16. AP, "Senator Scott's Estate Estimated at $66,850," *N&O*, April 25, 1958.

17. Dr. Charles Scott interview.

18. David Cooper, "Bob Scott Raps Utilities Ruling," *N&O*, December 19, 1962.

19. Text of speech, Norfolk Citizens for Democratic Government, April 1963, RWS Private Papers, Box 12, RWSFP.

20. RWS Diary, October 25, 1970, RWS Private Papers, RWSFP.

21. RWS to D. W. Colvard, June 16, 1958, Private Collection: Correspondence, Papers and Clippings, 1948–1960, RWSFP.

22. Ben Roney to RWS, June 18, 1959, RWS Private Collection, Box 8, RWSFP.

23. RWS interview, December 16, 1998.

24. Ibid.

25. RWS interview, December 16, 1998; Howard White, "Robert Scott—And His Future," *DTN*, December 28, 1962.

26. Jay Jenkins, "Another Scott Is Governor Like Father, Like Son?," *Atlanta Journal-Constitution*, January 19, 1969.

27. W. F. Wilson to RWS, October 24, 1963, RWS Private Collection, Box 3, RWSFP.

28. David Cooper, "Scott Nixes Governor's Race," *N&O*, January 8, 1964.

29. RWS oral history interview; Mitchell, *Addresses and Public Papers*, xxxii.

30. RWS statement, January 13, 1964, Box 12, RWSFP.

31. Richard W. Hatch, "Eure, Speaker Ban Was Born amid Racial Strife," *Raleigh Times*, June 2, 1965.

32. "Speaker Ban: An Outrage," *N&O*, September 27, 1962.

33. Jay Jenkins, profile of Ralph Scott, for a book by Albert Coats, 1978, Box 26, RSP.

34. Lambeth interview.

35. Ralph Scott interview with author January 7, 1978.

36. Newspaper advertisement, "Robert W. Scott, Democrat for Lieutenant Governor," *Perquimans Weekly*, May 22, 1964, Perquimans County Committee for Bob Scott, RWS Private Papers, Box 16, RWSFP.

37. AP, "Preyer Promises No Commitments," *High Point Enterprise*, May 27, 1964.

38. RWS, statement, and RWS, memo, RWS Private Papers, Box 11, RWSFP.

39. Raz Autry to RWS, September 1, 1963, RWS Private Collection, Box 5, RWSFP.

40. Ralph Scott to John Flannery, February 10, 1964, and Leola Flannery to Bob Scott, September 5, 1964, RWS Private Papers, Box 7, RWSFP.

41. AP, "Blue Calls for Runoff with Scott," *Charlotte Observer*, June 10, 1964.

42. Jordan interview.

43. RWS, letter, undated but probably around June 25, 1964, RWS Private Correspondence, Box 1, RWSFP.

44. UPI, "Lake Labels Preyer 'Captive' Candidate," *Daily Independent* (Kannapolis), June 25, 1964.

45. Jesse Helms, editorial, *Viewpoint*, WRAL-TV, June 29, 1964, Southern Historical Collection, University of North Carolina at Chapel Hill.

46. "Dan Moore's Big Victory Ends Long, Hard Campaign," *Charlotte Observer*, June 28, 1964.

47. J. Elsie Webb to RWS, August 3, 1964, RWS Private Papers, Box 7, RWSFP.

48. "It's Wrong to Tag Bob Scott as Leader of Liberal Wing," *DTN*, July 7, 1964.

49. Roy Parker, "Scott Heads Johnson's Rural Group," *N&O*, September 10, 1964.

50. Text of Goldwater speech, September 17, 1964, RWS Private Papers, Box 12, RWSFP.

51. Susan Lewis, "Scott Warns Farmers on Goldwater Plans," *N&O*, September 24, 1964.

52. David Cooper, "Speaker Ban Law Is Campaign Issue," *Winston-Salem Journal*, October 15, 1964.

53. Howard White, "The Career and Honor," *DTN*, n.d.

54. Eamon, *Making of a Southern Democracy*, 100–101.

55. Dan Moore, statement, June 1965, RWS Campaign Materials, 1968, Box 4.

56. "Senator Ralph Scott Rips Moore's Position on Gag," *Chapel Hill Weekly*, June 2, 1965.

57. Editorial, "The Welcome End of an Era," *Greensboro Daily News*, November 18, 1965.

58. Ralph Scott interview.

59. RWS, speech in Burlington, May 20, 1965, RWS Campaign Materials, 1968, Box 4.

60. RWS, speech to Radio-Television News Directors Conference, Greensboro, May 13, 1967, Lt. Gov. Speeches, 1967–68, Box 9.

61. Russell Clay, "Tar Heels Reject State's Label of No. 1 for Klan," *N&O*, October 24, 1965.

62. AP, "Bob Scott's Yard Gets Fiery Cross," *Robesonian*, July 1, 1966.

63. Lynn Nisbett, "Ruffled Moore Almost Lost His Temper," *Gastonia Gazette*, October 29, 1966.

63. Rob Wood, "Governor Asks for $748 Million for Education," *DTN*, February 9, 1967.

64. Cunningham, *Klansville, U.S.A.*, 6; AP, "King Decries Strange Mixture in N.C.," *High Point Enterprise*, May 9, 1966; AP, "Scuffles Mark Raleigh's KKK March," *Robesonian*, August 1, 1966.

65. Fuller, *No Struggle, No Progress*, 69.

66. Korstad and Leloudis, *To Right These Wrongs*, 303.

67. Donald Matthews to Sam Ragan, memorandum, July 28, 1967, RWS Gubernatorial Campaign Papers, Box 50, RWSFP.

68. RWS interview, December 16, 1998.

69. Cunningham, *Klansville U.S.A.*, 60–62.

70. Rob Wood, "400 National Guardsmen and Police Seal Off Section in Winston-Salem," November 3, 1967; Memorandum of the Governor's Committee on Law and Order, June 11, 1969, Gov. RWS General Correspondence, 1969, Box 33.

71. AP, "Scott Criticizes UNC for Hiring of Howard Fuller," *Richmond County Journal*, November 16, 1967; RWS speeches, lieutenant governor's office, general file, Box 56, RWSFP.

72. "Like Father, Like Son Doesn't Apply Here," *Charlotte Observer*, November 16, 1967.

73. "Mr. Scott in Harnett," *Greensboro Daily News*, November 16, 1967.

74. Jesse Helms, editorial, *Viewpoint*, WRAL-TV, November 16, 1967, Southern Historical Collection, University of North Carolina at Chapel Hill.

75. Jesse Helms, editorial, *Viewpoint*, WRAL-TV, February 25, 1969, Southern Historical Collection, University of North Carolina at Chapel Hill.

CHAPTER 9

1. Connor Jones, "Kerr Scott: Roads and Utilities," *DTN*, January 3, 1969.

2. RWS, address to N.C. Wholesalers Association, Jack Tar Durham Hotel, February 17, 1968, Lt. Gov. RWS Campaign Materials, 1968 Files, Box 3.

3. Wiseman, "New Politics in North Carolina," 37.

4. RWS, speech, December 14, 1967, Lt. Gov. RWS Campaign Materials, 1968 Materials.

5. Jeffreys, *I Never Promised Not to Tell*, 154, 170.

6. Wiseman, *James Gardner and the 1968 Governor's Race*, 38.

7. Ibid., 25.

8. Faulkenbury, "Telenegro."

9. Ibid., 86.

10. Wiseman, *James Gardner*, 36.

11. John F. Kraft Inc., "A Study of Attitudes of North Carolina Voters," November 1967, RWS Campaign Materials, 1968, Box 4.

12. Faircloth interview.

13. UPI, "14 Protesters Are Convicted," *Statesville Record and Landmark*, November 14, 1968; AP, "15 Persons Arrested in Dow Protest," *Asheville Citizen*, March 19, 1968.

14. Kaiser, *1968 in America*, 154.

15. "Scott Criticizes Student Boycotts," *N&O*, May 17, 1968.

16. Wellstone, "Black Militants in the Ghetto," 41.

17. Ibid., 45.

18. "Tear Gas Is Used on Mob," *N&O*, April 6, 1968; "Violence Hits State Cities," *N&O*, April 6, 1968.

19. Memorandum of the Governor's Committee on Law and Order, June 11, 1969, Gov. RWS General Correspondence, 1969, Box 33.

20. Wiseman, *James Gardner and the 1968 Governor's Race*, 30.

21. AP, "Order Theme Stressed by Scott," *N&O*, May 1, 1968.

22. Faulkenbury, "Telenegro," 117–18.

23. Jim Lewis, "Hawkins Changed Politics in NC, Atlantan Says," *N&O*, January 24, 1970.

24. Jeffreys, *I Never Promised Not to Tell*, 178–79.

25. Russell Clay, "Governor," *N&O*, May 6, 1968.

26. Jeffreys, *I Never Promised Not to Tell*, 179–80; RWS interview, May 8, 1968, North Carolina Division of Archives and History, Raleigh.

27. RWS interview, May 8, 1968.

28. Jesse Helms, editorial, *Viewpoint*, WRAL-TV, May 9, 1968, Southern Historical Collection, University of North Carolina at Chapel Hill; Jesse Helms, Lt. Gov. Robert W. Scott Campaign Materials, 1968 Files.

29. Kraft, "Study of Attitudes of North Carolina Voters."

30. UPI, "Violence Hit by Gardner," *Statesville Record and Landmark*, April 10, 1968.

31. Paul Jablow, "Gardner Straddling Fence on Unionism, Stickley Says," *Charlotte Observer*, April 19, 1968, Lt. Gov. Robert W. Scott Campaign Materials, 1968.

32. James Ross, "Polls: The Politician's Friend," *Greensboro Daily News*, June 23, 1968.

33. Viorst, *Fire in the Streets*, 406–20; Kaiser, *1968 in America*, 26–36.

34. Faulkenbury, "Telenegro," 136.

35. RWS, Lt. Gov. Speeches, 1968, Box 10; Wiseman, "New Politics in North Carolina," 58.

36. Roy Parker, "Happy Warrior Sanford Sympathizes with Scott," *N&O*, August 27, 1968; Covington, *Henry Frye*, 365; Under the Dome, "Sanford Friends Peeved by Scott's Uncertainty," *N&O*, August 22, 1968; AP, "Outsiders Pushing Sanford Drive," *Gastonia Gazette*, August 20, 1968.

37. Scott campaign release, August 8, 1968, RWS Campaign Materials, 1968 Files, Box 3.

38. AP, "Gardner Stands Firm for Nixon," *DTN*, March 15, 1968.

39. Gardner interview.

40. Ibid.

41. Kraft, "Study of Attitudes of North Carolina Voters."

42. Ibid.

43. Jack Childs, "Bob Scott Tours Onslow County," *N&O*, October 2, 1968.

44. Editorial, "Our Fair Weather Democrat," *N&O*, September 1, 1968.

45. Jack Holmes, "Nixon Appeals to Youth," *DTN*, October 16, 1968.

46. RWS Campaign Files, 1968, Box 4; *Charlotte Observer*, October 19, 1968.

47. AP, "Gardner Aide Tells of Stickers," *DTN*, May 29, 1972.

48. AP, "Literature Upsets Wallace Camp," *N&O*, August 24, 1968.

49. Jack Childs, "GOP Displays Unity as Gardner Attends," *N&O*, October 22, 1968.

50. James A. Shephard to J. Allen Adams, May 27, 1968, Robert W. Scott II Gubernatorial Campaign Materials, 1967–68, subject file, Broughton, ethnic, Box 51; AP, "Gardner Turns Down Frinks Offer," *DTN*, September 18, 1968.

51. Russell Clay, "SBI Findings Satisfy Scott," *N&O*, September 7, 1968; Bertrand M. Harding, acting director of OEO, to RWS, September 16, 1968, RWS Campaign Materials, 1968, Box 4; "Wake's Antipoverty Chief Quits: Cites Scott Charge," *N&O*, May 21, 1969.

52. "Committee for Truth," advertisement, *N&O*, October 22, 1968.

53. "Committee for Truth in Government," campaign flyer, Lt. Gov. Robert W. Scott Campaign Materials, 1968 Files.

54. AP, "Civil Rights Body Raps Gardner, Scott," *N&O*, October 24, 1968.

55. Jack Childs, "Scott Says Reject Negative," *N&O*, November 3, 1968.

56. "Gardner for Governor," news release, August 27, 1968, Lt. Gov. Robert Scott Campaign Materials, 1968 Files.

57. Wiseman, *James Gardner*, 64.

58. Jack Childs, "Won't Play upon Fears of Citizen, Scott Says," *N&O*, October 15, 1968.

59. Jack Childs, "Scott Says Reject the Negative," *N&O*, November 3, 1968.

60. RWS Gubernatorial Campaign Materials, 1967–68, Subject File, Absent Voters, Brain Trust, Box 50, Box 51; Roy G. Sowers to Key Scott People, memorandum, August 15, 1968, RWS Scott Campaign Materials, 1968, Box 4, RWSFP.

61. Pat Stith, "Morgan Says It's Late to Act on 1968 Gifts," *N&O*, January 29, 1972.

62. Jack Childs, "Campaign Spending: A Casual Attitude," *N&O*, November 15, 1970.

63. Faircloth interview.

64. Gardner interview.

65. Wiseman, *James Gardner*, 70; AP, "Gardner Defends Attitude towards News Media," *High Point Enterprise*, November 2, 1968.

66. Kraft, "Study of Attitudes of North Carolina Voters," October 25, 1968, RWS, 1964–79, Box 6.

67. Rob Wood, "Scott Criticizes Poster," *Raleigh Times*, October 16, 1968.

68. "No One Controls Gardner," *Gastonia Gazette*, November 1, 1968.

69. Miller, *Billy Graham*, 74.

70. Scott, Living the Vision Series.

71. Jack Childs, "Billy Graham, a Scott Family Admirer, Splits His Ticket," *N&O*, November 2, 1968.

72. Gardner interview.

73. James Graham to RWS, Nov. 2, 1968, RWS General Correspondence, 1969, Box 65.

74. Scott, *A Faith Established a Governor*, one of a series of booklets produced by the Evangelism and Church Development Program Area of the National Ministries Division, Presbyterian Church USA, June 2001.

75. Jay Jenkins, "Another Scott Is Governor—Like Father, Like Son," *Atlanta Journal-Constitution*, January 19, 1969.

76. Jesse Helms, editorial, *Viewpoint*, WRAL-TV, November 6, 1968, Southern Historical Collection, University of North Carolina at Chapel Hill.

77. Jim Gardner oral history interview by Jonathan Thomas Young Hougton, August 6, 1995, SOHP.

78. David M. McConnell to RWS, November 25, 1968, RWS General Correspondence, 1969, Box 81; James Johnson to RWS, January 24, 1969, RWS General Correspondence, 1969, Box 61.

79. Eamon, *Making of a Southern Democracy*, 121.

CHAPTER 10

1. RWS to H. G. Jones, August 1, 2005, H. G. Jones private papers; Robert W. Scott, Living the Vision.

2. Mitchell, *Addresses and Public Papers of Robert W. Scott*, 7.

3. Covington, *Henry Frye*, 123.

4. "New Sideburns, Oaths and Crowd of 50,000," *DTN*, January 4, 1969.

5. Mitchell, *Addresses and Public Papers of Robert W. Scott*, 140; RWS, speech, April 29, 1970, RWS General Correspondence, 1970, Box 243.

6. Liu, *Quality of Life in the United States*; Charles Angoff and H. L. Mencken, "The Worst American State," *American Mercury*, September–October 1931; Beyle and Black, *Politics and Policy in North Carolina*.

7. Bass and DeVries, *Transformation of Southern Politics*, 498.

8. Ibid., 500.

9. Jack Childs, "Scott's 70 Report Cites Environmental Progress," *N&O*, January 3, 1971.

10. Mitchell, *Addresses and Public Papers of Robert W. Scott*, xxxvi.

11. Claude Sitton, "Kindergartens for Tar Heel Stockings," *N&O*, November 26, 1972.

12. Mitchell, *Addresses and Public Papers of Robert W. Scott*, 36.

13. RWS to Bart Strickland, January 14, 1969, RWS General Correspondence, 1969, Box 53.

14. Report and Recommendations, Governor's Highway Study Commission, December 5, 1968, Box 23, RWSFP.

15. Mitchell, *Addresses and Public Papers of Robert W. Scott*, 29.

16. Russell Clay, "Scott Goes to People for Tax Bill Support," *N&O*, June 14, 1969.

17. Jesse Helms, editorial, *Viewpoint*, WRAL-TV, , June 16, 1969, Southern Historical Collection, University of North Carolina at Chapel Hill.

18. Mitchell, *Addresses and Public Papers of Robert W. Scott*, xxxvi.

19. AP, "Scott's Whirlwind Tour Strikes Poignant Note," *N&O*, June 15, 1969.

20. RWS Diary, May 27, 1969, RWS Private Papers, RWSFP.

21. RWS interview, December 16, 1998.

22. Howard Covington, "Tax Hikes to Haunt Democrats," *Charlotte Observer*, July 14, 1970, RWS General Correspondence, 1970, Box 242.

23. Russell Clay, "N.C. Assembly Quits at Last; 8 Percent Interest Approved," *N&O*, July 3, 1969.

24. Claude Sitton, "Scott's Success a Costly Thing," *N&O*, July 4, 1969.

25. "North Carolina's Financial State Outlook," RWS speech to Legislative Task Force of the Raleigh Chamber of Commerce, November 14, 1972, Gov. RWS, General Correspondence, 1972, Box 531.

26. Mitchell, *Addresses and Public Papers of Robert W. Scott*, xxxv.

27. Jack Childs, "Scott Offers Bond Plan for Low-Income Housing," *N&O*, May 9, 1969; Jack Loftus, "Scott Urges Establishment of Low-Income Home Unit," *N&O*, May 18, 1969.

28. Russell Clay, "Gov. Scott Favors Death Penalty Ban," *N&O*, March 19, 1969.

29. RWS Diary, June 29, 1972, RWS Private Papers, RWSFP.

30. Mitchell, *Addresses and Public Papers of Robert W. Scott*, 72.

31. Jack Childs, "Nixon Cheered by 15,000 in Rainy Asheville Visit," *N&O*, October 21, 1970.

32. RWS, speech at Valdese, October 22, 1970, RWS General Correspondence, 1970, Box 243.

33. "Mrs. Scott Uses Veep Verbiage," *N&O*, October 4, 1970.

34. Transcript of Spiro Agnew speech, October 26, 1970, RWS General Correspondence, 1970, Box 270.

35. RWS Diary, November 4, 1970.

36. Fleer, *Governors Speak*, 155.

37. RWS Diary, January 14, 1970, RWS Private Papers, RWSFP; "Possum Main Course," *N&O*, January 21, 1972; Sparrow, *Looking Back on 50 Years*, 12.

38. Charles Craven, "Governor Racks 'Em Up at the Mansion," *N&O*, February 8, 1971.

39. RWS Diary, September 2, 1972, RWS Private Papers, RWSFP.

40. McLamb interview.

41. AP, "No Tea for '71 Debutantes," *DTN*, May 24, 1971.

42. RWS Diary, May 18, 1971, RWS Private Papers, RWSFP.

43. RWS interview, December 16, 1998.

CHAPTER 11

1. Michael S. Lottman, "The GOP and the South," *Ripon Forum*, July–August 1970.

2. RWS General Correspondence, 1970, Box 242.

3. Biondi, *Black Revolution on Campus*, 114.

4. Knight, *Street of Dreams*, 135–36.

5. Fuller, *No Struggle, No Progress*, 94.

6. Report of the Adjutant General of the State of North Carolina, RWS General Correspondence, 1970, Box 286.

7. U.S. Army, "Counter Intelligence Spot Report."

8. Rod Cockshutt, "Guard Called," *N&O*, February 14, 1969.

9. RWS interview, Dec. 16, 1998.

10. "Scott: Duke Acted Fairly and Firmly," *N&O*, February 15, 1969.

11. Douglas Knight to RWS, February 19, 1969, Gov. RWS General Correspondence, 1969, Box 105.

12. Report of the Adjutant General of the State of North Carolina, July 1, 1969–June 30, 1970, RWS General Correspondence, 1970, Box 286; Bob Lynch, "Windows Smashed as Durham Rally Develops into Riot," *N&O*, March 12, 1969.

13. Knight, *Street of Dreams*, 139.

14. Charles T. Bowers to Charles Wade, February 17, 1969, Gov. RWS General Correspondence, 1969, Box 105.

15. Wayne Hurder, "White UNC Students March to Support Black Demands," *N&O*, March 8, 1969.

16. Link, *William Friday*, 149–50.

17. RWS Diary, March 5, 1969, RWS Private Papers, RWSFP.

18. Bob Lynch and Jack Childs, "Police Guard UNC Cafeteria," *N&O*, March 7, 1969.

19. Report of the Adjutant General State of North Carolina, July 1, 1969–June 30, 1970.

20. Jack Childs and Bob Lynch, "UNC Blacks Vacate Building," *N&O*, March 14, 1969.

21. RWS Diary, March 13, 1969, RWSFP.

22. RWS speech to Executive Committee of University of North Carolina trustees, March 14, 1969, Gov. RWS General Correspondence, Box 91.

23. RWS, speech, March 24, 1969, RWS General Correspondence, 1969, Box 82.

24. Shearon Harris to RWS, February 25, 1969, Gov. RWS General Correspondence, 1969 Box 65.

25. Jesse Helms, editorial, *Viewpoint*, WRAL-TV, March 20, 1950, Southern Historical Collection, University of North Carolina at Chapel Hill.

26. *Newsweek*, October 6, 1969, RWS General Correspondence, 1970, Box 179.

27. Josef Perry to RWS, March 16, 1969, Gov. RWS General Correspondence, 1969, Box 111.

28. American Association of University Professors to RWS, March 6, 1969, RWS General Correspondence, Box 12.

29. Ralph Scott oral history interview by Jacquelyn Hall and Bill Finger, April 22, 1974, SOHP.

30. Speck, *Gentleman from Haw River*, 112–14; UPI, "UNC Workers Agree to End Strike," *N&O*, March 23, 1969.

31. Speck, *Gentleman from Haw River*, 112; Fitzgerald, *Remembering a Champion*, 139; Ralph Scott oral history interview by Jacquelyn Hall and Bill Finger, April 22, 1974, SOHP.

32. Speck, *Gentleman from Haw River*.

33. "Marchers Met by Rain and Hope," *N&O*, April 19, 1969.

34. RWS Diary, April 21, 1969, RWS Private Papers, RWSFP.

35. "Police Arrest 15 Marchers for Blocking Assembly Door," *N&O*, May 3, 1969.

36. Shirl Spicer, "Golden Frinks: The Great Agitator, 1920–2004," *Tar Heel Junior Historian*, published by the Tar Heel Heel Junior Historian Association, January 1, 2004. N.C. North Carolina Museum of History, Raleigh; Rosen and Mosnier, *Julius Chambers*, 143.

37. Charles Craven and Bob Lynch, "Frinks Sentenced to Year in Jail," *N&O*, May 8, 1969; Charles Dunn to RWS, April 27, 1970, RWS General Correspondence, 1970, Box 176.

38. SBI Agent D. C. Marshall to the Director, memorandum, May 8, 1969, Gov. RWS General Correspondence, 1969, Box 79; RWS Diary, May 8, 1969, RWS Private Papers, RWSFP.

39. AP, "Guard Sent to Winston," *N&O*, April 30, 1969; AP, "Winston Curfew Lifted; Guard Stays," *N&O*, May 1, 1969.

40. Report of the Adjutant General of the State of North Carolina, July 1, 1969–June 30, 1970.

41. RWS Diary, May 16, 1969, RWS Private Papers, RWSFP.

42. Ibid., May 26, 28, 1969.

43. Biondi, *Black Revolution on Campus*, 158.

44. FBI Charlotte Office to J. Edgar Hoover, memorandum, May 29, 1969; Scott, Living the Vision pamphlet.

45. FBI Charlotte Office to Hoover.

46. RWS General Correspondence, 1969, Box 118.

47. RWS Diary, May 23, 1969, RWS Private Papers, RWSFP.

48. North Carolina State Advisory Committee on Civil Rights, *Trouble in Greensboro*.

49. RWS, transcript of news conference, April 1, 1970, RWS General Correspondence, 1970, Box 242.

50. Fleer, *Governors Speak*, 150.

51. David Newton, "The Day the National Guard Swept A&T's Scott Hall," *Greensboro Daily News*, May 20, 1979.

52. RWS Diary, February 6, 1971, RWS Private Papers, RWSFP.

53. Ibid., May 21, 1969.

54. Thomas J. White to Hector McGeachy, May 19, 1969, Gov. RWS General Correspondence, 1969, Box 78.

55. Rod Cockshutt, "Campus Unrest Spurs Bills," *N&O*, May 11, 1969.

56. Betty Crouch to RWS, May 23, 1969, RWS General Correspondence, 1969, Box 118.

57. North Carolina State Highway Patrol, "Summary of Activities and Performances, January–June 1969," RWS General Correspondence, 1969, Box 38.

58. Text of speech on new Highway Patrol antiriot unit, Gov. RWS General Correspondence, 1969, Box 91.2.

59. Lindsay Gruson and Stan Swofford, "Scott Was Briefed on Radical Groups," *Greensboro Daily News*, January 4, 1980.

60. Edmisten interview.

61. Military Intelligence Duty roster, February 23, 1970, RWS General Correspondence, 1970, Box 272.

62. Campbell, *Senator Sam Ervin*, 248.

63. Murray interview.

64. FBI SAC Charlotte to FBI Director, Counterintelligence Program, Internal Safety, Disruption of the New Left, memorandum, May 31, 1968. FBI Records: The Vault, (Online) Freedom of Information and Privacy Acts, Subject (COINTELPRO) New Left, Charlotte Division.

65. FBI Charlotte to Director, memorandums, April 6, 1971, October 13, 1969, October 15, May 31, 1968. FBI Records: The Vault, (Online) Freedom of Information and Privacy Acts, Subject (COINTELPRO) New Left, Charlotte Division.

66. Scott, *Reining in the State*, 90.

67. Intelligence Activities and the Rights of Americans, Book II, The Final Report of the Selection Committee to Study Governmental Operations with Respect to Intelligence (Church Committee Report), U.S. Senate, April 26, 1976.

68. Robert Morgan, memorandum to RWS, July 3, 1969. Gov. RWS General Correspondence, 1969, Box 79.

69. RWS Diary, March 19, 1969, RWS Private Papers, RWSFP.

70. Lee, *Courage to Lead*; RWS Diary, September 12, 1969, RWS Private Papers, RWSFP.

71. Copy of Asa Spaulding remarks made November 14, 1969, Colloquium for the Department of Afro-American Studies at Harvard, RWS General Correspondence, 1969, Box 118.

72. "Charlotte Negro Named to District Judge's Post," *N&O*, August 6, 1969.

73. AP, "Black Gets N.C. Parole Board Seat," *N&O*, June 15, 1971.

74. RWS Diary, July 1, October 10, 1971.

75. Ibid., June 25, 1970.

76. Richard Daw, "Repentant and Grateful, 5 Negroes Leave Prison," *N&O*, August 13, 1969; Sanders, "North Carolina Justice on Display."

77. UPI, "Agencies Told to Hire Blacks," *N&O*, October 6, 1972.

78. SBI Director Charles Dunn to RWS and Attorney General Robert Morgan, memorandum, January 20, 1969, RWS General Correspondence, 1969, Box 125; Civil Intelligence Report, May 29, 1969, SBI, Robert Morgan Papers, Joyner Library, ECU.

79. Jack Aulis, "Is U.S. Billboard Only Sign of Smithfield 'Klan Country'?," *N&O*, August 17, 1970.

80. RWS to Evelyn B. Hill of Coral Gables, Florida, July 15, 1969, RWS General Correspondence, 1969, Box 125.

81. Cecelski, *Along Freedom Road*, 145–56; "Arrests Continue Hyde Probe," *N&O*, July 8, 1969; Roy Hardee, "Klansmen, Negroes Plead Guilty in Hyde," *N&O*, July 20, 1969.

82. McAdams, *Comparative Perspectives*, 343.

83. "Tar Heels Divided in War Protest," *N&O*, October 16, 1969.

84. David Murray to RWS, memorandum, April 27, 1970, RWS General Correspondence, 1970, Box 162.

85. Broadhurst, "We Didn't Fire a Shot."

86. RWS Diary, May 1, 1970, RWS Private Papers, RWSFP.

87. RWS interview, September 22, 2005.

88. Rick Nichols and Rod Waldorf, "UNC Students March with Coffin," *N&O*, March 17, 1970.

89. RWS Diary, May 8, 1970, RWS Private Papers, RWSFP.

90. Louis N. Howard to RWS, telegram, May 7, 1970, RWS General Correspondence,1970, Box 260.

91. Brad Strickland to RWS, telegram, May 7, 1970, RWS General Correspondence, 1970, Box 260.

92. Mrs. Evon Ray to RWS, April 10, 1970, and RWS to Ray, April 14, 1970, RWS General Correspondence, 1970, Box 260.

93. Jesse Helms, editorial, *Viewpoint*, May 28, 1970, WRAL-TV, RWS General Correspondence, 1970, Box 274.

94. Claude Sitton, "Moderate's Role on Campus," *N&O*, May 31, 1970.

95. RWS, speech to honor POW/MIA families, Military Center, Raleigh, June 16, 1972, RWS General Correspondence, 1972, Box 540.

CHAPTER 12

1. Rosen and Mosnier, *Julius Chambers*, 162.

2. Cochran, "Desegregating Public Education in North Carolina," 192–213.

3. Ibid., 207; Roy Parker, "Student Integration in NC Reaches 28%," *N&O*, January 18, 1969.

4. Mrs. Robert G. Ferrell to RWS, February 12, 1969, RWS General Correspondence, 1969, Box 15.

5. Judy Bolch, "Private Schools under Public Eye," *N&O*, March 30, 1969.

6. "Warrenton Is Second Town Asking New School System," *N&O*, April 11, 1969; "Court Okays School Plan for Halifax," *N&O*, March 25, 1971; Rosen and Mosnier, *Julius Chambers*, 185.

7. SBI, Intelligence Section, to the Director, Subject: Reevaluation of School Opening and Violence Potential, August 28, 1969, RWS General Correspondence, 1969, Box 31.

8. Jack Childs, "Wilson Desegregation Effort Boosts Private Schools," *N&O*, September 9, 1969; "Black Enrollment Rises in Hyde: Unrest Elsewhere," *N&O*, September 4, 1969.

9. Mrs. Mack Webb to RWS, September 2, 1969, RWS General Correspondence, 1969, Box 50.

10. Edith Craft to RWS, January 9 and 19, 1970, RWS letter (no date), Gov. RWS General Correspondence, 1970, Box 152.

11. Mrs. A. C. Smith to RWS February 20, 1970, and RWS to Smith February 22, 1970, Gov. RWS General Correspondence, 1970, Box 152.

12. Jessie Rae Scott Diary, August 27, 1991, RWS Private Collection.

13. Ibid., August 30, 1971.

14. Ibid., June 2, 1972.

15. Jesse Helms, editorial, *Viewpoint*, WRAL-TV, October 31, 1969, Southern Historical Collection, University of North Carolina at Chapel Hill.

16. Gene Marlowe, "Jury Acquits Raleigh Man," *N&O*, March 1969.

17. Horace B. Caple to RWS, March 28, 1969, RWS General Correspondence, 1969, Box 120.

18. Gaillard, *Dream Long Deferred*, 53.

19. Jack Childs, "Scott Sets Day of Hope on Busing," *N&O*, October 7, 1970.

20. UPI, "Scott: I'm Opposed to Busing, but . . . ," *N&O*, January 23, 1970.

21. RWS Diary, January 29, 1970, RWS Private Papers, RWSFP.

22. Ibid., January 20, 1970.

23. Editorial, "Scott Position on Busing Sets Fine Example for State," *Raleigh Times*, January 23, 1970.

24. Judge James McMillan to RWS, January 23, 1970, RWS General Correspondence, 1970, Box 156.

25. Editorial, *Viewpoint*, WRAL-TV, February 3, 1970, Southern Historical Collection, University of North Carolina at Chapel Hill.

26. Betty Cain to RWS, n.d., RWS General Correspondence, 1970, Box 155.

27. RWS Diary, February 10, 17, 1970, RWS Papers, RWSFP; RWS, statement, February 11, 1970, General Correspondence, 1970, Box 156, RWSFP.

28. Gene Marlow, "New Push on Busing Seen Here," *N&O*, April 21, 1971; "High Court Upholds Busing, Other Methods for Integration," *N&O*, April 21, 1971.

29. Chicago Tribune, "Racial Balance Key to Bus Opposition," *N&O*, April 10, 1972.

30. Flood interview.

31. Mitchell, *Addresses and Public Papers of Robert W. Scott*, 473–74.

32. Gene Marlowe, "N.C. Schools Close to Cool Racial Temperature," *N&O*, November 29, 1970.

33. Cecelski, *Along Freedom Road*, 8.

34. Good Neighbors Council report, May 1970 RWS General Correspondence, 1970, Box 159.

35. Mitchell, *Addresses and Public Papers of Robert W. Scott*, 473–74.

36. RWS, address to Citizens Task Force on the Schools.

37. Text of RWS address to Citizens Advisory Council, May 26, 1972, RWS General Correspondence, 1972, Box 532.

38. Tyson, *Blood Done Sign My Name*, 258.

39. Rick Nichols, "Wilmington Chief of Police Criticized by District Judge," *N&O*, March 11, 1971.

40. AP, "Concord Remains Quiet, Tense after Racial Violence Flares Up," *Gastonia Gazette*, May 24, 1972.

41. RWS interview, September 22, 2005.

CHAPTER 13

1. University of North Carolina, *Statistical Abstract of Higher Education in North Carolina, 2012–13*, Table 21: Degree Credit Enrollment Trends, North Carolina Colleges and Universities, Fall 1920–Fall 2012.

2. RWS Speech to the State Higher Education Officers in St. Louis, August 1, 1972, RWS General Correspondence, 1972, Box 443.

3. "Scott Says Educators, 'Like Kids,'" *N&O*, May 23, 1971.

4. RWS to George Watts Hill, April 14, 1970, RWS General Correspondence, 1970, Box 264.

5. RWS Diary, November 25, 1970, RWS Private Papers, RWSFP.

6. Link, *William Friday*, 172.

7. Mitchell, *Addresses and Public Papers of Robert W. Scott*, 91.

8. Link, *William Friday*, 176.

9. RWS Diary, October 22, 29, 1971, RWS Private Papers, RWSFP.

10. RWS interview, September 22, 2005; RWS Diary, October 29, 30, 1971, RWS Private Papers, RWSFP; Link, *William Friday*, 183.

11. Editorial, *Chapel Hill Weekly*, November 24, 1971, RWS General Correspondence, 1971, Box 314.

12. Jack Aulis, "Big John Burney Admits He's Gonna Miss Senate," *N&O*, February 18, 1972.

13. Bartley, *New South*, 13; Fleer, *Governors Speak*, 269.

14. RWS, speech to Bankers Association, May 9, 1970, RWS General Correspondence, 1970, Box 243.

15. RWS Diary, May 24, 1972.

16. Roy Parker, "Money Returned to Castleberry," *N&O*, July 23, 1971.

17. Steve Berg, "Scott has 'No Apology" for Alamance Projects," *N&O*, September 16, 1972.

18. Speck, *Gentleman from Haw River*, 139.

19. RWS Diary, December 17, 1971, RWS Private Papers, RWSFP.

20. Ibid., September 21, 1972.

21. Ibid., July 26, 1970.

22. Noblin, *Hold High the Torch*, 123–24; Hunt interview, April 14, 2016.

23. RWS Diary, November 2, 1971.

24. Ibid., May 8, July 17, 1972.

25. Ibid., September 24, 1971, February 3, 1972.

26. Terry Sanford to RWS, April 2, 1972, Included with RWS Diaries.

27. Mitchell, *Addresses and Public Papers of Robert W. Scott*, 575.

28. Claude Sitton, "Wallace Busing Stand Called Strange," *N&O*, April 30, 1972.

29. RWS Diary, January 13, 1972, RWS Private Papers, RWSFP.

30. Mitchell, *Addresses and Public Papers of Robert W. Scott*, 578.

31. RWS Diary, August 15, 1972, RWS Private Papers, RWSFP.

32. Chafets, *Roger Ailes Off Camera*, 38–39.

33. Thrift, *Conservative Bias*, 183.

34. Eamon, *Making of a Southern Democracy*, 149.

35. RWS Diary, November 8, 1972, RWS PC.

36. Fleer, *Governors Speak*, 320.

37. "Scott Leaves Governmental Marks," editorial, *N&O*, January 5, 1973; Sparrow, *Old School Democrat*, 12.

38. RWS interview, Dec. 16, 1998.

39. Snider, "Scotts of Haw River," 521.

CHAPTER 14

1. RWS Diary, January 5, 1973, RWS Private Papers, RWSFP.

2. Ibid., January 8, 9, 1973.

3. FBI background check of RWS, April 26, 1977, when RWS was under consideration for presidential appointment as federal co-chairman of the Appalachian Regional Commission. FOIA request.

4. AP, "Scott Not a Candidate for Office," *High Point Enterprise*, August 12, 1975.

5. George Stein, "Jesse Scott Opens Campaign," *DTN*, April 28, 1976.

6. Ken Freidlein, "Bob Scott: Can He Leave the Farm and Ride Herd on State?," *Charlotte Observer*, November 4, 1979, RWSFP.

7. Hunt interview, April 14, 2016.

8. RWS interview; RWS interview with Joseph W. Westcott II, November 9, 2004.

9. RWS oral history interview.

10. RWS interview, December 16, 1998.

11. AP, "Hunt Organization Most Powerful," *Thomasville Times*, February 25, 1980; Stephen R. Kelly, "Hunt's Key People," *Charlotte Observer*, February 24, 1980.

12. Mann interview; RWS oral history interview.

13. RWS interview, December 16, 1998.

14. Mann interview.

15. Editorial, "Bob Scott's Flip-Flop," *N&O*, January 9, 1980.

16. Editorial, "Scott's Low-Voltage Idea," *N&O*, February 7, 1980.

17. Text of RWS news conference, April 21, 1980, RWS Papers, 1980 Campaign, RWSFP.

18. RWS, statement, May 5, 1980, RWSFP.

19. Fitzgerald, *Remembering a Champion*, 169.

20. Under the Dome, "Scott Staying Down on Farm," *N&O*, October 23, 1980; Hunt interview, April 14, 2016.

21. *DTN*, November 13, 1980.

22. William Porter, "GOP Brings Conservative Cause to Local Voters," *DTN*, October 29, 1980.

23. Rob Christensen, "State's Prominent Figures Pay Last Respects to 'Uncle Ralph,'" *N&O*, April 6, 1989.

24. Speck, *Gentleman from Haw River*, 181.

25. Eddie Marks, "Ex Gov. Scott Ends Dairying Tradition," *Greensboro Daily News*, August 3, 1982.

26. RWS interview, September 22, 2005.

27. Mike Wilder, "Always Governor," *Alamance News*, February 20, 1996.

28. North Carolina Department of Cultural Resources, *Kerr Scott Farm, Haw River, North Carolina*; Jones, *Robert W. Scott and the Preservation of North Carolina History*.

29. Corbitt, *Public Addresses, Letters and Papers of William Kerr Scott*, 8.

30. Mitchell, *Addresses and Public Papers of Robert W. Scott*, 413.

31. RWS, speech to N.C. Warm Air Heating and Air Conditioning Contractors Association, RWS General Correspondence, 1970, Box 242.

32. Erica Johnston, "Illiteracy Like a Cancer, Unseen, Eating Away," *Durham Morning Herald*, August 11, 1986.

33. Phipps interview.

34. RWS to former Rep. J. P. Huskins, June 9, 1999, Robert "Bob" Scott, 1999–2000 Personal Correspondence, SFC-ACC.

35. RWS to Tom Lambeth, November 29, 1999, Robert "Bob" Scott, 1999–2000 Personal Correspondence, SFC-ACC.

36. Crone interview.

37. Bob Williams, "Council of State," *N&O*, May 3, 2000.

38. Jesse Helms to RWS, January 27, 2000, Robert Bob Scott, 1999–2000 Personal Corr., SFC-ACC.

39. McLaurin, *North Carolina State Fair*, 40–80.

40. Bill Krueger, "Phipps Campaign Penalized," *N&O*, June 8, 2002.

41. Jay Price and John Sullivan, "Phipps' Dark Clouds Draw a Shaky Forecast," *N&O*, June 10, 2002.

42. Lynn Bonner and Dan Kane, "Shadow Falls on Ex Governor," *N&O*, October 25, 2003.

43. Crone interview.

44. Kristin Collins, "Phipps Jailed after Verdict," *N&O*, October 31, 2003.

45. Carroll Leggett, *Metro Magazine*, July 2011; Phipps interview.

46. Dennis Rogers, "Phipps Sent to jail; Extortion Scheme Brings 4-Year Term," *N&O*, March 3, 2004.

47. Phipps interview.

48. Mark Johnson, "Phipps Missives Tell of Life, Lessons in Prison," *Charlotte Observer*, April 22, 2007.

49. Mark Johnson, "Church Job, Ankle Bracelet Awaits Phipps after Prison," *N&O*, April 11, 2007.

50. Leggett, *Metro Magazine*.

51. Phipps interview.

52. Frank Porter Graham, article on WKS, Box 184, WKSP.

53. Ralph Scott funeral notes, prepared August 5, 1985, Box 26, RSP.

CONCLUSION

1. Badger, *New Deal/New South*.

2. Peele to WKS, July 12, 1951, Box 103, WKSP.

3. McAdam and Kloos, *Deeply Divided*.

4. "By His Own Reckoning, ERA Backer Is Saved," *N&O*, December 15, 1979.

5. Bureau of Economic Analysis, U.S. Department of Commerce; Price, *North Carolina during the Great Depression*.

BIBLIOGRAPHY

ARCHIVES

Alamance Community College, Haw River, N.C.
    The Scott Family Collection
        Robert "Bob" Scott, 1999–2000, Personal Correspondence
Federal Bureau of Investigation, Washington, D.C., and Charlotte, N.C.
    Investigative materials related to incidents of social unrest and protests via
        Freedom of Information Act requests
Joyner Library, East Carolina University, Greenville, N.C.
    Robert Morgan Papers
North Carolina Division of Archives and History, Raleigh, N.C.
    Ben Roney Papers
    Department of Agriculture Papers
    Jessie Rae Scott Papers
    Ralph Scott Papers
    Robert W. Scott Family Papers
    W. Kerr Scott Papers
Southern Historical Collection, University of North Carolina at Chapel Hill
    James C. Gardner Papers
    Southern Oral History Program interviews

BOOKS, ARTICLES, AND DISSERTATIONS

Ashby, Warren. *Frank Porter Graham: A Southern Liberal.* Winston-Salem, N.C.:
    John F. Blair, 1980.
Badger, Anthony. *New Deal/New South: An Anthony J. Badger Reader.* Fayetteville:
    University of Arkansas Press, 2007.
————. *North Carolina and New Deal.* Raleigh: N.C. Department of Cultural
    Resources, Offices of Archives and History, 1981.
Bartley, Numan V. *The New South: The Story of the South's Modernization, 1945–1980.*
    Baton Rouge: Louisiana State University Press, 1995.
Bass, Jack, and Walter DeVries. *The Transformation of Southern Politics: Social
    Change and Political Consequences since 1945.* New York: Basic Books, 1976.
Bell, John L. *Hard Times: Beginnings of the Great Depression in North Carolina, 1929–
    1933.* Raleigh: N.C. Department of Cultural Resources, 1982.

Berman, Ari. *Give Us the Ballot: The Modern Struggle for Voting Rights in America.* New York: Farrar, Straus and Giroux, 2015.

Beyle, Thad L., and Merle Black. *Politics and Policy in North Carolina.* New York: MSS Information, 1975.

Biondi, Martha. *The Black Revolution on Campus.* Berkeley: University of California Press, 2012.

Billinger, Robert D., Jr. *Nazi POWs in the Tar Heel State.* Gainesville: University of Florida Press, 2008.

Billingsly, William J. *Communists on Campus: Race, Politics, and the Public University in Sixties North Carolina.* Athens: University of Georgia Press, 1999.

Brisson, Jim D. " 'Civil Government Was Crumbling around Me': The Kirk-Holden War of 1870." *North Carolina Historical Review* 88, no. 2 (April 2011): 123–63.

Broadhurst, Christopher J. " 'We Didn't Fire a Shot, We Didn't Burn a Building': The Student Reaction at North Carolina State University to the Kent State Shootings." *North Carolina Historical Review* 87, no. 3 (July 2010): 283–309.

Bulla, Ben F. *Textiles and Politics: The Life of B. Everett Jordan.* Durham, N.C.: Carolina Academic Press, 1992.

Butler, Lindley S., and Alan D. Watson. *The North Carolina Experience: An Interpretive and Documentary History.* Chapel Hill: University of North Carolina Press, 1983.

Campbell, Karl E. *Senator Sam Ervin: Last of the Founding Fathers.* Chapel Hill: University of North Carolina Press, 2007.

Cash, W. J. *The Mind of the South.* New York: Vintage Books, 1941.

Cecelski, David S. *Along Freedom Road: Hyde County North Carolina and the Fate of Black Schools in the South.* Chapel Hill: University of North Carolina Press, 1994.

Chafe, William H. *Civilities and Civil Rights: Greensboro, North Carolina, and the Black Struggle for Freedom.* New York: Oxford University Press, 1980.

Chavets, Zef. *Roger Ailes Off Camera.* New York: Penguin, 2013.

Christensen, Rob. *The Paradox of Tar Heel Politics: The Personalities, Elections, and Events That Shaped Modern North Carolina.* Chapel Hill: University of North Carolina Press, 2008.

Clotfelter, James. *Frank Porter Graham: Service to North Carolina and the Nation.* Greensboro: North Carolina Service Project of UNC-Greensboro, 1993.

Cochran, A. B. "Desegregating Public Education in North Carolina." In *Politics and Policy in North Carolina*, edited by Thad L. Beyle and Merle Black, 192–213. New York: MSS Information, 1975.

Coon, John William. "Kerr Scott, the Go-Forward Governor: His Origins, His Program and the North Carolina General Assembly." M.A. thesis, University of North Carolina, 1968.

Cooper, Christopher, and H. Gibbs Knotts. *The New Politics of North Carolina.* Chapel Hill: University of North Carolina Press, 2008.

Cooper, William J., Jr., and Terrill, Thomas E. *The American South: A History*. New York: McGraw-Hill, 1991.

Corbitt, David Leroy. *Public Addresses, Letters, and Papers of William Kerr Scott*. Raleigh, N.C.: State Department of Archives, 1957.

Covington, Howard E. *Henry Frye: North Carolina's First African American Chief Justice*. Jefferson, N.C.: McFarland, 2013.

Covington, Howard E., Jr., and Marion A. Ellis. *North Carolina Century: Tar Heels Who Made a Difference, 1900–2000*. Charlotte, N.C.: Levine Museum of the New South, 2002.

———. *Terry Sanford: Politics, Progress, and Outrageous Ambitions*. Durham, N.C.: Duke University Press, 1999.

Culver, John C., and John Hyde. *American Dreamer: The Life and Times of Henry Wallace*. New York: W. W. Norton, 2000.

Cunningham, David. *Klansville U.S.A.: The Rise and Fall of the Civil Rights–Era Ku Klux Klan*. Oxford: Oxford University Press, 2013.

Daniels, Josephus. *Editor in Politics*. Chapel Hill: University of North Carolina Press, 1941.

Davis, Anita Price, comp. *North Carolina during the Great Depression: A Documentary Portrait of the Decade*. Jefferson, N.C.: McFarland, 2003.

D'Emilio, John. *Lost Prophet: The Life and Times of Bayard Rustin*. Chicago: University of Chicago Press, 2003.

Downs, Gregory P. *Declarations of Dependence: The Long Reconstruction of Popular Politics in the South, 1861–1908*. Chapel Hill: University of North Carolina Press, 2011.

Drescher, John. *Triumph of Goodwill: How Terry Sanford Beat a Champion of Segregation and Reshaped the South*. Jackson: University Press of Mississippi, 2000.

Eamon, Tom. *The Making of a Southern Democracy: North Carolina Politics from Kerr Scott to Pat McCrory*. Chapel Hill: University of North Carolina Press, 2014.

Edwards, Elizabeth. *Saving Graces: Finding Solace and Strength from Friends and Strangers*. New York: Broadway Books, 2006.

Egerton, John. *Speak Now against the Day, The Generation before the Civil Rights Movement in the South*. Chapel Hill: University of North Carolina Press, 1994.

Ehle, John. *Dr. Frank: Life with Frank Porter Graham*. Chapel Hill: Franklin Street Books, 1993.

Escott, Paul D. *Many Excellent People: Power and Privilege in North Carolina, 1850–1900*. Chapel Hill: University of North Carolina Press, 1985.

Faulkenbury, Terry Evan. "Telenegro: Reginald Hawkins, Black Power and the 1968 Gubernatorial Race in North Carolina." M.A. thesis, University of North Carolina, 2012.

Fergus, Devin. *Liberalism, Black Power, and the Making of American Politics, 1965–1980*. Athens: University of Georgia Press, 2009.

Ferguson, Ernest B. *Hard Right: The Rise of Jesse Helms*. New York: W. W. Norton, 1986.

Fitzgerald, Gayle Lane. *Recollections of Agnes White Scott Haesler and Elizabeth Hughes Scott Carrington*. N.p.: Published by the author, 1989.

———. *Remembering a Champion*. Raleigh, N.C.: Edwards and Broughton, 1988.

Fleer, Jack D. *Governors Speak*. Lanham, Md.: University Press of America, 2007.

Fuller, Howard. *No Struggle No Progress: A Warrior's Life from Black Power to Education Reform*. Milwaukee, Wis.: Marquette University Press, 2014.

Furman, Elizabeth White. *Grandfather's Letters: Letters Written to John Mebane Allen by Relatives from Friends of the Hawfields from 1852 to 1889*. N.p.: Published by the author.

Gardner, Michael R. *Harry Truman and Civil Rights: Moral Courage and Political Risks*. Carbondale: Southern Illinois University Press, 2002.

Golden, Harry. *The Right Time: An Autobiography by Harry Golden*. New York: G. P. Putnam's Sons, 1969.

Grantham, Dewey W. *The South in Modern America: A Region at Odds*. New York: HarperCollins, 1994.

Grimsley, Wayne. *James B. Hunt: A North Carolina Progressive*. Jefferson, N.C.: McFarland, 2003.

Gunther, John. *Inside U.S.A.* New York: Harper and Brothers, 1947.

Havard, William C., ed. *The Changing Politics of the South*. Baton Rouge: Louisiana State University Press, 1972.

Hayes, Anna R. *Without Precedent: The Life of Susie Marshall Sharp*. Chapel Hill: University of North Carolina Press, 2008.

Haynes, John Earl, and Harvey Klehr. *Venona: Decoding Soviet Espionage in America*. New Haven, Conn.: Yale University Press, 1999.

Helms, Jesse. *Here's Where I Stand: A Memoir*. New York: Random House, 2005.

Hester, James Earl. *More Wisdom than I Posses: Life at Hester's Store, North Carolina*. Roxboro, N.C.: Person County Museum of History, 2014.

Hobbs, S. Huntington, Jr. *North Carolina: An Economic and Social Profile*. Chapel Hill: University of North Carolina Press, 1930. Rev. ed., 1958.

Hodges, H. Luther, *Businessman in the State House: Six Years as Governor of North Carolina*. Chapel Hill: University of North Carolina Press, 1962.

Isenberg, Nancy. *White Trash: The 400-Year Untold History of Class in America*. New York: Viking, 2016.

Janken, Kenneth Robert. *The Wilmington Ten: Violence, Injustice, and the Rise of Black Politics in the 1970s*. Chapel Hill: University of North Carolina Press, 2015.

Jeffreys, Grady. *I Never Promised Not to Tell*. N.p.: CreateSpace, 2013.

Johnson, Sam. *A History of My Journey: From Life on the Farm to Many Adventures Worldwide and Back Home*. Raleigh, N.C.: Published by the author, 2007.

Johnson, Samuel W. "Kerr Scott and His Fight for the Improvement for the Improvement of North Carolina Roads." M.A. thesis, University of North Carolina, 1969.

Jones, H. G. *Robert W. Scott and the Preservation of North Carolina History*. Chapel Hill: North Caroliniana Society, 2009.

Kaiser, Charles. *1968 in America: Music, Politics, Chaos, Counterculture and the Shaping of a Generation*. New York: Grove Press, 1988.

Key, V. O., Jr. *Southern Politics in State and Nation*. New York: Vintage Books, 1949.

Kirkpatrick, Rob. *1969: The Year Everything Changed*. New York: Skyhorse, 2011.

Knight, Douglas M. *Street of Dreams: The Nature and Legacy of the 1960s*. Durham, N.C.: Duke University Press, 1989.

Korstad, Robert R., and James L. Leloudis. *To Right These Wrongs: The North Carolina Fund and the Battle to End Poverty and Inequality in 1960s America*. Chapel Hill: University of North Carolina Press, 2010.

Kurlansky, Mark. *1968: The Year That Rocked the World*. New York: Random House, 2004.

Lee, Howard. *The Courage to Lead: One Man's Journey in Public Service*. Chapel Hill: Cotton Patch Press, 2008.

Lefler, Hugh Talmage, and Albert Ray Newsome. *North Carolina: The History of a Southern State*. Chapel Hill: University of North Carolina Press, 1954.

Leuchtenburg, William. *Franklin D. Roosevelt and the New Deal, 1932–1940*. New York: Harper and Row, 1963.

Link, William A. *William Friday: Power, Purpose, and American Higher Education*. Chapel Hill: University of North Carolina Press, 1995.

Liu, Ben-Chieh. *The Quality of Life in the United States*. Kansas City, Mo.: Midwest Research Institute, 1973.

Lubell, Samuel. *The Future of American Politics*. New York: Harper and Row, 1951.

Matthews, Donald R. *North Carolina Votes: General Election Returns*. Chapel Hill: University of North Carolina Press, 1962.

Matthews, Donald R., and James W. Prothro. *Negroes and the New Southern Politic*. New York: Harcourt, Brace and World, 1966.

McAdam, Doug, and Karina Kloos. *Deeply Divided: Racial Politics and Social Movements in Post-War America*. Oxford: Oxford University Press, 2014.

———. McAdam, Doug, John D. McCarthy, and Mayer N. Zald. *Comparative Perspectives on Social Movements: Political Opportunities, Mobilizing Structures, and Cultural Framings*. Cambridge, UK: Cambridge University Press, 1996.

McCullough, David. *Truman*. New York: Simon and Schuster, 1992.

McGovern, George. *The Third Freedom: Ending Hunger in Our Times*. New York: Simon and Schuster, 2001.

———. *War against Want: America's Food for Peace Program*. New York: Simon and Schuster, 1964.

McLaurin, Melton A. *The North Carolina State Fair: The First 150 Years*. Raleigh: N.C. Office of State Archives and History, 2003.

McLendon, William W., Floyd W. Denny, and William B. Blythe. *Bettering the Health of the People: W. Reece Berryhill, the UNC School of Medicine, and the North*

Carolina Good Health Movement. Chapel Hill: University of North Carolina at Chapel Hill Library, 2007.

McMath, Robert C., Jr. *Populist Vanguard: A History of the Southern Farmers' Alliance*. Chapel Hill: University of North Carolina Press, 1975.

Myers, Andrew H. "Resonant Ripples in a Global Pond: The Blinding of Isaac Woodard." Paper prepared American Studies Association annual meeting, Houston, Texas, November 14–17, 2002.

Miller, Stephen P. *Billy Graham and the Rise of the Republican South*. Philadelphia: University of Pennsylvania Press, 2009.

Mitchell, Memory F. *Addresses and Public Papers of Robert W. Scott: Governor of North Carolina, 1969–73*. Raleigh: N.C. Division of Archives and History, Department of Cultural Resources, 1974.

Noblin, Stuart, and Bill Humphries. *Hold High the Torch: The Grange in North Carolina, 1929–1989*. Greensboro: North Carolina State Grange, 1990.

Parramore, Thomas C. *Express Lanes and Country Roads: The Way We Lived in North Carolina, 1920–1970*. Chapel Hill: University of North Carolina Press, 1983.

Pearce, Gary. *Jim Hunt: A Biography*. Winston-Salem, N.C.: John F. Blair, 2010.

Pierce, Neal R. *The Border South States: People, Politics, and Power in the Five Border South States*. New York: W. W. Norton, 1975.

Pietrusza, David. *1948: Harry Truman's Improbable Victory and the Year That Transformed America*. New York: Union Square Press, 2011.

Pleasants, Julian M. *The Political Career of W. Kerr Scott: The Squire of Haw River*. Lexington: University of Kentucky Press, 2014.

Pleasants, Julian, and Augustus M. Burns III. *Frank Porter Graham and the 1950 Senate Race in North Carolina*. Chapel Hill: University of North Carolina Press, 1990.

Powell, Willam S. *North Carolina through Four Centuries*. Chapel Hill: University of North Carolina Press, 1989.

Puryear, Elmer L. *Democratic Party Dissension in North Carolina, 1928–1936*. Chapel Hill: University of North Carolina Press, 1962.

Romerstein, Herbert, and Eric Breindel. *The Venona Secrets: Exposing Soviet Espionage and America's Traitors*. Washington, D.C.: Regnery, 2000.

Rosen, Richard A., and Joseph Mosnier. *Julius Chambers: A Life in the Legal Struggle for Rights*. Chapel Hill: University of North Carolina Press, 2016.

Sanders, Crystal R. "North Carolina Justice on Display: Governor Bob Scott and the 1968 Benson Affair." *Journal of Southern History* 79, no. 3 (August 2013): 659–80.

Scott, Katherine A. *Reinventing the State: Civil Society and Congress in the Vietnam and Watergate Eras*. Lawrence: University of Kansas Press, 2013.

Scott, Robert W. *A Faith Established a Governor*. Living the Vision Series. N.p.: Presbyterian Church (USA), 2001.

———. Living the Vision Series, pamphlets. N.p.: Presbyterian Church (USA), 1999.

Snider, William D. "The Scotts of Haw River." In *The North Carolina Century: Tar Heels Who Made a Difference, 1900-2000*, ed. Howard E. Covington Jr. and Marion A. Ellis. Charlotte, N.C.: Levine Museum of the New South, 2002.

Sparrow, J. Ray. *Looking Back on 50 Years as an Old School Democrat*. Raleigh, N.C.: Published by the author, 2017.

Speck, Jean. *The Gentleman from Haw River*. Raleigh, N.C.: Edwards and Broughton, 1990.

Thomas, Susan W. "Chain Gangs, Roads and Reform in North Carolina, 1900-1935." Ph.D. diss., University of North Carolina, 2011.

Thrift, Bryan Hardin. *Conservative Bias: How Jesse Helms Pioneered the Rise of Right-Wing Media and Realigned the Republican Party*. Gainesville: University of Florida Press, 2014.

Tindall, George B. *The Emergence of The New South, 1913-1945*. Baton Rouge: Louisiana State University Press, 1967.

Towe, William H. *Barriers to Black Political Participation in North Carolina: Voter Education Project, Inc*. Atlanta: VEP, 1972.

Troxler, Carole Watterson, and William Murray Vincent. *Shuttle and Plow: A History of Alamance County, North Carolina*. Pikesville, Md.: Port City Press, 1999.

Turner, Herbert S. *Church in the Old Fields: Hawfields Presbyterian Church and Community in North Carolina*. Chapel Hill: University of North Carolina Press, 1962.

————. *The Scott Family of Hawfields*. N.p.: Privately published, 1971.

Turner, Walter R. *Paving Tobacco Road: A Century of Progress by the North Carolina Department of Transportation*. Raleigh: N.C. Office of Archives and History, 2003.

Tyson, Timothy B. *Blood Done Sign My Name*. New York: Crown, 2004.

————. *Radio Free Dixie: Robert F. Williams and the Roots of Black Power*. Chapel Hill: University of North Carolina Press, 1999.

Viorst, Milton. *Fire in the Streets: America in the 1960's*. New York: Simon and Schuster, 1979.

Webb, James. *Born Fighting: How the Scots-Irish Shaped America*. New York: Broadway Books, 2004.

Wellstone, Paul. "Black Militants in the Ghetto: Why They Believe in Violence." Ph.D. diss., University of North Carolina, 1969.

White, Graham, and John Maze. *Henry A. Wallace: His Search for New World Order*. Chapel Hill: University of North Carolina Press, 1995.

Wicker, Tom. *Facing the Lions*. New York: Avon Books, 1973.

Wiseman, Jane Pettis. "The New Politics in North Carolina: James Gardner and the 1968 Governor's Race." M.A. thesis, University of North Carolina, 1971.

Woodward, C. Vann. *Origins of the New South, 1877-1913*. Baton Rouge: Louisiana State University Press, 1951.

GOVERNMENT DOCUMENTS

North Carolina Department of Cultural Resources. *Kerr Scott Farm, Haw River, North Carolina: State Historic Site Feasibility Report*. Division of Archives and History, Historic Sites Section, Architecture Branch, 1995.

North Carolina State Advisory Committee on Civil Rights. *Trouble in Greensboro: A Report of an Open Meeting Concerning the Disturbances at Dudley High School and North Carolina* A&T *State University*. March 1970.

President's Committee on Civil Rights. *To Secure These Rights: The Report of the President's Committee on Civil Rights*. Washington, D.C., October 1947.

United States Army. "Counter Intelligence Spot Report, Region II, 111th MI Group, Raleigh, Protest Demonstration at Duke University, Durham, North Carolina, February 13, 1969." FOIA request.

United States Army Corps of Engineers. Navigation and Civil Works Decision Support Center. *The U.S. Waterway System: 2016 Transportation Facts and Information*. Institute for Water Resources, October 2017.

United States Bureau of the Census. *Eighth Census of the United States, 1860*. Washington, D.C.: National Archives and Records Administration, 1860.

——. "Urban and Rural Population, 1900–1990." October 1995. https://www.census.gov/population/censusdata/urpop0090.txt.

United States Senate. The Final Report of the Select Committee to Study Governmental Operations with Regard to Intelligence Activities. Washington, D.C.: U.S. Government Printing Office, 1976.

——. *William Kerr Scott: Memorial Addresses Delivered in Congress*. Eighty-Fifth Cong., 2nd Sess. Washington, D.C.: U.S. Government Printing Office, 1958.

University of North Carolina. *Statistical Abstract of Higher Education in North Carolina, 2012–13*. Research Report 1–13. Chapel Hill: University of North Carolina, August 2013.

PERIODICALS

Agriculture Review
Alamance News
American Mercury
Asheville Citizen-Times
Atlanta Journal-Constitution
Better Roads Magazine
Carolina Israelite
Carolina Times
Chapel Hill Weekly
Charlotte News
Charlotte Observer
Christian Observer
Christian Science Monitor

Concord Tribune
Congressional Record
Daily Independent (Kannapolis)
Daily Times News (Burlington)
Durham Herald
Durham Herald Sun
Durham Morning Herald
Durham Morning Sun
Durham Labor Journal
Durham Sun
Fayetteville Observer
Gaston Gazette
Greensboro Daily News

Greensboro News and Record
Greensboro Patriot
Greensboro Record
Greenville Daily Reflector
Hartford Courant
High Point Enterprise
Jersey Bulletin and Dairy World
Journal of Southern History
Journal of Politics
Kiplinger Report
Mebane Enterprise
Metro Magazine
Morning Post (Raleigh)
News and Observer (Raleigh)
Newsweek
New York Herald Tribune
New York Post
New York Times
North Carolina Grange News
North Carolina Historical Review

North Carolina Roadways
Our State Magazine
Politico
Progressive Farmer
Raleigh Times
Richmond County Journal
Ripon Forum
Robesonian
Rocky Mount Telegram
Salisbury Post
Sandhills Citizen
The State (Columbia, S.C.)
Statesville Daily Record
Statesville Record and Landmark
Thomasville Times
Virginian-Pilot (Norfolk, Va.)
Washington Post
Wilmington Star-News
Winston-Salem Journal
Winston-Salem Journal and Sentinel

INTERVIEWS WITH THE AUTHOR

Bennett, Bert, April 28, 2016, Winston-Salem.
Bruton, Dr. David, April 7, 2016, Southern Pines.
Cochrane, Bill, date uncertain, Washington, D.C.
Cooper, Grady, April 20, 2016, Raleigh.
Creech, Sally Wood, February 28, 2017, Raleigh.
Crone, Brad, July 19, 2016, Raleigh.
Edmisten, Rufus, April 8, 2015, Raleigh.
Ellis, Tom, September 13, 2001.
Faircloth, Lauch, September 26, 2001, Clinton.
Flood, Dudley, April 3, 2015, Raleigh.
Fuller, Howard, June 8, 2014, Raleigh.
Furman, Grace, May 30, 2009, Raleigh.
Gardner, Jim, May 3, 2016, Raleigh.
Hill, Ethro, July 18, 2009, Pink Hill.
Hinton, Betsy, July 18, 2016, Raleigh.
Hunt, Jim, April 1, 2003; and April 14, 2016, Raleigh.
Jones, H. G., March 26, 2015, Chapel Hill.
Jordan, John, April 13, 2015, Raleigh.
Lambeth, Thomas, September 29, 2014. Winston-Salem.
Mann, Julian, June 20, 2016, Raleigh.

Massey, Raymond, November 12, 2003, Raleigh.

McLamb, Earl, April 15, 2016, Garner.

Mitchell, Burley, April 6, 2016, Raleigh.

Morrison, Fred, April 29, 2016, Raleigh.

Murray, David, August 28, 2014, Raleigh.

Pearce, Gary, March 1, 2017, Raleigh.

Phipps, Meg Scott, July 28, 2016, Haw River.

Roney, Ben, December 1978, Raleigh.

Sanford, Terry, February 1998, Durham.

Scott, Dr. Charles, May 2, 2016, Burlington.

Scott, Dr. Samuel, May 2, 2016, Burlington.

Scott, Ralph, December 1978, Haw River.

Scott, Robert W., December 15, 1994; December 16, 1998; and September 22, 2005, Raleigh and Haw River.

Sheffield, Dewey, July 13, 2014, Wilson.

Snow, A. C., May 27, 2010, Raleigh.

Wagstaff, D. B., April 6, 2016, Wendell.

Wilder, Roy, December 15, 2011, Rocky Mount.

ORAL HISTORIES

Boyce, Lena. Interview by Sue Beal, October 16, 1984. Southern Oral History Program, D-0005, University of North Carolina, Chapel Hill.

Covington, Jim. Interview by Peggy Boswell, November 14, 2000. Scott Family Collection, Alamance Community College.

Elliot, Mrs. W. D. Interview with Larry Johnson, June 6, 2005. Southern Oral History Program, D-0015, University of North Carolina, Chapel Hill.

Fleming, Neely N. Interview by Peggy Boswell, September 7, 2000. Scott Family Collection, Alamance Community College.

Gardner, James Carson. Interview by Jonathan Thomas Young Houghton, August 6, 1995. Southern Oral History Program, A-0378, University of North Carolina, Chapel Hill.

Johnson, Sidney Cecil. Interview by Peggy Boswell, November 3, 2009. Scott Family Collection, Alamance Community College.

Plexico, Dr. A. B. Interview by Peggy Boswell, September 12, 2000. Scott Family Collection, Alamance Community College.

Roodenko, Igal. Interview by Charles Adams, Joseph Felmet, Jacquelyn Dowd, and Jerry Windsor, April 11, 1974. Southern Oral History Program, B-0010, University of North Carolina, Chapel Hill.

Sanford, Terry. Interview by Brent Glass, May 14, 1976. Southern Oral History Program, A-0328-1, University of North Carolina, Chapel Hill.

Scott, Dr. Charles. Interview by Peggy Boswell, April 12, 2000. Scott Family Collection, Alamance Community College.

Scott, Ralph. Interview by Jack Bass and Walter De Vries, December 20, 1973. Southern Oral History Program, A-0141, University of North Carolina, Chapel Hill.

———. Interview by Jacquelyn Hall and William R. Finger, April 22, 1974. Southern Oral History Program, University of North Carolina, Chapel Hill.

Scott, Robert Walker. Interview by Karl E. Campbell, September 18, 1986. Southern Oral History Program, C-0036, University of North Carolina, Chapel Hill.

———. Interview by H. G. Jones, May 8, 1968. North Carolina Division of Archives and History, Raleigh.

———. Interview by Joseph W. Wescott, November 9, 2004.

———. Interview by Shannon Vickery, April 2004. Biographical Conversations with Bob Scott, UNC-TV.

Waynick, Capus M. Interview by William R. Finger, February 4, 1974. Southern Oral History Program, A-0332-1, University of North Carolina, Chapel Hill.

INDEX

Page numbers appearing in *italics* refer to figures.

feed manufacturing, 26
Ferrell, Mrs. Robert G., 212
fertilizer manufacturing, 26
financial aid termination for civil unrest, 203–4
Fitch, Milton "Toby," 223
Flannery, John and Leola, 141
Flav-O-Rich Dairies, 22
Flood, Dudley, 219
flood control, 114
Food for Peace program, 112–13
Fountain, L. H., 151
4-H Clubs, 16
Fourteenth Amendment, 118
Fourth U.S. Circuit Court, 223
Freedom of Choice plans, 156, 169, 211–12, 216
Friday, William C., 191, 210, 226–27
Frinks, Golden, 168, 171, 196, 221–22
Frye, Henry, 174, 175–76, 199, 201
Frye, Shirley, 176
Fuller, Howard, 149–50, *150*, 151–53, 188, 192, 222, 223
fundamentalism, religious, 3–4
Fusionists, 10

Galifianakis, Nick, 232
Gans, Curtis, 164
Gardner, Jim, 151–52; gubernatorial general campaign of, 166, 167–68, 169–70, 171–72, 173–74, 179; gubernatorial primary campaign of, 155, *157*, 162–63; presidential support of, 165–66, 167, 237
Gardner, O. Max, 23–24, 30–31, 78
gas tax, 53, 54, 55, 56, 91, 178–80, 181
Gavin, Robert, 145, 162
German, Finley L., 54–55
GI Bill of Rights, 225
Gibson, O. W., 117
Gilmore, Voit, 68
Gleaves, J. H. R., 107, 108

Godwin, Philip P., 228
Go Forward program, 3, 50, 97, 259
Golden, Harry, 2, 66–67, 123
Goldwater, Barry, 144, 145, 151
Good Health Plan, 28–29
Goodman, R. W., 143
Good Neighbors Council, 220
government: as foe, 3–4, 238; reorganization of, 229–30
Governmental Relations and Assistance Group, 241–42
governor campaign of 1948: main campaign, 46; primary, 30, 31–36, 41; primary run-off, 37–39
governor campaign of 1952, 97–100
governor campaign of 1960, 127, 133
governor campaign of 1964, 142–43
governor campaign of 1968, 147, 152–56, *157*, 159–62, 165, 166–74
governor campaign of 1972, 232
governor campaign of 1980, 244–46
Graham, A. H. "Sandy," 24, 25
Graham, Billy, 172
Graham, Frank Porter, 77–80, *79*, 90; Committee on Civil Rights and, 40–41; as president of UNC, 1; Scott as Senate candidate and, 101, 110; Senate appointment of, 77, 80–81, 84; as Senate candidate, 81–82, 83–88, 89–90, 98, 107
Graham, Jim, 250
Graham, William A., Jr., 23–24, 25
Graham, William A., Sr., 11, 16, 23
Grange, the, 3, 18–19; Bob Scott and, 131–33, 135, 179, 258; Hunts and, 232–33; Kerr Scott and, 19–20, 21, 23, 28, 39; telephones and, 68–69
Great Bull Calf Walk, 103, *104*
Great Depression, 17, 20–21, 24, 51
Greene, Daniel, 186
Greensboro Daily News, 95, 146, 154, 167, 201, 231
Green's Grill, 74